THE REPUBLIC ACCORDING TO
# John Marshall Harlan

STUDIES IN LEGAL HISTORY

*Published by the*

*University of North Carolina Press*

*in association with the*

*American Society for Legal History*

*Thomas A. Green and Hendrik Hartog, editors*

THE REPUBLIC ACCORDING TO

# John Marshall Harlan

LINDA PRZYBYSZEWSKI

The University of

North Carolina Press

*Chapel Hill & London*

© 1999 The University of North Carolina Press
All rights reserved
Manufactured in the United States of America
Set in Janson type by Tseng Information Systems, Inc.
The paper in this book meets the guidelines for permanence
and durability of the Committee on Production Guidelines
for Book Longevity of the Council on Library Resources.
Library of Congress Cataloging-in-Publication Data
Przybyszewski, Linda.
The republic according to John Marshall Harlan / Linda Przybyszewski.
    p.   cm. — (Studies in legal history)
Includes bibliographical references and index.
ISBN 0-8078-2493-3 (alk. paper). —
ISBN 0-8078-4789-5 (pbk. : alk. paper)
1. Harlan, John Marshall, 1833–1911.   2. Judges — United States —
Biography.   3. Constitutional law — United States.   [1. United States.
Supreme Court — Biography.]   I. Title.   II. Series.
KF8745.H3P79   1999
347.73′14′092 — dc21
[B]                              99-13686
                         CIP


03   02   01   00   99   5   4   3   2   1

FRONTISPIECE
This tintype of Justice John Marshall Harlan seated in front of a set of
mirrors was taken at Atlantic City, N.J., circa 1903. (Courtesy of the
Library of Congress)

FOR MY PARENTS

# CONTENTS

## ILLUSTRATIONS

# ACKNOWLEDGMENTS

Many people know that Virginia Woolf believed that a writer needs "a room of one's own." She also suggested an income of £500. I would add to Woolf's list of necessities a circle of supportive family members, friends, colleagues, and mentors. I am grateful to have had all of these.

My graduate work at the History Department at Stanford University was made possible by a Mellon Fellowship in the Humanities and by funds from the History Department and the Office of Graduate Studies. The Northern California Association of Phi Beta Kappa also awarded me a graduate scholarship.

In addition, I received a Littleton-Griswold Research Grant from the American Historical Association. Generous postdoctoral fellowships from the Charles Phelps Taft Memorial Fund at the University of Cincinnati and the Institute for Legal Studies at the Law School of the University of Wisconsin–Madison furthered my research. The first year I was at Cincinnati, the Law School graciously offered me space in its library. The Society of Fellows in the Humanities at the Heyman Center at Columbia University gave me time to revise the manuscript in the final and crucial stages. I am grateful to the staff of the center for their help, especially the director of the society, Marsha Manns. At the center, I enjoyed the stimulating intellectual company of Michael Anderson, Leo Shin, and Richard Serrano. My many discussions and friendship with Anne Waters made my time at Columbia precious.

As a faculty member at the University of Cincinnati, I have received technical help, financial support, and leave time from the university. I thank especially the Taft Memorial Fund, the Department of History, the Dean's Office of the McMicken College of Arts and Sciences, and the Office of Research and Advanced Studies.

Many people have helped me find resources on John Marshall Harlan, including the staff of Stanford University's Green Library, especially Jim Knox; the staff of the Manuscript Division of the Library of Congress; James J. Holmberg of the Filson Club Historical Society in Louisville, Kentucky; the archivists at the Chicago Historical Society; Gene Teitelbaum of the University of Louisville Law Library; and Thomas J. Culbertson of the Rutherford B. Hayes Presidential Center in Fremont, Ohio.

Robert F. Peckham, who was then chief judge of the U.S. District Court for the Northern District of California, was kind enough to arrange my first contact with the Harlan family. Several descendants of Harlan, including Elizabeth Derby Middione, Eve Harlan Dillingham, Edith Harlan Powell, and Roger A. Derby, did me a great service by gathering the materials they possessed.

Many historians and legal scholars have helped me at conference sessions, through correspondence, and in conversation. I am especially grateful for the chance to discuss my work at the Biography Seminar at Stanford University organized by Barbara Babcock and Diane Middlebrook, with the fellows at the Heyman Center at Columbia University, with the historians led by Phil Gleason at the Young Scholars in American Religion seminar sponsored by the Center for the Study of Religion and American Culture at Indiana University–Purdue University at Indianapolis, and with my colleagues in Cincinnati at the History Department research seminar.

My greatest intellectual debts are to my mentors. As an undergraduate, I took a course in legal history at Northwestern University taught by Arthur McEvoy. His friendship has helped me through my hardest moments, and his example as a teacher, scholar, and colleague is always with me. Robert Gordon and George M. Fredrickson helped me immeasurably as I was writing my dissertation. Carl N. Degler, my graduate adviser, was generous with his time and attention and even let me sit in his endowed chair, which inspired me to no end.

Years ago, I met Lewis Bateman of the University of North Carolina Press, and one of my pleasures in finishing this manuscript has been placing it in his hands. G. Edward White served as a perceptive reader of the manuscript. The editors of the Studies in Legal History series, Dirk Hartog and Tom Green, read several versions of the manuscript and offered advice of the kind few authors receive and from which most could benefit. I am especially grateful to Dirk for his willingness to wait while I found my voice and his faith that indeed I would. Paula Wald at the press has proved an encouraging and keen-eyed project editor.

My friends Nancy Spatz, Wayne Durrill, Maura O'Connor, and Bill Novak have listened to and read many a Harlan story and kept my spirits up throughout the work. Daniel Ernst's friendship has been as invaluable as his advice. During my final push to finish the book, David Lazar refreshed me with his wit and learning, provided smart editorial advice that eventually sank in, and proved to be a steadfast and cheerful companion during my many bouts with ill-health. My father and stepmother, Adam and Ying Przybyszewski, have offered their love as well as much-needed technical help with computers. My mother, Carol Adams, has always made my way easier with her love, encouragement, and good humor.

THE REPUBLIC ACCORDING TO
# John Marshall Harlan

*Enable the younger generation of Thy servants, upon whom must now fall the burden and the heat of the battle, to quit ourselves like men. As true lovers of Liberty, may we like-wise be obedient servants of the Law. Help us ever as wise stewards of the gifts of Freedom, to be soldiers of the Common Good, so that in all things we may show ourselves worthy of the fathers and of our high calling as citizens of this favored land.*

*Thus may we establish the Republic upon a Rock, and build in America the Holy City, foretold and dreamed of by the prophets and sages of all races since the world began.*

*We ask it of Him Who maketh man to be of one mind in the house; Who giveth integrity to states. Jesus Christ, the desire of all nations, the memory of whose birth among men fills the heart of this world, this night, with gladness and immortal hope. Amen.*

—Prayer delivered by Reverend Richard D. Harlan
  at a banquet honoring his father, Justice John Marshall Harlan,
  1907

# Introduction

*I doubt whether you know as much as one of your age
should about the history of your own country, & the lives of
the great men who founded the government, & have since
illustrated the principles which distinguish American
civilization from that of every other country on the earth.*
—John Marshall Harlan to his son,
  James S. Harlan, 1880

Anyone working on a book has a short explanation of it. I
was giving mine to a curious tablemate at a crowded luncheon several years
ago. John Marshall Harlan, I said, is best known for his dissent in *Plessy v.
Ferguson* in 1896 when the rest of the Supreme Court allowed the states to
segregate people according to their race despite the Fourteenth Amendment's
guarantees. I described the most striking feature of Harlan's life: that he was
born into a slaveholding family in Kentucky in 1833, that he fought for the
Union during the Civil War but opposed emancipation. I was going to add
that I was interested in explaining this change in his beliefs when a young
lawyer at the table interrupted me. "But Harlan was a great judge," she said.
As my listener was marveling at Harlan's early opposition to the Fourteenth
Amendment, the lawyer interrupted our conversation again to repeat, "But
Harlan was a really great judge." In her eyes, knowing that Harlan had once
held views now considered unacceptable was less important than knowing that
he was a great judge. Our conversation broke up amid these interruptions and
drifted to other topics.

What this lawyer had learned in the course of her education demonstrates
something I had noticed while researching Harlan: that the usual purpose of
judicial biography is to prove that a judge was great and that this is somehow more important than our knowledge of the judge's life. It is true that
many nineteenth-century judges wanted to be remembered as great men by
their fellow citizens. But our failure to continue this discussion illustrates the
problem with the search for greatness: it tends to end the conversation.

This book argues that the search for greatness hobbles historical work on judges because it is a mistaken attempt to transcend history itself. Instead of trying to prove that Harlan was a great judge, I focus on certain aspects of Harlan's life and beliefs using sources that have been neglected by other scholars. In these sources and topics lies an explanation for Harlan's transformation and its limits. This is not an exhaustive account of Harlan's life or of his work on the Court. It is an attempt to begin a new conversation.

Most people have heard of Justice John Marshall Harlan because he dissented in *Plessy v. Ferguson*. He wrote in that dissent the words for which he is best known today: "Our Constitution is color-blind, and neither knows nor tolerates classes among citizens." He raged at the idea of separate but equal accommodations, saying, "The thin disguise of 'equal' accommodations for passengers in railroad coaches will not mislead any one, nor atone for the wrong this day done." Harlan warned that the contempt for black citizens expressed by the Court by this decision "will not only stimulate aggressions, more or less brutal and irritating, upon the admitted rights of colored citizens, but will encourage the belief that it is possible, by means of state enactments," to defeat the purposes of the Thirteenth, Fourteenth, and Fifteenth Amendments.[1]

This was not the first time that Harlan dissented in defense of civil rights protections for blacks. In fact, the public reaction to *Plessy* was muted because most white Americans considered the question of segregation to have been settled by the *Civil Rights Cases* in 1883. *Plessy* became the Harlan dissent known best by recent generations because the decision in *Brown v. Board of Education* in 1954 specifically rejected the idea that separate accommodations could be equal.

Harlan repeatedly protested from the bench against racial discrimination.[2] When the Court allowed the state of Kentucky to force segregation on a private Christian college in 1908, Harlan dissented.[3] And he voiced his disappointment when the Court did not come to the aid of black plaintiffs facing violence and the semislavery of peonage.[4] Harlan demanded broad interpretations of the Civil War amendments so that the national government would act on behalf of blacks seeking to exercise their rights.[5]

But two decisions do not follow Harlan's color-blind rule. One is an 1882 decision testing a state law that punished interracial adultery more severely than same-race adultery. The entire Court agreed that such discrimination did not violate the Constitution.[6] Then there was an 1899 decision about the closing of a public high school for black students for financial reasons while the white high school was kept open. Harlan's opinion for the Court said nothing about segregation, but it did say that the decision by the local board of education to close the school was not in itself proof of ill-intent.[7] What did Harlan think he was doing in these two decisions? How can they be reconciled with his famous dissents?

A similar puzzle emerges when it comes to economic issues. Harlan became famous during his lifetime as a defender of the people because he argued that the federal income tax law was constitutional in 1895. It would force the wealthy to pay their share of taxes. His reputation was clinched by a series of antitrust decisions in the late nineteenth and early twentieth centuries that targeted corporate monopolies. Conservative newspapers condemned him, and grateful Progressives wrote letters of praise. Yet Harlan also supported doctrines that benefited large property holders. He wanted to strike down state laws that favored locals over out-of-state producers; this encouraged the rise of giant companies that came to dominate the nation's markets. Harlan supported substantive due process, a doctrine that benefited railroad corporations by making federal judges—not state legislators or state railroad commissioners—the final arbiters of shipping rates. Justice Felix Frankfurter wondered aloud in 1948 why "Harlan, who thought himself a tribune of the people," "gave comfort" to the interests of property.[8] Just whose side was he on?

It is possible to reconcile these decisions by looking to the larger patterns of Harlan's thought. These patterns can be traced by using Harlan's public speeches and private papers as well as his judicial writings. True, the private papers have enormous gaps. For example, very few survive from Harlan's pre-Court days, when he was changing his opinions on civil rights for blacks. We have most of his wife's letters to him in later periods but far fewer from him to her. And Harlan felt compelled not to discuss publicly or privately most of the issues of the day until he had expressed his opinion officially. He once advised Justice Horace H. Lurton that the safest bet when making speeches was to "put yourself in the attitude of expressing the *substance* of what has already been declared by the Court."[9]

Still, some extraordinary documents have been neglected. One such document is a verbatim transcript of Harlan's 1897–98 lectures on constitutional law taken down by two of his students practicing their shorthand. Another is a list drawn up by Harlan in 1910 of opinions that he wanted republished together in a single volume. Since these documents are obviously relevant to explaining Harlan, there must be a reason for their neglect.

Harlan's biographers were distracted from these treasures by their efforts to prove that Harlan was a great judge. Sources that seemed irrelevant to proving his greatness were ignored. Evidence that did not seem to support Harlan's greatness troubled them. In effect, Harlan's latest biographer, Tinsley E. Yarbrough, noticed that Harlan did not seem to meet all of the criteria for judicial greatness and concluded that he was an enigma. So powerful is the idea of greatness that Yarbrough declared that this enigma was indeed great.

Some may argue that biographers need to make their judges great in order to justify their own years spent in libraries, but I believe something more is at stake. The pursuit of greatness is almost irresistible because it justifies judicial biography itself. If judges' personal beliefs do not affect the decisions they make on the bench, their biographies are unimportant to legal history. Only the rare jurist who laid out new doctrines single-handedly deserves one. The details of other judges' lives could be mentioned in passing in histories of courts and doctrines. On the other hand, if judges' personal beliefs affect the decisions they make on the bench, more judicial biographies are needed, but the law itself becomes suspect. Law becomes what the judge had for breakfast, as the legal realists of the early twentieth century put it. Judges do not discover the law deep in tomes but create it themselves. How can we be "a government of laws, not of men," under such circumstances?

Morton J. Horwitz pointed out in 1973 that this was a general problem in legal history. Instead of using the insight of the legal realists, lawyers wrote history as if the bar was made up of neutral experts. Legal thought was described as progressing ever onward and upward, unaffected by social, political, or economic pressures: "The main thrust of lawyer's legal history, then, is to pervert the real function of history by reducing it to the pathetic role of justifying the world as it is." [10]

The problem of the relation between the law and the world is even more acute in judicial biography. Carl B. Swisher presents one of the clearest examples in his 1930 book on Justice Stephen J. Field, a colleague of Harlan's who sat on the Court from 1863 to 1897. He sums up Field's decisions on the Civil War Confiscation Act this way: "He gave different reasons for dissenting in different cases, and from a standpoint of law these opinions are no doubt worthy of study." Swisher continues, "In a biography of the man, however, they are less important than the fact that he usually found one legal reason or another for arguing and voting in favor of the rights of the original owners of the properties." [11] Swisher treats Field's legal reasoning with an off-handedness bordering on contempt. The aim of biography is to uncover the human purpose hidden behind the mask of judicial talk. The study of the life and the study of the law are at odds.

This is an unnerving conclusion for judicial biographers. In order to avoid it, many of them acknowledge the realist insight into the worldly sources of legal doctrine but remain intent on reaching for something that transcends those petty realities. Greatness is what they have taken hold of. Swisher enjoyed casting Field in a bad light yet called him a great judge. Paul Kens, who shares this distrust of Field in his 1997 book, wants to move him from the "near-great" to the "great" category.[12] Even Horwitz was more displeased with the yardstick being applied by biographers than dismissive of any yardstick.

What is greatness? By my reckoning, five tests usually surface in twentieth-century judicial biographies: wisdom, economic progressivism, vindication by history, integrity, and Holmes. Let me explain how they work.

Willard Hurst demanded wisdom in a talk entitled "Who Is the 'Great' Appellate Judge?" given at a symposium on judicial biography in 1948.[13] By wisdom, Hurst meant that judges were aware of the consequences of their actions and appreciated both the potential and the limits of their power. Hurst also required craftsmanship, which has a touchy relationship with wisdom. Charles Fairman noted in 1939 that Justice Samuel F. Miller had troubles here and characterized him as "a man of wisdom rather than of knowledge."[14] Horwitz thought that the obsession with craftsmanship left out "some of the best judges" of the early bar, but he did not go on to tell us what they had instead, although apparently it was something of Chief Justice John Marshall's.[15] Harlan scholars have sometimes taken this tack. An early one wrote that in Harlan's dissents there was "a consistent policy of progressiveness and a lofty idealism which in a technical sense may not be good law, yet which is founded upon broad principles of humanity and of fundamental justice."[16] On the other hand, Alan F. Westin wrote in 1957 that Harlan's interpretations of the Thirteenth and Fourteenth Amendments "still have not impressed the Supreme Court, nor should they; honest and well-intentioned as they were, they rest upon a misreading of language and of legislative history which, if adopted as proper technique, would confuse and stultify the interpretive process."[17]

Harlan's mixed record on economic issues poses a similar problem. Legal progressives were angry at the turn-of-the-century Supreme Court for striking down laws aimed at controlling corporate power and protecting workers. They accused the Court of clinging to outmoded economic beliefs about individualism and distorting the Constitution in order to oppose legislation that acknowledged the realities of industrialization. The influence of the progressives lives on. Applause greets any judge who is seen as ahead of the economic curve and hisses anyone who falls behind.[18] For example, Swisher defined Field as great by virtue of being "one of the master-builders of the legal structure needed for the housing of a particular economic order through a dramatic era of our history"—the mid-nineteenth century. But Field fell behind the times by "labor[ing] stubbornly to keep the country chained to the old order of legal relationships, in spite of the new social and economic conditions which had already come, and others which were to follow." [19] Field failed to recognize that industrialization had created enormous corporate power that the government had to control. For this, Field is scolded by Swisher. On the other hand, Swisher is gentle with Roger Taney because he was born into an aristocratic, Federalist family but saw the light. He became a Jacksonian Democrat who fought that bastion of moneyed privilege, the Bank of the United States. When Swisher wrote on Taney in 1936, support for a man who pitted himself against "predatory financial interests" was in the air.[20] Frankfurter's impatience in 1948 with Harlan for having given comfort to the interests of property is part of this progressive–New Deal tradition. So is Kens's recent criticism of Field for believing in a "radical form of individualism." [21] The great judge should cooperate in inevitable and desirable social and economic change by modifying legal doctrines. This has a suspiciously confident ring to it.

Another test for greatness, vindication by history, raises the same suspicion. Biographers eagerly point out that modern problems would have been avoided if their judge's reasoning had been followed earlier. What Judge Lemuel Shaw did during the nineteenth century, Leonard Levy implies, a later Court should have done when faced with New Deal legislation.[22] John Reid praised Joseph Doe in 1967 for anticipating procedural code simplification.[23] Fairman thought we owed Justice Joseph P. Bradley a vote of thanks for twentieth-century federal regulation of labor relations because Bradley led the Court in promoting a national economy in the 1870s and 1880s.[24] Clearly, Harlan's biographers have had an easy time with this one. A year after *Brown*, Loren P. Beth wrote of Harlan that "a dissent is an appeal to the conscience of the future: it is thus to be judged on whether it correctly divined that conscience." [25]

Integrity raises a different problem from that of vindication by history and for that reason interests me more. Integrity covers easy and hard instances. An easy instance would be that of simple corruption. Another is the decision to let stand a law that one thinks is stupid but constitutional. Fairman notes that one of Justice Miller's letters records his personal disapproval of a statute that he refused to strike down when it was challenged before his Court.[26] Judges of integrity are supposed to be able to distinguish between what they think is good policy and what they think is good law.

Then there are the hard cases. Sometimes a judge approves a course of action both personally and judicially, and the biographer cannot distinguish between the two. Charles W. McCurdy argues that far from being a running dog for the capitalist class, Justice Field was a man of principle. All of his life, Field adhered to a constitutional theory rooted in the Jacksonianism of his boyhood teacher Theodore Sedgwick II.[27] But the fact that a judge had a larger purpose may not decide the hard cases of integrity. When Levy wrote, "Stated crudely, the [Lemuel] Shaw Court [of Massachusetts in the mid-nineteenth century] favored railroads over shippers," he added a note for us crude-minded types explaining that he had looked for evidence on whether or not Shaw owned railroad stock and found none.[28] He left Shaw his integrity while acknowledging his bias: "The Chief Justice, like so many of his time, linked that which was beneficial to railroads with industrial expansion, which in turn was linked with the grand march of the Commonwealth toward a more prosperous life."[29] Most people need to believe that what benefits their class is good for society. This is the difference between favoring railroads because you and your friends own stock and favoring railroads because their success will bring prosperity to all *and* because you and your friends own stock. But did Shaw have integrity if his decisions followed or broke with precedent, so long as the railroads always won?

Therein lies the threat to our hope that the courts treat people fairly. One doesn't need overt bias to favor one group over another. Men of good conscience can do terrible things to other people. Even Justice Oliver Wendell Holmes Jr. couldn't crack this nut, according to G. Edward White in 1993. Holmes is famous for saying that the life of the law has not been logic but experience. Yet Holmes himself worked hard to distinguish the correct logic by which law should be systematized.[30] In other words, Holmes thought that other people's law had been experience; *his* would be logic.

Holmes himself is the final test for judicial greatness. Biographers often search for proof that their subject was like Holmes or was praised by Holmes and therefore worthy of being called great. R. Kent Newmyer wrote, "Without fanfare or theorizing, [Judge Joseph] Story operated regularly on the practical principle—one that Oliver Wendell Holmes, Jr., rediscovered in his *Common Law* (1881) and that modern legal historians have begun to explore—that law must serve the needs of society."[31] Reid made comparisons between Joseph Doe and Holmes whenever possible. And Willard L. King bestowed the ultimate compliment on Bradley by calling him "the Justice Holmes of [an earlier] Court."[32] Yarbrough suggests that Harlan's dissent in a famous labor decision was "arguably" just as good as Holmes's.[33] Even Beth felt compelled to invoke Holmes in his 1992 biography of Harlan, although it is hard to think of two judges with less in common.[34]

One of G. Edward White's purposes is to undermine this practice by explaining that Holmes was vindicated through misinterpretation before he even became history by young legal scholars attracted to his status in the Boston upper class and eager to use him for their own ends.[35] So successful were they that in my youth I sponged up an impression of Holmes as a warm humanitarian, only to encounter the actual cold-blooded Holmes with a shock.

White explains that the making of the Holmes myth relied on a definition of judicial greatness that existed only at a particular point in time: "Holmes came to be regarded as 'great' in large measure because this group [of younger legal scholars] attributed qualities of 'greatness' in a judge to him, and those qualities—philosophical skepticism, deference to the legislature in constitutional cases, a direct, 'literary' style of opinion writing—would not have been identified with judicial distinction two decades before."[36] Although the biographies I have mentioned date from the mid- to late twentieth century and largely share a common definition of greatness, White is right. Not having existed earlier, this definition of greatness may one day disappear.

The history of Harlan's reputation shows how later generations thrust greatness on him. Although it is true that during his lifetime, Harlan was called the Great Dissenter because of his dissents in the antitrust and income tax cases, he was considered something of an eccentric until *Brown v. Board of Education* sent scholars scrambling to study him in 1954.[37] A flurry of articles followed, and the lone champion of black civil rights on the turn-of-the-century Court was hailed as a prophet. An entire issue of the *Kentucky Law Journal* was devoted to him in 1958.[38] Harlan's reputation changed accordingly. Although a 1953 edition of the *Encyclopedia of American History* did not even mention Harlan's dissents on civil rights in its short biography, Harlan made it onto a list of great judges in 1958 primarily on the weight of those dissents.[39] Harlan has appeared regularly on such lists ever since.

Harlan's evolving reputation demonstrates what some judicial biographers seem unaware of: that the definition of greatness they happen to be using is a historical artifact. The result of this anachronistic approach is that topics that fall outside the current twentieth-century definition of judicial greatness, such as religious faith or literary accomplishments, are neglected despite the importance they had for their subjects.[40] Instead of solving the dilemma of judicial biography, the pursuit of greatness tempts biographers to overlook historical circumstances that would undermine their effort. To paraphrase Horwitz, this reduces judicial biography to the pathetic role of justifying the judges as they were. Instead of proving that Harlan was a great judge, this book tries to put to use the legal realists' insight into the worldly origins of the law.

My quarrel is more with the problem of greatness in conventional judicial biographies than with their usual structure. Most of them are organized largely chronologically. The judge is born in the first chapter and dies in the last. In between are the obligatory precourt chapters, followed by doctrinal chapters. Nonjudicial activities are set to the side. Wonderful books have been written this way. But the tendency to separate judicial and nonjudicial thoughts and actions from each other can be misleading. Also, a flowing narrative tends to smooth over unanswered questions and the difficulties of interpretation. For these reasons and since narrative has not served Harlan all that well so far, I have decided to try something different.

Instead of presenting a chronological or doctrinal narrative, this book first treats Harlan's general ideas about law and nation and then looks at how those ideas were expressed in specific instances. Instead of placing off-the-bench activities to the side, I move between life and law in each chapter. This book notes connections between ideas not usually considered part of the legal realm and those that usually are. In order to make these connections, it moves about in time, breaking from chronological order.

Each chapter relies on particular primary sources that have been neglected by other historians. In these sources, we can see that Harlan inherited certain traditions; that he reshaped them in light of his experiences as a lawyer, a political candidate, and a judge; and that he justified the vision of law that resulted. I would rewrite Holmes's saying that the life of the law has been experience, not logic. In this life in the law, experience created logic.

My editors and I have puzzled over what to label the result. Like an intellectual biography, this book focuses on Harlan's ideas and their relationship to his experiences. Yet its emphasis on sources and their interpretation is not exactly what one expects in a biography.[41] Whatever its proper designation, I take heart in J. Woodford Howard Jr.'s suggestion at a 1995 symposium on judicial biography that "rather than contend over the superiority of competing styles of research, the wise course is to strengthen each mode, giving due regard for what others provide, and . . . thereby advance the whole."[42] Many aspects of Harlan's life and work remain unexplored in this volume. Their absence is an invitation for others to join the conversation I have tried to begin.

Chapter 1 uses the memoirs of Harlan's wife, Malvina, to show how the family members created a mythic identity for themselves as paternalists. Whites wielded benevolent power over blacks, and white men did the same for white women. The Civil War destroyed this supposedly happy household. In the political chaos that followed, John Harlan was forced to choose between the two values on which paternalism rested: white supremacy and white forbearance from the abuse of power. He chose the latter and embraced legal equality of the races but never completely abandoned the idea of racial difference inherent in paternalism.

Chapter 2 introduces the other two traditions that influenced Harlan—religious faith and constitutional nationalism—by using a set of law lectures he gave during the 1897–98 academic year. Harlan's faith in the unquestionable truth of Christian orthodoxy underlay his faith in the law. Harlan was a legal formalist who believed that the rules of judicial interpretation remained fixed despite contemporary controversies. He neither struggled with the intellectual problems that formalism created nor examined the theological difficulties that religious orthodoxy faced. Harlan interpreted events within this cosmic framework. He could account for the Civil War and the constitutional revolution that followed it by identifying racial egalitarianism as the fixed goal toward which the country was divinely directed. His national myth of the founding fathers as reluctant slaveholders paralleled the family myth the Harlans had created for themselves. Both demonstrate Harlan's ability to explain change by reference to unchanging principles.

These early chapters lay out the traditions on which Harlan relied. Chapter 3 serves as a transition to more specific treatments of legal decisions. It explains how Harlan was appointed to the Supreme Court and examines the moral and civic meaning he gave to his position. The three chapters that follow show how the traditions of racial paternalism, legal formalism, and religious orthodoxy shaped Harlan's understanding of specific legal issues brought before him as a judge.

I turn first to Harlan's civil rights decisions not only because they are the decisions for which he is known but also because they were central to his thought. The status of blacks was the foremost issue for Harlan as a new member of the Republican Party in the late 1860s and early 1870s, and determining exactly which rights they possessed would be one of his major judicial tasks. Harlan's loud demands for a broad, national standard of rights were voiced most obviously on behalf of these new citizens.

Chapter 4 shows how remnants of paternalism—in particular, a belief in racial identity—limited Harlan's effort to ensure equal rights to blacks. Taking a cue from Harlan's identification of law and religion, I use three stories about race and religion to explain the inconsistency of his judicial record on black rights. Although Harlan went further than any other Supreme Court justice in extending civil rights to blacks, he balked at the interracial social intimacy that might result in the blurring of racial identity. Racialism gave rise to Harlan's support for legal equality by making it the duty of all Anglo-Saxons to refrain from the abuse of power and his particular duty as a judge to see that they did so. But racialism also limited Harlan's support for legal equality by requiring the persistence of Anglo-Saxons as such.

Chapter 5 demonstrates the broader implications of Harlan's belief in the national mission led by Anglo-Saxons by looking at how it determined his reaction to the Spanish-American War and its aftermath. Harlan's response to the war was enthusiastic because he believed that his country was fighting for liberty as it had done during the Revolution and the Civil War. By using this typology, Harlan distorted contemporary fact. Eventually, Harlan's judicial duty required him to test America's actions against the standards of the national mission in the Insular Cases. Harlan dissented passionately when a majority of the Court refused to extend the Bill of Rights to the inhabitants of the new colonies won from Spain.

Whereas these two chapters explain that Harlan approached the question of the status of the new black citizens and the question of the status of the insular inhabitants from the same direction, chapter 6 traces the links between civil and economic rights by examining a list of favorite decisions drawn up by Harlan near the end of his life. Harlan's list reveals that the logic that justified federal protection for black men seeking the right to vote could also be used to protect corporations from unreasonable state regulation. In effect, the Fourteenth Amendment gave Harlan a way to renew the antebellum Whig belief that economic ties helped foster unionist sentiment.

One of the results of Harlan's efforts to facilitate this national marketplace was the growth of corporations of unprecedented size. Harlan was sure that the men who created these giants had somehow violated the natural laws of the economy. He condemned their ambitions in the language of antislavery protest. What was needed was not a new economic system like socialism but effective regulation to ensure free competition of labor and capital in the national marketplace. When a majority of the Court struck down such legislation, Harlan accused them of failing to recognize, as their brethren had before the Civil War, that slavery—this time economic slavery—threatened the Union.

Chapter 7 brings us back to the household where we began. Although classical republican thought holds that all male citizens must be willing to sacrifice self-interest to the greater civic good, Harlan made financial sacrifice the special responsibility of lawyering men like himself. He built on his family's history of service to the Republic by valuing it more than the financial success that eluded him. In doing this, Harlan made his life into a model for the men of his family as well as a legacy to the nation.

In addition to suggesting a new approach to the study of judges, this book offers an alternative to the two standard interpretations of the effect of the Civil War on legal thought. One stresses the persistence of Jacksonian individualism long after the economy had become dominated by industrial corporations.[43] Old Jacksonians feared class privilege created at the hands of legislators more than they feared the power of economic giants created by market forces. For example, Justice Stephen J. Field once objected to a provision of the 1884 California constitution that gave municipalities the power to set water rates. Field argued that the new law violated the rights of the owners of the waterworks. He wrote: "The pearl at the bottom of the sea belongs to no one, but the diver who enters the waters and brings it to light has property in the gem. He has, by his own labor, reduced it to possession, and in all communities and by all law his right to it is recognized."[44] This inapt analogy between a pearl diver at the bottom of the sea and a waterworks corporation chartered by the state to serve the city of San Francisco demonstrates that Jacksonian individualism persisted in the face of economic change. The Civil War only made such men more conservative. Having seen the social order disrupted violently, they clung to the vision of the Constitution they had known in peace.[45]

The other interpretation of the effect of the Civil War on legal thought identifies a profound change that would become part of the revolt against formalism.[46] The war taught sentimental individualists that to simply "feel right," as Harriet Beecher Stowe urges her readers to do at the end of *Uncle Tom's Cabin*, was not enough to win a war.[47] Power had to be centralized, bureaucracies created, procedures followed. Ideals were not as important as practical organization. The legal mind best known for learning the hard lessons of war was that of the wounded Oliver Wendell Holmes Jr. He declared in 1895 that obedient, unthinking service to the nation-state was the soldier's faith.[48]

The Jacksonian mind of Field survived the Civil War intact; the skeptical mind of Holmes learned that the world was indifferent to his fate. What of Harlan's mind? For him, the war became a moral touchstone. Instead of seeing emancipation as a mere tactic in the grand strategy for saving the Union, he saw it as the reason why the Union had to be saved. The country had a mission: setting an example for the world as a republic where men were free and equal. The moral lesson that Harlan drew from the war was that the Union had to be preserved against the threat of tyranny, whether it came in the form of white supremacy or corporate power.

In creating this alternate postwar jurisprudence, Harlan was not alone. The judges of the lower federal courts acted on the belief that the Civil War amendments had worked a revolution in federalism until 1873, when the Supreme Court told them they were mistaken.[49] Some persisted in their mistake. Judge Lorenzo Sawyer of the Ninth Circuit told historian H. H. Bancroft in 1890 that since the Civil War, he had "stricken the word 'Federal' from my vocabulary" and used "the word 'National' in its place."[50] In states where Republicans ruled, blacks seeking civil rights protections before state courts were more often successful than not.[51] And in the long run, nationalism gained the upper hand as well as the high moral ground.

Although Harlan altered the ideas he had been taught, the most striking thing about his life is the persistence of tradition. Historians tend to be more interested in new ideas emerging than in old ones hanging on. As a result, they can underestimate the lasting power of ideas. But what better proof is there of the persistence of the republican requirement that men serve the state and of the formalist desire to transcend history than today's judicial biographers who continue their pursuit of greatness?

# CHAPTER I

# The Best Type of Slave-holders

## A Family Ethic of Paternalism

*The destinies of the two races, in this country, are indissolubly linked together, and the interests of both require that the common government of all shall not permit the seeds of race hate to be planted under the sanction of law.*

—John Marshall Harlan,

  *Plessy v. Ferguson,* 1896

The main riddle of John Harlan's life is how a former slave-holder and an opponent of emancipation came to support the legal equality of blacks. Although the rest of the Supreme Court dashed the hopes blacks had placed in the Civil War amendments, Harlan delivered dissents that condemned state-sponsored racial segregation. He wrote in 1896 in *Plessy v. Ferguson,* "Our Constitution is color-blind, and neither knows nor tolerates classes among citizens."[1] He expressed disgust at the idea that the states could force apart members of different races when they sought each other's company in the pursuit of worthy goals.

Some scholars have tried to solve this riddle by playing up his prophetic vision on civil rights and other issues. For example, one argues that Harlan "can properly be regarded as a 'founding father' of modern constitutional law."[2] But if we see Harlan as a man before his time, a twentieth-century liberal mysteriously born in 1833, we overlook the sources of his thought. Other historians have looked to his early experiences. One suggested that Harlan's pro–civil rights decisions were based on his realistic understanding of race relations as a former slaveholder.[3] Contact with slavery is hardly enough of an explanation, however; most white Kentuckians were familiar with the institution and still opposed giving equal legal status to blacks.

And we must account for another side to Harlan's judicial record. He did not always follow his own color-blind rule. He agreed to allow the states to punish miscegenation. He dealt clumsily with a case that seemed to authorize segregation in the public schools. How can we make sense of his record as a whole?

In order to explain how Harlan came to support legal rights for blacks and the limits of that support, we need to know how Harlan experienced slavery, how he interpreted that experience in light of the Civil War amendments, and how that early understanding shaped his later judicial interpretation of civil rights. Finding all of this out is difficult. Very little evidence exists on what life was like in the slaveholding Harlan households. The Harlan papers from the decades when John Harlan was on the Court are voluminous, but only a handful of letters date back to the 1860s and earlier. So how can we explore this border-state politician's experience with slavery?

A voice rises out of this silence; it belongs to Harlan's wife of over fifty years, Malvina Shanklin Harlan. Her memoirs, "Some Memories of a Long Life, 1854–1911," contain the only surviving descriptions of her husband's relations with blacks, slave and free. Although some recent biographers of judges have looked at their subjects' marriages, most have treated wives as one of those off-the-bench activities put to the side. But I argue that these memoirs, if used with caution, illuminate Harlan's understanding of the proper exercise of power inside and outside the household. Because the Harlan household contained not only blood relatives but also relatives by marriage and "servants," as the slaves were called, we must look to the interlocking hierarchies of race and gender in order to understand the sources of Harlan's political thought.[4] Malvina Harlan's memoirs offer unparalleled information on these issues.

Using memoirs written in 1915 to understand experiences from decades earlier is a tricky process—even more so when they were written not by the judge in question but by his wife. The human mind apparently constructs memory as part of an ongoing process, so that Malvina's memories of the prewar period were filtered by her concerns in 1915.[5]

Consider, for example, the tableau of womanly sacrifice that Malvina drew when recounting what happened when her husband decided to join the Union army in 1861. Malvina tells us that he said "he would leave the matter entirely to me" because "his first duty was to me and his children." She in turn asked him what he would do if he had no family; "he said at once with great earnestness, 'I would go to the help of my country.'" Malvina responded that he should go: "I could not stand between you and your duty to the country and be happy."[6] It would be a mistake to take this story at face value.[7] By 1915, all Americans would have been familiar with similar tales of the Civil War sacrifices of women that were told and retold as history and in fiction.[8] Knowing that Malvina's story shared the central features of a host of similar accounts should make us cautious.

We should be especially cautious since we know that the formula of the self-effacing woman did not always work so straightforwardly in Malvina's life. For example, John made arrangements to be buried in Arlington National Cemetery just outside Washington, D.C., and he assured Malvina that there would be room for her in the cemetery as well. When he died in 1911, she defied his wishes. She had him buried in Rock Creek Cemetery in Washington, D.C., in a family plot where there was enough room for herself and all of their children. By doing this, she made clear that John was not in the end a soldier of a nation but the patriarch of a family. Here her determined actions speak louder than her remembered description of the self-effacing incident. By keeping in mind the need to test the tales in the memoirs against the available facts, we can use them to understand the identity the Harlan family created for itself.

Malvina's identification of her husband in death as a patriarch is one we should heed. Historians have recognized the importance of the links between private and public life for nineteenth-century women. Malvina Harlan's memoirs show the importance of such links for men as well. The rhetoric of separate spheres, which created a "polarity" between the household (where women stayed behind) and the world (into which men sallied forth), has misled us.[9] Although Harlan moved in the public world of electoral politics and law, he never strayed far emotionally from the family relations in which he grounded his identity.

John Harlan is the subject of Malvina's memoirs. Consider Malvina's choice of time period in the title. The memoirs begin in 1853 when Malvina first spotted through a window a tall stranger in her small hometown of Evansville, Indiana; she remembered "his magnificent figure, his head erect, his broad shoulders well thrown back—walking as if the whole world belonged to him."[10] They met the next year, the first year in her title. She ends the memoirs with the prayer said at John's burial in 1911. Indeed, Malvina's claim to a public audience rested solely on her position as John's wife. Their private correspondence displays a deep emotional bond between them. When consulting with John about a suitor for their eldest daughter, Malvina questioned the match because the girl did not exhibit "the true all absorbing love that one must feel for a life companion."[11] The week of John's burial, Malvina consoled herself that she could "truthfully say, that never *knowingly* did I do anything that I thought he would not approve!" Even as she mourned, she tried to follow his wishes. Malvina wrote her children: "I am trying to be brave, as I know he would have me be, but the wakening in the morning to find him *gone* is heartbreaking."[12] Malvina recorded her remembrances in order to honor her life's companion. She wanted to present to the world a

Malvina Harlan wrote her memoirs, "Some Memories of a Long Life, 1854–1911," in 1915 as a tribute to her husband, John Marshall Harlan. They contain the only surviving descriptions of her husband's relations with blacks, slave and free. (Courtesy of Edith Harlan Powell)

portrait of their family life that he would approve. These memoirs were not so much a record of past reality as a record of the stories the "Harlan tribe" told in order to identify itself before the world.

Other scholars have used Malvina's memoirs in a far less cautious way because of their desire to prove that John was a great judge according to the late-twentieth-century definition of the term. They have quoted it as fact whenever it might serve to establish John as a precocious racial egalitarian.[13] The wish to create the kind of hero that would have been vindicated by *Brown v. Board of Education* has led to a neglect of other incidents described by Malvina.

For all of the goodwill she expresses toward the slaves and freedpeople, Malvina obviously sees them as fundamentally simpler folk than whites. Because of this difference, the two groups live in stratified yet mutually devoted company. Harlan learned a sense of white obligation to black dependents in his father's house. The tone set in Harlan's ancestral household resonated through his actions in the political community. His demand for the legal equality of blacks rested on this paternalism, which in turn rested on an assumption of fundamental differences between the races. This accounts for the limits of his defense of black civil rights as well. When Harlan warned his brethren that the destinies of the two races were indissolubly linked together, his intention was not to make a prophecy but to state an old truth.

Malvina's memoirs record her husband's belief in a second kind of fundamental difference that reinforced the racial paternalism of the southern patriarch. The Harlan family believed that white women were fitted solely for the domestic sphere. In turn, white men had duties in the public world as well as personal responsibility for their womenfolk. This idea was not peculiar to the Harlans. Some southern law codes even grouped husband and wife, parent and child, and master and slave all under the heading of domestic relations.[14] Thus a second social hierarchy based on mutual devotion persisted essentially unaltered through the Harlans' lifetimes. The paternal relationship of husband and wife served to bolster that between white and black. Each exhibited Harlan's loyalty to the ways of his father's household.

In order to explain the riddle of Harlan's life, we must stop treating him as a lone individual. To focus on his political and judicial life and neglect his family life is to make him into an isolated eminence handing down decisions from on high. The brilliant light shone on the great judge leaves in the shadows two members of what he called his family, one a white woman, the other a black man. Without their stories, Harlan remains an unexplained judicial anomaly. With them, he becomes a member of a tribe steeped in traditions

James Harlan (1800–1863), the father of John Marshall Harlan, was a lawyer who held both state and national offices. His family remembered him as a slaveholder who condemned the cruelties of slavery, but records from the antebellum period indicate that he traded in slaves and he may have fathered one of his own slaves, Robert James Harlan. (Courtesy of the collection of the Kentucky Historical Society)

and legends who carried these older ways with him even as he entered the revolutionary era of legal equality.

When Malvina married John Harlan in 1856, she left her hometown in the free state of Indiana and crossed over the Ohio River to the slave state of Kentucky. There she came face-to-face with the peculiar institution of slavery she had feared from a distance but grew to cherish. Her depiction in 1915 of relations between masters and slaves within the Harlan household is one of interdependence and affection. It was a vision created by the Harlan family that survived long after slavery itself was abolished.

Malvina admits in her memoirs that she traveled South with some trepidation since "all my kindred were strongly opposed to Slavery." In fact, one of her uncles was an abolitionist who "would rather have seen me in my grave than have me marry a Southern man and go to live in the South." [15] She loved the man in question enough to defy this opposition. "Following the patriarchal custom that was quite common in Kentucky at the period — in accordance with which a son brought his bride home to live under his ancestral roof," Malvina moved into the home of James and Eliza Harlan. [16] She immediately became dependent on the slave labor system since "each daughter and daughter-in-law in the Harlan family had her own special maid, with whom she was most familiar." [17]

James Harlan was a successful Whig politician and a crony of Henry Clay's. He had gathered under his roof a population worthy of a patriarch: one unmarried son, two unmarried daughters, two married sons and their wives, and a married daughter who brought her children to spend summers. [18] Although he was a lawyer and a town dweller for most of the year, James owned some dozen slaves. This was the typical form of slaveholding in Kentucky, which had very few plantations. No Kentuckian owned more than 300 slaves in 1860, and only a handful owned more than 100. [19] Kentucky slaves generally lived in groups of less than twenty.

James was no radical on race issues, but he seems to have had more sympathy than the average white Kentuckian for blacks. After all, he was allied with Clay, who supported gradual emancipation. When James was running for state attorney general in 1851, a friend warned him that supporters of his Democratic rival had spread "a report of a most slanderous character . . . to the effect that you have an agent travelling over the State hunting up negroes claiming their freedom for the purposes of instituting suits in their behalf." That was not the worst of it: "It has also been stated that you are an *abolitionist*." His supporter called desperately for a denial of "these ridiculous statements." [20]

James assured his friend that "the term 'Abolitionist' has no terrors for me" since "he who applies it to me lies in his throat." Abolition, unlike gradual emancipation, was a radical movement demanding an immediate end to an intolerable crime against nature. To moderates like James Harlan, it represented a threat to the political and social order. Abolitionist William Lloyd Garrison had shocked many white Americans by calling "the compact" between the North and the South—that is, the Constitution, with its clauses protecting slavery—"a covenant with death and an agreement with hell." This was hardly the kind of sentiment likely to play well in Kentucky among Whigs devoted to the Constitution. James denied the "palpable falsehoods" linking him to abolitionism with care; his letter is blotted with corrections. He admitted to taking on freedom cases. His personal integrity demanded it: "I cannot be deterred from engaging for or against any person on account of any public clamor." The code of his profession also supported his decision to take on such cases: "Nothing which may emanate from Negro traders or [others?] will ever prevent me from instituting a suit for *freedom* if I believe the laws authorize it."[21] James took on freedom suits not because he opposed slavery but because he upheld the law—in particular, the kind of laws designed to "domesticate" slavery by making it seem less cruel and arbitrary.[22] By allowing persons held in bondage to sue for freedom on the grounds that they were wrongly held, state lawmakers merely reaffirmed that most slaves were rightly held while giving themselves credit for their scrupulousness.

In like fashion, James was apparently trying to domesticate the peculiar institution in his home. The Harlan "servants," as Malvina always calls them, lived in one wing of the "Big House" and "in the cabin at the back of the lot." The female slaves were personal servants and household help, and the male slaves worked in the large gardens surrounding the house. Malvina tells us that to her surprise "I was often obliged to admit to myself that my former views of the 'awful Institution of Slavery' would have to be somewhat modified." She noted with "great wonder" "the close sympathy existing between the slaves and their Master or Mistress."[23] She insists on this all-pervading sympathy between the two races throughout her account.

Malvina's memoirs record the same picture elaborated before the war by southern white men who feared abolitionists and after the war by whites of both regions who found the image of moonlight and magnolias appealing—"the image of a beautifully articulated, patriarchal society in which every Southerner, black or white, male or female, rich or poor, had an appropriate place and was happy in it," as one historian puts it.[24] Unlike their early-eighteenth-century predecessors, whose casual cruelty indicated that they did not see themselves as paternalists, nineteenth-century white southern men, influenced partly by their evangelical faith, changed the slave codes "to curtail once unbounded power" to murder and maim.[25] Although few successful prosecutions resulted, slaveholders justified the exercise of their enormous power by denouncing the worst cruelties.[26] Their rule was supposed to be benign, even beneficial to the slaves. According to Malvina, the Harlan slaves were devoted to their masters' interests and in return received paternal care. "Most of the property of my Father-in-law consisted in slaves," she explains, "and he felt that there was nothing for him to do but to accept the responsibility for these human souls, doing for them as best he could."[27]

In effect, Malvina justifies slavery, as had the antebellum planters, by pointing out that blacks differed essentially from whites. She notes the native artistry of blacks, all of whom "at least have some ear for music," and "the poetic touch that seems to be inborn in so many of that race."[28] She blames the death of one black woman, who slept too close to the hearth and burned to death, on the fact that she was unconscious "of the heat that would have quickly awakened one of another race."[29] Other characteristics of the slaves, such as their ignorant "fondness for large words," might be explained by their situation rather than by any innate difference, but Malvina makes no distinction.[30]

Above all, "the servants of that time" impressed her with their "very close and affectionate interest . . . in the affairs of their Master and Mistress."[31] She notes "the pride which the maid took in the fine clothes of her 'Young Missus.' "[32] As remembered by its privileged half, the relationship between master and slave was one of sentiment and not production in the Harlan household. A rare surviving letter from the Civil War years reveals that Malvina oversaw dairying, but her "Memories" push work to the background.[33] We hear that "Uncle" Lewis "wielded the spade or hoe" only en route to a description of the song he sang as he worked.[34] She states that "Aunt" Charlotte was her cook only in order to tell us that one evening when she went to give orders for breakfast she found Charlotte praying "for every member of the family by name." Returning to her bed, Malvina told her husband that she "did not care whether we had any breakfast or not, so long as there were such prayers going up for us from the kitchen."[35] When Malvina writes of slave labor generally, she is careful to avoid any mention of unpleasantness. Slaves made work arrangements on their own terms, she says, since "a good slave-owner never forced good servants to hire themselves to any household that was objectionable to the servants."[36] There is no mention of punishment of these members of the household for insubordination or misbehavior.

In fact, slavery comes across more as a form of social welfare than as a labor system in Malvina's memoirs. The Harlan slaves "were all carefully looked after, not only physically but morally," Malvina assures us. She insists that the Harlan family never thought of abandoning their older slaves. Malvina recalls her visits to "Uncle" Joel and his wife, both in their nineties: "They were cared for like two babies; and the almost daily visit that was made to their cabin, by one or more from the 'Big House' kept them in good cheer and full of interest in what was going on in the 'Family.' "[37] Here, Malvina tells, were caring whites dedicated to the welfare of even their aged slaves. From her "Memories" alone, one would scarcely suspect that their relationship had ever been based on the labor of one for the benefit of the other. But there was trouble in paradise: some people did not seem to belong there.

The gifted slave required more than paternalism could offer. James Harlan, "with his sympathy for the unfortunate [black] race, was always quick to recognize anything like unusual ability in them," Malvina writes. Unlike average slaves, exceptional ones deserved an opportunity to earn their freedom. Accordingly, James "made it possible for two of his men servants to purchase their own freedom, by giving them, each year, for several years, the money equivalent to half-a-year's hire."[38] One of them found a place as a railroad porter after his release. The other, Robert James Harlan, who was seven-eights white in ancestry, had been allowed "unusual freedom" from the first and was "taught the elements of an education by Mr. Harlan's older sons" after the local public school learned he was partially black in ancestry and refused him further admittance.[39]

Robert may have been an example of what Anne Firor Scott calls "the fatal flaw" in the southern paternalist order: miscegenation.[40] At least one newspaper article implied that this octoroon slave was in fact James's illegitimate son, fathered by James before his marriage when he was only fifteen years old.[41] Malvina's references to Robert suggest that she did not know he was a Harlan by blood. (She arrived eight years after his departure from the house.) Robert and John remained friends and political allies throughout their lives.[42] Whether or not Robert was James's son, he must have made an indelible mark on the Harlan family's memories. He physically represented the interdependence of the two races, and his personal history after leaving the household proved that race was no bar to success. Allowed to travel on his own, Robert made a fortune during the Gold Rush of 1848 and finally settled in Cincinnati to pursue a political and business career after paying $500 for formal freedom papers. The exceptional slave called on the paternalist to acknowledge their essentially monetary relationship in order to end it. Other slaves were supposed to be satisfied with their lot.

Central to Malvina's memoirs and to the Harlan family's identity as pater-

Robert James Harlan (1816–1897) was born a slave. The *Cincinnati Daily Gazette* of 15 October 1881 wrote that he, "on the paternal side, is a son of one of the best Kentucky families." He lived in James Harlan's household until 1848, when he traveled to California and made a fortune in the Gold Rush. He then bought his freedom for $500 and settled in Cincinnati, where he pursued a career in business and politics. (From William J. Simmons, *Men of Mark, Eminent, Progressive, and Rising* [1887]; courtesy of the Library of Congress)

nalists is a story she tells about James Harlan. John told the same story to a newspaper interviewer in 1906.[43] It describes James's anger at the spectacle of blacks suffering under less benevolent care than that which he was supposed to have accorded his own slaves.

According to Malvina, one Sunday morning John was walking to church with his father down the main street of Frankfort, Kentucky. They encountered a group of chained slaves and a "brutish" white slave driver whose "badge of office was a long snake-like whip made of black leather, every blow from which drew blood."[44] James was reminded that "the peculiarly close relations that existed between Master and slaves in the case of the best type of Slave-holders in the South" were an ideal not always reached.[45] Malvina testifies to his outrage: "The sight stirred my Father-in-law to the depths of his gentle nature." James and his son saw before them "the awful possibilities of an institution which, in the division of family estates, and the sale of the slaves, involved inevitably the separation of husband and wife, of parent and children."[46]

James gave the slave driver a piece of his mind. "My Father-in-law could do nothing to liberate the poor creatures then before him," Malvina explains, "but he was so filled with indignation that any one calling himself a man should be engaged in such a cruel business that, walking out to the middle of the street and angrily shaking his long fore-finger in the face of the 'slave-driver,' he said to him, '*You are a damned scoundrel. Good morning, sir.*'" It was the closest thing to "swearing" that young John had ever heard from his father's mouth. "After having thus relieved his feelings," Malvina continues, "he quietly pursued his way to the House of Prayer."[47] With that said, she or another family member telling this tale probably would have sat back and waited for a murmur of appreciation from the listener.

We can regard this tale as an indication that the Harlans recognized on some level of consciousness the central flaw in their myth. James and his family condemned the slave trade because it demonstrated just how fragile white paternalism was. When John recalled in 1898 slavery-era "practices that were horrible to the rights of the Christian man," it was the slave trade that came to his mind. Neither physical abuse nor cheating laborers of their hire made as great an impression on his memory as the sight of a slave family "divided and separated" on the courthouse steps, "the father sold to one man and the mother to another in a distant part of the country, and the children sold one by one, and separated, one to be sent to one state, and one to another."[48] The familial feelings of interracial affection and obligation the Harlans claimed to have fostered in their household could not survive this threat. When masters exercised their right to trade in slaves, the notion of an integrated household was exposed for the lie it was. By his very existence, the slave driver betrayed the white paternalist. In Malvina's memories, he embodied "the worst aspects of the system."[49]

Clearly, James could have done more than curse the slave trader. Kentuckians like Henry Clay and Robert J. Breckinridge worked for gradual emancipation during the campaign for a new state constitution in 1849.[50] More impressively, Cassius M. Clay, Henry's nephew, freed his own slaves, paid them wages, and presented himself as an abolitionist candidate for governor in 1851, although he lost spectacularly.[51] That was the same year James denied that he was an abolitionist. Nor was the younger Clay the only white person to risk his safety in the abolitionist cause in Kentucky.

Unlike these men, James merely cursed a slave trader for his cruelty. By doing no more than that, he did nothing to stop a growing trade that "virtually converted" his state "into the slave mart for the lower South."[52] Because it had few plantations, Kentucky had less need for slave labor, and the excess, as it were, could be sold. Although white southerners often denounced the slave trade itself, they appear to have accepted the traders socially.[53] Apparently, only the slaves truly hated the traders.

James Harlan's curse was not his only contact with the slave trade. One scholar's study of tax and census records from the prewar period has revealed that James did indeed buy and sell slaves.[54] Also, a rare surviving letter written by one of his sons in 1845 refers to a boy who was "not in condition to sell" and comments on the price of slaves.[55] So stories about the Harlans' complicity with the slave trade must have been pushed from the family's memory in order to make room for this one about the cursing of the slave trader.

James's curse earned him biblical stature in his family's eyes. Malvina writes that "like some Old Testament prophet he seemed to be calling down Heaven's maledictions upon the whole institution of Slavery."[56] After John's father condemned a slave driver in the street that morning, he slept the righteous sleep of a slaveholder that night in his own bed. His family felt no need to apologize for his restraint. They shared his belief that he taught the virtues of benevolent mastery in his own household.[57]

In Malvina's memoirs, the family has no other real contact with the slave trade. Malvina assures us that John "never forgot the impression that was made upon him by his [father's] sudden indignation at the brutal and typical incident."[58] His father confirmed in public the lessons emphasized at home. Anyone worthy of "calling himself a man" did not deal in human flesh. Good slaveholders sabotaged chattel slavery from within by cherishing blacks as inalienable members of their households. Malvina characterizes the taint of the original purchase as so ancient that both John Harlan and the black "Mammy" who nursed him considered themselves born into their relationship. The slaves Malvina had known were "inherited from both sides of the Harlan family," she tells us.[59] Masters could sell slaves by right, but no Harlan was ever supposed to have sold a slave. Malvina insists that John learned this lesson from his father and practiced it himself. She mentions the purchase of a slave only once: when John bought a cook in order to save her from being sold away from her husband.[60] She tells us that when the death of James in 1863 threatened the comfort of his widow (who by law could inherit only one-third of his estate) and the stability of his household by forcing the sale of slaves, "promptly, and without a thought of himself and of the burden he would have to carry," John "made himself responsible to the Estate for the value of the rest of those slaves."[61] So Bob, Lewis, Henry, Sarah, Jenny, Silva, Maria, and Ben—listed on the inventory of his father's estate alongside his household goods—became John's.[62] In the name of a paternalistic trinity—his father, his mother, and the slaves themselves—John Harlan preserved the "family."

The visions conjured up by Malvina Harlan in 1915 could not be further from the fears voiced by Thomas Jefferson in 1789 in his *Notes on the State of Virginia* of the nasty white boy who learns from his tyrannical parents' example to put "on the same airs in the circle of smaller slaves" and let loose "the worst of his passions." As Eugene Genovese has observed, "Notwithstanding its ideological rationalizations, its gaping contradictions, and its dose of hypocrisy, [the phrase 'our family, white and black'] lay at the core of the slaveholders' world view and sense of themselves as good and moral men who walked in the ways of the Lord."[63] In this remembered household, whites neither denied the humanity of blacks nor indulged in brutality. The Harlans told themselves that they had prevented their children from learning the ways of racial despotism.

If white paternalism was the foundation of the antebellum Harlan household, male paternalism was the crossbeam. Malvina was destined for domestic duties and subordinated her wishes to those of her husband in return for his protection. The bond was sealed with proper womanly affection. As with slavery, the marriage described by Malvina was far less coercive than the laws governing it. But the similarity ends there. John Harlan never had to face the decision of what to do when the institution of marriage was dismantled as he had to do with slavery. Instead, the basic shape of his marriage remained essentially unchanged for fifty-five years.

The woman who spent her life identified as Mrs. John Marshall Harlan was born the daughter of a schoolteacher and a wealthy merchant. In 1854, John Harlan was a graduate of Centre College and just out of Transylvania University's Law School. He was a junior partner in his father's law office. After a two-week acquaintance with Mallie, as she was nicknamed by her family, he wrote her father for her hand in marriage. She was then fifteen years old. She recalls in her memoirs her favorable impression of his good looks—"his fine blue eyes" and "his beautiful sandy hair"—and their evening conversations. Although Malvina makes a point of telling her readers that "I never heard any questions from either of my parents as to what he had in worldly goods or prospects—his character and habits being their one and only thought," they must have been pleased at an offer from a young man of a prestigious Kentucky family. They did think Mallie too young to marry immediately, however, and insisted on an engagement of two years.[64]

Despite her long engagement, Malvina entered marriage at a disadvantage. At twenty-three, John was a college and law school graduate who had already begun a professional career and made a name for himself as a Whig orator; at seventeen, Malvina had finished a year of the slight education afforded to girls and had been quietly practicing housekeeping under her mother's guidance.[65] Malvina acknowledges this disadvantage when she writes that John "had taken me into his life when I was still a child, having little or no confidence in myself and no knowledge of the world."[66] Her relative immaturity confirmed the dictates of her society. Women were relegated to the private sphere of domesticity as junior partners in the marital enterprise. She testifies that John made an effort to assure her of his confidence.

Malvina accepted the idea that women were suited to their role as housewives. Like many of her peers, she endorsed what historians call the cult of true womanhood, which held that women had innate tendencies toward "piety, purity, submissiveness, and domesticity."[67] Their belief in it was the logical result of their upbringing, and they did not see the limitations it imposed as an insult. A scholar of domesticity notes that "for the first time in American history, both home and woman's special nature were seen as uniquely valuable."[68] A poem written for the Harlans' golden wedding anniversary described the fulfillment a woman like Malvina expected:

> *1856*
> A Bride is starting—crowned with hope,
> Starting to read her horoscope:—
> Life's promises are sweet.
> *1906*
> A Wife is standing, crowned with love
> And motherhood—both from above:—
> Life's promises complete.[69]

John Marshall Harlan of Frankfort, Kentucky, and Malvina French Shanklin of Evansville, Indiana, were married on 23 December 1856 after a two-year engagement. He was a twenty-three-year-old lawyer, and she was seventeen. When John died in 1911 after almost fifty-five years of marriage, Malvina wrote, "The wakening in the morning to find him gone is heartbreaking." (Courtesy of Edith Harlan Powell)

Admittedly, it is a bad poem, but its very triteness recommends it as a description of the nineteenth-century view of domesticity: a woman defines herself as wife and mother by divine command. The ideal of companionate marriage, which held that a life partnership was built on affection, separate spheres, and treasured children, demanded a measure of subordination from women.[70] To Malvina, this was altogether natural.

At the age of seventy-six, she testifies that she is still "impressed by the wisdom of the parting advice which my mother gave me as I left for my new home in Kentucky." Her mother told her, "You will miss us terribly." "But never," Philura French Shanklin warned her daughter, "let your husband know that you are mourning for your girlhood's home." As a good wife, Malvina was supposed to hide her tears. "Often you will have to relieve your home-sickness with a good cry," said her mother, "but wait until your husband is out of sight and have it over and out of the way before his return, and have nothing but smiles to greet him when he comes home." Philura instructed her daughter that self-effacement was a requirement when a woman loved a man "well enough to marry him." Echoing Ruth of the Old Testament, she said, "Remember, now, that *his* home is YOUR home; *his* people, YOUR people; *his* interests, YOUR interests—you must have *no other*."[71] Whatever Malvina might have lost in doing this, she was supposed to have gained a protected place within John's household.

A husband could sabotage the legal hierarchy of marriage, just as the Harlans were supposed to have sabotaged the legal hierarchy of slavery. According to Sir William Blackstone in the eighteenth century, women suffered "civil death" upon marriage. They could neither contract nor sue without the consent of their husbands. They lost control of even the property they had owned before marriage. "Neither the culture nor the law viewed [a wife] as a free individual, nor did many women themselves glimpse such a possibility."[72] But if a husband refused to exercise his legal prerogatives, he could undermine marital hierarchy. Suzanne Lebsock observes that "the maintenance of a companionate marriage . . . depended on the voluntary compliance of the husband, on his willingness to refrain from using the many clubs his society handed him."[73] Just as John Harlan was never supposed to have raised the lash that slavery put in his hands, so he was never supposed to have lifted the club that the law of marriage gave him. On both fronts, paternalism required the patriarch to ignore his legal power (even though his very status was sustained by it) in favor of self-restraint.

To equate marriage with slavery would be a gross oversimplification. Marriage was a civil contract that could be enforced by the authorities or broken if one side failed to fulfill its obligations. Fear of scandal, lack of money, and legal rules hampered the ability of wives to enforce the contract on wayward husbands, but over the course of the nineteenth century, judges and legislatures in America "riddled" civil death with exceptions, thereby "domesticating" patriarchy.[74] John, who coauthored a technical treatise on the law of marriage, was aware of the many rulings and laws that limited the male's power.[75] Woman's rights advocates had some hand in bringing about these changes but less than one might have expected; even conservatives wanted to curtail the abuse of male power in order to protect their own daughters.[76] Over the course of the century, white women were free to express their contempt for white men who did not live up to the ideal.[77] This placed them on a completely different plane from slaves of either sex.

Another poem read at the Harlans' fiftieth wedding anniversary celebration in 1906, described as a grand affair in the papers, refers to the religious prototype of marriage. Adam, lonely for a mate, is given Eve. Her creation from his rib indicates that their relations are unequal but not grossly so:

> The Woman was not taken from Adam's *head*, we know;
> So she must not rule over him — 'tis evidently so.
> The Woman was not taken from Adam's *feet*, we see;
> So he must not abuse her — the meaning seems to be.
>
> The Woman was extracted from under Adam's *arm*;
> So she must be protected from injury and harm.
> The Woman was extracted from near to Adam's *heart*;
> By which we are directed that they should never part.[78]

At the risk of appearing to recommend the Victorian ideal of marriage and its poetics, let me suggest its possible appeal. Putting aside the question of love, we could say that Malvina Shanklin made a deal with John Harlan. She would run his household, bear his children, and support him in his public efforts while he earned a living for all of them and repaid her faith with his success. There is nothing inherently wrong with this deal; the problem is that it was virtually the *only* deal a woman could make at the time, and often she had no way of enforcing the bargain.

The memoirs' account of Malvina's only trip to Europe indicates how the deal worked in practice. When Malvina was offered a last-minute opportunity to take a side trip to Italy, she hesitated to go. In John's "absence it seemed at first impossible for me to decide such an important matter for myself for I had always looked to him for advice and guidance." When she decided to go, "this exhibition of independence was so new and surprising to my daughters, that they called my Italian trip, 'Mother's Revolt.' " The joke indicates that the whole family recognized Malvina's willingness to defer to her husband's judgment. That same European trip was the occasion for an argument with a drunken Prussian officer. Malvina congratulated herself on her refusal to yield before his imperiousness. "It was evident that, in *his* world, 'the Frau' was compelled to know her place and to keep it," she remarks.[79] Evidently, Malvina felt that it was not her place to be squelched by a male ego.

If the term "unequal partnership" described Malvina's marriage, her emphasis would have been on "partnership." She explains that "in the old days, the 'Help-mate' idea entered more universally into the marriage relation than is now the case. The man was not only the bread-winner, but the *name*-maker for the family, and an ambitious wife felt that no sacrifice on her part was too great that would in the slightest degree make the way to the desired goal for her husband." She says she was glad to help copy John's legal briefs into a legible hand while he was establishing his practice. "When my husband appealed to me for assistance in this regard, my exultation of feeling, in thus being able to help him, made a large part of my happiness in those days."[80] Malvina's understanding of her role explains her approving reference to James M. Barrie's play, *What Every Woman Knows*, first performed in 1908. The wife's last speech runs: "Every man who is high up loves to think that he has done it all himself; and the wife smiles, and lets it go at that. It's our only joke. Every woman knows that." The moral of the play was voiced by a character commenting on a joint enterprise of a husband and wife: the effort of each was not enough by itself, but together they were irresistible. Together, the Harlans reached the dizzying heights of the "Court circles," where Malvina entertained several hundred people at her Monday afternoon at-homes and visited the White House, offering her "ponderously cordial" greetings.[81]

Even in her descriptions of the success of their marital enterprise, her efforts centered on John. The wife's role was to sacrifice, to help. In effect, Barrie's play and Malvina's memoirs made two points: first, that private wifely support was essential to public husbandly success and, second, that wifely support should not presume to be more than just that. Woman's effort was to be expended on behalf of man, not in her own name.

The memoirs show that Malvina knew of the New Woman, college educated, independent, taking a place on a public stage, yet she never embraced the change.[82] While explaining her role as John's copyist, Malvina acknowledges that the idea of the helpmate existed in the past. When she tells the story of the Court's refusal to help Belva Lockwood gain admission to the bar, Malvina notes that the request "was an unprecedented proceeding at that time."[83] When Malvina accepted the appointment by Governor Augustus Willson, an old friend of John's, as Kentucky's representative to a conference held under the auspices of the National Congress of Mothers (which would evolve into the Parent-Teacher Association) in 1908, she wrote that he might better have chosen a New Woman.[84] This may have been Malvina's only sustained contact with women reformers who had moved into policy-making roles in the name of separate spheres. The argument for mother-voters would have given someone like Malvina a mental handle on the need for women's suffrage for the first time. This foray into the public sphere in the name of the very traits that fitted her for the domestic one seems to have left Malvina essentially unchanged.

Few pressures prompted John Harlan to rework the ideas that had governed his vision of women's role in the household or in the polity. He was not yet on the Court when it delivered *Bradwell v. the State* in 1872, but he would have agreed with Justice Joseph P. Bradley that "the paramount destiny and mission of woman are to fulfill the noble and benign office of wife and mother. This is the law of the Creator."[85] Not that Harlan was unaware of what he termed "radical" statutory change in the position of married women. In *Thompson v. Thompson*, decided in 1910, Harlan dissented when the Court majority refused to interpret a federal statute giving wives contractual powers as authorization for a battered wife to bring a tort action against her husband. Harlan's main complaint was that the majority had usurped the legislative authority, but he opened his dissent with the ugly charges: "The first, second and third [counts] charge assault by the husband upon the wife on three several days. The remaining [four] counts charge assaults by him upon her on different days named—she being at the time pregnant, as the husband then well knew."[86] Clearly, Thompson had failed as a companionate husband. Like the married women's property acts of the nineteenth century, which were passed in order to protect the daughters of legislators' from their wayward husbands rather than to empower women as a class, Harlan's acceptance of legislative change in *Thompson* may have sprung more from his paternalism than from a desire to see wives freely contracting.

We can see the persistence of Harlan's traditional attitude toward women in his response to a genealogical inquiry in 1911. He gave full descriptions of the educations and careers of his three sons, James, John, and Richard, then he mentioned his surviving daughters and granddaughter without bothering to record even their names.[87] We may never know the fate of daughters Laura and Ruth, who defied Providence and never married.[88] Overshadowed by the public activities of their male relatives, they have left little behind save a reputation for gumption among their grandnieces and grandnephews. Harlan loved them dearly, but they did not exist in the public sphere, according to him. Renovations of the sexual wing of household paternalism were made by other Americans but not by the Harlans.

The main difference between John's view of race and his view of sex may be that political events forced him to reexamine where he stood on the civil status of the black race, whereas he never had to confront a strong challenge to women's subordinate status. Yet even as he faced the changes wrought by the Civil War, Harlan remembered the paternalistic ideal his father had taught him. When emancipation became a fait accompli, Harlan tried to preserve the reciprocal goodwill that he believed had marked the relations between kind master and loyal slave. Racial paternalism was responsible for his decision to accept the revolutionary changes brought by the Civil War amendments to the Constitution.

Harlan would have inherited his father's spot in the Whig Party if the party had not collapsed along sectional lines in the 1850s under the weight of arguments over slavery. He briefly took up the banner of the antiimmigrant Know-Nothing Party because it seemed to appeal to native-born voters regardless of section. Yet even as a Know-Nothing, Harlan accused immigrants in 1855 of being "almost invariably prejudiced against the institution of slavery." [89] White Kentuckian voters were not particularly interested in the issue of immigration, despite the Know-Nothing state victory in 1856. After a stint as an Opposition Party member, Harlan became a supporter of the Constitutional Union Party, which offered Tennessean John Bell as its candidate for president in 1860.[90] Bell won Kentucky's electoral votes but came in last in the four-way race.

When southern whites panicked at the election of Republican Abraham Lincoln and began to support secession, most white Kentuckians were devoted both to the Union and to slavery. Blacks made up 25 percent of the total population, and the vast majority of them were slaves.[91] The natural result, as Harlan wrote Secretary of War Joseph Holt in March 1861, was that "no earthly power will prevent the people" of the border states "from sympathizing and to a great extent taking part with 'their brethren of the South' against what is called an 'abolition' administration." Harlan recommended that Lincoln remove the federal troops from the harbor forts of Sumter in South Carolina and Pickens in Florida or risk losing the Upper South, especially Kentucky, to secessionist sentiment.[92] Lincoln hesitated to advocate emancipation early in the war because of his fear of losing the support of the border states; he is supposed to have said that he would like to have God on his side but he *must* have Kentucky.[93]

The ensuing fight in Kentucky between the Unionists and the Southern

Rights Party was close. Just a few days after the attack on Fort Sumter in April 1861, Governor Beriah Magoffin responded to a federal demand for regiments: "I say, *emphatically*, Kentucky will furnish no troops for the wicked purpose of subduing her sister Southern States."[94] Harlan and other Unionists feared that Magoffin's stated position of "armed neutrality" camouflaged his pro-Confederate feeling. Two sets of state militia organized and drilled: the Unionist Home Guards, in which Harlan was a captain, and the Southern Rights State Guards. Harlan helped distribute guns among Unionists.[95] "Nearly every afternoon," he and other Unionists spoke on street corners "standing on a pine box" accompanied by a crowd-drawing brass band.[96] The Union army approached Kentucky's borders by installing its native sons as commanders of recruitment camps in neighboring states.[97]

When Confederate troops marched into Kentucky in late August, the state legislature abandoned neutrality in favor of Unionism. But every kind of social institution from family to church divided between Unionist and Confederate sympathizers. Even the two Kentucky senators chose different routes: John Cabell Breckinridge resigned to join the Confederate army in 1861 and became Jefferson Davis's secretary of war in 1865, whereas Lazarus Powell completed his full term. Harlan and his father found themselves "differing from many warm and dear friends" because of their Unionist sentiments, he recalled later.[98] Harlan raised his own Union regiment of over 800 men, the 10th Kentucky Infantry, in September 1861.[99] He and his men took part in several skirmishes and chased the famous Confederate cavalry raider, John Hunt Morgan.[100]

Meanwhile, the federal army wore out its initial welcome and came to be viewed as an annoying occupying force. The state legislature became a Unionist stronghold under the eye of Union troops. It banned Confederate sympathizers from holding public office, from teaching in public schools, and from publishing newspapers; they were arrested for speaking against the federal government.[101] Still, newspapers kept up criticisms of the federal forces, as did individuals. Several months after the war ended, in September 1865, Kentuckians had some 3,000 civil suits pending against Union officers, most of which were probably for destruction of property.[102] Many whites in the border state could not forgive the federal government for the wrongs they thought it had done to them.

Their main complaint was emancipation. Unionists like Harlan had argued against secession on the grounds that Lincoln's election was not a threat to slavery. This was a war for union, not emancipation. In fact, just two weeks before the state legislature abandoned the policy of armed neutrality, Kentucky Unionists had driven an abolitionist minister, John G. Fee, out of the

Harlan raised his own Union regiment, the 10th Kentucky Infantry, in September 1861. He fought to defend the Union and his home state. Harlan resigned his commission in early 1863 shortly after his father's death in order to handle the family law practice. He assured his superior officer that his decision "is from no want of confidence either in the justice or ultimate triumph of the Union cause." (Courtesy of the Library of Congress)

state under threat of hanging.[103] But the federal government moved steadily toward emancipation. In July 1862, Lincoln asked the border states to consider compensated emancipation, and the Kentucky legislature rejected the idea.[104] Then came the president's preliminary emancipation proclamation in September 1862. E. Merton Coulter writes that a "storm of disapproval" immediately gathered and broke over Lincoln's head.[105] The subsequent efforts of Union officers to free slaves clinched the white population's alienation from the federal government. Like many other Unionist slaveholders, Harlan felt betrayed.

The shock of the Emancipation Proclamation had yet to wear off when Harlan resigned his commission in 1863, shortly after his father's death. He assured his commander in his letter of resignation that the Union cause "will always have the warmest sympathies of my heart." [106] Decades later, he explained to his son Richard in an autobiographical letter that "my only remaining brother had become incompetent for business" and the family law firm was suffering.[107] Although Harlan did not resign to protest the proclamation, he made his unhappiness with Lincoln clear on his return to civilian life.

Harlan went back to lawyering and politicking. In 1863, he won the office of state attorney general, a post his father had held before him, running on the Union ticket. Harlan campaigned for Democratic candidate General George B. McClellan in the 1864 presidential election. McClellan's calls for peace were increasingly appealing to Kentuckians. The voters went for McClellan by 57 percent despite an enormous drop in voting due to military interference and wartime confusion.[108]

Harlan believed the federal government had abused the trust of the border state's white population by bringing on emancipation. He explained to an Indiana crowd in 1864 why the people of the Union states had risen against secession: "It was for the high and noble purpose of asserting the binding authority of our laws over every part of this land." He scarcely had to remind them that "it was not for the purpose of giving freedom to the Negro." [109] The national government was interfering with a local institution. In 1865, Harlan complained in a public letter that the national government had transgressed its rightful powers and left the state unable to cope with "the ruinous effects of such a violent change in our social system." Harlan suggested a seven-year plan of gradual emancipation but wanted to leave the final decision to white voters.[110] The value of the slaves was irrelevant to the constitutional question. He declared that he would still oppose the Thirteenth Amendment as "a flagrant violation of the right of self-government" even if only a dozen slaves lived in Kentucky.[111] Harlan urged whites to organize to prevent blacks from gaining political rights.[112] In 1866, he cursed the abolitionists Charles Sumner and Thaddeus Stevens for their invention of constitutional amendments that "would work a complete revolution in our Republican system of Government."[113] The war was fought to prevent the secessionists from destroying the Union. Now the federal government threatened to violate the very principles of the Union.

Harlan carried on the fight against political revolution as Kentucky's attorney general. He helped in the state's effort to control Union officers bent on furthering emancipation before the Thirteenth Amendment was ratified. Union general John M. Palmer instituted a pass system in May 1865 that allowed slaves to travel out of the state to freedom, and he recruited slaves as soldiers after the war ended under a congressional act passed in January 1865 that freed recruits and their families.[114] The local civil authorities were beside themselves. Harlan brought an indictment against Palmer in 1866 for "violating the slave code of Kentucky."[115] The state legislators refused to ratify the Thirteenth Amendment. As late as 1867, Harlan argued that the Thirteenth Amendment, now part of the Constitution, did not invalidate a state law that discounted the word of a black witness against that of a white witness.[116] White Kentuckians were not going to give up their slaves without a fight.

Politically, Harlan found himself between a rock and a hard place. He tried to make do with the Conservative Union Party from 1865 to 1867, but the Democrats won the governorship in 1866. While still denouncing civil rights for blacks, Harlan joined other former Conservative Unionists in an attempt to steal some of their opponents' votes by creating the Conservative Union Democratic Party in 1867. That year's August elections proved that Kentucky voters preferred true Democrats, including former Confederates, over the remnants of the Unionist Party. Most Conservatives gave up their isolated efforts after that defeat and joined the Democrats. Only a few chose to go over to the side of the Radical Republicans.

Harlan had long despised the Democratic Party. He described his father as "an intense Whig of the old School" who had seen "very little in the Democratic party that was good."[117] John was speaking of constitutional interpretation, but the family's dislike of their political opponents was general.[118] A fellow Unionist named J. S. Sinclair described their dilemma in 1869: "If we continue to keep up our separate party, we count, in numbers, to nothing, and become a stumbling block to some good end." But conversion to either of the remaining parties was unacceptable. "To go with the Radicals I can't & will not do," declared Sinclair; "to go with the Reb. Democracy, would be my humiliating." The result "virtually *disenfranchises me*," Harlan's friend complained, "for with my present convictions and prejudices against both, I can't feel satisfied to identify myself with either."[119] Harlan too felt torn, but he ended up making a choice. In January 1868, his cousin Wellington Harlan wrote to say that when asked, he ventured that John supported Ulysses S. Grant for president. "How near am I right?," he asked.[120]

Although Wellington may have known of the paternalism and anti-Democratic sentiments of James Harlan, he probably based his guess about John's political future on the company his cousin had chosen to keep. It seems no accident that Harlan had entered into a law partnership with Benjamin H. Bristow, then U.S. attorney for the Kentucky district. Bristow was one of the Kentucky Republicans whose efforts were "striking exceptions" to the general failure of southern federal officers to enforce the Civil Rights Act of 1866.[121]

Harlan explained years later in an autobiographical account why he had voted Republican in 1868: "There was nothing else to do" since the "general tendencies and purposes of the Democratic Party were mischievous."[122] Only one party seemed intent on upholding the standards he was supposed to have learned in his father's house.

Although several factors pushed Harlan in the direction of the Republican Party, the most important was his revulsion to the racial violence orchestrated by the Democrats.[123] People joked at the time that Kentucky had waited to secede until after the war was over. Throughout the late 1860s and early 1870s, bands of marauding whites—called Regulators or, after their leaders, Rowzee's Band or Skagg's Men—ran rampant over the Kentucky countryside, attacking whites and blacks alike.[124] White terrorism led a group of Frankfort blacks to petition Congress for protection; they detailed sixty-four attacks that had occurred from November 1867 through December 1869. Despairing of getting help from either local or national authorities, about 30,000 blacks left the state from 1860 to 1870, a number far out of proportion to other border-state migrations.[125] Could the boy who remembered his father's disgust at the brutality of a white slave driver become a man willing to embrace the political company of men who murdered blacks in the dead of night?

Decades later, Harlan wrote of his disappointment when his son John Maynard was thrown out of Princeton University for hazing. Harlan took the opportunity to give his son James a lesson about bullying. "The spirit out of which Hazing comes," he explained, "is that kind of low brutality which comes out finally as robbery, burglary & murder." "You can rely on it," he continued; "if you find any boy in your class who is continually & *deliberately* pulling indignities upon others, he is a mean cowardly fellow who will turn pale & cower when confronted by a brave, self-respecting, justice-loving comrade who has the courage to resent personal insult."[126] And so the son passed on to the grandson the patriarch's lesson. Anyone worthy of calling himself a man did not brutalize the weak. In fact, a true man, an American who loved justice, had a duty to fight those who did. Harlan had never wanted emancipation, but it had come. In the late 1860s in Kentucky, whites who rejected freedom and civil rights for blacks made the very survival of blacks impossible. The result was a lowering of white standards of behavior to a level Harlan found contemptible. He had to decide which tradition of the peculiar institution deserved his loyalty: the unlimited legal control of the master that gave rise to white supremacy or the ideal of private restraint that required white men with power not to abuse it. The only way Harlan could find to preserve some semblance of white paternalism was by embracing a party that championed revolutionary legal change.

As a Republican, Harlan argued that white terrorism posed a threat to whites as well as blacks. He reentered the campaign life he had known before the war, traveling on horseback with the opposing candidate and speaking outdoors for up to two hours, his audience made up of "people from the whole surrounding country coming on horseback and in waggons and buggies to attend." [127] "These KuKlux are enemies of all order," he declared in a town in western Kentucky in 1871 just a month before the gubernatorial election. They must be "extirpated" by the authorities, "else civil society, in all its parts, is in danger, and the lives, liberty and property of the people put in peril." Any "citizen who proposes to deny" black males their rights under the national Constitution "is no friend of the law, is an enemy of our free institutions, and no friend of peace," he insisted during his 1875 campaign for the governorship.[128] Harlan reported to Bristow that he had discovered while traveling to Frankfort in 1871 a "universal dread" among Republicans regardless of color. Yet no one dared to act on the local level because "their lives and property would probably both be destroyed if they publicly warred against the KuKlux." [129] Although Bristow once drew cold comfort from the idea that the "chief strength" of the Republicans over the Democrats was that "no matter how badly we act, they are sure to do something worse," he must have grown worried when Harlan reported the hopes of the southern Democratic leaders in 1874.[130] "Their plan," Harlan asserted, "is to force Colored people [in the] South into the Democratic ranks, or drive them from the polls." [131] He warned Bristow that the return of the Democratic Party to national power "would make the condition of the Union men and the negroes of the South as intolerable as that of the children of Israel during their bondage in Egypt." [132]

Harlan made a good showing for a Republican when he ran for governor in 1871 and 1875, but he could not shake the Democratic hold. In 1870, a friend had written to mourn the demise of Louisville as a "Union City." "Alas," he sighed, "if the falls of the Ohio River were to run through the City of Louisville, the waters thereof would not drown the rebelism therein." [133] Another supporter preferred to blame Harlan's defeat in 1875 on fraud. The leap in the number of Democratic votes defied logic, he wrote, so that "I am almost persuaded to believe in the Darwinian theory that the very animals are developing into men and all Democrats at that." [134] Harlan did not *startle the country*" in 1875 as he had hoped, but he did attract the national attention that would eventually help him gain a spot on the U.S. Supreme Court. [135]

However, when President Rutherford B. Hayes nominated Harlan to the Supreme Court in early October 1877, his early opposition to emancipation attracted congressional scrutiny. [136] Harlan drafted a letter to Kentucky senator James B. Beck detailing his political history, including how he had voted in each presidential election since 1852. [137] Harlan assured the Judiciary Committee of his conversion to Republican principles (his gubernatorial platforms in 1871 and 1875 had endorsed the Civil War amendments), but he had to overcome attacks based on his prior history. Kentuckian Speed S. Fry, once a political ally but now an enemy, wrote in a letter that was forwarded to the chair of the Senate Judiciary Committee that Harlan had been "very bitter" about the Emancipation Proclamation and had declared in 1866 that "he had no more conscientious scruples in buying and selling a negro than he had in buying and selling a horse." [138] The doubts raised by such letters and congressional squabbling about petty issues delayed Harlan's confirmation until late November.

Among the crowds he had worked as a Conservative Unionist, Harlan could hardly reconcile his former position on slavery with his new Republican beliefs. Nor did he try. Pointing to the upheavals all Kentuckians had withstood during and after the war years, Harlan owned up to his uncertain course in a speech in 1871. He took a page from the book of Henry Clay and declared, "Let it be said that I am right rather than consistent." He had been inconsistent, but by 1871, he had staked out a position on slavery that would serve him the rest of his days. "It is true that I was at one time in my life opposed to conferring these privileges [of citizenship] upon [blacks]," he acknowledged to the Kentucky crowd, "but I have lived long enough to feel and declare, as I do this night, that the most perfect despotism that ever existed on this earth was the institution of African slavery." Slavery wronged blacks, but it also oppressed whites. "With Slavery it was death or tribute." "It was an enemy to free speech," he reminded them; "it was an enemy to a free press." He was glad that "these human beings are now in possession of freedom, and that that freedom is secured to them in the fundamental law of the land, beyond the control of any state." Both the Thirteenth and the Fourteenth Amendments had his entire support. Harlan's voice rang out over the crowd, and emancipation took on a glorious hue: "I rejoice that it is gone; I rejoice that the Sun of American Liberty does not this day shine, upon a single human slave upon this continent." [139] And so he would continue to rejoice.

Harlan embraced a political party that championed revolutionary legal change in order to preserve some semblance of the paternalism he had learned in his father's house. The Democratic Party was intolerable to a man who had prided himself on the kind treatment of his "servants." Even the shock of emancipation could not erase the habits of his upbringing. And just as Harlan could not abandon the idealized standard of goodwill and care exercised by the best type of slaveholders, he could not surrender completely its assumptions of racial hierarchy and separation.

The ties between master and slave did not dissolve with the Thirteenth Amendment. John received a letter in 1877 in which his former slave, "Aunt" Charlotte, pleaded for "some close for the wihnter" and asked him to "give me love to the Children." She addressed him as "Mr. Mars John." [140] Malvina Harlan's memoirs offer a description of John's relationship with a black man, James Jackson, that proves that neither the slaveholder nor the slave were yet dead. Her account suggests the strength of John's paternalism and how it limited his vision of race relations in a free, republican country.

Her portrayal of John's relationship with Jackson, a "court messenger" assigned by the Supreme Court to help with menial tasks, rests on the same premise as her depiction of slavery: the naturalness of a stratified household based on mutual devotion. She tells us that "the fine Old Maryland family in which he was brought up as a slave in the antebellum days" endowed Jackson with "dignified and courtly manners." Malvina describes with delight Jackson's success at self-effacement. "By the time Jackson had been in the service of my husband for two or three weeks, he had so thoroughly identified himself with my husband and all our family interests, that, whenever he spoke to others about my husband or addressed him personally, he always used the pronouns, 'We,' 'Us,' and 'Ours.' " [141] While writing of the slaves who acted as maids to the Harlan women before the war, Malvina had noted that "the familiarity was never abused by the maid, and the real affection which each had for the other showed itself in many ways." [142] She praises Jackson in similar language: "While he was on peculiarly friendly and even affectionate terms with his employer, he never for one moment forgot his place, nor the respect that was due from him to all the members of the family." Jackson "was in a real sense a member of our household" and accompanied the family to Murray Bay in Canada, where John gathered the "Harlan tribe" every summer. All of the children and servants were not under one roof as in James Harlan's day, but John surrounded himself with his married sons and their offspring.[143] "Jackson took so much pride in all the members of 'The Family,'" Malvina assures us.[144] She recounts Jackson's reaction to the news that her son John Maynard had won a golf tournament at the resort: "With his kindly, ebony countenance fairly shining with affectionate pride, [Jackson] grasped my son's hands in both of his and said, 'Mr. John, *when* will *these people* around here understand what kind o' stock *we* come from?'"[145] Obviously, Jackson was accustomed to the emotions and expectations of a paternalist household. Jackson and John Harlan were devoted to one another, Malvina tells us—so much so that Jackson mourned alongside the family at John's deathbed. He had served fifteen years in their midst.

This is not the kind of relationship one would expect the dissenter from *Plessy v. Ferguson* to be involved in, but its combination of racial hierarchy and devotion was altogether natural in Malvina's eyes. In fact, her relationship with John followed a similar pattern. She praised her mother for advising her to make her husband's interests her own. Marriage made her and John into a legal "we," of which John made up the greater part. For Jackson and Malvina, subordination was exchanged for protection and care. Altered as this pattern was by evolutionary and revolutionary changes in black and female status, it was never erased from John Harlan's mind.

Although we cannot confirm independently the workings of paternalism in the slaveholding household of John's father, we can see that remnants of the idea survived the elevation of blacks to citizenship. In considering Harlan's judicial record on civil rights, we should keep in mind the power structure of the household in which he lived. We must also understand how this family identity converged with constitutional order. Just as the Harlan tribe treasured its legend of paternalism over uglier truths, so John Harlan recounted a civic myth of egalitarianism at odds with the full reality of national history. Both myths would shape Harlan's legal thought.

# CHAPTER 2

# Little or No Scope for Originality

## Law, Religion, and the Union

*They meant to set up a standard maxim for free society, which should be familiar to all, and revered by all; constantly looked to, constantly labored for, and even though never perfectly attained, constantly approximated, and thereby constantly spreading and deepening its influence, and augmenting the happiness and value of life to all people of all colors everywhere.*

—Abraham Lincoln on the founders and the

Declaration of Independence, 1858

In 1955, the grandson and namesake of John Harlan, now himself a justice on the U.S. Supreme Court, received a letter from a former law student of his grandfather's. It seems that during the 1897–98 academic year at Columbian University in Washington, D.C., later George Washington University, he and another student had taken down the first Justice Harlan's lectures on constitutional law in shorthand and then typed them up. He asked if the second Justice Harlan would like to have their transcriptions.[1]

So some 500 pages of lectures were deposited at the Library of Congress along with other Harlan papers. Although scattered reports of Harlan's public addresses are available, no other documents of the length or nature of these lectures exist. Because they are a verbatim transcript, they reproduce the cadences of speech, the run-on sentences, the questions and answers of the classroom. Of course, the tone is lost in print. After describing one of his dissents, Harlan sometimes remarked, "But of course I was wrong." A former student reminisced about the laughs Harlan got with that sarcastic line.[2] A newspaper account from 1895 described Harlan's appearance before a college auditorium of law students, mostly government clerks by day, and above them a gallery filled with old lawyers, shorthand novices, and gentlemen and ladies on their way out for the evening. This sets the scene:

> Promptly at 7 o'clock Justice Harlan enters and takes his seat on the platform. His appearance is greeted with cheer after cheer from the students and visitors. He must needs wait a minute or two before he can make his voice heard above the clamor of approval. Then his great form, clad fre-

quently in evening dress, rises amid the hisses of the boys for silence, and by the time he has uttered his familiar greeting—"young gentlemen of the law class"—the dropping of a pin can almost be heard, so still is the room and close the attention paid him, which continues to the end of the lecture, though interrupted with popular applause, or laughter, at the frequent fine points scored, and witty thrusts.[3]

If one listens to the lectures as one reads, a nineteenth-century voice rises off of the page. It is the same voice recorded in accounts of Harlan's delivery of opinions from the bench.[4] A reporter once wrote of it: "He has a slight Southern drawl in his conversational voice, but when he speaks from the bench his voice is sonorous."[5]

Almost as remarkable as the survival of these lectures is historians' neglect of them.[6] Teaching was important to Harlan. He taught for twenty years at Columbian, and when he gave up his position reluctantly in 1909 after a dispute with the university administration over pay, he wrote a friend that he "regarded my connection with the University as a part of my life-work—and the most interesting part." He was "buoyed up with the thought that my lectures had much to do with spreading safe and sound thoughts about our National Government and the Constitution under which it was organized."[7] And these lectures were given during a historic year. Harlan makes clear references to the events that provoked the Spanish-American War.

This neglect has occurred despite the tremendous importance of the Constitution to Harlan. One evening, Harlan ended his lecture by reading aloud. He read out the supremacy clause of the Constitution, which declares that all local laws are subordinated to the national Constitution and any treaties ratified under its authority. He must have looked at his watch and realized that the hour was almost over because he paused to ask his students to let him continue. Harlan confessed to them, "I love to read these clauses. Let me read one more before we close." The class apparently settled down and Harlan continued with the next clause, which demands that all officers of any branch, national or local, swear to uphold the Constitution. He stopped reading and asked, "Is there any country on the earth that has in its statutes or laws a provision like that? Not one."[8] Harlan marveled over the Constitution and invited his students to do the same.

The reason for the neglect of this extraordinary source may lie in a comment I received from a reader of an earlier manuscript; he wrote that there was "nothing" in the lectures. Legal historians who can find nothing in the lectures are looking for the wrong thing. Perhaps they hope to find what Oliver Wendell Holmes Jr. had offered in his 1880 lectures at Harvard Law

School: an ambitious correction of legal history and an even more ambitious systematization of legal theory. Holmes's lectures, published as *The Common Law*, signaled a new movement in legal thought that would flower into legal realism in the twentieth century. Legal realists would argue that law must be understood as the product of social conditions and political choices. Law was man-made, as it were. In contrast, Harlan's lectures show that he remained a legal formalist who believed that the rules of interpretation, clear and fixed, lay beyond the tussles of everyday political life. This old-fashioned approach led to criticism. A newspaper story recounted that Harlan loaned a copy of his lectures to Justice David J. Brewer, who also taught at Columbian University, only to find this written on the flyleaf when he got it back:

> Lucubrations of Mr. Justice Harlan on constitutional and other
>     law, intended for the young and inexperienced,
> Take it up tenderly,
> Touch it with care,
> Fashioned so slenderly,
> So crude and so bare.[9]

Such criticisms arise because Harlan simply went through the Constitution clause by clause describing the interpretations of the Supreme Court and any objections he had made to them in dissent.

Such an approach makes vindication by history doubly impossible for Harlan. Because he believed that judges do not make law but only apply it to the case at hand, Harlan appears naive in the eyes of many legal scholars. At this point in time, Harlan did not even have the saving grace of using the new case method of teaching begun at Harvard Law School under Christopher C. Langdell in 1870, a method that still reigns in law schools today.[10] The premise of the case method was that the firsthand analysis of selected decisions would lead students to the few principles that underlay private law. But even Langdell did not think that one could find principles in constitutional cases; public law was all politics.[11]

As a teacher, Harlan represented the old ways because he was also a sitting judge. Law professors were busy organizing themselves into a discipline of specialists devoted exclusively to scholarship and teaching. By teaching working men at night, Harlan was also at odds with the efforts to do away with night schools on the grounds that their admission standards and requirements were too low.[12] By the early twentieth century, law professors had mostly succeeded in standardizing themselves and their students.[13] When George Washington University joined the Association of American Law Schools in 1902, night classes were ended.[14]

So Harlan's philosophy of law, his approach to teaching, his professional standing, and his classroom's occupants all made him the old-fashioned man he often proclaimed himself to be. Perhaps Harlan's biographers have neglected these lectures because they offer no evidence that he was in the vanguard. His lectures cannot help prove his greatness through vindication by history.

Rather than making history in his lectures, Harlan recounted it. Despite their lack of theoretical innovation, the lectures are valuable because they contain Harlan's fullest account of the nation's history. He told this history in episodes from lecture to lecture as he explained the writing of particular clauses and amendments. Taken together, they form a coherent and consistent explanation for the country's purpose. We must understand Harlan's vision of his country's history in order to explain the reasoning of his judicial decisions.

Just as the legend of James Harlan and the slave driver became *the* story of slavery for the Harlans despite whatever else had actually happened, so the legend of the founding fathers as reluctant slaveholders became Harlan's national story despite the more complicated historical facts. James Harlan was the literal father from whom John drew lessons for personal behavior; the founders became the metaphorical fathers from whom he drew lessons for the nation. The constitutional amendments that followed the Civil War answered the founding fathers' demand that their descendants remove the blot of slavery from the Republic.

In his lectures, Harlan used typology, the religious theory that events in the Old Testament foreshadow events in the New Testament, in order to explain American history. Many Americans, both black and white, used the Bible this way, as "the story above all other stories." [15] In Harlan's hands, the Revolutionary War became a type for the Civil War. With the help of God, Americans had first overthrown the hierarchy of monarchy and nobility, then they overthrew the hierarchy of race. In this, they were divinely destined to serve as an example to the world. True, God did not interfere in human events by way of miracles as he had in biblical times, but he had laid down a plan into which human efforts fell.

Perhaps historians have overlooked the significance of Harlan's national myth because civil religion is an uncomfortable topic for legal scholars. A Supreme Court justice who believed that his country's destiny was determined by Providence defies the clear-cut separation of church and state that late-twentieth-century academics have defined as ideal. But the fact that wrongs have been inflicted in the name of religion should not stop us from recognizing the importance of faith in our subjects' lives.

Harlan taught the Bible long before he taught law. He began by teach-

Harlan was serving as an elder of the New York Avenue Presbyterian Church in Washington, D.C., when this photograph was taken in 1903. He organized a Sunday school class of middle-aged men in 1896, which he taught until his death in 1911. Malvina Harlan wrote in 1915 that it was still called the "Harlan Bible Class." (Courtesy of the New York Avenue Presbyterian Church)

ing Sunday school to young women in Kentucky shortly after his marriage. "From that time on and throughout his entire life, in any church with which he was connected," writes Malvina Harlan, "my husband always taught a Bible Class."[16] John organized a Sunday school class of middle-aged men at the New York Avenue Presbyterian Church in Washington, D.C., in 1896, which he taught until his death in 1911.[17] Malvina tells us proudly that it was still called the "Harlan Bible Class" in 1915.[18] In light of John's belief that the United States was a providential nation, we should consider the connections between his faith and his law.

Perhaps historians have overlooked Harlan's myth because they know it to be one. They hesitate to take seriously the stories they try to dispel from the minds of their own students every term. However, the myth's very success demands attention. Harlan played a role in the lengthy and complex historical process that gave the North what Robert Penn Warren called the "Treasury of Virtue."[19] Before the war, most white northerners considered the abolitionists dangerous radicals; during the war, they identified the preservation of the founding fathers' Union as the moral justification for the war.[20] But by the late 1880s, many had come to define slavery as a blot the war had removed from the nation's history. In Lincoln's martyrdom, his misgivings about blacks were forgotten as he became the Great Emancipator who made good on the promises of the Declaration.[21] The myth of an egalitarian national mission grew in the version of history recounted by Union veterans like Harlan and black leaders like Frederick Douglass, whose race had the most to gain from its widespread adoption.[22]

Although Harlan is known for his dissents, his lectures show how much he shared a common culture. The idea that the United States was on a divinely appointed mission dated back to colonial times; each generation rephrased the mission in order to make sense of its situation. Harlan's belief that God had established a moral foundation for law was shared by many nineteenth-century legal writers. More specifically, Harlan thought that the Civil War amendments constitutionalized the egalitarian spirit of the Declaration of Independence. Here he followed the tradition of legal nationalism championed by Justice Joseph Story, his own father, and his law teachers at Transylvania University, a tradition that held the Declaration to be the true founding document, and grafted onto it the abolitionist arguments that gained in respectability as slavery receded into the past.

Of course, the myth of the egalitarian mission had competition. Myths of the Old South and the Lost Cause may have had stronger appeal among whites. During the war, secessionists argued that the founding fathers were on the side of the rebellion; afterward, even some northerners agreed that Robert E. Lee resembled George Washington.[23] Southern orators recalled the charms of the Old South.[24] White audiences in the North, becoming uncomfortable as cities and factories grew and multiplied, enjoyed reading romantic stories about the lost world of country plantations, languid southern belles, and devoted black slaves.[25] Stories about the corruption, folly, and bestiality of blacks during Reconstruction appealed to northerners of Anglo-Saxon ancestry now faced with unfamiliar-looking immigrants from eastern and southern Europe. Even members of the Grand Army of the Republic, the veterans' organization for Union soldiers (largely limited to native-born whites), reconciled with their Confederate brothers, at least to acknowledge that they had fought well if none too wisely for the Lost Cause.[26] And the Spanish-American War marked for many Americans an occasion for ending sectional differences for good.[27]

Harlan shared these ideas. The happy relations between master and slave described by Malvina Harlan fit into the Old South myth. And Harlan wanted reconciliation with the Confederates. In 1893, he wrote Alabama senator John T. Morgan, a rabid racist who was a fellow U.S. representative at the Bering Sea arbitration with Great Britain in Paris, that "one of the pleasantest reflections I have in connection with the work here is that you, an ex-Confederate soldier, and I an ex-Union soldier, have sat side by side, in a foreign land."[28] He expressed regret in an 1898 letter that he could not attend the Grand Army of the Republic encampment "where veterans who wore the Blue and veterans who wore the Gray will stand together under one flag and renew their pledges of devotion to the Union."[29]

The emphasis of Harlan's reconciliatory gestures, however, was on the rightness of the Union cause, just as the emphasis of Malvina's memoirs was on the antislavery impulse in the slaveholding household. The Confederates had been wrong; they were welcome to repledge themselves to the Union. In the same 1898 letter, Harlan criticized the suggestion that the U.S. government should return to Confederate veterans the flags captured from them during the Civil War. *All* was not forgiven.

Only after we have understood Harlan's vision of his country can we begin to explain the decisions he made about its founding document. Just as Harlan justified his choices by reference to his father, so he justified his decisions on the bench by reference to the founding fathers. If the best type of slaveholders had practiced paternalism while hoping for the end of slavery, the Civil War and the amendments to the Constitution fulfilled their desires. Unlike politicians of the antebellum generation who felt they would never live up to the founders' achievement, Harlan fit himself into the republican myth unselfconsciously.[30] The Civil War generation had answered the nation's call for emancipation, and Harlan would spend his life continuing to serve.

Harlan's lecture on the first day of class in October 1897 made clear his belief in the finite nature of legal knowledge. After advising his students to read American and English history, Harlan stated: "You well understand that there is little or no scope for originality for anything that I can present to you as to our constitution. The whole thing seems to have been fully covered by treatises and judicial decisions. These lat[t]er must be our guides in ascertaining what that instrument means." Harlan was confident in the Court's ability to cope with change without having to alter legal principles. He cautioned his students not to misunderstand his statement: "Now do not understand me to say that every possible question has been determined. From the very nature of things as our civilization advances and broadens, new phases of questions supposed to have been settled will arise and present difficulties of a very serious character. All that I mean to say is that most every position relative to the power of the Federal Government have been defined in their scope, so that all that remains to be done is to apply the rules to new phases of old questions."[31] Like Joseph Story, who had argued that there were nineteen rules of constitutional interpretation, Harlan advocated the formalist belief that the rules of law remained unchanged by social life.[32] The founders had set forth a plan that simply had to be followed. Harlan concluded his last lecture on 7 May 1898 by telling his students that he hoped his lectures had induced them "to study the history of this instrument, and read the lives of the men who laid the foundation of this government, read their letters, and their speeches, from which light will come on the words of this instrument."[33] Between the founders' words and the Supreme Court's decisions, the rules were clear. Perhaps this faith was what allowed Harlan to joke about his dissents; not only did he know that he was right, but also he knew that right was unchanging and would prevail eventually.

Even when discussing instances in which it was difficult to apply the rules, Harlan refused to make a break from formalism. He had trouble explaining to the class how the Constitution remained undisturbed when the state of West Virginia broke off from Virginia during the Civil War even though Article 4, Section 3 expressly forbids the creation of a new state in this way. No lawsuit had ever challenged the existence of the new state before the Court. Harlan's first instinct was to avoid the issue. He told his students, "It is just one of the things that resulted from that war, which the less said about the better for the country." But one of his students persisted with questions.

Here was a point at which Harlan could have admitted the extraconstitutionality of the event and agreed with Holmes that the life of the law had not been logic but experience. The same year that Harlan began these lectures, Holmes published *The Path of the Law*, which urged judges to acknowledge their role in making policy. Instead, Harlan tried to explain "the theory that the old state for the time being had committed suicide, and that there was no state of Virginia left as a part of the United States." He must have recognized that his listener wasn't satisfied because he added, "Now if you tell me that you don't quite understand that, I am quite ready to agree with you it is not easy to understand." In response to yet another question, he replied, "Let me, Yankee fashion, answer that question by putting another," and he posed a series of hypothetical questions about the constitutionality of the effort of some Kentuckians to organize a new state and then compared that to the West Virginian situation. His treatment did not so much clarify "the legality of any movement which proposed to take a state bodiatiously, if I may coin a word, out of the Union" as much as it laid out the problem. He confessed at last, "I do not know whether I have made myself clear. I am not sure that I understand myself on that question."[34] Harlan knew there was a problem, but to solve it would have required him to create a new rule or to embrace a hard-nosed legal realism. To not solve the problem troubled him less.

Harlan presided over the celebration of the centennial of the New York Avenue Presbyterian Church in 1903. He appears seated, second from the left, in this portrait of the Centennial Bench of Elders. To Harlan's right is C. H. Fishbaugh; to his left are Wallace Radcliffe, the pastor of the church, Charles B. Bailey, and S. L. Crissey. Standing from left to right are Joseph C. Breckinridge, W. B. Gurley, H. L. Bruce, W. D. Hughes, J. W. Dawson, Charles A. Baker, and T. H. Herndon. (Photograph by Prince; courtesy of the New York Avenue Presbyterian Church)

Harlan's refusal to make this intellectual leap can be explained by looking at the religious basis of his legal thought. He was a Presbyterian Church elder who spent his Sundays at church and reading the Bible. The story that Harlan turned down Sunday night dinner invitations because he had a "*standing engagement for the Sunday Evening Service*" was well known in Washington, D.C.[35] He thought others should do the same.[36]

Like many Protestant Americans, Harlan thought of his country in religious terms. When Justice Brewer declared from the bench in 1892, "This is a Christian Nation," he was correct in identifying Protestantism as an informally established religion during the nineteenth century. As Brewer pointed out, oaths and wills referred to the Almighty, most legislatures and conventions began with prayers, all public and most private businesses closed on Sundays, and churches and Christian organizations dotted the landscape.[37] Justice William Strong even supported a movement to amend the preamble to the Constitution to read, "We the people of the United States, humbly acknowledging Almighty God as the source of all authority and power in civil government, the Lord Jesus Christ as the Governor among the nations, and

His revealed will as of supreme authority, in order to constitute a Christian government . . . do ordain and establish this Constitution."[38] Perhaps the effort failed because it was overkill. As Harlan noted in a 1906 interview in the *Washington Post*, "Let any public man openly denounce the Christian religion or avow himself to be an infidel, he will soon find that such views will be an insuperable obstacle to success in public life, although the law will not technically disqualify him from holding office."[39]

The informal establishment of Protestantism created a constitutional dilemma, but it could be sidestepped. Harlan once upheld a state law that punished a railroad superintendent named Hennington for running a freight train on Sunday. Hennington complained that the law violated the interstate commerce clause. Harlan must have realized that a Sabbath law was at odds with the constitutional prohibition on the establishment of religion. Although he acknowledged that "the day on which the running of freight trains is prohibited is kept by many under a sense of religious duty," he emphasized the state's interest in providing its citizens with a day of rest.[40] Missing was the religious sentiment Harlan voiced in other public forums: "When the mail carriers deliver mail on Sunday, they violate the holy day," or "A people without a Sabbath have a rotten social organization and cannot exert a beneficent or permanent influence upon the world."[41] Harlan respected disestablishment in *Hennington*, but his heart lay with the Christian nation. He mixed biblical language into political discussion; he quoted the Bible in explaining the political fate of the United States. He used the same word—"fathers"—when speaking of the founding fathers and the church fathers.

At times, he spoke literally of the connections between his denomination and his country, such as when he noted to a group of Presbyterians in 1905 the "striking similarity between the fundamental principles of the Presbyterian Constitution and the fundamental principles of the American Constitution." Both were representative in nature and barred arbitrary authority. Both had a final court to which even the most humble could plead their cases. Presbyterianism was particularly conducive to freedom because "it teaches man to read the Bible, and invites every one to freely utter his opinions, despite any authority that may attempt to control his thoughts. Aye, it teaches him to resist, as did his fathers, any authority that would assume to trample upon the rights of man."[42] During a newspaper interview in 1908, Harlan discussed the role of Presbyterianism during the Revolutionary War: "Did you ever hear of such a thing as a Presbyterian Tory? I never did, and I have searched history carefully. If there was one, he kept well out of view. Presbyterianism was the very basis of that contest, and it was even called a Presbyterian rebellion."[43]

Such claims were commonplace. An 1893 volume designed for "church members, officers and busy pastors" marveled that so few Presbyterian ministers were killed in the Revolutionary War "considering their exposure."[44]

Although these were exaggerations, it was natural for Harlan to note the historical interdependence of church and state. Many of the large Protestant sects had split before the Civil War. During the controversies that would divide the Presbyterians into the (mostly southern) Old School and the New School in 1837 and then split the two schools yet again in the 1850s, "prominent Presbyterians confessed their awareness that a division of the church could precipitate a crisis in the political compact."[45] Harlan worked with Unionist minister Robert J. Breckinridge after the war to defeat the plans of southern-sympathizing Presbyterians in a church property suit that ended up before the Court. Church and state intertwined in theory and in practice for Harlan. To make this identification of the Presbyterian Church with the Republic plain to all, Harlan worked on a project to build a Presbyterian cathedral in Washington, D.C.[46]

Harlan's contemporaries remarked on his identification of law and faith. During a banquet to celebrate Harlan's twenty-fifth year on the Supreme Court, Justice Brewer teased that Harlan "goes to bed every night with one hand on the Constitution and the other on the Bible, and so sleeps the sweet sleep of justice and righteousness."[47] A journalist brought up the remark in 1906, and although Harlan bristled a bit at the comic image, he embraced the parallel: "The Bible is supreme in respect of all matters with which it deals, and the Constitution is supreme in this country in respect to all civil matters of national concern."[48] Harlan found power and meaning in the Constitution and in the Bible. In fact, his faith explains his legal formalism. His belief in a transcendent God who ordered the universe lay behind his belief in a transcendent law that ordered the nation.

The way Harlan dealt with the constitutional problem of West Virginia reflected his approach to theological issues. In 1880, he learned from his wife that their son James had been arguing with another college student about the question of eternal punishment. Harlan wrote James that "it seems to me that this is not a question which need concern us very much in this life." The degree of punishment had been an issue between the boys, but Harlan dismissed it: "I don't think it material for you to inquire as to the degree or extent of the punishment which will be inflicted. Whatever may be the punishment it is certain to be more than you or Dave will like, and more than you will, even in that supreme moment, admit you ought to have." Harlan turned to the Bible to answer his son's questions. He quoted the story in the Gospel of Luke of the rich man who is surprised to find himself in hell and to see the beggar Lazarus in Abraham's bosom in heaven.[49] The rich man was "anxious to change his base of operations," as Harlan put it. But Abraham replied to him that "between us and you there is a great gulf fixed; so that they which would pass from hence to you cannot; neither can they pass to us, that would come from thence." Harlan took this passage as a literal account of what happens after death. There was a hell and there was a heaven, and each of us was sent to one or the other. The Bible's account was not a metaphor or a possibility; it was the truth.

Harlan concluded that since the Bible contained no other relevant story, Abraham's words were the end of the matter. There was no way to cross from the one place to the other. "The thing is not to get into the torment at all" because "it is certain that if we are comforted, as the beggar was, we will not know what torment is, will have no occasion to bother our brains with determining the question as to how long the 'tormented' will be punished."

Harlan must have been taken with the idea that those in Abraham's bosom did not raise such questions because he repeated the phrase. "I do not bother my brain with these subtle inquiries," he wrote; "if we could solve them all we should know as much as God does, and would claim ourselves to have had some hand in creating the Universe." Harlan took his son's questioning as a sign of rebellion rather than intellectual curiosity. He chided, "Do not fall into the habit too common among young collegians of calling into question the fundamental ideas upon which all religion rests." Perhaps he thought this severe because he added, "You are not bound to accept blindly what the fathers have taught but you ought to be slow in striking down the old landmarks, or ploughing up the old ways."[50] As a father, Harlan ordered his son to behave; he made himself an example of the virtue of ceasing to inquire as well.

Harlan's conservative method of biblical exegesis places him within the tradition of Scottish commonsense realism (no relation to legal realism), which he would have learned while attending Centre College in Danville, Kentucky. At the time he graduated in 1850, the college president was John C. Young. A chronicler of the college writes, "It has been well stated and repeated that during this long period of his administration (1830–1857) Centre College was John C. Young and John C. Young was Centre College."[51] Young had graduated in 1828 from Princeton Theological Seminary, where students had been learning how to interpret the Bible by applying the principles of Scottish commonsense realism since the late eighteenth century.[52] A list of books recommended by another of Harlan's Centre College professors included such Scottish philosophers as Dugald Stewart.[53]

Commonsense realism held that human beings had the capacity to understand the world through the use of their five senses. The proper way to study the natural world was to begin with the physical facts and then discover general principles or laws. Although the Princeton theologians insisted on the empirical method, they assumed the existence of God to begin with.[54] Harlan voiced the idea that God ordered the natural world in an 1892 letter to his wife. "In the midst of a furious gale" while waiting to sail across the Atlantic Ocean, Harlan wrote that "the man who can stand in such a gale and doubt that there is a sublime [?] providence which holds all in his hand, is to be pitied if not regarded as a fool."[55] The natural world was proof of human helplessness and divine power. The Princeton theologians also believed that God had implanted a moral sense in the human soul and that the Bible contained a body of moral truths palpable to the moral sense just as the natural world revealed its general laws to the physical senses. The Princeton theologians' preference for facts over "speculation" displayed what Theodore Bozeman calls "the psychology of humility."[56] Just as they were humble before God, so they were humble in inquiry. Charles Hodge, who taught at Princeton Theological Seminary for some six decades before his death in 1878, once boasted that "a new idea never originated in this seminary."[57]

The parallel between the study of the natural world and the the study of the Bible went even further since scientists who were Christians believed that the laws of nature confirmed the existence of God. The creator had endowed human beings with reason, and they could best use this capacity by trying to understand and appreciate his marvelous creation and by following his moral laws. President Young announced in his inaugural address at Centre College in 1830 that "an instructor has daily opportunities of aptly and unobtrusively interweaving sanctifying truth into all the studies he directs; for religion is not a thing apart from life—it connects itself with every science."[58]

Harlan would have taken the moral philosophy class with Young his senior year. This course was usually taught by the college president.[59] It was the climax of a college career and was designed to show that the principles of commonsense realism applied to a range of practical issues. It demonstrated how revelation and reason dovetailed, and its textbooks displayed "almost an obsession" with "the legal model of morality."[60] Obedience to the moral laws set down by God would benefit both the individual and the community.

Although virtually every American college graduate would have been taught some version of Scottish commonsense realism, some did not remain as attached to its teachings as others did. New scientific knowledge indicated that revelation was at odds with reason. Geologists determined that the earth was far older than the 6,000 years accounted for by the Bible.[61] Charles Darwin's theory of natural selection and evolution did more than give humans common ancestry with apes. It replaced the Christian creator of infinite love, designer of a beautifully functioning world, with a being who watched unmoved as humans, like other animals, battled for life.[62] Although most Christians remained true to their faith and university scholars worked at reconciling the new scientific discoveries with religious faith, as the Princeton theologians had been doing since the late eighteenth century, what was called "the unity of truth" had taken a serious blow.[63]

Harlan scoffed at the intellectual forces shaking up religious orthodoxy. While speaking at a ceremony at Centre College honoring Young and other teachers in June 1891, Harlan criticized the " 'higher critics' of these modern days, vain of their scholastic attainments."[64] Traditional criticism of the Bible had contented itself with textual analysis, but higher criticism, which originated in Germany, treated the Bible as a historical literary document. Higher critics noted that the Bible contained discrepancies that might be explained by the historical circumstances under which it was written. Some argued that these discrepancies proved that it was not the divinely revealed word of God.[65] They treated the Bible as a historical document instead of a transcendent one, just as the legal realists would see the Constitution as historical rather than providential. Harlan may have heard of higher criticism from his sons, who, like many upper-class American men of the late nineteenth century, studied at the University of Berlin, and from Richard in particular, who earned a doctorate of divinity from Princeton Theological Seminary in 1885.[66]

Higher criticism troubled all conservative Presbyterians. One historian writes that "there can be little doubt that biblical criticism was responsible for the hardening of the Princeton position" of biblical inerrancy.[67] Minister Charles A. Briggs had provoked the wrath of Presbyterian orthodoxy by praising higher criticism in his inaugural address, "The Authority of Holy Scripture," at Union Theological Seminary in New York City just months before Harlan's speech at Centre College. Briggs ended up being convicted of heresy by the Presbyterian General Assembly.[68]

According to Harlan, the higher critics were "over-anxious to find errors, however insignificant, even at the risk of undermining the settled faith of others in the essential truths of religion."[69] Like other believers in biblical inerrancy, Harlan thought such errors petty.[70] He had counseled his son James to abandon his questioning, and he advised the students of his alma mater to do the same. The issues that troubled other believers and led them to religious liberalism or even agnosticism were waved away by Harlan.

Harlan served on a committee that worked on revising the Presbyterian confession of faith in light of challenges from people like Briggs. After surveying the presbyteries, the committee members made several suggestions. The most important were that Presbyterians make clear that they did not believe in infant damnation and drop the identification of the pope as the Antichrist.[71] The General Assembly of 1902 adopted the report unanimously, apparently relieved that it might avoid radical change.

Harlan's faith determined his understanding of his place in the world as a man and as a judge. Although the higher critics used reason to test revelation, Harlan recognized the limits of human reason. If we could solve all of the subtle inquiries, he told his son, we would know as much as God does and would claim to have had some hand in creating the universe. Similarly, he told his law students that the case of West Virginia was not easy to understand, but he was willing to leave it at that. Harlan's faith in God determined the shape of his intellectual understanding, just as the agnosticism of Holmes and the legal realists would determine theirs. We might say that Harlan knew that he had not had a hand in creating the universe, whereas the legal realists knew that they had. Agnosticism made inquiry imperative; faith made it less necessary.

Harlan's belief that judges declare law but do not make it was shared by nineteenth-century legal traditionalists of all stripes.[72] When judges announced a change in a legal rule, they were simply correcting mistakes. Chief Justice Samuel F. Miller, under whom Harlan served for many years, explained to a law class in 1890 that "it has been long since discovered" that knowledge of a crime and the accused disqualifies a person from jury duty, "yet it is an undoubted fact that the principle of the trial by a jury of the vicinage was founded" precisely on the idea that neighbors would have such knowledge.[73] Historical change meant only that the true principles of law were eventually "discovered." As George Robertson, Harlan's law teacher at Transylvania University, put it, judges "both make laws and repeal them" only when they did their jobs badly—"by a hasty, ill considered, illogical conclusion, by overlooking authorities or disregarding facts."[74] Langdell of Harvard argued similarly that "law, considered as a science, consists of certain principles or doctrines" that could be identified through the close reading of select, correctly decided cases.[75] Whatever method they used, orthodox legal thinkers believed that good judges merely applied the principles of law.

Where Langdell differed from people like Harlan was in refusing to invoke the commonsense belief in an innate moral sense as an explanation for the principles they had found.[76] In contrast, Story had announced in his inaugural address at Harvard Law School in 1829 that Christian morality was the foundation of common law.[77] Legal treatise authors like Thomas M. Cooley and John Norton Pomeroy were certain "that a transcendent Christian God ruled both heaven and earth."[78] Like the Princeton theologians, who modeled their method on the natural sciences, judges investigated the facts of the cases before them to try to discover the principles of law that applied to

Unlike most nineteenth-century lawyers who studied for the bar in a law office, Harlan attended the Law School of Transylvania University in Lexington, Kentucky, in the early 1850s. In 1908 he paid a visit to the school in the company of his old friend Augustus E. Willson, then governor of Kentucky. In this photograph commemorating the visit, Harlan is wearing a top hat and holding a cane and Willson is standing to Harlan's right. (Courtesy of the Library of Congress)

them.[79] Joel Bishop, the writer of several widely read legal treatises, made the analogy between discovering law and the ordering of the natural world plain in 1868: "Where there is a concurrence of all the circumstances essential to a sound administration of justice . . . 'Almighty God' appears in the midst of the tribunal where it sits and reveals the right way to the understandings of the judges, as surely as he appears in the tempest on the ocean and teaches each water-drop where to lie."[80] Even when they described legal change at the hands of humans, traditional legal writers placed God somewhere in the background as the author of it all. Law served human purposes while reflecting higher ones. As Philomon Bliss asked in 1884, "Is there anything in jural society, when it answers its ends, that does not spring from the will of God? . . . Who but God is sovereign?"[81]

The lack of talk about science in Harlan's 1897–98 lectures on constitutional law may be a reaction to the stresses that scientific discoveries had been putting on the assumption that the study of the natural world revealed God's works. Just as the Princeton theologians responded to higher criticisms by hunkering down and refusing even to contemplate the possibility that copyists' errors were explanations for discrepancies in the Bible, so Harlan may have been hunkering down in reaction to attacks on his vision of constitutional law.[82] Langdell and his colleagues at Harvard left God out of the story of legal principles and dismissed constitutional law as mere politics unworthy of scientific study. The lack of scientific talk and the abundance of providential talk in Harlan's lectures may be the result of his perception that the links between faith and law needed a stronger defense.

Instead of offering his students a sustained inquiry into the logic and history of constitutional interpretation, Harlan delivered an unremarkable exposition of the Supreme Court's decisions. He followed the structure of the third book of the first volume of *Commentaries on the Constitution of the United States*, Joseph Story's standard statement of legal nationalism, which Harlan assigned as a textbook at least through 1904, according to Columbian University's *Bulletin*. He started with the preamble, commented on the historical situation at the time of the Constitution's writing and on later interpretations, and then went on to the next clause.

Harlan's exams reflected his view of legal knowledge. Some questions required mere memorization: "1. In whom is the Executive Power vested by the Constitution? 2. What are the qualifications required in the President?" Sometimes he led the student to the right answer: "What was the power *to regulate foreign commerce* submitted to the Federal Government?," followed by "What was temporarily excepted from its exercise? When did that exception cease to operate?"[83] Any student who could not come up with the importation of slaves and the year 1808 must have slept through the lectures. Other questions required the students to go further by explaining the Court's interpretations: "State the *general* rule defining the extent of the power of Congress? What is the test for determining whether a particular statute is within or beyond the power of Congress? Give reasons."[84] Just as Harlan limited his own inquiry into constitutional puzzles, so he limited that of his students.

Despite this or maybe because of it, the students appear to have enjoyed his lectures. When Harlan had to miss the commencement in 1894, his wife and daughter Ruth went instead and reported happily that his congratulatory telegram was "overfuriously applauded by the young men." One of the "*fresh*" ones, as Malvina Harlan put it, started up "the refrain with which every [faculty member's?] name was sung 'What's the matter with Harlan—He's all right' but cooler & wiser heads rather quashed it in the beginning, letting only the 'Harlan's all right' really come out in full."[85] Of course, as a sitting justice on the Supreme Court, Harlan must have been a natural draw. He could describe national controversies in which he had played a part. He could tell of his meeting with English judges and their discussion of the differences between Parliament and Congress.[86] In addition to teaching constitutional law at Columbian University from 1889 to 1909, he taught domestic relations, torts, and commercial law, but we have no record of his lectures in those classes. He also guest lectured at Northwestern University and other law schools and was invited to join the summer law school at the University of Virginia.[87]

Harlan's demeanor while lecturing was unpretentious. An undated newspaper clipping preserved in a family scrapbook described him as arriving at evening class "immaculately dressed, white tie, the freshest of linen, full evening suit, a smoothly shaven face just from the hands of the barber." His formal appearance was softened by his physical habits: "Then from the rear pocket of his swallow-tail coat he draws a good old-fashioned bandana handkerchief, which he knows how to use, and from his capacious mouth he occasionally expectorates real genuine tobacco juice."[88] Despite his birth into a politically elite family, his education, and his high position, Harlan always called himself a plain man. One student recalled years later that Harlan once admitted to being unable to answer a question but promised to look it up: "For one of the greatest judges of the Supreme Court to avoid any degree of evasion, and to tell a class of greenhorns that he was not positive as to the answer of one of their questions, naturally gave the students confidence that anything he told them in the future would be a thing to be relied on."[89] Harlan gave his students homely advice. After describing the *Federalist Papers*, he told them, "If you have not got it in your library I advise you to look tomorrow in the secondhand book stores and see if you cannot buy one for half price, for it is worth its weight in gold."[90] By taking into account their situation—they were night students who had to work during the day to support themselves—Harlan exhibited an appealing practicality.

Harlan's language was also without ceremony. The lectures read as spoken, not written, speech that displays all of the basic techniques of stump speaking. This simple style may be another reason the lectures have been neglected. Unlike Holmes's famous 1880 lectures, which must have demanded extraordinary powers of comprehension on the part of his listeners if the book that resulted is any indication, Harlan's lectures were easy to follow. He used rhetorical questions, parallel construction, and repetition in order to make important points easier to remember. Other practices made his words more immediate and persuasive, such as using the present tense when the subjunctive was grammatically correct. He used vivid imagery and the second-person pronoun—"you" instead of "one"—in order to involve his students. And he employed humor as a way of encouraging students to join him in opposing ideas, at least through their laughter.

Harlan's main point was that the U.S. Constitution was superior to any other plan of government that had ever existed. He often used the pronoun "we" to include his students in this belief. After describing the federal judicial system, he explained that it was unclear how the idea of it had arisen: "We are amazed that these men were as wise as they were. . . . Where the thought originated of one Supreme Court, I do not know. They certainly did not borrow it from any country on the earth. . . . It seems to have come providentially into this instrument."[91] The Court's most important role was as protector of the rights and liberty that the United States alone offered its citizens. Harlan reminded his students again and again of their country's exceptional nature. On the first day of class, he declared, "It [i]s the only government on the face of the earth where man and man are equal before the law, and with all that large liberty we are stable and strong."[92] As he lectured, Harlan told the story of his country's unique mission.

Harlan once proclaimed, "I never tire of reading about the great men who laid in this goodly land the foundations of free republican government."[93] As he explained the various clauses of the Constitution and the amendments that altered them, he described the progress of equality. In order for all Americans to claim civil rights, the Civil War had to be fought and the slaves freed. Far from disrupting the course of American history, these events fulfilled the country's providential mission. The emancipation of blacks answered the wish of the founders.

Harlan did not actually portray American history as a historical or human-driven process of cause and effect. Like many Americans, he believed that the United States had escaped the classical cycle of history in which republics like Rome rose only to fall because of internal decay.[94] Instead, the history of the United States was the inevitable fulfillment of a divine plan. History became religious myth in Harlan's hands.

The notion that the United States had a divinely ordained destiny that placed it outside the usual cycles of history was deep-rooted and widespread.[95] The revolutionary generation built on the Puritans' identification of themselves as God's chosen people.[96] Just as the Israelites had made a covenant with God, so Americans believed they had made a national covenant. They appropriated millennialism for civil ends as well. According to the Book of Revelation, Christ would reign on earth for 1,000 years of perfect rule. Adapting this imagery, Americans came to believe that the United States would usher in an era of perfect liberty.[97] When the Civil War came, people on both sides identified themselves as God's chosen people who were scourged for their sins.[98] For some on the Union side, the sin was slavery.[99] The version of history that Harlan told after the war was similar to that put forth by the abolitionists before it.[100]

The apology for chattel slavery displayed in Malvina's descriptions of the Harlan household found its civic counterpart in John's depiction of the revolutionary generation in his lectures. In order to make his history of egalitarian progress coherent, Harlan had to show that later events had been anticipated by earlier ones, so he emphasized the antislavery aspects of early American history. In January 1898, Harlan stood before his students and tried to erase from their minds "the impression that the people of the South were unitedly in favor of the extension of slavery" at the time of the Constitutional Convention.[101] Harlan depicted white southerners as guiltless. He voiced their predicament as they had explained it at the Constitutional Convention: "These people are not here of our seeking; they were brought here against our will. . . . Here they are. What are we to do with them?"[102] Their unheroic but excusable passivity made emancipation impossible at the time of the convention: "Anything in the constitution here that would uproot that institution all at once would disturb all of our local affairs, produce infinite confusion."[103]

In Harlan's mythology, the founding fathers' hesitation to uproot this labor system was matched by their dislike of it. "It is not stating it too strongly," he informed his students, "to say that all the leading statesmen of the South, with few exceptions, were opposed to the institution of slavery, and regretted that it was there."[104] Harlan challenged his students to find "in the writings or letters or speeches of any statesmen of the South during the Revolutionary period and before the constitution was adopted any defense of the institution of slavery upon moral or economic grounds."[105] He noted that both Thomas Jefferson and George Washington opposed slavery. He pointed out that George Mason, author of the Virginia Bill of Rights, gave "the most terrific arraignment of the institution upon high moral and public grounds" at the convention, stronger even than those made later by abolitionists William Lloyd Garrison and Wendell Phillips. Mason condemned slavery, "yet he was a man who had the confidence and affection of all men in the state of Virginia."[106] Harlan pushed some of the responsibility for slavery off of the shoulders of white southerners.[107]

By emphasizing that complicity in slavery was a *national* rather than a southern phenomenon, Harlan was trying to undercut any feelings of sectionalism among his students. He prevented them from identifying slaveowning southerners as the sole cause of the Civil War. Harlan portrayed slavery as widely if reluctantly supported by whites in one way or another. He told his students that at the time of the founding, "there were persons even in Boston" who "engaged in and profited by the importation of slaves from Africa." [108] Any student who questioned this might "turn to the newspapers published in Boston about the time of the Declaration of Independence, and even after that," where they would find advertisements for runaway slaves.[109] Harlan had some reservations about spreading responsibility for slavery to northern whites. He conceded that in the North "the great masses of people were hostile to that institution." [110]

The fact that whites of neither section were particularly supportive of slavery explained the Constitution's handling of the subject. Harlan focused on the words used in the document in order to argue that emancipation was latent in the very clauses that gave protection to slavery. The Constitution refers to persons "held to service or labour" and "the migration or importation of such persons" and never uses the words "fugitive slave" or the "slave trade." "It is a curious fact," Harlan told his students after reading aloud the fugitive slave clause, "that you do not find the word 'slave' anywhere in the constitution of the United States; they did not mention it, and yet there were slaves when the constitution was adopted . . . and that clause that I have just read had reference primarily to slaves." [111] Harlan drew an antislavery lesson from the founders' language. The slave-trade clause was "an illustration of the hesitancy on the part of the men who framed this instrument about using any word that indicated the recommendation in the constitution of the institution of slavery in mere words." [112] The writers of the Constitution might have felt helpless to oppose slavery, but they made sure that its sordid name did not stain their new republic, at least not in print. Harlan implied that the founders had left it to their descendants to answer the Constitution's tacit request for abolition.

Harlan elevated the revolutionary spirit of the Declaration of Independence above the complacency of the Constitution. The pronouncement of universal equality found in "our political bible," as he called the Declaration, embodied the founders' wishes better than the constitutional system they had actually constructed.[113] The main reason Harlan admired Mason was his authorship of the Virginia Bill of Rights.[114] In Mason, Harlan also found an alternative to Jefferson, whom his father had disliked as the opponent of the Whig Party's hero, Alexander Hamilton. Since Mason's Bill of Rights predated the Declaration of Independence and since Jefferson drew on it, Harlan could pay homage to a slightly more original document and snub Jefferson at the same time. So strongly was Harlan attached to the Virginia Bill of Rights that he included it on a list of writings that he wanted published in an appendix to a volume of his judicial decisions.[115] The Virginia Bill of Rights contained, according to the judge, "all the ideas that were established after several hundred years of trial for the vindication of the inalienable rights of man." In its sixteen propositions, his students would "not find absent a single idea that we to-day regard as essential to freedom in this country."[116] Members of the revolutionary generation had drawn up a blueprint for their descendants to follow.

By identifying the Declaration of Independence as the original founding document, Harlan was following the nationalist school of legal thought he had inherited as a Whig. (His father had not named him after Chief Justice John Marshall for nothing.) Democrat John C. Calhoun had tried to repudiate the Declaration of Independence in order to argue two related things: that slavery was a positive good and that the states retained their sovereignty after they created the Union. Story had tackled the state sovereignty issue by arguing that "from the moment of the Declaration of Independence . . . the united colonies must be considered as being a nation *de facto*, having a general government over it, created and acting by the general consent of the people of all the colonies."[117] Harlan had attended the Law School of Transylvania University, which taught the same brand of constitutionalism.[118] One of his teachers, George Robertson, had opposed the Virginia and Kentucky resolutions of 1798 because "it is not true, that the States, in their sovereign political capacity alone, made the Constitution of the United States."[119] The people had made the Constitution, according to Robertson, and "the citizen should hold the Constitution as the Christian does the decalogue, sacred and inviolable."[120] Harlan drew his students' attention to the "peculiar force in these words 'We the People of the United States.'"[121]

Harlan took up this constitutional tradition and grafted abolitionism onto it.[122] After burning a copy of the Constitution on the grounds that it protected slavery, William Lloyd Garrison had asked, "What is an abolitionist but a sincere believer in the Declaration of '76?"[123] Frederick Douglass had drawn the same antislavery directive from the founders' unwillingness to use the word "slavery" in the Constitution.[124] Abolitionists and Radical Republicans proclaimed the Civil War a second American Revolution that made good on the Declaration. When Harlan emphasized the Declaration's assertion of the equality of all men in his lectures, he nurtured this graft onto the tradition of legal nationalism. Abraham Lincoln had followed this path earlier.[125]

Of course, the story Harlan told in his lectures favored certain aspects of the founders' history and neglected others. It was similar to Free-Soiler Salmon P. Chase's reading of the Constitution in its emphasis on Jefferson's opposition to slavery.[126] Winthrop Jordan agrees that at least "during the Revolutionary War . . . no one in the South stood up to endorse Negro slavery." [127] But the Virginians amended Mason's propositions in May 1776 in order to make it clear that equality existed in a state of nature and not in the state of Virginia. And Harlan failed to acknowledge Jefferson's suspicion that blacks were less rational than whites. In fact, David Brion Davis describes Jefferson as having had "only a theoretical interest in promoting the cause of abolition." [128] Harlan never mentioned that early support of emancipation was always linked to the deportation of freed blacks to African colonies. Nor did he speak of the next generation of southern leaders, like John C. Calhoun, who defended slavery instead of apologizing for it, or the attacks on newspaper editors in Kentucky and elsewhere who dared to speak out against slavery. [129] These historical facts did not fit into a story of progress toward emancipation.

Harlan's history skipped from the founders to some indeterminate period of antebellum history and then zeroed in on the 1850s. He offered no clear explanation for why abolitionists and slaveholders came to blows when they did. Seemingly out of nowhere "the desire for liberty and freedom throughout the whole land had increased, abolitionists springing up everywhere to place their opposition to slavery upon high moral grounds." [130] Soon the arguments were so heated that "there was no such thing as freedom of thought, when it bore on this institution." Anyone who denied that God had blessed the institution "was looked upon with distrust and suspicion" in some parts of the country; in other regions, people found it "very difficult" to treat the advocates of slavery "with Christian moderation." [131] Although Harlan depicted both sides on the slavery question as deaf to each other, his sympathies clearly lay with the abolitionists. He even praised John Brown, whose attack on the federal armory at Harpers Ferry in 1859 had horrified white southerners. The true aggressor in Harlan's history remained the institution of slavery, which "had got its hand upon the throat of this country" and "adopted the motto 'Death or Tribute.' " [132] Slavery seemed to rise up from where the founding fathers had left it to threaten their descendants. "It had come to this," Harlan explained: "this country had to perish under that institution, or that institution had to die." [133]

When Harlan explained the political situation of the 1850s, he focused on its most anti-egalitarian aspects. The Compromise of 1850 allowed California to enter the Union as a free state in exchange for a law that ordered federal officials to capture slaves who had escaped to the North. Harlan passed over any further particulars. He explained to his class that the enforcement of the fugitive slave law meant that "men of the colored race that had been in the North for years were arrested . . . and brought back by the orders of courts of justice to states of slavery." The "political contest" thus provoked "never ended until Sumter was fired upon, and until the close of the war at Appomattox."[134]

Similarly, Harlan interpreted "probably the greatest judicial contest this country has ever witnessed," *Dred Scott v. Sanford*, as primarily a decision about citizenship.[135] The case had raised a number of issues in 1857, the most important of which was whether Congress had the power to outlaw slavery in the western territories as it had done for the northern part of such territories in the Missouri Compromise of 1820. But in Harlan's account, there was only one issue: who made up "We the People of the United States" who had established the Constitution. Dred Scott was a black slave whose owner had brought him into a free state and free territory before settling in Missouri, a slave state. A test suit for freedom based on the argument that Scott was a citizen of Missouri was brought first in the state courts and then in the federal courts and ended before the Supreme Court. Chief Justice Roger B. Taney, whose decision papered over various concurring opinions, declared the Missouri Compromise of 1820 unconstitutional. This caused more public uproar at the time, but to Harlan the most important aspect of Taney's decision was his denial that Scott could ever be a citizen because of his race. Harlan noted that "according to [Taney's] understanding of the history of the period," Taney wrote "that the men who adopted that constitution did not intend by the phrase 'We, the people of the United States' to include the colored man of African descent." Harlan explained that when Taney declared this, there arose "an excitement at that time that you at this day can scarcely understand." The political parties broke apart; antislavery advocates "abused" federal judges. When he added that "out of this came the Republican party of to-day," his students burst into applause. Harlan hushed them with, "I am not talking about politics, but about the constitution of the United States."[136]

*Dred Scott*, the catalyst for the war, was raised to providential status in Harlan's eyes. He noted that "we are in the habit in our ordinary conversation of speaking of particular things which have occurred as Providences." He then linked the founding fathers and the Union leaders as similarly bestowed from on high: "We say that George Washington was a special Providence, and that no other man could have done the work so far as we can tell that he did. We say that Jefferson was a special Providence, and that no other man could have performed the work that he did. We talk in the same way about Abraham Lincoln, about Ulysses S. Grant in the same sense." These men had served God's purpose by taking part in forwarding the American mission. Then Harlan raised *Dred Scott* up to the same height: "I think I may say that that case was a work of special Providence to this country, in that it laid the foundation of a civil war which, terrible as it was, awful as it was in its consequences in the loss of life and money, was in the end a blessing to this country in that it rid us of the institution of African slavery." [137] Just as God had raised up the founders and Harlan's generation to fulfill the mission of emancipation, so he had created even something as contrived as *Dred Scott* in order to further his cause.

Harlan's generation responded to the wishes of God and the fathers by glorying in emancipation. "People of all sexes, and all states are glad of it," he declared to his students. Again, he pushed aside sectional feeling in favor of nationalism. Even white southerners, he told his students, "have come to the conclusion that the best thing that could have happened to them was the defeat of the South." He had "no doubt that each one of them would vote against" reenslavement "if the question were submitted to-day." [138] There was no turning back from this mission.

The Civil War turned egalitarian spirit into constitutional word. The Fourteenth Amendment fixed the people's identity in the double sense of clearing away error and settling the argument. It assured that "now there cannot be any dispute as to who constitute the people of the United States who ordained and established this constitution." [139] Harlan's use of the past tense of the preamble's "ordain and establish" demonstrates how fundamental his reconstruction of the Constitution and his rejection of *Dred Scott* were. He gave blacks a constitutional role that history had largely denied them; they became part of the people who *had* ordain*ed* and establish*ed*. In like manner, Harlan placed an amendment at the Constitution's very base. "Equality before the law," he assured his students, "is the fundamental underlying principle upon which our constitution rests, and it rests there securely." [140] His version of history did away with the messy struggles over power and wealth and race. It was simply the unfolding of events as ordained by the original plan.

Harlan adopted the arguments of Free-Soilers and Republicans, who had declared before the war that slavery degraded even free labor by its example. The ideology of free labor held that the system of wage labor allowed worthy men to better themselves, eventually working their way from hired hand to employer. Harlan now applied these ideas to race relations in the era of emancipation. Unlike most antebellum Republicans who had doubted that blacks could take full advantage of any opportunities offered them, Harlan thought their progress in the postwar era inevitable.[141] He told his students to pay no attention to white people who thought it "unfortunate" even in 1898 "that this institution of African Slavery went down." Harlan admitted that "of course there is before us the probability of trouble, on account of this race," but he made it clear that "some people talk about it more than they ought to." Most of the uneasiness in interracial relations arose when shiftless whites tried to tear down hardworking blacks. "You occasionally meet with a [white] man," Harlan explained, "as I did about a year ago, who never did an honest day's work in his life, and who never earned the salt that he ate on his food. That was his only aim in life, to live upon somebody else." Having little else to pride himself on save his color, "this man was greatly disturbed at the probability, that that race would come into contact with the Whites in this country." But no white man of ability wasted time trying to undermine black efforts at self-improvement. "Well the white man who has got self-respect," Harlan emphasized to his students, "that has got humanity in his nature, who has respect for a human being, because he is one, wherever he sees him; that sort of man is not much disturbed by the fact, that the black man is bettering himself, here and there, taking an education, laying up a little property, learning a trade, and are advancing." With slavery destroyed, the entire black race started out on the life of free labor by which all men proved themselves in a republic. Harlan launched blacks into this new life with the rhythm of his sentences: "Every human being, since the addition of the [Thirteenth] Amendment is free to do as he pleases, to work for his own salvation, so far as more worldly affairs are considered. To make this way in their lives as far as they can. To aspire as other people who are free. To do what they can for themselves, and their race."[142]

Without explicitly exhorting them, Harlan invited his students to follow his example and take a role in the national mission. "I am ready to say," he declared from his podium, "that if there is a black man who can get ahead of me, I will help him along, and rejoice, and his progress in life does not excite my envy." He proclaimed this sentiment practically universal among whites. He was "glad to feel and know that it is the desire of the white people in this country, that that race shall push themselves forward in the race of this life."

Out of the racist rhetoric of manifest destiny, Harlan carved an egalitarian future. Although white Americans had long justified taking land from the Native Americans on the grounds of racial superiority, Harlan described egalitarianism as a consequence of the great size of the country that had resulted.[143] The availability of land in the United States was seen as the reason why Americans could break from the European feudal past to set up a republic. Now Harlan used sheer geographical scale to ease the relations of blacks and whites. "This world is big enough for us all," Harlan asserted, "and this country is big enough for us all. And if a man gets along, whether he be white or black, there is room enough in this broad free land of ours, for all of us."[144] Harlan integrated his students rhetorically with the race that his university refused to enroll.[145] Blacks and whites formed an "us" that could glory in their country and the freedom and opportunity it offered.

These safe-and-sound thoughts were not just for public consumption or for young and inexperienced minds. Harlan's private correspondence also invoked egalitarianism and the ideology of free labor. After the son of the Russian czar, Grand Duke Alexis, was "received with distinguished honors" in Louisville in 1872, Harlan and Benjamin Bristow shared an indignant exchange of letters.[146] "Altogether it was to my mind a very ridiculous demonstration, and to my republican mind," Harlan wrote, "a very offensive one." The duke had no claim to distinction other than blood: "Here was a young man who had not made a character & who was received with the most distinguished consideration because he was a nobleman, the son of the most absolute monarch on Earth." Harlan was quick to explain that although he was listed as a member of the Committee of Reception, "I had nothing whatsoever to do with the 'tom-foolery.'" Rather, "the honors of the occasion were 'done' by the Southern Rights gentlemen."[147] Bristow responded that he was unsurprised at this "disgusting exhibition of American toadyism." The states' rights men "never were real republicans or believers in free government." Echoing the arguments of Free-Soilers who had identified slavery as a source of undemocratic feeling before the war, Bristow wrote that the states' rights men had "fought for slavery not so much because of the dollars at stake as because of their love of the aristocracy of which it was the main stay and support."[148]

Just as the states' rights men had identified with aristocracy, so Harlan equated aristocracy with white supremacy. In 1885, a newspaper article that reported that English aristocrats had bowed out of the memorial service to Ulysses S. Grant at Westminster Abbey and sent equerries (substitutes) in their place stirred Harlan into a fierce denunciation. "The 'bloods' of Old England are laying up for themselves wealth against the day of wrath," he wrote Chief Justice Morrison R. Waite. "It will not be long before they will come down with a crash," he warned, "and as a plain man, who is no respecter of persons, I do not care how soon the overthrow comes; for, out of the destruction of royalty will come the regeneration & elevation of the masses." As in his law lectures, Harlan used religious language to sanction his republicanism. The day of wrath meant the end of the world and the Final Judgment. "God is no respecter of persons," Peter concludes when told that a Gentile, not a Jew, has been sent to him by God; he "judgeth according to every man's work."[149] So the English nobles disgusted Harlan because they "never did an honest day's work & live upon taxes wrung from the people." Paraphrasing Taney's statement in *Dred Scott* that blacks had no rights that a white man was bound to respect, Harlan fumed over the nobility's opinion of commoners, "whom they regard as inferior, with no rights that people of royal blood are bound to respect."[150] God and the force of history were on the side of the republic and the free laboring man.

It is not exactly clear when Harlan began telling the history that would culminate in his constitutional law lectures. When Harlan rejoiced in 1871 that the sun of American liberty no longer shone on a single human slave, he was already recounting this history. It was part of his effort to make sense out of his own past as a Whig, then a Know-Nothing, then a Constitutional Unionist, and then a Republican and to make sense out of the country's past. The providential mission was a way to explain himself to others and to reassure himself that the future was secure despite the recent disputes, battles, and deaths.

John Harlan, his face flushed as he addressed a Kentucky crowd whose votes he desperately needed, and Justice Harlan, behind the podium in a college auditorium before rows of respectful students, melt into one image. The tone differed, but the ideas, in fact, the very language, were the same. The justice elaborated the history by starting at the beginning and placing the war generation within the flow of egalitarian history. In a letter written to his son James on his birthday in 1880, Harlan characterized the Civil War as a conflict in which "the nation was then struggling [for] its life against traitors." Then he added, "But in another sense, it was struggling for a new life which would come after the destruction of slavery, and the incorporation into our Constitution, of the equality, before the law, of all citizens, without reference to their race, color, or previous condition."[151] The United States was a messianic nation in Harlan's account. Like Christ, it suffered and died only to rise and live again. There was no place in this new republic for white supremacists who, like the aristocrats defeated long ago, attempted to substitute their ancestry for the honest labor that the republic demanded of all men. The inexorable workings of Providence had shown how wrong they were.

As God's chosen people, Americans were destined to serve as an example to the world. At a public dinner in 1901, Harlan responded to a toast to the judiciary by saying, "To-day, the Government established by that Constitution is regarded by thinking men everywhere as the most marvelous that has existed at any time in the history of the world."[152] He believed that England was destined to follow the American example. The House of Lords would be replaced by a Senate, and a Supreme Court of the American type would be created, he explained in a letter to a friend: "All this may be far in the future, but that the final result will be an enlargement of the principles of popular government I do not doubt."[153] The United States was "a light to guide the oppressed of all lands in their struggle for freedom."[154]

Harlan's faith in this version of the mission is all the more conspicuous considering the growing racism among white Americans by the turn of the century. Most had come to believe that Reconstruction was a failure because blacks weren't up to the demands of citizenship. Novels like *The Clansman* by Thomas Dixon (made into the film *The Birth of a Nation* in 1915 by D. W. Griffith) depicted foolish and depraved blacks manipulated by corrupt northerners. White historians were at best ambivalent on the equality of the races.[155] By the end of the 1890s, white men had succeeded in stripping most black men of their right to vote. Over 1,000 lynchings occurred between 1882 and 1900, and most of the victims were black men.[156]

Harlan never mentioned these issues except to condemn the racist who had never done an honest day's work. Instead, he told the story of a providential mission in such a way as to recruit his students to the project of moving the country toward its ultimate goal. His own particular duty was to do this on the bench.

The version of history that Harlan recounted in his lectures has been neglected up to now, despite the frequency with which legal scholars have described Harlan as being a results-oriented judge with a loose grip on the technicalities of doctrine.[157] A vague desire to do justice has been cited as the explanation for Harlan's embrace of several doctrines rejected by the rest of the Court.[158] But before concluding that Harlan did not understand the technical details of some legal arguments, we should consider the possibility that he understood and rejected the doctrinal logic advocated by his brethren because he believed he held something that trumped that logic: his country's mission. We cannot understand his desire to do justice until we appreciate that he defined justice by reference to the national mission. By ignoring the lectures because of their prosaic, mythic nature, historians have failed to recognize the moving force in Harlan's legal thought.

# CHAPTER 3

# An Opportunity to Make a Record

## The Judge's Role

*Mr. Justice Harlan has a hobby—
a judicial hobby—and that is the
Constitution of the United States.*
—Justice David J. Brewer

The first two chapters of this book do not resemble a conventional judicial biography. Instead of a chronological narrative of Harlan's pre-Court career, they have laid out the most important intellectual traditions Harlan inherited and have shown how he altered them. Chapter 1 recounted the family myth of the paternalist and what Harlan did with it as he lived through the political confusion of the 1860s and 1870s. Chapter 2 explained the parallels between this family myth and the national myth. It also explored the religious beliefs that underlay his civic ideals.

Although these traditions of paternalism, nationalism, and religious faith had their origins in the antebellum period, I have used documents from later decades to describe them. Malvina Harlan's memoirs record stories that were doubtless elaborated over the years; the law lectures date from 1897–98. Partly this is out of necessity since very few early personal papers have survived. Also, the later documents can show us what the Harlans chose to remember out of all of their experiences.

The rest of this book continues the close reading of neglected sources while narrowing the focus. It will consider how Harlan's understanding of the three traditions affected his jurisprudence. I will focus on certain decisions and justify my choices by their importance to Harlan's thought. I will make a bow to convention now by describing how Harlan got on the Court and explaining what he's known for doing there.

Harlan's nomination was a political reward that he saw as a way to rise above politics. Although Harlan lost his bid for governor of Kentucky in 1871 and 1875, he remained the state's leading Republican politician. He led the

Kentucky delegation to the national convention that nominated Rutherford B. Hayes for president in 1876. Kentucky gave its votes to Hayes after giving up hope on Harlan's friend Benjamin H. Bristow, a reform candidate. Harlan wrote a political ally that after the convention, "a nephew of Gov[ernor] Hayes hunted me up and said that his uncle was indebted to us Kentucky fellows for his nomination, and he intended to let his uncle know all about it."[1] Hayes appointed Harlan to a commission sent to Louisiana in 1877 to sort out a disputed state election. In an effort to gain the goodwill and eventually the votes of white southerners, the president wanted to ease out the Republican candidate and the federal troops who might protect him.[2] The commission reported as he wished, but Harlan wrote Bristow from New Orleans that the state's "politics were in utter confusion, and it will puzzle anyone to get at the exact truth." He was sure that "the wrongs done . . . in the name of Republicanism" had taught the Democrats to respect the new black citizens.[3] Hayes thought about giving Harlan a cabinet position but finally settled on the U.S. Supreme Court nomination.[4] As a southern Republican, Harlan bridged sectional differences. In a private letter, Hayes asked: "Confidentially, and on the whole, is not Harlan the man? Of the right age—able—of noble character—industrious—fine manners, temper and appearance. Who beats him?"[5]

Critics charged that Harlan had never fully accepted the Civil War amendments, but his supporters countered with articles recalling the speeches he had made championing Republican positions.[6] Harlan was confirmed by the Senate on Thanksgiving, 1877, and seated on 10 December.

A place on the bench fulfilled an ambition Harlan had had for some time. Harlan confided to Bristow in 1870, "I know of no more desirable position than that of a Judge of the Supreme Court, especially if the Salary should be increased to $10,000." The money would end his dependence on clients' fees and Kentucky voters. A federal judgeship "lifts a man high above the atmosphere in which most public men move, and enables him to become, in every sense, an independent man, with an opportunity to make a *record* that will be remembered long after he is gone." Harlan foretold the fate of one of his state's politicians: "Crittenden, great as he was will be known fifty years hence only in Madison [County], while the name of a Judge of the Supreme Court, who has proven himself to be an able upright man will be familiar to every lawyer in the land."[7] (John J. Crittenden was a U.S. senator and attorney general and a governor of Kentucky.)

Life tenure as a federal judge gave Harlan independence in return for service to the high cause of the law. In a lecture in March 1898, Harlan detailed the difference between an appointed federal judge and an elected state judge. If the latter "is a weak man, or a little timid, he will trim his way" and allow fears about his political future to affect his decisions. But the federal judge with life tenure and an untouchable salary "is in a condition where he can say to the politicians, 'do what you want, do as you will, you cannot hurt me, I am here to administer the law, and I am going to give the law whatever may be the consequences to my political associates or to my party.'"[8] The federal judge played an essential role in the constitutional system. In ringing phrases, Harlan insisted on the independence of the federal judiciary: "When that Judge sits in the courthouse trying a case according to law and under the constitution of the country he knows nobody, neither the President of the United States, nor the whole Congress of the United States; he is there representing the majesty of the law, and that law is above everybody; it is above Presidents; it is above Congresses; it is above all the seventy millions of people."[9]

By serving on the Court, Harlan rose above the petty struggles of local politics. He moved into a national arena where he could act in the name of the law. The law was above everybody, as he put it, and he was its guardian. When Harlan urged a reluctant Melville Weston Fuller to accept the chief justiceship in 1888, he called the Court "the most elevated place on the earth."[10] The Court met in a room in the Capitol that had once served the Senate. An 1889 guidebook to Washington, D.C., described it this way:

Entering you find yourself in a large semicircular chamber, with a lofty, dome-shaped ceiling. The walls are supported by marble pilasters, and adorned with the busts of stately, distinguished-looking gentlemen—the deceased chief justices. At the rear of the room, facing the entrance, is the long judicial bench, where the judges sit. Over it is a wide arch, hung with looped velvet curtains, concealing a deep recess, supported by a series of pillars of variegated marble, with white marble capitals. The central part of the room is occupied by the seats and desks of the lawyers who practise before the court, and outside of this bar are tiers of seats upholstered in red velvet for the use of visitors.[11]

The guidebook noted the dignity of the robed justices as they proceeded into the room and seated themselves at the bench.

Harlan intended to remain at his post until he was removed feet first. In 1896, he wrote Fuller, "I am seriously considering various plans for such reforms in my mode of living as will enable me to carry out my earnest wish, which is, not to surrender my office until the 10th day of December 1927."[12] This would have given Harlan an unprecedented fifty years on the Court and brought him to the age of ninety-four. As it turned out, he served until only a few days before his death in October 1911 at the age of seventy-eight. A newspaper reporter described Justice Harlan in the spring of that year as almost

Harlan is standing second from the right in this 1882 photograph of the U.S. Supreme Court. Already some of the men who were on the Court when he started in 1877 were gone. To Harlan's right are William B. Woods and Horace Gray; to his left is Samuel Blatchford. Seated from left to right are Joseph P. Bradley, Samuel F. Miller, Chief Justice Morrison R. Waite, Stephen J. Field, and Stanley Matthews. (Photograph by C. M. Bell; courtesy of the Library of Congress)

bald and with few teeth left but still erect in carriage, elastic of step, and attentive in conversation.[13] Some complained, however, that he and some of the other older justices nodded off now and then while on the bench.

Harlan served under three chief justices: under Morrison R. Waite until 1888, under Melville Fuller until 1910, and briefly under Edward D. White. He began in 1878 sharing the bench with Joseph P. Bradley, Nathan Clifford, Stephen J. Field, Ward Hunt, Samuel F. Miller, William Strong, and Noah Swayne. All were gone by 1911. Harlan ended his career alongside William R. Day, Oliver Wendell Holmes Jr., Charles E. Hughes, Joseph R. Lamar, Horace H. Lurton, Joseph McKenna, and Willis Van Devanter. He started with men who had lived through the Civil War and ended with some who would witness the New Deal.

Harlan's tenure on the Court was indeed one of the longest. He voted in some 14,000 cases. Some attracted national attention and caused reporters to race out of the courtroom to spread the news, whereas others interested only a handful of people.

Harlan is seated second from the left in this 1911 photograph of the U.S. Supreme Court. Harlan died in October of that year. To his right is Oliver Wendell Holmes Jr.; to his left are the new Chief Justice Edward D. White, Joseph McKenna, and William R. Day. Standing from left to right are Willis van Devanter, Horace H. Lurton, Charles E. Hughes, and Joseph R. Lamar. (Photograph by Harris-Ewing; courtesy of the Library of Congress)

Depending on whether it was written in the first or second half of the twentieth century, an account of Harlan's decisions would either indulge or applaud his arguments on behalf of civil rights for blacks. As I noted early on, he dissented in the *Civil Rights Cases* in 1883 and *Plessy v. Ferguson* in 1896. In both, the majority of the Court held that the Thirteenth and Fourteenth Amendments did not prohibit racial segregation in public accommodations. Harlan also dissented in *Berea College v. Commonwealth of Kentucky* in 1908 when the Court ruled that a state law that prohibited interracial teaching in a private school was not unconstitutional. He exhibited a similar concern for national protection of civil rights in *Baldwin v. Franks* in 1887. Here, he dissented when the Court refused to categorize an attack on Chinese immigrants as a wrong falling under national jurisdiction.

Harlan's broad application of the Fourteenth Amendment was evident as well in his failed attempts to use it to apply the Bill of Rights to the states. His effort began as several of the states were experimenting with more efficient criminal procedures. Harlan dissented first in *Hurtado v. People of California* in

1884 on the grounds that the Bill of Rights required that the states use an indictment by a grand jury for capital crimes. Similarly, he argued in dissent in *O'Neil v. Vermont* in 1892 that the Eighth Amendment's ban on cruel and unusual punishment applied to the states. He tried to do the same with the Fifth Amendment's protection against self-incrimination in *Twining v. New Jersey* in 1908. He made a similar attempt to extend the full protection of the Bill of Rights to all persons subjected to the authority of the U.S. government in his dissents in the Insular Cases in 1901. Here, he joined several of his colleagues in insisting that the islands taken by the United States during the Spanish-American War must be protected by the Constitution. Harlan continued this effort to extend rights to the island inhabitants in *Hawaii v. Mankichi* (1903) and other dissents.

The Insular Cases serve as a turning point in this short list of Harlan's decisions because imperialism involved economic expansion as much as civil rights. The Insular Cases were actually about tariffs. The Civil War not only had produced constitutional amendments but also had precipitated economic growth. Charles Francis Adams Jr. blamed it for giving men the idea of large-scale corporations: "The great operations of war, the handling of large masses of men, the influence of discipline, the lavish expenditure of unprecedented sums of money, the immense financial operations, the possibilities of effective cooperation, were lessons not likely to be lost." [14] Both the states and Congress attempted to control corporate power in the late nineteenth and early twentieth centuries through regulation, but the majority of the Court did not always find their efforts constitutional.

Harlan argued repeatedly in dissent that the Interstate Commerce Commission had broad regulatory powers over the railroads, as in *Interstate Commerce Commission v. Alabama Midland Railroad Company* in 1897. He also supported a broader reading of the Sherman Anti-Trust Act than that of the rest of the Court. When the Court distinguished between commerce, which Congress could regulate, and manufacturing, which it could not, in *United States v. E. C. Knight Company* in 1895, Harlan dissented. He did deliver a majority opinion upholding the Sherman Act in 1903 (*Northern Securities Company v. United States*) but then dissented in part in the Great Trust Cases of 1911 (*Standard Oil v. United States* and *United States v. American Tobacco*). Harlan feared that the reference to "the rule of reason" in deciding antitrust cases was the majority's attempt to claim a discretion that Congress had not intended it to have in interpreting the Sherman Act. These cases brought popular attention to Harlan, as had his angry dissent in the *Income Tax Case* in 1895, when the Court struck down a federal law taxing incomes of over $4,000.

Harlan's concern for the states' police power is demonstrated by his dissents from decisions in which the Court struck down prohibition laws, such as *Bowman v. Chicago and Northwestern Railway Company* in 1888, and his victory in upholding a prohibition law in *Mugler v. Kansas* in 1887.

Lastly, his opinions in two decisions on labor laws and their seeming contradiction should be noted. Harlan dissented when the Court struck down a state law regulating the working conditions of bakers in *Lochner v. New York* in 1905. He delivered a majority opinion in *Adair v. United States* in 1908, which condemned as unconstitutional a federal law banning so-called yellow-dog contracts—that is, labor contracts in which the worker promised not to join a union on pain of dismissal—for interstate railroad workers.

These are the decisions discussed in any sketch of Harlan's work. The next three chapters focus on some of these decisions, but the treatment differs in important ways from that in the standard accounts. Like the authors of those accounts, I focus on constitutional issues. For readers in the late twentieth century, this seems natural because the Constitution is at the center of so many contemporary controversies. It makes sense to focus on it in explaining Harlan for several reasons. The judges of the late nineteenth century were called on to determine the meaning of new amendments to the Constitution. Of course, our view of Harlan may be skewed by the chance preservation of his constitutional law lectures. After all, he also taught domestic relations, commercial law, and torts, and this book would look different if we had the lectures from those courses. Still, it is hard to imagine Harlan declaring that he loved to read the clauses of some tort statute in the same way that he said he loved to read the supremacy clause of the Constitution. According to Harlan, the Constitution distinguished the United States from other countries and contained provisions for a federal judiciary the likes of which the world had never known. Determining constitutional controversies was Harlan's professional mission.

The next chapters differ from conventional accounts of Harlan's decisions in three ways. First, I break from chronological order in order to explain patterns in Harlan's thought. The very nature of judicial work on the Constitution warrants this approach. Cases do not usually come up so frequently and in such an order as to allow a judge to determine systematically all aspects of a particular issue, especially when litigants lack funds, time, and attorneys, as blacks did at the turn of the century.

Second, I look to expressions of Harlan's thought in nonjudicial forums. This approach is what justifies judicial biography in the first place, and it is particularly useful in explaining Harlan. Here was a man who thought that his place on the bench gave him duties that transcended history. The Constitution was more to him than a document to organize a government; it recorded a divine purpose. Examining Harlan's religious beliefs and activities helps us understand his judicial ones.

Third, I explore Harlan's understanding of race. Although the inconsistencies of Harlan's civil rights record have attracted some attention, they have not been fully explained. On one level, they can't, and I don't want to try to make doctrinal logic out of doctrinal illogic. But judicial decisions are made by minds with ideas broader than doctrines. Chapter 4 explains how Harlan's understanding of race determined the legal arguments he made in various civil rights decisions. Chapter 5 also deals with race but focuses on how Harlan came to his decision in the Insular Cases. It is unusual in offering an opportunity to see how Harlan tested political and judicial decisions by measuring them against the requirements of the American mission.

Although civil rights and the Insular Cases make a tidy package in any account of Harlan's decisions, chapter 6 tries to cross the boundary between decisions on civil rights and those involving economic issues. The first Supreme Court ruling on the Fourteenth Amendment in 1873 actually involved white men complaining that the state had snatched away their economic opportunities. Still, its outcome would clearly affect the status of blacks. Chapter 6 shows how patterns of thought repeated themselves in Harlan's decisions, whether they involved civil rights or property rights. The same logic that drove Harlan to argue for nationalization of the Bill of Rights appears in his decisions on substantive due process. Whereas the first doctrine would have protected criminal defendants from the states, the second protected railroad corporations from the states. Similarly, the free labor ideology that inspired Harlan to condemn corporate giants as a new slave power also justified his support for liberty of contract that benefited corporations. The first meant that the government might control corporations through regulation, whereas the second prevented the government from using regulation to control how corporations treated their workers. Harlan's records on civil rights and property rights are of a piece.

When scholars characterize Harlan as a results-oriented judge, they neglect the larger legal principles he sought to follow. Of course, adhering to these larger principles could lead to doctrinal inconsistencies. We will see in the next chapter that Harlan's understanding of race prompted his lapses from his support for a color-blind Constitution. Still, I am less interested in condemning such lapses as the result of nonlegal ideas interfering with the internal logic of legal thought than in showing how the very meaning and purpose of the law grew out of these broader ideas. Harlan created the logic of his law out of his traditions and his experience.

# CHAPTER 4

# Every True Man Has Pride of Race

## Civil Rights, Social Rights, and Racial Identity

*The subject was brought up as to what was the most important question before the American people.*

*"It is difficult to say," the Justice said musingly. "But perhaps it is the relation of the races. The question presents a grave situation. . . . But I cannot go into details of such subjects because in one form or another, they are likely to come before the Court."*

—Interview with John Marshall Harlan,

*New York Herald,* 1908

According to Harlan, the central event of the Civil War was the destruction of slavery. His generation had replayed the Revolution and forwarded the country's mission by fighting the war and adopting the Thirteenth Amendment. Under the Fourteenth Amendment, blacks were made part of the people who had ordained and established the Constitution. Blacks now had rights that a white man was bound to respect. The question became just what those rights were.

Republicans of the 1860s tried to answer that question even as their belief in the God-given nature of rights made it impossible for them to do so definitively. "Because they were learning intensively from their historical experience in the Civil War and Reconstruction, [Americans] were also coming to see, none too clearly, that the rights of black people were expanding and developing over time," write Harold M. Hyman and William M. Wiecek.[1]

Figuring out how Harlan answered the question is the problem his biographers face. There are two difficulties. One is understanding a nineteenth-century vocabulary of rights that has disappeared from common usage. The other is coping with a lack of sources. Harlan refused to discuss topics that might come up before him on the bench, and when civil rights cases did come up, they touched on only particular issues.

Nineteenth-century white Americans spoke of three kinds of rights: civil, political, and social. Civil rights included at minimum personal liberty and the right to hold property, make contracts, and testify in court. The Republicans in control of Congress thought they had endowed blacks with basic civil rights by freeing them with the Thirteenth Amendment in 1865. But southern white legislators countered that amendment with state black codes on vagrancy, labor contracts, and apprenticeship designed to preserve their power over the former slaves. Pressed to consider just what rights blacks now had, Congress passed the Civil Rights Act of 1866 and then proposed the Fourteenth Amendment that same year because many feared that the act was unconstitutional. Suffrage qualifications remained under state authority; a state willing to forgo a proportion of its representation might exclude any men over twenty-one. Although many whites believed that blacks were not up to exercising civil rights properly, the Fourteenth Amendment indisputably granted them. Congressional Democrats and white southerners condemned these efforts as attempts to centralize power in the hands of the national government.[2]

But national guarantees of civil rights seemed inadequate to protect blacks from whites determined to regain control over them. In order to protect themselves and their families (not to mention the Republican Party), black men needed political rights, which included the right to vote, hold public office, and serve on juries. So Congress proposed the Fifteenth Amendment in 1869, which barred the states from using race or previous condition of servitude as a factor in determining voting qualifications. Black men with the power of the ballot should be able to make the state respond to their complaints. The former Confederate states were required to ratify these amendments before being readmitted to the Union. When violence continued in the South, Congress passed the Enforcement Acts of 1870 and 1871 to protect those trying to exercise their civil and political rights.

The term for the third category of rights, "social rights," "was a misnomer," according to Charles W. McCurdy; "it referred not to rights but to legal disabilities."[3] Although they were called social, such activities fell under state control in some way. In the name of prohibiting social equality, whites argued that the states had the power to prevent the two races from mixing, whether in public places like schools and railroad cars or in marriage. Debates in Congress over whether granting civil rights amounted to extending social rights as well were bitter.

The issues associated with social rights were a mixed bag. If a state provided a public school, it determined whether whites and blacks would sit together, and any student's preferences would be ignored.[4] The same might be said of public accommodations, which were licensed, regulated, and sometimes subsidized by the states. The usual justification for segregation was that innate racial differences meant that everyone preferred or should have preferred separation. The usual argument for integration stressed the fundamental importance of equality of all citizens before the law. Charles Sumner argued this in *Roberts v. City of Boston* in 1849 when he tried and failed to have the Massachusetts Supreme Judicial Court declare segregation in Boston schools unconstitutional under state law.[5] As a congressman during Reconstruction, Sumner tried to shift public schools and accommodations from the category of social rights to that of civil rights. But so many northern states had segregated schools that few Republicans supported his plan.

Marriage was also considered a social right, but it was different. After all, if the state allowed interracial marriages, no one had to be part of such a union. But if the state prohibited such marriages, some couples could not unite. One of the oddities that popped up in white minds was the idea that the state's options on interracial marriage were equivalent. That is, the state's power to bar interracial marriage was somehow equal to its power to force people into such unions. During the congressional debates on the Fourteenth Amendment and its Enforcement Acts, some Democrats accused Republicans of encouraging or requiring miscegenation. Only a handful of Republicans spoke against antimiscegenation laws instead of just flinging the charge back.[6] Whatever they tell us about the tangled issue of sex and race, such fears indicate that whites saw these disparate issues as falling into the same legal category. To integrate or to segregate and to allow intermarriage or to bar it were similar issues in their eyes.

Harlan distanced himself from attempts to alter the three-part system of rights as a politician in the 1870s. After the war, nothing seems to have riled up white Kentuckians more than blacks claiming social rights, and Democrats charged white Republicans with encouraging them to do so. Blacks in Harlan's hometown of Louisville won a federal suit against segregation in city streetcars in 1871.[7] Despite fears of white violence, the rail companies complied. When Harlan campaigned for governor that summer, he asked a crowd: "What do they mean by this cry of Negro equality? Do you suppose that any law of the State can regulate social intercourse of the citizen?"[8] He told another audience that "no law ever can or will regulate such relations. Social equality can never exist between the two races in Kentucky."[9]

Harlan's friend Benjamin H. Bristow wrote in 1872 of his frustration with congressional Republicans like Sumner who tried to reposition the line between social and civil rights. "I have stood up for the negro ôn principle & have advocated every measure to secure his civil & political rights," he told Harlan, "but we always insisted on leaving his *social* relations with the whites to regulate themselves." Bristow's desire was to "give the freest and fullest scope to the maxim *de gustibus non disputandum.*" Although this Latin phrase is usually translated as "there's no accounting for taste," here it meant more literally "one should not argue about taste." "If white people want to go to churches, theatres, schools & hotels with negroes or *even to marry them,*" Bristow explained, "I would not prohibit them by law." "But," he added, "I will not consent to law *forcing* anybody to do either." [10] Of course, marriage laws did not force one white person to marry another, but the specter of forced intermarriage flitted through white imaginations. And segregation and anti-miscegenation laws punished the very interracial choices that Bristow wished left alone.

Harlan knew the political cost of asking for social rights. In 1874, his friend William C. Goodloe complained to him about the bill that would become the Civil Rights Act of 1875. Its requirement for integrated public accommodations had "played havoc, and under its shadow it will be as difficult to gather Republican recruits as Free Love followers from among virtuous women." [11] Harlan wrote Bristow that year that he objected to the bill's provision for integrated public schools. The remedy for white political violence "lies [not] in mixed schools, as contemplated by the last Civil Rights bill—but in an exhibition of Federal power for the protection of life, liberty and free elections." [12] The schools provision would be stripped out of the final version. [13] When a federal judge in Memphis, Tennessee, declared the act unconstitutional, Harlan praised the decision in a campaign speech. He did "not believe that the Amendments to the Constitution authorize the Federal Government to interfere with the internal regulations of theatre managers, hotel keepers or common carriers within the State in reference to the colored man, any more than it does in regard to white people." [14]

As a politician, Harlan supported the common three-part system of rights, but as a judge, he expanded his definition of civil rights to include public accommodations. When the Court declared the 1875 act unconstitutional in the *Civil Rights Cases* in 1883, Harlan dissented alone. He protested that "the substance and spirit of the recent amendments of the Constitution have been sacrificed by a subtle and ingenious verbal criticism." [15] When the Court decided in *Plessy v. Ferguson* in 1896 that a state law segregating train passengers by race violated neither the Thirteenth nor the Fourteenth Amendment, Harlan dissented in the words for which he is best known today. [16] Harlan dissented in 1890 when the Court allowed a state to punish a railroad that did not want to bother to segregate its facilities and in 1910 when it allowed a railroad conductor to force a black interstate passenger to remain in a segregated car. [17]

In expanding his definition of civil rights to include a right usually considered a social right, Harlan demonstrated that ideas about rights had a dynamism of their own. [18] He may have reasoned that if segregation in public accommodations constituted a state-sponsored insult to blacks, as its advocates often openly argued, then the right to equal accommodations was civil rather than social. In expanding his own definition, Harlan differed from most of his Republican peers, who eventually sacrificed their commitment to black rights in pursuit of the votes of white southern men. Of course, he also differed from most of his Republican peers by sitting in a place where he could say, "Do what you want, do as you will, . . . I am going to give the law whatever may be the consequences to my political associates or to my party."

But Harlan was unwilling to make further alterations in the three-part system of rights. In two decisions involving what most nineteenth-century white Americans considered social rights, Harlan did not speak out against discrimination. One was an 1889 decision in which Harlan ruled in favor of an all-white public school board sued by black parents for closing the black high school.[19] Harlan's decision was cited later as proof that the Court had no objection to state-ordered racial segregation.[20] In an 1882 decision in which Justice Stephen J. Field approved a law that punished an adulterous interracial couple more harshly than an adulterous couple of the same race, Harlan voted with a unanimous Court.[21] If the Civil War amendments had "removed the race line from our governmental systems," as Harlan wrote in *Plessy v. Ferguson*, then he should have held these laws unconstitutional.[22]

These two decisions helped lead one biographer to conclude that Harlan was "an enigma." Aside from the question of doctrinal logic, the failure to find in Harlan the kind of hero that would make him the prophet of *Brown v. Board of Education* creates uneasiness in biographers concerned with proving his greatness. One writes, "An admirer of Harlan would at least wish that he had refused to be the Court's spokesman" in the public school case.[23]

We may end the confusion by looking more closely at Harlan's understanding of race and its relationship to rights. Dispelling the disappointment of his admirers is another matter. In fact, clutching at greatness is especially inappropriate here because it turns out that the beliefs that made Harlan's famous dissents possible also underlay his less-admired decisions.

We can use Harlan's legal opinions to help explain his understanding of race and rights, but the two troubling decisions concerned issues raised rarely before the Court. In Harlan's thirty-four years on the bench, he heard only two cases involving segregated schools, and almost a decade separated them. The single miscegenation case came early in his tenure.

We find more if we look beyond the decisions to other legal sources, such as his constitutional law lectures. Unfortunately, no notes or lectures on Harlan's domestic relations course at Columbian University, which started in 1891, seem to have survived.[24] We do have a treatise on the law of marriage in 1907 he coauthored with Supreme Court reporter Charles Henry Butler that explains that the state's concern in marriage gave it the power to void unions tainted with "incest, polygamy, or miscegenation."[25] Unfortunately, it is the most utilitarian sort of treatise (I would guess it was a purely moneymaking venture). It records the current state of marriage law without comment of any kind.

To learn how Harlan viewed the black race and the rights it possessed, we need to turn to his efforts at doing "Christian justice to the negro race."[26] These efforts are described in three stories that indicate how Harlan's religious and legal ideas reinforced each other. Admittedly, there are problems in using them. They are scattered across time; they come to us secondhand; what each tells us about Harlan is open to some debate. Still, these stories are one of the few entries into his thoughts on race. And since his civil rights decisions are what have attracted attention, the risk of overinterpretation seems worth taking.

By the turn of the century, most white Americans were convinced by a combination of racial science and tales of Reconstruction-era corruption that the new black citizens were a hopeless cause. Anglo-Saxons had invented free institutions and were the only people up to running them.[27] As one author put it in 1912, "The adoption of the Fourteenth Amendment could not make Anglo-Saxons out of Africans."[28]

These stories place Harlan among the few whites who believed otherwise and who worked at uplifting the black race after the war. The paternalism he had learned in his father's house was reprised in his activities within the Presbyterian community. Most religiously inspired paternalists were culturalists. They believed that the culture of white, middle-class Protestants was superior to other cultures but that anyone could learn it and rise in the world.[29] Harlan welcomed blacks to the struggle for self-improvement, but he remained a romantic racialist. He harmonized the two systems of belief by identifying the peculiar genius of the Anglo-Saxon race as its willingness to extend civil rights and economic opportunities to people of other races. His culturalism grew out of his racialism.

The first story is about the struggle of Harlan and his black ally Reverend Francis J. Grimké to prevent segregation in the Presbyterian Church in 1905. It helps us understand Harlan's two most famous civil rights dissents: the *Civil Rights Cases* in 1883 and *Plessy v. Ferguson* in 1896. In all three instances, Harlan proclaimed color-blindness part of the historical mission and applied it to a particular issue, yet color identity remained essential to his effort. Harlan and Grimké's cooperation played out against a background of voluntary separation that ensured the preservation of racial identity. In the two decisions, Harlan demanded a color-blind Constitution in the name of Anglo-Saxonism.

The second story helps explain Harlan's decisions in the two school cases: *Cumming v. Richmond County Board of Education* in 1899 and *Berea College v. Commonwealth of Kentucky* in 1908. This story involves the attempts of Harlan and other white Presbyterians to uplift and evangelize blacks while maintaining a clear social separation from them. It suggests that Harlan had trouble treating public schools the same way he treated public accommodations because the specter of social equality haunted the issue.

The third story is the most poignant, not for Harlan's sake but for that of the man who retells it—Grimké. I use it to try to account for Harlan's silence in *Pace v. Alabama*, the miscegenation case of 1882. In this story, both Harlan and Grimké demonstrate their ambivalence about the issue of interracial sexual relations. For Harlan, this ambivalence flowed naturally from his concern for the preservation of Anglo-Saxon identity. Grimké's ambivalence grew from his birth to a black woman owned by his white father.

These stories tell us that Harlan could not abandon the three-part system of rights completely because he continued to believe in racial identity. He broke his own color-blind rule as a result. Although Harlan moved public accommodations out of the category of social rights and into that of civil rights, he shied away from doing the same with the more intimate contact of schooling, which might result in friendships and more, and marriage, in which racial identity could indeed be lost. His handling of these issues indicates some uneasiness, and possibly he recognized that social rights were misnamed.

As a political candidate in 1875, Harlan told a crowd gathered in Elizabethtown, Kentucky, that "the testimony of candid men must be that the white and black races can move along in this free land of ours, each cherishing, if you please, the prejudices of race without at all interfering with the just rights of the other."[30] We may find it hard to reconcile race prejudice with legal equality, but Harlan voiced virtually the same idea in his famous dissent from *Plessy v. Ferguson* in 1896. There he wrote, "Every true man has pride of race, and under appropriate circumstances when the rights of others, his equals before the law, are not to be affected, it is his privilege to express such pride and to take such action based upon it as to him seems proper."[31] These are not the words for which Harlan is remembered, but they are important for understanding how he fought for the color-blind Constitution.

The first story begins in 1904 when the white Cumberland Presbyterian Church asked to join the northern General Assembly of the Presbyterian Church in the United States of America without having to associate with local black churches. (The Cumberland Presbytery had split off in 1810 because of a dispute over ordination standards and formed its own church.) The General

Assembly's Committee on Overtures recommended the reunion since its own southern churches were already segregated. White Presbyterians had barred freed blacks from sitting in the pews on the main floor and refused to welcome them as pastors or elders after the war. So missionaries from the North helped set up new churches where the ex-slaves could take up the practice of self-government that was the essence of Presbyterianism.[32] By looking after the interests of the newly freed slaves, the white leadership authorized racial separation.

The Committee on Overtures argued that the Cumberland whites' "unwillingness to accept [blacks] on equal social standing . . . must be taken into account and some solution of the difficulty must be found which will bring the two races together in terms of mutual respect and reconciliation." The committee argued that most black Presbyterians understood this and felt "that their best interests are to be secured by their segregation, under certain limitations."[33] If separate churches had allowed blacks leadership roles, the committee reasoned, then separate presbyteries would allow blacks their own space on the local level as well. (Indeed, the Afro-American Presbyterian Council, created in 1894, worried that blacks wielded little power in integrated synods.)[34] Separate presbyteries "will tend to foster a proper race pride, self-respect and independence" among blacks and thus aid in their "development" as a race, according to the Committee on Overtures.[35] These "developed" blacks, it implied, might eventually win the approval of southern whites.

As Harlan was always eager to point out, the organization of the Presbyterian Church resembled a federal republic. The battle over this amendment paralleled the Union's own struggle. But whereas the Civil War amendments had been passed in order to counter the hostility of southern whites toward their former slaves, this amendment to the Presbyterian constitution would cater to their prejudices.

In the black newspaper the *New York Age*, Archibald H. Grimké, the first black graduate of Harvard Law School, reported on an April 1905 Washington City Presbytery meeting at which the main speaker on the topic of the amendment was his brother, Francis Grimké. The Grimké brothers had been born into slavery in South Carolina. Their mixed-race mother was a slave, but their white father, who owned them and and their mother, treated them as free. After their father's death, a white half-brother forced them into slavery, but the Grimké brothers eventually made contact with their famous abolitionist aunts, Sarah and Angelina Grimké. Upon learning that they were indeed blood kin, Angelina wrote the boys that "duty calls upon us now, so to use the past as to convert its curse into a blessing."[36] Both Francis and Archibald worked at freedpeople's schools sponsored by the church. Francis went on to Princeton Theological Seminary and married Charlotte L. Forten of the wealthy black abolitionist family. In 1878, he became the pastor of the prestigious Fifteenth Street Presbyterian Church in Washington, D.C., whose congregation was made up of affluent, well-educated blacks whose light skin color indicated that they, like the Grimké brothers, were probably of mixed ancestry.[37]

When he came before the Washington City Presbytery in 1905, Francis Grimké was already well versed in the arguments against segregated presbyteries and synods. He had opposed them during negotiations between the northern and southern branches of the church in 1888.[38] Grimké again declared his opposition to segregation: "It may not be popular but we must stand up for principle and there is no option left to us as Christians." It was "unchristian" to humiliate people on account of their race and to order them to stand apart. The segregation overture was "simply a movement to cater to Southern sentiment which holds that the white man disgraces himself by any sort of affiliation with the black man." Grimké made it clear that he thought separate presbyteries were inherently unequal.

The article continued that there then arose "the venerable form of the famous Supreme Court judge and grand old friend of the Afro-Americans, Mr. Justice Harlan." Harlan praised Grimké's speech and seconded his sentiments. He then took aim at the consent clause of the overture. "Judge Harlan proceeded to put himself on the record . . . saying that he was against separate Presbyteries for whites and blacks even if the whites and blacks were to agree mutually to have them." The report paraphrased his explanation: "Christianity has nothing to do with race but only with men." " 'Let us,' " he concluded with weighty words, " 'stand in the way of the fathers, and say to the world that as far as our church is concerned, we are race blind and color blind.' "[39] The church fathers had written that God had made of one blood all nations of men, and no matter what had happened in the meantime, that meant that presbyteries should not be segregated.

The article in the *New York Age* tells us that "long continued applause" followed Harlan's speech, but the Washington City Presbytery nevertheless approved the overture.[40] Archibald Grimké entitled his account of the meeting and its outcome "The Presbyterian Fall." His title implied that, like Adam and Eve in the Book of Genesis, Washington, D.C., Presbyterians were warned, but their imperfect nature led them to sin. The majority of presbyteries, but none that were black, approved the overture.

Although the story of Harlan's fight against segregated presbyteries contains elements found in his famous dissents—the demand for equal status, an appeal to a historical mission, defiance of majority opinion, condemnation of the wrong done—it also reminds us to consider the context. The debate over segregated presbyteries for the Cumberland churches masked the fact that the churches of the Presbyterian Church in the U.S.A. were segregated in practice, even if their presbyteries were not. When Harlan attended services at Grimké's church along with other prominent whites, he was a guest, not a member. His regular church was the white New York Avenue Presbyterian Church. Grimké had "little or no social contact with white people" in Washington, D.C.[41] In fact, his biographer calls Harlan and other white guests at his church "visiting dignitaries."[42] I imagine them as ambassadors whose presence was marked precisely because they served as liaisons between the two races.

It may be hard to imagine why integrated presbyteries for the Cumberland churches were controversial since they meant that only ministers and elders of both races would have regular contact. In fact, integrated presbyteries did not produce good race relations. Grimké came to boycott Washington City Presbytery and Baltimore synod meetings because of the prejudice he encountered.[43] But we should not underestimate their symbolic significance. To the Cumberland church leaders, integrated presbyteries were the thin edge of the wedge of racial equality. Integrated churches or worse might follow.

Similarly, desegregated public facilities accounted for only casual interracial contact on terms of equality. But to white state legislators and others, even such limited contact threatened white supremacy. It did not threaten racial identity, however, which may be why it did not bother Harlan.

The *Civil Rights Cases* of 1883 were five separate suits brought by or on behalf of blacks complaining that owners of inns, theaters, and a railroad had excluded or segregated them on account of their race in violation of the Civil Rights Act of 1875. The act clearly prohibited racial discrimination in public accommodations, but the question was whether Congress had the right to pass the act in the first place. The first section of the Thirteenth Amendment declares that "neither slavery nor involuntary servitude, except as a punishment for crime whereof the party shall have been duly convicted, shall exist within the United States" or under its jurisdiction. The second section gives Congress the power to enforce the first through legislation.

Speaking for the Court, Justice Joseph P. Bradley asked, "What has [segregation] to do with the question of slavery?"[44] Revealing the awkwardness of the three-part system of rights, Bradley declared that "Congress did not assume, under the authority given by the Thirteenth Amendment, to adjust what may be called the social rights of men and races in the community."[45]

Bradley also rejected the idea that the Fourteenth Amendment prohibited racial discrimination in public accommodations. Its first clause declares "all persons born or naturalized in the United States, and subject to the jurisdiction thereof," to be citizens of both the United States and the state they live in. But the rest of its clauses target state action: "*No state shall* make or enforce any law which abridges the privileges or immunities of citizens of United States; *nor shall any state* deprive any person of life, liberty, or property, without due process of law; nor deny to any person within its jurisdiction the equal protection of the laws" (emphasis added). Bradley argued that the Fourteenth Amendment authorized Congress to prohibit actions by the state or its agents, not actions by private citizens. He put aside the question of whether a state law ordering segregation in public accommodations would violate the Fourteenth Amendment. (It would be answered in *Plessy*.)

Harlan dissented alone in an opinion more than twice as long as the majority opinion. His answers to the legal questions were the opposite of Bradley's. Discrimination in public accommodations was a badge of slavery prohibited by the Thirteenth Amendment. Access to public accommodations was a civil right. The first clause of the Fourteenth Amendment applied to private actions. The actions of owners of public accommodations licensed by the state amounted to state actions. Harlan's use of both amendments and his insistence that the denial of public accommodations was both a state and a private action call to mind the language of the Fourteenth Amendment itself. Like the Republicans of the 1860s, he used overlapping arguments and language in order to corner his opponents.

Harlan's and Bradley's legal arguments differed because their accounts of history differed. Their disagreement centered on two historical questions: What was slavery and what was the intent of Congress in passing constitutional amendments to end it?

The line Bradley drew between freedom and slavery was based on the idea of chattel slavery, whereby a slave was treated (as much as humanly possible) as just another piece of personal property. The line Harlan drew between freedom and slavery was based on the idea of both chattel slavery and civil slavery, under which even free blacks were subordinated to all members of the white race.

The term "civil slavery" is not a common one. In fact, Harlan doesn't even use it (it will come up in our second story, but the words aren't necessarily his). But the idea itself is familiar, and it seems the most accurate expression for what Harlan was describing for two reasons. First, the term we often use to express the idea today—"second-class citizenship"—is probably derived from the segregation decisions themselves. Second, "civil slavery" reminds us of the position of free blacks before the war. St. George Tucker used the term in 1796 in his *Dissertation on Slavery*, in which he argued for the abolition of slavery in Virginia and the colonization of free blacks. Civil slavery "exists in most, if not all of [the American states], at this day, in the persons of our free Negroes and mulattoes; whose civil incapacities are almost as numerous as the civil rights of our free citizens."[46] Frederick Douglass helped draft "An Address to the Colored People of the United States" in 1848, which voiced the same idea: "In the Northern States, we are not slaves to individuals, nor personal slaves, yet in many respects we are the slaves of the community."[47] Harlan recalled these prewar experiences in his dissent from the *Civil Rights Cases*, and he found constitutional justification for doing so in the most infamous decision of the nineteenth century—*Dred Scott v. Sanford*.

Bradley made no mention of *Dred Scott*. Instead, he found his definition of slavery in the list of "burdens and incapacities" found in the state codes on slavery. These included "compulsory service of the slave for the benefit of the master, restraint of his movements except by the master's will, disability to hold property, to make contracts, to have a standing in court, to be a witness against a white person."[48] Congress did away with all of that in the Civil Rights Act of 1866. "The essential distinction between freedom and slavery" was clear.[49]

Bradley noted a possible similarity between the cases at hand and an element of "the Black Code (as it was called), in the times when slavery prevailed."[50] The code had forbidden the owners of public accommodations to serve blacks because they might be helping fugitive slaves. "This was merely a means of preventing such escapes, and was no part of the servitude itself."[51] With slavery gone, such a law—and no law was at issue here, only the private decisions of owners of public accommodations—could not have that purpose and therefore could not be struck down by the Thirteenth Amendment. (One can see the *Plessy* decision foretold here.)

Bradley pointed to the "thousands of free colored people in this country before the abolition of slavery, enjoying all the essential rights of life, liberty and property the same as white citizens" but barred by law from exercising all of the privileges guaranteed to whites. Indeed, the northern states offered blacks only segregated schools, if any; denied black men the franchise while easing voting qualifications for white men; and even forbade blacks from crossing into their borders in the first place.[52] In the South, freed blacks were ordered to leave their home states or threatened with arrest if they could not prove that some white person employed them.[53] Bradley presumed to speak for these people and to express their reaction to these degrading experiences: "No one, at that time, thought that it was any invasion of his personal status as a freeman because he was not admitted to all the privileges enjoyed by white citizens, or because he was subjected to discriminations." [54] He ignored decades of efforts by blacks who petitioned their legislatures, wrote newspaper editorials, spoke from public platforms, and, last but not least, filed lawsuits in the courts in order to protest their awkward status under civil slavery as neither slaves nor citizens. Frederick Douglass lamented in 1853, "Aliens we are in our native land." [55]

Bradley's inability to grasp the significance of civil slavery was common. Before the war, white abolitionists had viewed slavery and freedom as opposites, whereas black abolitionists saw them as points along a continuum.[56] Some whites did come to recognize the situation. A Freedmen's Bureau officer noted in 1865 that some southern white men "who are honorable in their dealings with their white neighbors" could cheat, kill, seduce, or rob free blacks without a twinge of shame; "they still have the ingrained feeling that the black people at large belong to the whites at large." [57] When Bradley referred to antebellum laws that discriminated against free black travelers as the "Black Code," his language betrayed the fact that southern law had identified blacks as a slave race.[58] But he nevertheless concluded that "it would be running the slavery argument into the ground to make it apply to every act of discrimination" against blacks in "matters of intercourse or business." [59] Chattel slavery did not cover such actions.

But civil slavery did, and Harlan used constitutional history to argue that free blacks had been treated as civil slaves prior to the Civil War amendments. He found his proof in Chief Justice Roger B. Taney's opinion in *Dred Scott*. He took Taney's description of the subordinate status of both enslaved and free blacks as what the postwar amendments had undone.

The reasoning of Harlan's dissent clearly plays off of Taney's *Dred Scott* opinion, yet the briefs filed in the case do not bring it up.[60] Malvina Harlan's memoirs tell us what did: an inkstand that had once belonged to Taney. The marshall of the Court had given it to Harlan, but when a female descendant of Taney's asked for it, Malvina hid it. "He values it more than it is possible for any woman to do," she reasoned, "for he appreciates the part it played in the history of the Nation." So did Malvina. She thought of the inkstand when her husband was wrestling with his dissent in the *Civil Rights Cases*. "He had reached a stage when his thoughts refused to flow easily," she tells us; "he seemed to be in a quagmire of logic, precedent and law." As the youngest member of the Court "and standing alone, as he did in regard to a decision which the whole country was anxiously awaiting, he felt that, on a question of such far-reaching importance, he must speak, not only forcibly but wisely." She took the inkstand out of hiding and placed it on Harlan's desk as "a bit of inspiration." Malvina recalls that "the memory of the historic part that

Taney's inkstand had played in the Dred Scott decision, in temporarily tightening the shackles of slavery upon the negro race," clarified "my husband's thoughts." Harlan quickly finished the dissent. The use of the inkstand was "poetic justice."[61]

Harlan quoted Taney at length to disprove Bradley's statement that no one had thought free blacks were less than citizens before the war. Taney had announced that at the time of the drafting of the Constitution, blacks "had for more than a century before been regarded as beings of an inferior race, and altogether unfit to associate with the white race, either in social or political relations, and so far inferior that they had no rights which the white man was bound to respect."[62] Whether they were held in chattel slavery or not was irrelevant since all blacks were subordinated to all whites. Harlan quoted Taney's explanation that "whether emancipated or not," blacks "remained subject to [white] authority, and had no rights or privileges but such as those who held the power and the government might choose to grant them."[63] Although Taney did not use the term, he was describing civil slavery. Harlan quoted Taney's declaration that "neither the class of persons who had been imported as slaves, nor their descendants, whether they had become free or not, were then acknowledged as a part of the people" who had ordained and established the Constitution of the United States.[64]

This was the situation targeted by the Thirteenth Amendment, Harlan explained. He offered this historical account so that "we may better understand what was in the minds of the people" when that amendment was proposed and adopted.[65] Its purpose was, as the other brethren had allowed, the establishment of "universal *civil freedom*," which meant not only the end of chattel slavery but also the end of racial discrimination by the states.[66] Discrimination in public accommodations was included in this prohibition: "The authority to establish and maintain them comes from the public. The colored race is a part of that public."[67]

As I mentioned above, Harlan was unwilling to limit the Fourteenth Amendment's scope to state action. He argued that its first clause, which granted citizenship, applied to private actions as well. He explained that at the time of its passage, "it was perfectly well known that the great danger to the equal enjoyment by citizens of their rights, as citizens, was to be apprehended not altogether from unfriendly State legislation, but from the hostile action of corporations and individuals in the States." This interpretation did not mean, as Bradley charged, that Congress was authorized to pass what amounted to a municipal code covering every aspect of life, liberty, and property. Harlan explained that "the States possess the same authority which they have always had to define and regulate the civil rights which their own people, in virtue of State citizenship, may enjoy within their respective limits; except that its exercise is now subject to the expressly granted power of Congress, by legislation, to enforce the provisions of such amendments."[68]

Harlan had opened his dissent with the complaint that "the substance and spirit of the recent amendments of the Constitution have been sacrificed by a subtle and ingenious verbal criticism."[69] He warned that the Court's decision was as great an error as *Dred Scott*. In fact, Harlan wrote former president Rutherford B. Hayes to "confess some surprise when I found myself alone in these cases."[70] If Noah Swayne and William Strong had still been on the Court, he might not have dissented alone.[71]

Harlan ended his dissent with what may have been a veiled reference to his own checkered political past. He noted that to the constitutional decree "that no authority shall be exercised in this country upon the basis of discrimination, in respect of civil rights, against freemen and citizens because of their race, color, or previous condition of servitude . . . every one must bow, whatever may have been, or whatever now are, his individual views as to the wisdom or policy" of the amendments.[72] Of course, Harlan may have been referring here to the prejudices of some of his fellow judges. Chief Justice Morrison R. Waite, for example, regarded "the Negro as somewhat inferior," according to his biographer,[73] and Justice Stephen J. Field had condemned Reconstruction entirely.[74]

Harlan's own history was thrown in his face by southern newspapers as proof that he was not sincere in his defense of black rights.[75] But a witness of his delivery of the dissent recalled it years later as impassioned. Although the tradition was to read decisions in a low, monotonous manner, "his great voice rang through the little court room . . . filled with tones of feeling, while from time to time he gesticulated and even struck the desk before him in his earnestness."[76]

As the first important segregation decision before the Court, the *Civil Rights Cases* attracted enormous attention. The Harlan family filled a scrapbook with letters of thanks from attorneys, political allies, whites, blacks, and even children.[77] Frederick Douglass, who was engaged in his own struggle over the meaning of the Civil War, wrote an emphatic letter of praise.[78] He compared Harlan's dissent to one made by Justice Benjamin R. Curtis in *Dred Scott*, in which he argued that free blacks were citizens of the United States.[79]

Unlike the *Civil Rights Cases*, *Plessy v. Ferguson* did not attract much public attention.[80] As far as most whites were concerned, the issue of segregation, whether by a private owner or by state law, was already settled. But in the earlier case, Justice Bradley had noted that he was not ruling on the issue of state-ordered segregation. Still, the Court had already tipped its hand. In the *Civil Rights Cases*, Bradley referred to public accommodations as a matter of social rights. Earlier decisions indicated a preference for segregated facilities. Just before Harlan arrived, the Court struck down a Louisiana state law (passed when Radical Republicans were still in control) that banned segregated facilities on common carriers on the grounds that they violated the interstate commerce clause.[81] But then in 1890, with Harlan and Bradley dissenting, the Court declared that a Mississippi law requiring equal but separate accommodations on railroads did not violate the interstate commerce clause.[82] Despite this discouraging record, a group of black men from New Orleans supported the bringing of a suit to challenge an 1890 Louisiana law requiring "equal but separate accommodations for the white, and colored races."[83] *Plessy* forced the issue of whether the Fourteenth Amendment prohibited state laws requiring segregation in public accommodations.

Behind Harlan's and the majority's opinions lay their different definitions of slavery. Following Bradley's reasoning in the *Civil Rights Cases*, Justice Henry B. Brown dismissed the Thirteenth Amendment as inapplicable, whereas Harlan warned that the Court's decision was as bad as *Dred Scott*. Perhaps more important to their interpretations was the meaning of segregation itself. And most important to Harlan was the question of what the future would hold if whites were allowed to segregate their fellow citizens on account of their race.

Brown declared that public accommodations, even those segregated by state law, were a matter of social rights. He admitted that the purpose of the Fourteenth Amendment was "undoubtedly to enforce the absolute equality of the two races before the law." But he insisted that "in the nature of things it could not have been intended to abolish distinctions based upon color, or to enforce social, as distinguished from political equality, or a commingling of the two races upon terms unsatisfactory to either."[84] He cited as support the *Roberts* decision on segregated schools in Boston, state laws against miscegenation, and Supreme Court and state decisions approving segregation.

Brown may have recognized the conceptual unsteadiness of the idea of social rights because he stressed the reasonableness of the state's choosing forced separation over forced integration. "In determining the question of reasonableness," the Louisiana state legislature "is at liberty to act with reference to the established usages, customs and traditions of the people, and with a view to the promotion of their comfort, and the preservation of the public peace and good order."[85] Forced separation was thus not only historically preferred but somehow a public good in itself. It satisfied "racial instincts."[86]

Although Brown denied repeatedly that segregation laws were based on a belief in black inferiority, he stressed that "social prejudices" could only be overcome by "natural affinities, a mutual appreciation of each other's merits and a voluntary consent of individuals." To force "commingling of the two races" would only accentuate "the difficulties of the present situation."[87] So segregation in public accommodations, although not an insult to blacks, was a result of white prejudice that the state would do well to accommodate. "If one race be inferior to the other socially," Brown concluded, "the Constitution of the United States cannot put them upon the same plane."[88]

For Harlan, segregation remained an incident of slavery and a violation of personal liberty. He attacked Brown's statement that segregation laws did not imply the inferiority of blacks by reference to both history and contemporary understanding. The precedents cited by Brown were meaningless because some of them predated the Civil War amendments and even those that didn't "were made at a time when . . . it would not have been safe to do justice to the black man; and when, so far as the rights of blacks were concerned, race prejudice was, practically, the supreme law of the land."[89] Again he quoted Taney in *Dred Scott* that blacks were treated "as a subordinate and inferior class of beings, who had been subjugated by the dominant race, and, whether emancipated or not, yet remained subject to their authority, and had no rights or privileges but such as those who held the power and the government might choose to grant them."[90] This history informed contemporary understanding. So when the state argued that the law affected whites and blacks equally, its lack of candor was obvious. "Everyone knows," Harlan insisted, "the thing to accomplish was, under the guise of giving equal accommodation for whites and blacks, to compel the latter to keep to themselves while traveling in railroad passenger coaches. No one would be so wanting in candor as to assert the contrary."[91] One of the basic attributes of civil freedom—the personal liberty of locomotion—had been violated.

Whereas Brown used racial instinct to justify state-ordered segregation, Harlan argued that racial instinct was no bar to the possibility that "a white man and a black man [might] choose to occupy the same public conveyance on a public highway."[92] Such an exercise of personal liberty fell into the category of civil, not social, rights, "for social equality no more exists between two races when traveling in a passenger coach" than it existed between races on streetcars, in jury boxes, at public assemblies, on the street, or at the ballot box.[93]

Early in his dissent, Harlan had declared that the "pride of race" possessed by "every true man" was irrelevant to state action for no "legislative body or judicial tribunal may have regard to the race of citizens when the civil rights of those citizens are involved."[94] But as Harlan developed his argument, he made white racial pride essential to the preservation of the Civil War's constitutional achievements and to the fulfillment of the American mission. Harlan made it the means to his end. He wrote, "The white race deems itself to be the dominant race in this country. And so it is, in prestige, in achievements, in education, in wealth and in power." Notice that here he did not say that the white race was superior; he said it was dominant. It had controlling influence or power and surpassed blacks in prestige, achievements, education, and wealth. This dominance may have resulted merely from history and numbers, but Harlan held out the carrot of future dominance in exchange for loyalty to the nation's mission. Harlan continued, "So, I doubt not, it will continue to be for all time, if it remains true to its great heritage and holds fast to the principles of constitutional liberty." The ultimate test of the greatness of the Anglo-Saxons was not how they looked but how they behaved. Harlan appealed to white racial pride in his demand for a legal system blind to race. He then wrote the passage for which he is best known: "But in view of the Constitution, in the eye of the law, there is in this country no superior, dominant, ruling class of citizens. There is no caste here. Our Constitution is colorblind, and neither knows nor tolerates classes among citizens."[95] The peculiar heritage of whites was to express whatever racial superiority they might claim by yielding legal power.

This was why whites damaged themselves by wronging blacks. Harlan assured his audience that "the presence here of eight millions of blacks" posed no danger to the dominance of 60 million whites. He then insisted that "the destinies of the two races, in this country, are indissolubly linked together, and the interests of both require that the common government of all shall not permit the seeds of race hate to be planted under the sanction of law."[96] The danger to whites lay not in the presence of blacks but in their own failure to welcome blacks as part of the "People" of the Constitution. Like the prewar paternalist who was required to forbear from exercising his full legal power in order to be worthy of his position, the postwar generation of whites had to control their exercise of raw power in order to fulfill their destiny.

Harlan foretold the sorry result of the Court's decision: "The judgment this day rendered will, in time, prove to be quite as pernicious as the decision made by this tribunal in the *Dred Scott* case."[97] It would "stimulate aggressions, more or less brutal and irritating, upon the admitted rights of colored citizens," behavior at odds with the Anglo-Saxon heritage. And it would "encourage the belief that it is possible, by means of state enactments, to defeat the beneficent purpose, which the people of the United States had in view when they adopted the recent amendments of the Constitution" making blacks part of their number.[98] By failing to live up to their own racial heritage, the brethren thwarted the republican mission.[99]

Harlan's famous civil rights dissents made racial identity both essential and irrelevant. Racial identity was essential to the means because whites expressed their racial identity best by extending civil rights to others regardless of race, and it was irrelevant to the end for the very same reason. Harlan declared the Constitution color-blind in the name of his racial heritage. He continued to work within the basic framework of the three-part system of rights that was premised on separate racial identities. Harlan did not reject the concept of social rights outright in the *Civil Rights Cases* and *Plessy v. Ferguson;* he merely redefined free access to public accommodations as a civil right. But he found it impossible to expand the category of civil rights further because he continued to value racial identity.

Whereas Harlan's dissents from the *Civil Rights Cases* and *Plessy v. Ferguson* share much in logic, historical understanding, and tone, his two opinions on schools could not be more different from each other. *Cumming v. Richmond County Board of Education* in 1899 is a short, stiff decision for the majority in which he refused to grant an injunction to make the school board close its white public high school until it reopened the black one. *Berea College v. Commonwealth of Kentucky* in 1908 is a lengthy, impassioned dissent in which Harlan condemned the Court's unwillingness to consider how a state law barring interracial teaching affected individuals. For historians looking to Harlan as the prophet of the 1954 *Brown v. Board of Education* decision, *Cumming* is a disappointment. Why did he deliver it? Is there a strictly doctrinal explanation? Was it the pleading or the situation? Didn't he care about education?[100] These questions presume that Harlan thought of public education the same way he thought of public accommodations, but he probably didn't. In order to suggest how he may have thought about schooling, I will link the two opinions with a story about race and religion. This story demonstrates that white efforts to uplift the black race could go hand in hand with a rejection of interracial social contact, that is, a rejection (to use the nineteenth-century vocabulary) of social equality. This story leads me to believe that Harlan understood the public school case within the three-part system of rights, which meant that he could not square it with the color-blind Constitution.

Before the war, public schools in the North were often segregated or exclusively white. Integrated public schools were virtually unknown in the ex-Confederate states save for unusual areas like New Orleans where a black middle class had some temporary political clout.[101] Before the Civil War, Harlan's home state of Kentucky closed its public schools to blacks—remember Robert J. Harlan had been thrown out of one. The Freedmen's Bureau set up black public schools in Kentucky paid for by black poll taxes kept separate from other state funds until 1882.[102] On the national level, Charles Sumner tried to make equal integrated schools part of congressional Reconstruction until his death in 1874, but his Republican colleagues "used the mixed school question merely as a party stalking horse." [103] Some mention of the issue would keep black votes, but no action was broadly supported. Most of them simply refused to speak about it. By the 1880s, most northern states had prohibited segregated schools and southern and border states required them.[104]

As a politician in the 1870s, Harlan had objected to mixed schools, but he had also objected to integrated public accommodations back then. As a judge, he decided to move public accommodations into the category of civil rights. He does not seem to have done the same with public schools.

Harlan did not mention schools in his dissents from the *Civil Rights Cases* and *Plessy v. Ferguson*, which is striking because the Court majority did. Justice Brown cited state laws and decisions segregating public schools and banning interracial marriage in *Plessy*.[105] Harlan mentioned neither subject in his dissents. Instead, he listed streetcars, open vehicles on public roads, public streets, turnpikes, public markets, public buildings (courthouses, post offices, legislative halls, voting places, jury boxes), and public assemblies as places the state could segregate if it had the power to segregate public accommodations.[106] The fact that he did not mention public schools indicates that he did not expect to treat them the same way he treated public highways.

Since Harlan did not list public schools as one of the areas covered by the color-blind Constitution, we might conclude that he believed that the states could segregate them. He never said that, however, despite the fact that he had opportunities to do so. In *Cumming*, Harlan noted that George F. Edmunds, the attorney for the black parents, had argued before the Court that racial segregation was "the vice in the common school system of Georgia" but that segregation was not the actual complaint made in the pleadings. Harlan concluded, "We must dispose of the case as it is presented by the record," and he said nothing about segregation.[107] Similarly, he concluded his angry dissent from the *Berea College* decision in 1908: "Of course what I have said has no reference to regulations prescribed for public schools, established at the pleasure of the State and maintained at the public expense. No such question is here presented and it need not be now discussed." [108] In short, Harlan never said from the bench whether or not racial segregation in public schools was constitutional.

Public schooling presented Harlan with a problem. Clearly, it was an action taken by the state, so it should have fallen under his color-blind rule. But Harlan seems to have had trouble extracting public schooling from the category of social rights. He possibly did not come out clearly against single-race schooling because it was a way to preserve racial identity, not for the racist reason that a separate and unequal system of education would keep blacks down but for the racialist reason that schooling was a far more intimate activity than riding a streetcar and could lead to friendship and marriage. Historian Louis R. Harlan (a distant relation) writes that whites in New Orleans in the 1870s "never really surrendered their concept of the public school as a sort of private club." [109] Harlan may never have surrendered this concept either, but his unwillingness to say anything about public schools indicates that he knew he had a problem. What he did not have was a solution.

The public school case began in 1897 when the Richmond County Board of Education closed its small black high school and allocated the building and funds to the overwhelmed black grammar schools. Black parents asked for an injunction to force the board to stop spending tax money on the white high school until it was ready to reopen the black one. [110] Speaking for a unanimous Court, Harlan affirmed the judgment of the Georgia Supreme Court that the board had not violated the Fourteenth Amendment.

Instead of taking the opportunity to declare that segregation in public schools was an incident of slavery, as he had done with segregation in public accommodations, Harlan saw the white board's decision to fund the black grammar school rather than the black high school as a good-faith effort. If the plaintiffs had tried to have the black high school reopened (instead of trying to have the white one closed), "and if it appeared that the Board's refusal to maintain such a school was in fact an abuse of its discretion and in hostility to the colored population because of their race, different questions might have arisen in the state court." [111] The scholar who suggested that Harlan was attempting to stave off outright approval of segregated public schools by the Court and directing future plaintiffs in how to win their cases attributes an incredible amount of shrewdness to him. [112] When public accommodations were at issue, Harlan had no trouble denouncing the hostility to the colored population that had inspired segregation. But in *Cumming*, Harlan was unable to find "a clear and unmistakable disregard of rights secured by the supreme law of the land." [113]

J. Morgan Kousser suggests that Harlan "was eager to defend the largely symbolic exercises of their rights by the few turn-of-the-century blacks who could afford to attend integrated colleges, to patronize integrated theaters or hotels, or to buy first-class railway tickets" but that he was "either blind to the much more practical problem, which directly affected much larger numbers of Negroes, of obtaining a decent education, or he opposed, at this time in his career at least, granting equal public services to blacks." [114] This characterization of Harlan's civil rights record ignores his condemnation in *Clyatt v. United States* and *Bailey v. State of Alabama (I)* of peonage and racial violence.[115] Harlan may have emphasized the power of the first clause of the Fourteenth Amendment even in the public accommodations decisions because he believed it was also designed to control white terrorism.

The situation in Richmond County was not that black teenagers could no longer obtain a decent education. The distinction between public and private was blurred there. Private schools got public funds, and public schools received private donations.[116] The black public high school had charged tuition as did the white high schools, and three private high schools enrolled blacks for the same fees. Black tax dollars were going to a public high school not open to black children, but black parents would not be paying more tuition for the privilege of sending their children to private high schools. This was why Harlan could write in *Cumming*, "So far as the record discloses, both races have the same facilities and privileges of attending them." [117] The Richmond County School Board did not treat black children the same way it treated white children. As Edmunds argued before the Court, the board admitted that "the public funds have been devoted to the complete provision for all the white children, when they had not for the colored children." [118] But the existence of private high schools open to blacks allowed Harlan to avoid facing that discrimination squarely.

The second story of Harlan's involvement with the Presbyterian Church may be useful at this point because it reminds us that even whites committed to helping blacks could value racial identity. Harlan attended the 1905 meeting of the General Assembly of the Presbyterian Church in the U.S.A. as a member of the Standing Committee on Freedmen. Every year's report was different, a reflection of the turnover of the committee members. Most reports simply appealed for funds; others argued for the importance of black uplift to the church and the Republic; only a few expressed an opinion about the proper relations of the races, as the 1905 report did.

It is hard to estimate how much influence Harlan had on this report. On the one hand, there were ten other elders and a dozen ministers on the committee.[119] On the other, Harlan was a justice on the Supreme Court with a reputation for his civil rights dissents and was vice-moderator of the assembly that year. His comments during the assembly were not recorded, but a church newspaper reported approvingly that Harlan's "remarks . . . especially on the obligations of Christian justice to the negro race were self-evidently out of his life and not expressions concocted for the occasion." [120] Although the committee report was not necessarily written by Harlan, he may have had some influence on its shape. In any case, the report reveals how white Presbyterians talked about race. Its demands for Christian justice to blacks and its insistence on social separation may help us understand why Harlan hesitated to speak out in the public school case but dissented passionately in the private school case. Whereas public schools invoked the dreaded coercion of social equality, private schools required only the liberty needed for the effort of uplift. Uplift did not have to lead to social equality.

The report displayed the combination of paternalism and optimism that makes for culturalism. "The Negro must be taught self-respect and race-respect," it reads, "for often he hates his own kind, and therefore hates every other kind." Presbyterian missionaries were asked to "bear with his childishness, bear with his backwardness, bear with his stubbornness, bear with his indifference, restrain firmly his immorality, curb greatly his self-assertiveness." This effort assumed a superiority of culture and even of force over benighted blacks that was similar to paternalism in the antebellum household. But it relied on a faith in change to come that was missing from that older tradition. It might take "generations of Christian education," but eventually "the virility of freedom" would eliminate "the puerility of slavery."[121] Change was slow—some forty years after emancipation this committee was still called the Committee on Freedmen—but the effort was based on faith in improvement.

In order to ensure that future, the committee recommended equal educational opportunities for blacks. The committee criticized the emphasis on industrial education that had made Booker T. Washington of Tuskegee Institute so popular with white conservatives.[122] It acknowledged the usefulness of industrial education for both races, "but we believe also in higher education for the white man that he may have educated teachers and doctors and lawyers and preachers—educated leaders." Blacks deserved the same and needed it more. "The Negro also needs more than industrial leaders," the report insisted. "He needs educated leaders. He needs educated doctors, for his death rate is much higher than that of the white! He needs educated teachers to lead him out of ignorance; he needs educated preachers to lead him out of immorality."[123] This emphasis on higher education fits the character of the American Presbyterian church, which required its clergy to obtain a college education. Like W. E. B. Du Bois, who wanted a "Talented Tenth" of the black population to raise up the rest, the Presbyterian committee believed that blacks were capable of taking on the task of uplift themselves. The committee exhorted, "Educate him, not for a civil slave, but to give him an equal chance with every other man—laborer with laborer, artisan with artisan, doctor with doctor, teacher with teacher, preacher with preacher and leader with leader." Interracial economic competition would allow talented blacks to lift up themselves and others.

The committee nevertheless insisted on social separation of the races. The report identified "a mighty question to be solved in the treatment of the Freedman" and offered five possible answers: "export him, destroy him, assimilate him, enslave him, or save him." The first possibility harked back to the old plan of colonizing blacks in Africa and was rejected as unacceptable ("He does not want to be exported") and impossible ("There is no place to put him. He is too large"). The report then rejected in a matter-of-fact way the next possibility: "For the same reason it would be difficult to destroy him."

The third possibility was assimilation, which the committee declared to be "as destructive as it is repugnant." Intermarriage or assimilation is destructive to both races only if each has valuable characteristics that would be lost through intermixture. The committee also found the idea of intermarriage offensive. Some whites' habit of imagining that social equality led somehow to forced intermarriage may have been at play here, and a racist dislike for dark skin and African features stirs within their words.

The committee found a way to reconcile its dislike for assimilation with goodwill between the races. Its fourth possible solution, slavery, was "not to be dreamed of in this land of liberty." But its last solution for what to do with the freedman was to "save him." "Can we save him?," the report asked; "we must, or he will destroy us." The committee wondered, "Can two races live together, and both be independent and their identity be preserved?" It suggested that for an answer we "look at the Jew." [124] The committee explained no further, but we can consider what it meant.

White Christians of the nineteenth century displayed "especially diverse and conflicting attitudes" toward Jews. [125] As God's chosen people, Jews were venerated in a country whose people believed that they too were on a providential mission. At the same time, Jews had failed the ultimate test by refusing to accept Jesus Christ as the Messiah and were targeted by Christian missionaries. [126] English and American Christian novelists—including the two Harlan recommended to his sons, Sir Walter Scott and William Thackeray—presented a range of stereotypes from the grasping miser to the beautiful and virtuous Jewess. [127] Christian literature focused on Jews in order to depict their conversion to Christianity. [128]

Although clearly freer than their European counterparts, American Jews had encountered discrimination since colonial times. [129] When Harlan stressed the similarities between Presbyterianism and republicanism or demanded that there be no mail delivery on Sunday, he promoted the informal establishment of Protestant Christianity that led inevitably to both thoughtless and deliberate discriminations against Jews. [130] When Harlan brought up in an 1898 lecture "the fantastic trial" of Émile Zola for his criticisms of the French court-martial of Alfred Dreyfus, who was framed because he was a Jew, it was only in order to point out the superiority of the American judicial system. Like many American lawyers, he condemned Zola's prosecution as a "complete farce," but he ignored the religious issue.[131] Anti-Semitism became more visible in the United States between 1870 and 1900 as poor European Jews poured into the cities and a class of nouveaux riches claimed status on par with their wealth. Accounts of denials of their social rights began appearing in the newspapers.[132] A few Christian political writers began blaming Jews for all of society's ills.[133] If blacks were to become like Jews, this was hardly the time.

But enslaved blacks had long identified with the Jews of the Old Testament. Like Harlan, they believed in typology. Just as Moses had led the Jews out of Egypt, they too were a chosen people who would one day be led to freedom.[134] A Union army chaplain noted that "there is no part of the bible with which they are so familiar as the story of the deliverance of the children of Israel. Moses is their *ideal* of all that is high, and noble, and perfect, in man. I think they have been accustomed to regard Christ not so much in the light of a *spiritual* Deliverer, as that of a second Moses who would eventually lead *them* out of their prison-house of bondage." [135] When emancipation came, it was a day of jubilee, a term in the Old Testament for the day on which slaves were freed every fifty years.[136] The parallels seemed even plainer as Jews experienced what was called emancipation during the mid-nineteenth century when European governments lifted the civil and economic disabilities imposed on them.

Black leaders drew lessons from Jewish experience. Frederick Douglass pointed to American Jews as models—in their self-respect, their demand for rights, their economic success—to be imitated by blacks.[137] Booker T. Washington "found in their history of persecution and cultural nationalism a kinship with the black experience." When asked in 1906 whether the social separation that he advocated did not always lead to injustice, Washington responded, "May we not become a peculiar people—like the Jews?" [138] Southern blacks generally had good relations with Jews, whom they regarded as more courteous than white Christians.[139]

In turn, Jewish leaders and Jewish newspapers were more interested in the fate and accomplishments of blacks than in any other ethnic group.[140] Although some resisted identifying themselves as a race rather than a religion, other American Jews used the language of race to describe themselves in the late nineteenth century.[141] Jewish philanthropists such as Julius Rosenwald supported black education by making donations to Tuskegee Institute and Howard University.[142] Jews were among the early supporters of the National Association for the Advancement of Colored People because they saw racism as akin to anti-Semitism.[143]

At the turn of the century, American Jews were a striking example of a minority that enjoyed political rights and economic success yet often rejected assimilation. As Jews broke down professional barriers and educational quotas, many feared that acculturation and intermarriage would destroy their community. Traditionalist Jews and immigrant Catholics would invent the term "cultural pluralism" in the early twentieth century for the idea that peoples of various origins could retain their traditions while enjoying civil equality.[144] So by choosing the Jew as its example, the Committee on Freedmen tapped into streams of American culture other than white racism.

Still, choosing the Jew also indicates the limit of the committee's thought. After all, the Presbyterian mission was founded on the idea that the Jews had got it wrong. The Presbyterian Board of Home Missions did not target Jews for conversion until 1908, but from 1914 to 1938 it was "the most vigorous denominational organization seeking to proselytize American Jews."[145] The 1905 report of the Committee on Freedmen suggested that "the only effective rule for the solution of the Southern Negro problem" was to "preach the pure Gospel of Jesus Christ, and apply the principles thereof, in the church, home and school, to the heads, hearts and hands of the Negroes who, under the Holy Spirit, will hear, believe and practice."[146] By urging blacks to become like Jews and disciples of Christ, the Committee on Freedmen did more than mix metaphors. It demonstrated the difficulty of coupling equality of opportunity with social separation.

The private school case of 1908, *Berea College v. Commonwealth of Kentucky*, raised this difficulty as well. Harlan recounted in his dissent that the founders of Berea had sought "to establish and maintain an institution of learning, 'in order to promote the cause of Christ,'" and had been doing this interracially since 1866.[147] The Day Law, named after its sponsor, was designed to drive blacks out of the college to make way for the whites of the mountain counties.[148] It barred any corporation or individual from running "any college, school or institution where persons of the white and negro races are both received as pupils for instruction."[149] The legal question centered on whether the statute's impact on corporations (which had few rights) and its impact on individuals (who had many) were separable. Justice David J. Brewer, speaking for the Court, said that the law applied to corporations but declined to rule on its effects on individuals. Harlan insisted that the Kentucky courts had not considered the law separable and demanded that the Supreme Court "directly meet and decide the broad question."[150]

When Harlan condemned the law as unconstitutional, he joined tacitly in a discussion of the meaning of interracial religious and educational cooperation for the future of racial identity. The attorneys for the Commonwealth of Kentucky argued that the Day Law was passed under the state's police power in order "to foster and promote the happiness and general welfare of its people." This law and laws segregating public accommodations and public schools, prohibiting interracial marriage, and disinheriting the children of such marriages "had but one common purpose and end—to preserve race identity, the purity of blood, and prevent an amalgamation."[151] Ending interracial education at Berea was just one more way to prevent social equality. The attorneys for the college responded that the state should be neutral on interracial social intercourse, as it was on intraracial social contact: "Social equality between persons of the white and colored races, or between persons of the same race, cannot be enforced by legislation, nor can the voluntary association of persons of different races, or persons of the same race, be constitutionally prohibited" unless there was some justification on grounds of immorality or public disorder.[152] Notice that they didn't try to use the phrase "social equality" in a positive sense but instead used the term "voluntary association," which carried with it no historical connotation of coercion or intimacy.

Harlan did not mention the state's fear of social equality and the danger it posed to racial identity, but his dissent picked up the college's argument on the limits of the police power. Harlan denounced Kentucky for violating the Fourteenth Amendment by imperiling the "right to impart and receive instruction not harmful to the public," which he identified as a right to property and a right to liberty akin to liberty of contract.[153] Harlan did not usually invoke God in his dissents, but here he declared, "The capacity to impart instruction to others is given by the Almighty for beneficent purposes and its use may not be forbidden or interfered with by Government—certainly not, unless such instruction is, in its nature, harmful to the public morals or imperils the public safety."[154] If the state could interfere with private education in this way, then "it is difficult to perceive why it may not forbid the assembling of white and colored children in the same Sabbath-school, for the purpose of being instructed in the Word of God, although such teaching may be done under the authority of the church to which the school is attached as well as with the consent of the parents of the children." It might go so far that "white and colored children may even be forbidden to sit together in a house of worship or at a communion table in the same Christian church."[155] In answer to those who claimed that "no government, in this country, can lay unholy hands on the religious faith of the people," he responded that "the right to enjoy one's religious belief, unmolested by any human power, is no more sacred nor more fully or distinctly recognized than is the right to impart and receive instruction not harmful to the public."[156] Under the Court's decision, the state could require private schools to separate students according to their national origins or religion.

Whereas the Kentucky brief put private schools in the social rights category along with public accommodations, public schools, and marriage, Harlan's dissent put private schools in the same category as Sunday schools, churches, public markets, and public assemblies, all of which were covered by civil rights protections. But apparently he could expand the category no further. The heartfelt conclusion to his paragraph denouncing the Day Law—"Many other illustrations might be given to show the mischievous, not to say cruel, character of the statute in question and how inconsistent such legislation is with the great principle of the equality of citizens before the law"—was followed by the remark quoted earlier: "Of course what I have said has no reference to regulations prescribed for public schools, established at the pleasure of the State and maintained at the public expense. No such question is here presented and it need not be now discussed."

How could Harlan argue that private schools were covered by civil rights protections but refuse to do the same for public schools? Although he must have had trouble disentangling public schools from the issue of social equality, the Committee on Freedmen report indicates how he might have separated private schools from that issue. Berea College was a counterpart to the committee's efforts. Its leaders argued for the need to educate blacks for all levels of society.[157] Harlan noted over and over again in his dissent the voluntary, private, harmless, and innocent character of the activity targeted by the state. According to the report of the Committee on Freedmen, such efforts had nothing to do with social intermixture. Blacks could be educated to full equality with whites, and the races could still preserve their separate identities. According to this view, Berea College posed no danger to racial identity.

But the issue of the social effects of interracial education could not be avoided, and not just because white supremacists had long attacked missionary educators for encouraging social equality and miscegenation.[158] A white Presbyterian who spoke out in 1867 against the ordination of black men by the southern church pointed out the difficulty of drawing the line between interracial cooperation and racial separation. He asked his fellows, "So you tell me that after you have admitted this negro thus to your . . . pulpits, your sick and dying beds, your weddings and funerals, you will still exclude him from your parlors and tables?"[159] Bereans had previously been charged with "racial contamination."[160] In 1872, members of the college's Board of Trustees had had to confront the issue of intermarriage in light of the relationships some of their students wished to pursue. They decided that interracial couples might date as long as their motives were pure, their parents were told, and their actions provoked no violence.[161]

Interracial Christian efforts inevitably led to social contact between the races. When intermarriage arose from such contact, racialists might object. When the question became whether the state should do anything about it, the racialist faced a difficulty. How could a statutory prohibition be social in its character? How could a law banning intermarriage not be an insult to blacks when such laws originated from their former status as chattel and civil slaves? Harlan preferred to change the subject rather than answer these questions.

This chapter has moved about in time. The story from 1904 introduced Harlan's famous dissents in 1883 and 1896. The 1905 Committee on Freedmen's report linked his 1899 public school decision with his 1908 private school dissent. In order to explain the 1882 decision on miscegenation, I now want to consider the possible meanings of an incident that probably occurred in the 1870s when Harlan was still a Kentucky politician. He recounted the incident after he became a judge, and it comes to us secondhand in a letter written by Reverend Francis J. Grimké in 1916. I say possible meanings because the incident may have meant one thing to Harlan in the 1870s, something else after he became a judge, and something entirely different to Grimké. The plot may be thickening, but my point is that faced with the most provocative of the so-called social rights, Harlan dodged the issue. To see how he did this, we should reacquaint ourselves with the decision and Reverend Grimké.

In *Pace v. Alabama*, Tony Pace, a black man charged with living with a white woman, challenged the constitutionality of a law that punished adultery and fornication by an interracial couple more harshly than adultery and fornication by a same-race couple. (The law also punished interracial marriage.) Justice Field spoke for a unanimous Court. The law did not violate the equal protection clause of the Fourteenth Amendment because both the black and the white partners of the interracial couple were punished equally. "Whatever discrimination is made in the punishment prescribed . . . is directed against the offence designated and not against the person of any particular color or race," he concluded.[162]

Alabama's ban on interracial marriage was not uncommon. Marriage had been a private civil contract in English common law, but American judges treated it as a legal status open to state intervention during the antebellum period.[163] Harlan and Butler explained in their 1907 treatise that the "contractual elements" of marriage "are important only in its inception; for once entered upon it becomes a relation rather than a contract, and invests each party with a status toward the other and society at large, involving duties and responsibilities which are no longer matter for private regulation but concern the common wealth."[164] When judges ruled that the Fourteenth Amendment had not altered each state's power to define who could or could not marry, they fit antimiscegenation laws into this general framework.[165] The northeastern states repealed such laws after the war. Some southern states repealed them during Reconstruction only to pass them again later. By 1910, thirty-two states outlawed interracial marriage.[166] Such laws were sometimes justified by the conclusion of white scientists that the children of mixed-race couples were "physiologically inferior to both of the original stocks."[167]

Although *Pace* only confirmed the constitutionality of Alabama's ban on interracial extramarital sex, its reasoning might be applied to its ban on interracial marriage. Both the black and the white partners would be barred equally from marriage, according to the logic of *Pace*. In effect, by acquiescing to *Pace*, Harlan agreed that marriage was a status rather than a contractual right. It remained one of those social rights that blacks could not claim. The Court never passed judgment on such a law during Harlan's tenure, but the story that Reverend Grimké retells indicates that he might have had trouble condemning such a law.

Grimké was dubbed the Black Puritan by his congregation.[168] The name was probably inspired by his resemblance to the early English Puritans who fought for the Lord; Grimké fought for the Lord and against racial discrimination. "We must agitate, and agitate, and agitate, and go on agitating" until blacks were accorded their full rights, he declared in 1902.[169] Grimké later wrote that World War I was "making the world safe for white supremacy."[170] For Grimké, Christianity was a color-blind religion, and any white Christian who expressed race prejudice was nothing but a hypocrite.

The retelling of Harlan's story begins when Grimké published a sermon in 1916. He criticized white Christians who could not throw off their "color-phobia." Grimké quoted the Apostle Paul's statement that "there can not be Greek and Jew, circumcision, and uncircumcision, barbarian, Scythian, bondman, freeman; but Christ is all and in all."[171] Then Grimké related how a white man had rebuked a black friend of his for introducing himself as "Mr." because the title indicated that he considered himself the white man's "social equal."[172] Grimké condemned this and other instances of Christian hypocrisy, including the separate presbytery overture of 1905.

Among the people who read the tract was Reverend Solomon C. Dickey of Winona Park, Indiana, who wrote Grimké to ask "if you really insist on social equality, by which is meant intermarriage of the races."[173] Grimké had had enough of such questions from "you white people." He chastised Dickey for being "determined to make Christianity conform to your notions rather than make your notions and prejudices conform to its teachings." Instead of worrying about intermarriage, Dickey should worry about "the illicit intercourse between the races, which has gone on for centuries, and still goes on." Then Grimké quoted Harlan, whom he described as "one of the truest, squarest, noblest types of a Christian that the Presbyterian Church has produced in this country." Harlan had told this story "in an address which he made here some years ago":

> "In Kentucky, when I began insisting upon according to colored men the same treatment, civilly and politically, that was accorded to other men, I was charged with encouraging and teaching social equality with Negroes. The man who made the charge was, at the very time, living with a colored woman." The Judge then asked the question: "If that isn't social equality, what is it?" and followed with the remark, "If I was teaching social equality, he certainly was practicing it." [174]

Harlan must have been referring to an incident that occurred in the early 1870s when he was a politician. Back then, he came out against social equality and defended segregated public schools and accommodations as constitutional. By accusing his critic of practicing social equality, Harlan implied that he wasn't interested in teaching it.

He was also engaging in a familiar tit for tat between supporters of black civil rights and white supremacists. White southerners began by accusing white abolitionists of desiring black wives.[175] William Lloyd Garrison responded to a slaveholder who asked if he wanted a black man to marry his daughter that "slaveholders generally should be the last persons to affect fastidiousness on that point; for they seem to be enamoured with amalgamation."[176] Except for the Garrisonians, most abolitionists did not speak out against laws prohibiting intermarriage because of their own prejudice or their fear of the reactions of other whites.[177] During the 1864 presidential campaign, two journalists tried to coax abolitionists into revealing their conspiracy to force racial amalgamation by publishing *Miscegenation: The Theory of the Blending of the Races* (the first appearance of the word).[178] During the congressional debates on the Fourteenth Amendment and its Enforcement Acts, the Democrats cried miscegenation whereas only few Republicans spoke against antimiscegenation laws instead of just flinging the charge back.[179]

As Garrison's remark makes clear, the story that Harlan recounts is as much about white hypocrisy and sin as about white fears of interracial mixture. It isn't clear if Harlan criticized his challenger publicly, but in the 1870s, Harlan sought the votes of white men who wanted him to condemn social equality and those of black men who would have been pleased to hear criticism of this kind of interracial immorality from a white Republican leader. In condemning his accuser's hypocrisy, Harlan was joining in the chorus of criticism of the sexual exploitation of black women that dated back to before the war. This abuse horrified the abolitionists, who treasured virtuous family life and personal self-control above all else.[180] Angelina Grimké had shocked observers by speaking out against the sexual exploitation of slave women by white men in her *Letters on the Equality of the Sexes.*

Harlan's story would have had particular appeal to Grimké because both he and his brother Archibald followed in this family tradition. Grimké once asked his congregation, "Where did all the mulattoes in the south come from? Were the masters forced by their black slaves to part with their virtue, or was the reverse true? Were the slaves the aggressors, or the masters?" He mocked the white South that now "holds up its hands in holy horror at the thought of miscegenation" but "thinks nothing of the illicit intercourse between white men and colored women."[181] Archibald identified "the heart of the race problem" in 1906 as the double standard of moral behavior created under slavery. The result was an "under world of the under race" where white men preyed on black women, provoking resentment from black men and white women. This "vicious circle of moral ruin for both races in the South" could only be broken by allowing intermarriage.[182]

Indeed, although state laws had long declared all interracial sex a crime, the real concern of white legislators was the control of white women's sexuality, especially after emancipation undid one of the linchpins of the South's social hierarchy.[183] Like Ida B. Wells, Francis Grimké explained that lynching, although invariably justified by whites as the result of the anger that followed the rape of a white woman by a black man, was often provoked by consensual sexual relations between black men and white women.[184] Such violence was designed to keep both groups in line.[185] At the same time, white men were not prosecuted for having sexual relations with black women. In fact, southern judges made sure that their illegitimate children inherited the property destined for them.[186] Fornication with a black woman was not social equality in the eyes of many white men. As W. E. B. Du Bois put it in 1913, "We must kill [antimiscegenation laws], not because we are anxious to marry white men's sisters, but because we are determined that white men shall let our sisters alone."[187]

The opening of Grimké's response to Dickey—his reference to "the illicit intercourse between the races"—places Harlan's story within this effort to end the hypocrisy of white men. Remember that the Harlan household had included Robert James Harlan, a light-skinned slave who was educated by the older Harlan boys and allowed to buy his freedom. If Robert didn't gain these privileges because he was James Harlan's child, he was undoubtedly some white man's bastard born of a slave mother. Robert would go on to work for the repeal of an intermarriage ban while serving in the Ohio State House in 1886.[188] The sin and hypocrisy of white patriarchs cut close to the bone for the Grimké brothers as well. South Carolina law prohibited the marriage of their white father and their slave mother (who was apparently the result of such a union herself) but was uninterested in the dishonor represented by the birth of her three brown-skinned sons.[189] When Grimké asked his mostly light-skinned congregation where all the mulattoes in the South came from, he knew they already knew the answer.

Harlan's comments may have been part of the effort to end the sexual exploitation of black women, but that does not mean he agreed with the Grimkés that the solution was the repeal of laws banning intermarriage. He might have come to regret his silence in *Pace* over the years, but no later decisions tested this. Nor does he make any comments in his writings. The way Grimké uses the story indicates that Harlan was dodging the issue, and that's exactly what Grimké does in retelling it.

Grimké laid out the moral of Harlan's story for Dickey. "What Judge Harlan was insisting upon, in regard to the treatment of colored people, had no more to do with the question of social equality than the position which I am taking in regard to the Church's treatment of colored people has to do with it." Grimké took Harlan's remark as the civil counterpart of his own effort in the Presbyterian Church. As Harlan had done in his story, Grimké responded to Dickey's question about whether he advocated "intermarriage of the races" with questions of his own. "Why do you ask that question?," Grimké demanded. "Have you ever seen any statement of mine, in any shape or form, intimating in any way that such a thought was even remotely in my mind?" Grimké considered Dickey's question insulting as well as inappropriate. He scolded: "You seem to be possessed with the idea that [blacks] are extremely anxious to be affiliated socially with white people. In this you are entirely mistaken. The colored people have no desire to force themselves socially upon anybody." Unlike white Americans who defined social equality as a kind of compulsory intimacy between the races, Grimké argued for what we might call social freedom (and what the Berea College legal brief called voluntary association): "Social intercourse is a matter to be determined entirely by the individual choice. Each one is left free to choose his own associates." Grimké reminded Dickey that "all white people are not on terms of social equality, as you well know, and it is a mere subterfuge, a mere dodging of the question, touching the treatment of colored people, to lug it in here." All he asked was that blacks "be treated as Jesus Christ would treat them." He ended his letter with harsh words on Dickey's "pusillanimous spirit" in dealing with the "Negro question" and insisted that he avoid "mixing it up with the matter of social equality and the inter-marriage of the races." [190]

Grimké must have heard Harlan tell his story after they both came to Washington, D.C., in the late 1870s. In the account, Harlan tried to defuse the issue of social equality by distinguishing it from civil and political equality. When Harlan moved public accommodations into the category of civil rights in his dissents, he insisted that social rights were another issue entirely. Grimké used the story for the same purpose. Considering the effect the term "social rights" had on white minds, the tactic made sense. Kelly Miller, professor and dean at Howard University, noted in 1908 that the term "arouses the deepest venom of race, which slumbers only skin deep beneath a thin veneer of civilization." It was "a savage warwhoop" made by white southern politicians bent on keeping blacks as an underclass stripped of political power, that is, as civil slaves.[191] Let black men vote, the argument ran, and they'll soon be wanting a place at your table or worse. White Democratic politicians used the specter of the black rapist bent on obtaining social equality to rally white men across class lines to one purpose.[192] Remove the sexual component from the debate by distinguishing the three kinds of rights from one another, and the political discussion became far less explosive.

The trouble for Harlan's doctrinal consistency was that bans on interracial marriage had always been a part of civil slavery. When Justice Taney examined the status of blacks in his *Dred Scott* opinion, he noted that both a colonial Massachusetts law of 1705 and a colonial Maryland law of 1717 had prohibited mixed-race marriages. These laws proved that "a perpetual and impassable barrier was intended to be erected between the white race and the one which they had reduced to slavery, and governed as subjects with absolute and despotic power, and which they then looked upon as so far below them in the scale of created beings." Since the laws made no distinction between the chattel slave and the free black or free mulatto, "this stigma, of the deepest degradation, was fixed upon the whole race." [193] Harlan was inspired by Taney's decision, as we have seen, and relied on Taney's general depiction of the degraded status of even free blacks before the war as proof that the Civil War amendments undid not only chattel slavery but also civil slavery. Yet Harlan steered clear of the issue of marriage in his dissents from the *Civil Rights Cases* and *Plessy*. In fact, Harlan condemned the Court's decision in *Plessy* in the name of Anglo-Saxon identity itself. If the physical appearance of men such as Francis and Archibald Grimké and Robert Harlan was not enough, intermarriage of the races proved the shakiness of racial identity.

Grimké's letter recounting Harlan's story indicated that he, like many turn-of-the-century black leaders, shied away from the issue of social equality. When he suggested that he had never supported intermarriage, he was being dishonest. Grimké had performed the marriage ceremony for Frederick Douglass and his second wife, a white woman, in 1884.[194] In a 1903 sermon, Grimké had criticized a white minister who was embarrassed to discover that he had unknowingly married a light-skinned black man to a white woman.[195] In a 1910 sermon, he included laws against intermarriage on a list of the discriminations blacks faced.[196] Few blacks were willing to follow the example of Frederick Douglass, who touted his own mixed-race heritage as the physical embodiment of "our composite nationality."[197] As one historian puts it, "Most articulate [nineteenth-century] Negroes . . . seemed to say that while intermarriage ought to be an undisputed right, it was a right better left unexercised."[198] Some blacks at the turn of the century discouraged their daughters from marrying white men because they believed such unions carried the taint of racial oppression.[199] Archibald Grimké had had an unhappy marriage to a white woman whose family had objected to their union.[200] When Francis Grimké recollected Douglass's second marriage in 1934, he wrote, "The intermarriage of the races may not be a wise thing, in this country, in view of present conditions, but the right to marry if they want is inherent, God-given."[201] He also noted that many blacks took Douglass's choice as an insult.

Indeed, black leaders reacted to the failure of Reconstruction by placing a renewed emphasis on black solidarity and identity. In his 1897 speech before the fledgling American Negro Academy (founded with the help of Francis Grimké), W. E. B. Du Bois argued for "the conservation of races." Since most discussions of racial identity stressed black inferiority, "the American Negro . . . has, consequently, been led to deprecate and minimize race distinctions, to believe that out of one blood God created all nations," but each race had something distinct and valuable to contribute to the world.[202] Du Bois asked, "Have we in America a distinct mission as a race . . . or is self-obliteration the highest end to which Negro blood dare aspire?"[203] He opposed intermarriage but saw no reason why racial identity and legal equality might not flourish together.[204] Grimké's experience with white hostility may have led him to shift his emphasis even as he, like Du Bois, continued to criticize laws that banned intermarriage. After all, in the mid-twentieth century, blacks ranked the ban on intermarriage as the least important discrimination they faced.[205]

It would have made sense as legal doctrine for Harlan to move marriage out of the category of social rights and into that of civil rights. In doing so, he would have followed his own color-blind rule. Every aspect of civil slavery would have been erased if social rights ceased to be an object of state concern.

But Harlan understood the mission of the United States as a free, republican nation propelled by its Anglo-Saxon heritage. Since one of the sources of Harlan's support for civil and political equality was his own racial identity, he continued to believe in the third component of the three-part system of rights: social rights. Like the Committee on Freedmen, he must have thought that civil slavery could be abolished at the same time that social separation was upheld.

All of Harlan's decisions on civil rights, from the famous dissents to those that have left his other biographers puzzled, grew out of his understanding of his own and his country's history. Harlan built on what he knew. The paternalism that the Harlan family remembered as James Harlan's legacy prompted his son to join the Republican Party and to embrace the Civil War amendments. The paternalist's refusal to abuse power became the racialist's model. The Anglo-Saxon yielded legal power in order to prove the superiority of his racial legacy. Racialism made egalitarianism possible.

In an 1880 birthday letter to one of his sons, Harlan dreamed that the United States was "destined, perhaps, to revolutionize the world so far at any rate as to compel a fuller recognition of the rights of man."[206] The Civil War was a sign that this dream might come true. The amendments had made blacks "part of the political community called the People of the United States, for whom, and by whom through representatives, our government is administered," he wrote in his dissent from *Plessy*.[207] But the Court had shirked its duty just as it had in *Dred Scott*. Harlan wrote: "We boast of the freedom enjoyed by our people above all other peoples. But it is difficult to reconcile that boast with a state of the law which, practically, puts the brand of servitude and degradation upon a large class of our fellow-citizens, our equals before the law. The thin disguise of 'equal' accommodations for passengers in railroad coaches will not mislead any one, nor atone for the wrong this day done."[208] Harlan's statement elsewhere in *Plessy* that "every true man has pride of race" tells us that he thought that behavior rather than anatomy established manhood. So too behavior rather than color made the Anglo-Saxon. A white man could fail to live up to his racial heritage.

It is hard for us to deal fully with this phenomenon because the source of Harlan's egalitarianism troubles the late-twentieth-century mind.[209] We are so used to seeing racial identity as a barrier to civil equality that we have trouble conceiving of it as a bridge between the two.

Harlan's racialism also accounts for the inconsistencies in his civil rights decisions. Because his support for legal equality grew in part out of his belief in an Anglo-Saxon heritage, he hesitated to apply his color-blind rule when so-called social rights were at issue. Racial identity would have been lost if social equality existed. Yet state laws barring interracial marriages or schools were clearly remnants of the civil slavery that Harlan condemned. His preference for avoiding a direct discussion of the issue of social equality may indicate that he understood the logical difficulty he had created.

Despite these inconsistencies, Harlan stands out in the historical record. Thomas F. Gossett writes that "American thought of the period 1880–1920 generally lacks any perception of the Negro as a human being with potentialities for improvement."[210] Harlan was one of a small band of whites who thought otherwise. Among the boxes of Harlan's family papers is a program for a memorial service for Harlan held at the Metropolitan African Methodist Episcopal Church in Washington, D.C., in December 1911. On the cover is a photograph of Harlan, and beneath it are the words "A True Friend of the People." The service began with Beethoven's "Upon the Death of a Hero."[211]

Harlan wanted to be remembered for only some of his civil rights decisions. Consider the decisions he listed with the instructions, "In book containing my opinions & dissenting opinions publish the following."[212] The dissents in the *Civil Rights Cases, Plessy v. Ferguson,* and another public accommodations case are there,[213] as are several dissents in which Harlan argued that the Fourteenth Amendment authorized the national government to act against individuals depriving others of their civil rights.[214] The dissents in *Berea College v. Commonwealth of Kentucky* and the peonage decision, *Bailey v. State of Alabama (I),* are also listed. One of Harlan's majority decisions in a jury discrimination case is included as well.[215] But *Cumming v. Richmond County Board of Education* is missing. Even an Anglo-Saxon may come to recognize his failures.

# The Hopes of Freemen Everywhere

## Anglo-Saxonism and the Spanish-American War

*It has been said that the flash of Dewey's guns at Manila Bay revealed to the American people a new mission. I like rather to think of them as revealing the same old mission that we read in the flash of Washington's guns at Yorktown.*
—Benjamin Harrison,

    *North American Review,* 1901

Harlan often spoke of the equality of *all* races before the law, but white paternalism and Anglo-Saxon racial identity both justified his famous dissents and limited his definition of civil rights. Harlan included blacks among the people of the Constitution by relating a particular version of American history. Blacks, present at the creation as slaves, witnessed the Union's rebirth as free men and women. By focusing on *Dred Scott*, Harlan made the citizenship of blacks central to the nation's mission. But who else could claim the nation as their own?

In a 19 March 1898 lecture, Harlan explained the origins of the Fourteenth Amendment's clause granting citizenship to all persons born and naturalized in the United States. It had arisen in response to the special Providence of *Dred Scott* that had provoked the war. Blacks were citizens of their states and the Union. Opposition was fruitless. Then a student asked, "Judge, does that include Indians?" Like blacks, Native Americans were present at the time of the founding, but unlike blacks, they remained victims of history. Harlan agreed with the Court that they had become wards of the United States, tribal nations in name only.[1] But he excluded those who acted like the people of the Constitution. Harlan explained sarcastically to his class that in "a very learned opinion," the majority of the Court had determined that Native Americans could not become citizens. "I had the misfortune to differ from the court upon that question," he joked, "and of course I was wrong."[2]

Harlan had dissented from *Elk v. Wilkins* in 1884 when the Court declared that an assimilated, tax-paying Native American male did not have the right to vote because he was not a citizen. Harlan argued that citizenship was the right of Native Americans "who, by becoming *bona fide* residents of States and Territories within the complete jurisdiction of the United States had evinced a purpose to abandon their former mode of life and become a part of the People of the United States."[3] Elk had become part of Harlan's mythic people because he had been willing to *behave* like them; his color or blood became irrelevant. Harlan concluded angrily in his dissent that if assimilated Native Americans were not granted citizenship under the Fourteenth Amendment, "there is still in this country a despised and rejected class of persons, with no nationality whatever," who had to bear the burdens imposed by the American government.[4]

Although Harlan's dissent in *Elk* rested in part on his belief in culturalism, he also voiced the widely shared racial myth that Native Americans were a doomed people. The expansion of the United States had always been intertwined with racism since westward movement meant taking land from native peoples.[5] It was the manifest—that is, providential—destiny of Americans to control the entire continent, including lands belonging to Native Americans and Mexicans. The historians that Harlan had read as a boy and cited in his own speeches as a man—William Hickling Prescott, George Bancroft, and John Bach McMaster—described Anglo-Saxons as progressing through time and space, fulfilling a providential plan.[6] They believed in the romantic notion of national character: "The Frenchman was mercurial, the Spaniard, romantic, haughty, sometimes chivalrous, often cruel, fanatical; the Italian, subtle and crafty; the Dutchman and the Englishman, frank, manly, self-reliant, enterprising, vigorous."[7] Those of African descent were supposed to make especially good Christians because of their "meek, long-suffering, loving virtues."[8] Because of the superior nature of the Anglo-Saxons, the continent belonged to them. Even when these historians acknowledged the abuse that Native Americans had suffered at the hands of European settlers, they played it down in favor of the larger process of racial destiny.[9]

Harlan did the same. During one lecture, he noted how badly Native Americans had been treated by the U.S. government and then announced that "it is a race that is disappearing and probably within the lifetime of some that are now hearing me there will be very few left in this country."[10] He expanded on this point: "To my mind, to my apprehension it is certain as fate that in the course of time there will be nobody on this North American continent but Anglo-Saxons. All other races are steadily going to the wall. They are diminishing every year."[11] Even as Harlan condemned the shameful behavior of the national and state governments toward native peoples, he implied that impersonal forces were responsible for their demise. Harlan may have been influenced by the 1890 census, which showed (inaccurately, it turned out) that whites were growing in numbers and all other races were shrinking.[12] He may have heard of sociologist Benjamin Kidd's *Social Evolution*, published in 1894, which argued that the Anglo-Saxon race, although the most altruistic of all the races, "had a degenerating effect on the inferior races."[13] Of course, these predictions had an unreal air about them in light of the hundreds of thousands of non-Anglo-Saxon immigrants pouring into the country in the late nineteenth century.

One of the biographies Harlan recommended to his sons, an 1850 volume on William Wirt, took an identical position.[14] Wirt, an attorney general of the United States and opponent of Andrew Jackson, had defended Cherokees in their land claims against the state of Georgia in 1830. His biographer, John P. Kennedy, condemned the state's behavior but wrote that Native Americans were doomed to be moved out of the way of white progress. (Wirt himself placed all of the blame on the white government in his argument before the Supreme Court.)[15]

After Harlan explained that he was "wrong" in *Elk*, another student asked, "Would a Chinaman born in this country be a citizen?" At that moment, the case of a man born in the United States in 1873 to Chinese nationals was before the Court. Wong Kim Ark's parents could not become U.S. citizens because Congress had rejected Charles Sumner's attempt in 1870 to change the naturalization laws to include the Chinese.[16] The senators considered the Chinese too different morally, politically, and temperamentally to be fully assimilable. Still, Chinese immigrants came to the United States to work and eventually became the target of white working-class resentment. Congress passed exclusion acts in 1882, 1884, 1888, and 1892 that made Chinese immigration and reentry increasingly difficult.[17] Wong Kim Ark was detained by customs officers in San Francisco in 1890 after a trip to China with his parents.

Harlan told his students that he could not answer the question because the decision was pending. After stressing that he was "now giving the argument for one side," he noted that the Chinese had long been excluded "upon the idea that this is a race utterly foreign to us and never will assimilate with us." They were pagans. Neither the Chinese nor the Americans wanted to intermarry. "And when they die, no matter how long they have been here, they make arrangements to be sent back to their Fatherland."[18]

He then asked his students "what would be the condition to-day" of the western slope without the exclusion acts. He answered that vast numbers of Chinese "would have rooted out the American population." The attorneys for the United States had argued that if Wong Kim Ark became an American citizen "by accident of his birth," not only would Congress's power over naturalization be curtailed, but also children born to Americans traveling abroad would not be American citizens. Harlan concluded his discussion by saying, "Now those questions are involved I say in that case, and I do not think I can answer it yet." He promised to tell the class when it was decided. Harlan had spent several minutes laying out the legal arguments against Chinese American citizenship. He ended the discussion with this one comment on the argument for citizenship: "Of course, the argument on the other side is that the very words of the constitution embrace such a case."[19] The Court declared in May 1898 that indeed they did.

Harlan joined Justice Melville Weston Fuller's dissent in *United States v. Wong Kim Ark.*[20] Fuller reviewed the history of citizenship in the United States and noted the rejection of the English rule that anyone born within its borders remained the monarch's subject even if that person swore allegiance to another country. Chinese law, he noted, took a similar position. Fuller argued that children born to foreign nationals were not, in the language of the Fourteenth Amendment, "subject to the jurisdiction of the United States." Harlan reported back to the class in May that he had been "wrong" again. But he made his case by offering possibilities that flowed from the Court's position. "Suppose an English father and mother went down to Hot Springs" for a cure and had a son while there. He would be an American citizen "by the mere accident of his birth." Recognizing that Wong Kim Ark was an American citizen meant that "when that man goes back to China, and the emperor should conclude to cut his head off, a custom which prevails to a very great extent among these people," the United States would have to act. The United States would also have to do something if he was impressed into the Chinese army.[21]

Harlan had drawn attention to Chinese exclusion in his dissent to *Plessy* in 1896. He had noted that the Chinese, "a race so different from our own" that they are not allowed to naturalize, "can ride in the same passenger coach with white citizens of the United States while citizens of the black race in Louisiana, many of whom, perhaps, risked their lives for the preservation of the Union," faced imprisonment if they did so.[22] This passage, which scholars of the legal status of Asian Americans have noted, confirms my account of the origins of Harlan's commitment to black rights.[23] In it, he juxtaposes a race kept alien by national law with a race he considered central to the Union's history. Black Louisianans perhaps had risked their lives to preserve the Union, whereas Chinese Americans had no role in his version of the country's history.

Harlan did not come to proclaim a commitment to the equality of all men before the law because of some abstract Enlightenment ideal of a universal human identity. He defended legal equality in the name of three traditions. One was familial, one historical, and one racial: his father's paternalism, Unionism cleansed of the stain of slavery, and a romantic Anglo-Saxonism that made him a hereditary protector of a precious form of liberty. It was as if history had provided a special dispensation that allowed black Americans to join the Anglo-Saxons in their mission.

Although Harlan understood the flow of history as controlled by racial destinies, he also shook behavior loose from its racial origins. Elk was entitled to citizenship for the same reason that Anglo-Saxons had acted badly in deciding *Plessy v. Ferguson*. There was play in the link between race and behavior.[24] One sees this in the lectures when Harlan discussed his fears of immigration. On the one hand, he could make that most racist of remarks—that the Chinese "all look alike"—and note with apparent approval that "we could exclude any particular race anywhere on the earth from our country by act of Congress."[25] "All the nations of Europe" were sending over their criminals, he complained. On the other hand, his demands that immigrants be qualified for American citizenship focused on behavior. He objected to immigrants who were "not born and reared under our institutions; not born and reared under the institutions of other countries like England that understand what life, liberty, and property mean, but born under despotisms; who have been in the habit all of their lives of bowing to titles and powers that did not know what liberty was, and who come to this country mistaking liberty for license and license for liberty."[26] Language issues seem to have bothered him especially because an immigrant who did not know English "cannot read a single word in the constitution."[27] This criticism was cultural rather than biological. At times he indicated that American ways could be learned. "The True American," he announced at a banquet at the Union Club of Chicago in the early 1890s, "whether native or naturalized, stands, under all circumstances, for the law and for the rights of his fellow-men as recognized and defined by the law."[28]

The most striking example of the play in the link between race and behavior in Harlan's lectures actually concerned Anglo-Saxons. As the academic year ended in the spring of 1898, the sequence of events that led to the Spanish-American War began. The lectures record Harlan's initially wary reaction to intervention in Cuba and end with his wholehearted embrace of a global vision of American military might. Harlan's interpretation of the Spanish-American War grows out of the lectures both literally and figuratively. The national myth that Harlan recounted in his lectures was more than just a vision of the past. It dictated his understanding of the present.

Harlan used typological thought, which had allowed him to explain the past, in order to explain the present. Just as the Revolutionary War had been a type for the Civil War, so the Revolutionary War and the Civil War were types for the Spanish-American War. First, Americans had defeated the British monarch, then they had defeated the slave aristocracy, and now they were destined to defeat the tyrannical forces of Spanish imperialism. Blinded by his typological vision of history, Harlan interpreted contemporary events in ways that distorted reality.

Another neglected document allows us to see how Harlan put his mythic history to use. On 21 February 1900, Harlan delivered an address at the dedication of the new law building at the University of Pennsylvania in Philadelphia that was published in the *American Law Review*, a leading law journal. Harlan's topic was James Wilson, a founding father, the first professor of law at the University of Pennsylvania in 1790, an associate justice of the Supreme Court, and a source for Joseph Story's constitutional nationalism. Wilson had believed in the "intimate connection and reciprocal influence of religion, morality, and law." [29] Roman republican virtue was Wilson's ideal. Harlan's speech on Wilson contained the same prehistoricist view of American history that he expressed in his lectures. It also presented a critique of the American antiimperialist movement and of the Filipino independence struggle that was notable for its unwillingness to confront facts.

Harlan's speech on Wilson has been neglected because the Insular Cases, decided in 1902 before a rapt nation, overshadow all other documents.[30] In these two close decisions, the Court settled a debate that had been raging in the newspapers and the law journals. It determined that Congress could treat the island territory gained in the Spanish-American War—the insular possessions—in ways other than those dictated by the Constitution. This meant that the inhabitants of such territory did not have the protections of the Bill of Rights. Harlan dissented angrily and stubbornly.

Harlan's speech from 1900 reveals that he struggled over several years to understand American imperialism within the framework of his national myth. His dissents in the Insular Cases should be viewed within that framework. Mythic history determined Harlan's judicial position: the United States could not have colonies because of its divinely ordained mission.

Harlan's evolving interpretation of American foreign policy allows us to see how the prehistoricist view of the American past shaped political understanding at the turn of the century. Although European historians discarded religious explanations in favor of scientific ones and influenced some Americans, who in turn challenged the idea of the country's providential mission in the late nineteenth century, Harlan remained prehistoricist in his view of the past, just as he remained orthodox in his religion and formalist in his legal theory.[31] By giving lectures and speeches, Harlan encouraged prehistoricism among his listeners and readers. In fact, the vision of the United States as being on a mission (sans God) of liberty and progress persists to this day in high school textbooks.[32]

Whereas other men in the American political elite announced that they had to have complete control over the former Spanish colonies in order to teach the inhabitants the virtues needed to exercise self-government, Harlan took the national mission literally. Colonialism was at odds with republicanism. When Harlan used words such as "dependencies" or "outlying possessions," "subjects" or "dependent peoples," he placed them in quotation marks as if handling them with fire tongs.[33]

On the first day of class, 14 October 1897, Harlan admitted that England had not treated the United States well in the past but emphasized that "the English and the Americans . . . are leaders of the Anglo-Saxon people of the world. . . . They are the custodians of the principles of liberty which must prevail to the end, that men shall enjoy that freedom of speech and action which is essential to the security of life, liberty and property."[34] Anglo-Saxons were supposed to spread the principles of liberty and make possible the exercise of rights. Harlan demanded that the Supreme Court take part in this effort by applying all of the Constitution to the insular territories. By defining the distinguishing characteristic of Anglo-Saxons as their willingness to apply their system of rights and liberties to other races, Harlan put to egalitarian use an idea that was often employed to justify racial hierarchy. Just as Harlan used paternalism in order to embrace civil rights for blacks, so he managed to use Anglo-Saxonism in order to extend rights to the insular inhabitants.

Harlan was not alone in endowing Anglo-Saxons with a universalist duty, in trying to stop the creation of an American empire, or in invoking history to justify his opposition.[35] But there is something especially poignant in his journey from champion of the Spanish-American War to the last antiimperialist holdout on the Supreme Court. Harlan's early enthusiasm for the war and his prehistoricist interpretation of it have been overlooked, but the intellectual origins of Harlan's dissents lie in his historical and racial myths. The past was not dead. It was not even past.

The question of Cuba entered American political debate after Cubans rebelled against Spanish rule in February 1895. Yellow journalists fanned the flames of public opinion by describing the Spanish concentration camps and the vicious behavior of the general in charge. Public meetings were held by Cuban sympathizers in New York City, Atlanta, Chicago, Washington, D.C., and even Harlan's hometown of Frankfort, Kentucky. A *New York World* editorial demanded, "How long shall the United States sit idle and indifferent within sound and hearing of rapine and murder?"[36]

Harlan cautiously came to the conclusion that the United States should intervene. His analysis was shaped by his vision of the American mission.

In January 1898, while discussing Congress's power to declare war, he commented that if war should come, "all that any of us can hope and desire is that we shall be on the right side, that our cause shall be just." Harlan then moved from morality to aggression; if Congress did declare war, he told them, "why, I take it for granted that the world will find out, if it does not know now, what it is possible for this American people to do if they are brought to war."[37]

After the American battleship *Maine* blew up in the harbor at Havana on 15 February, the U.S. public grew furious with Spain. The *New York Herald* reported the story the next day under the headline, "Spain's Populace Hostile to the United States." Underneath the headline was the threat, "Bombardments of our coast discussed—Spaniards counting upon the supposed helpless condition of all American towns except New York."[38] But Harlan counseled caution. It was essential to "keep cool, and not to pass judgments upon grave questions when you have not the facts before you." Facts alone were a lawyer's business. "It is idle for any man to say that he knows how that calamity occurred," the judge told them four days after the explosion, "and any man belittles his nature and lowers himself in the estimation of his fellow-men if he expresses the anxiety that it will turn out that that was treachery rather than an accident." Harlan appealed to his students' self-respect: "Brave, generous men do not want to think so badly of their fellow-men."[39] Harlan was trying to calm down his audience.

By early April, Harlan was entertaining the idea that after the war, if "an island down southwest" "should become part of the United States, no matter how, it could be organized as a territory, and after a while if we saw proper it could be admitted into the Union as one of the states of the Union."[40] The phrase "if we saw proper" indicates that Harlan was imagining that territory not intended for statehood might be taken.[41]

By the last day of class on 7 May 1898, Harlan drew a dizzying picture of the international destiny of the United States. The concluding passages of his lecture show both his view of history and his ability as an orator. Harlan connected America's distinctive history to its future glory. He explained that the English historian Thomas Babington Macaulay had once written "that our constitution was all sail and no anchor" and had foretold the fall of the American Republic. Macaulay compared the United States in the twentieth century to the Roman Republic in the fifth, "but only with this difference, that whereas the Huns and Vandals who destroyed Rome came from without, our Huns and Vandals will come from our own institutions." Macaulay had invoked the classical theory that republics naturally cycled through growth and decay, but Harlan, like many nineteenth-century Americans, believed that the United States had escaped history.[42] The Roman Republic may have risen and fallen;

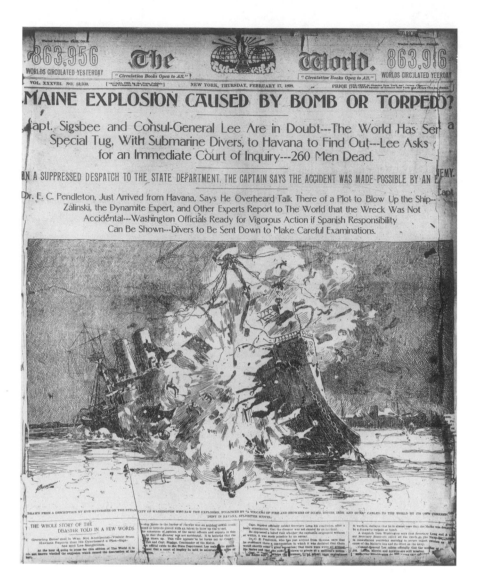

The front page of the 17 February 1898 issue of the *New York World* depicted the explosion of the U.S. battleship *Maine* in the harbor at Havana, Cuba. "Remember the *Maine!*" became a rallying cry for U.S. intervention in Cuba. Harlan gave his wholehearted support to the Spanish-American War as part of the American effort to lessen "the burdens which have been imposed upon man by despotic governments." (Courtesy of the Library of Congress)

the American Republic was all rise. Prophecies such as Macaulay's had been proven wrong, Harlan argued, because the country was "more closely united than ever before in our past history." There was no need to worry even in the midst of war, Harlan told his students: "As we stand at the close of this century, and think as to what will be our condition in the next century, there is nothing to disturb our vision." Harlan made his own prophecy: the war with Spain was only the first mark America would make on world affairs. He finished with a rousing declaration that ended with a reference to the United States so as to give the clearest opportunity for patriotic cheers: "If the world never knew so before, they have become convinced within the last fortnight that this great republic of ours, in all the future destinies of the world, is to be reckoned with, in the government of European affairs, and that the power on this earth to-day that is likely to shape the destinies, of Europe, and the far Eastern Countries, and of the whole human race, in the next century, are the United States of America."[43] Members of the class of '98 must have come to their feet with a shout.[44]

When the academic year and judicial term ended, Harlan traveled to his summer home in Point-au-Pic, Quebec, and waited for signs of the fulfillment of his prophecy. Interviewed by the *Montreal Daily News* in June, he explained that the war was popular "because it is a war of emancipation." Indeed, the war was popular, although historians argue over why. Progressives and New Left scholars believe the war to be the work of businesspeople keen on opening new markets abroad.[45] The people had been fooled into war hysteria by the yellow journalists. When Americans like Harlan's son described the war as a struggle for "humanity and honor," they were simply being naive.[46] More conservative scholars depict the public as confused by war fever and see the empire that resulted as a mistake, a betrayal of American innocence.[47] James A. Field Jr. stresses the accidental nature of the entire chain of events leading to the war—"a sunken *Texas*, say, would have contributed little to the torchlight parades of chanting patriots."[48]

In Harlan's eyes, these events were providential, not accidental. We can see him in his interview with the Canadian paper trying to work out how the turn of events might be understood. He realized that foreign wars were at odds with George Washington's advice to avoid entangling alliances and still sounded wary: "Whether it would be advisable to follow that dictum or to exercise the power resulting from our community of interests with the entire world, I am unprepared to say. History will tell the story and its verdict will be impartial." He expected that the United States would have to take responsibility for the former Spanish colonies and was sure that "the American people will be equal to the task."[49] Harlan invoked the judgment of history here as though he believed that the United States was like other nations whose leaders chose among various political options. But he was not embracing a historicism that allowed for human choice and mortal causation. His confidence that the American people would be equal to the task was an expression of his unflagging faith in the American mission. Within days, Harlan was celebrating more proof of the country's glorious destiny.

On 5 July, Harlan wrote a jubilant letter to President William McKinley congratulating him "on the glorious news [from Cuba] of the recent victory resulting in the destruction of the Spanish fleet at Santiago." Harlan wrote that he hoped "the next news will be that our gallant army entered Santiago on the 4th day of July, and that on the same day Dewey took possession of Manilla [*sic*] despite the presence of European war ships."[50]

The power of typology is obvious here. The Fourth of July had always been *the* national holiday in the United States.[51] On the Fourth, Americans gathered together to remember the Declaration, its proclamation of inalienable rights, and the legend of the founding fathers. It is no accident that Harlan wrote an autobiographical letter to one of his sons on the Fourth in 1911.[52] Harlan recorded his own efforts as a citizen and civic leader. He made himself part of the nation's story in a private ritual.

Military victories on the Fourth of July would confirm the providential nature of the Spanish-American War for Harlan. Neither the Spanish fleet nor other European warships could halt such a process. Harlan was certain that the United States was going to spread the liberties dear to Anglo-Saxons across the globe. He assured McKinley of his "firm conviction . . . that your Administration will have the honor of inaugurating a New Era for our country, and of lessening the burdens which have been imposed upon man by despotic governments, administered in the interests of the few without any reference to the welfare of the many."[53] Harlan was not alone in thinking this. Speakers from the Grand Army of the Republic saw the American victory as "the overseas extension of the Union army's millennial crusade."[54]

The hoped-for coincidence of dates had not occurred. U.S. ships destroyed the Spanish fleet at Santiago, Cuba, on 3 July and occupied the town on 17 July; U.S. troops occupied Manila on 13 August, and the Spanish surrendered in the Philippines the next day. But Harlan remained firm in his belief that the past determined the present. The increasing inappropriateness of Harlan's historical analogies shows how typology dictated his understanding.

Although most Americans supported the Spanish-American War, its results were not universally welcomed. The Senate fight over whether to ratify the Treaty of Paris, which lasted from December 1898 to February 1899, was one of many public contests between expansionists and antiimperialists. The original American declaration of war contained an amendment disclaiming any intention of controlling Cuba. So when Spain "relinquish[ed] all claim of sovereignty over and title to Cuba" in the treaty, the United States did not gain title to Cuba. Spain "ceded" Puerto Rico and the Philippines, two places most Americans were ignorant of until the war, and the United States paid $20 million for the Philippines. Already some Americans were questioning the wisdom and constitutionality of extending American sovereignty to far-away territories peopled by alien races.

Meanwhile, some Filipinos rejected the exchange of one ruler for another. Emilio Aguinaldo was a voluntary exile who had returned to fight alongside the U.S. forces but turned against them when it became obvious that the U.S. government was set against independence. Admiral George Dewey later denied that he ever "considered [Aguinaldo] as an ally, although I did make use of him and the natives to assist me in my operations against the Spaniards." In June 1898, Aguinaldo organized ceremonies for the declaration of Philippine independence, which American officials ignored. Dewey reported to an investigating commission that he "never received Aguinaldo with military honors, or recognized or saluted the so-called Filipino flag."[55] McKinley approved of Dewey's behavior and declared American sovereignty over the islands in December 1898. Confrontation was unavoidable. On 4 February 1899, American and Filipino soldiers first fired on one another in a war that would last until 1902 and turn popular opinion against expansion.[56]

This conflict inspired Harlan to turn again to history for a type. Two days after the shooting, he wrote McKinley "to express my cordial approval of your course in the struggle now going on over the ratification of the Treaty with Spain." The judge had worked out a new analogy based on the Civil War experience. "In 1861," he recalled, "the so-called Peace men of the Northern and Border States came perilously near inducing the Government to 'let the wayward sisters depart in peace.' But misguided men having fired upon our flag, loyal citizens everywhere arose as one man to vindicate the national honor and to preserve the Union." Focusing on the image of "misguided men" firing on the American flag, Harlan associated the shots fired at American patrols in the Philippines with those fired at Fort Sumter. "History is repeating itself," Harlan told the president. "The recent attack on our troops at Manilla [sic] is an indignity that should not be forgotten nor go unpunished." Like the secessionists in 1861, the Filipinos were rebels whose defeat was assured if all Americans rallied around the flag and stood together "without regard to party affiliation," he concluded.[57]

Only the powerful appeal of typology can account for the violence Harlan did to the facts in making this analogy. The Filipinos were not secessionists since they had never been part of the Union; nor was the city of Manila anything like the federal property of Fort Sumter. But Harlan's view of American destiny required that present events resemble past ones. He needed a type, a historical analogy. The one he found called for universal popular support for the Union, precisely the kind of feeling missing at the time of the Civil War.

Harlan had told his law class just days after the sinking of the *Maine* that war would end sectionalism. If the people rallied against a common enemy, "we will not hear any more of North, South, East, or West in this country, but we will only hear of Americans."[58] Once the war began, Harlan felt that his dramatic prophecy had been fulfilled. "Veterans who wore the Blue and veterans who wore the Gray" no longer saw themselves as enemies, he wrote in a letter in August 1898. Which side a man had taken during the Civil War no longer mattered because "we now measure every man's Americanism by his present attitude towards the Government of the Union."[59] The nationalism of the New Era had put the Civil War to rest. History did not merely repeat itself. It improved. Harlan was not alone in making this historical analogy; some called the antiimperialists what they had called Confederate sympathizers: copperheads.[60]

Antiimperialists also used history to understand the present. They were a mixed lot. White southern Democrats thought imperialism was a mistake because it meant taking into the country yet another inferior race, and Reconstruction had proven the folly of that.[61] Many white northerners shared their prejudices and fears. The more egalitarian opponents of empire drew on the traditions of classical republicanism and American abolitionism. At the founding of the Anti-Imperialist League in November 1899, Moorfield Storey, who would go on to help organize the National Association for the Advancement of Colored People, reminded his audience that "when Rome began her career of conquest, the Roman Republic began to decay." "Let us once govern any considerable body of men without their consent," he warned, "and it is a question of time how soon this republic shares the fate of Rome."[62] The meeting site was Faneuil Hall in Boston, where abolitionists had once gathered. Like the presence of William Lloyd Garrison Jr., the setting urged Americans not to make the same mistake twice. But the league remained a small, divided band with no political influence.[63]

Whereas Harlan believed that the British practiced a backward constitutionalism destined to be replaced by features of the American system, some antiimperialists insisted that the United States was becoming more like its parent country, regressing to despotism. When Mark Twain recommended in the February 1901 issue of the *North American Review* that the United States clothe its soldiers in khaki, the fabric used in the British imperial army uni-

This cartoon by Grant Hamilton on the cover of the 11 June 1898 issue of *Judge* depicts the Philippines, which were won from the Spanish during the Spanish-American War, as a dark-skinned, primitive, and noisy infant. Uncle Sam asks, "Now that I've got it, what am I going to do with it?" The Supreme Court ruled on the constitutional aspect of that question in the Insular Cases in 1902, a decision from which Harlan dissented. (Courtesy of the Library of Congress)

form, he mocked those who believed that the United States was fundamentally different from other nations.[64] Such criticisms denied the inevitability of American destiny. Harlan's public response to the antiimperialists was hostile precisely because they had dared to question the country's destiny.

Harlan's February 1900 address at the University of Pennsylvania, "James Wilson and the Formation of the Constitution," resembled traditional Fourth of July orations he must have heard as a child and given as a politician.[65] Instead of dwelling on the Revolution, Harlan emphasized the founding fathers' role in creating the Constitution and the lessons to be drawn from them. Harlan also stressed a less common theme: the importance of racial equality to the American mission.

After congratulating those who had built the new law building for being lovers of liberty, he defined that liberty for them. "This fair land is in a peculiar sense the home of freedom," he told his listeners, "the freedom that takes account of man as man, that tolerates no government which does not rest upon the consent of the governed, and recognizes the right of all persons within its jurisdiction, of whatever race, to the equal protection of the law in every matter affecting life, liberty or property."[66] As he began his discussion of James Wilson, he announced that he would recount "the principles by which [Wilson's] public career was guided." He cited a 1774 pamphlet by Wilson entitled *Considerations on the Nature and Extent of the Legislative Authority of the British Parliament*, which concluded that Parliament had no authority over the colonies. Harlan drew the audience's attention to Wilson's declaration that all men are by nature equal and free. As he had during his law lectures, Harlan focused on the egalitarian nature of the phrase: "all men — not some men, not men of any particular race or color, but '*all* men are by nature equal and free'—the same great principle subsequently embodied in the Declaration of Independence."[67] The logical result of the Revolution was the Fourteenth Amendment. Typology made history into a package.

In discussing Wilson's constitutional nationalism, Harlan invoked typology as well. In effect, the Civil War had proven that Wilson was right. For proof of the need to give Congress the powers it had lacked under the Articles of Confederation, Harlan quoted Joseph Story, the constitutional nationalist he had relied on in his law lectures. Wilson had influenced Story, and Harlan quoted Wilson's arguments as well. During the ratification convention in Pennsylvania, Wilson declared himself "astonished . . . to hear the ill-founded doctrine that States alone ought to be represented in the Federal government; these must possess sovereign authority, forsooth, and the people be forgot!" The Constitution was "ordained and established by the people themselves;

and we who give our votes to it, are merely the proxies of our constituents."[68] As Harlan moved from the founding period, he emphasized the direct relationship between the citizenry and the nation and between the nation and the world. Localism, a natural tendency, should never allow Americans to forget "that our all, and perhaps the hopes of freemen everywhere, depend upon the recognition of the right of the national government to exercise the powers belonging to it under the Constitution."[69] Harlan had expanded the republican mission from a national one to a global one—the hopes of freemen everywhere. The Spanish-American War was a replaying of republican history on a larger scale.

Harlan ended with the lesson he thought his listeners should draw from the founders' story, one that some people had forgotten. The lesson was "absolute fidelity to country and unflinching adherence to principles that must be regarded and enforced, if government of the people, by the people and for the people is not to disappear." This paraphrase of Abraham Lincoln's address at Gettysburg was surely deliberate since it was in keeping with Harlan's view of the Filipino insurgency as a repeat of secession. Gettysburg recalls to mind a period when the country was struggling, and Harlan identified 1900 as a time "now more than at any period in our history" when it was necessary to "be faithful to sound principles of government and of liberty under law." He then chided those who refused to take part in public affairs, but his main targets were those who "strengthen the hands of the enemies of the Republic"—critics of America's actions in the Philippines.[70]

Harlan spoke scathingly of people who said that "those who from jungles ambush and shoot down our brave soldiers" were "fighting the battles of liberty and doing only what they have a right to do, what their honor requires."[71] In the spring of the previous year, Edward Atkinson, a member of the Anti-Imperialist League, had attracted national attention by mailing pamphlets critical of American imperialism to officials in the Philippines in defiance of the McKinley administration's military censorship policies designed to forestall mutiny.[72] Expansionist newspapers condemned Atkinson and the league as traitorous supporters of Aguinaldo, although other antiimperialists tried to distinguish criticism of the government from criticism of the troops.[73] Harlan continued: "These men are never happier than when attempting to persuade their fellow-citizens that America is entering upon a dark and perilous future, and that all so far accomplished for the liberty and well-being of the people will be lost if the nation does not retrace its steps."[74] What evidence did Harlan offer to counter the antiimperialists' view of the present and the future? How did he respond to the criticisms of the United States made in the name of the very principles of self-government and liberty that he himself championed? Did he describe the military situation in the Philippines or defend the administration's policies?

Harlan offered only dogged assertions of republican faith. His reading of the present was controlled by the idea of the republican mission. Having rejected the sorry future foretold by the antiimperialists, Harlan explained that "for my own part, I believe that a destiny awaits America such as has never been vouchsafed to any people, and that in the working out of that destiny, under the leadings of Providence, humanity everywhere will be lifted up, and power and tyranny compelled to recognize the fact that 'God is no respecter of persons,' and that He 'hath made of one blood all nations of men.' "[75] Harlan could not have made plainer his faith in the American mission of racial egalitarianism. He quoted the same biblical passage that he had used when condemning English aristocrats, the same passage once favored by abolitionists. The founders had practiced these biblical lessons, and the present generation had to apply them to the world. Harlan urged his listeners to join him: "Let us have an abiding faith that our country will never depart from the fundamental principles of right and justice, or prove recreant to the high trusts committed to it for the benefit, not alone of the American people, but of all men everywhere." Other "political storms" had made some people doubt their country's destiny, "but those storms passed away."[76] He commanded his audience: "Take courage in the belief that the American people are pure in heart, and have no desire or purpose other than to maintain the authority of the nation wherever our flag floats, and to preserve unimpaired to the latest generation the free institutions given them by the fathers." History had taught Americans that they should have "a firm conviction that the kind Providence that has always watched over this people will preserve our heritage of constitutional liberty."[77] Harlan had no need to cite facts or explain policies because republican faith determined the future. The United States could not be doing wrong because it had a destiny. Although the emphasis on racial egalitarianism that Harlan expressed was rare, many Americans justified involvement in the Philippines on the grounds of national honor and duty.[78] Even among missionaries troubled by the war with the Filipinos, "the single most dominant mood was that of determined optimism."[79]

Harlan did acknowledge the possibility of error on the part of the nation or its people in this speech. He used the qualification "if this people remain true to their great destiny" in describing the future glory of the country; he spoke of "an evil hour" when the people might lose sovereignty.[80] But his ultimate message was the unshakable faith that ended the lecture and that he tried to impart to his listeners. The words he used indicated that current troubles could not undermine this faith. He believed that a destiny awaited

America; his listeners should have an abiding faith in their country's purposes; they must take courage in the belief that the American people are pure in heart. His final words were a quotation from the popular play *William Tell* by James Sheridan Knowles, first performed in 1825. When the Swiss patriot finds himself in a storm in the mountains of Switzerland he says:

> I thought of other lands, whose storms
> Are summer flaws to those of mine, and just
> Have wished me there: the thought that mine was *free*
> Has checked that wish; and I have raised my head,
> And cried in thraldom to that furious wind,
> "Blow on: this is the land of Liberty!"[81]

Political storms were necessary, Harlan had noted earlier, because "nothing worth preserving has ever been achieved by individuals or by nations except through trials and sacrifices."[82] Harlan had lived through the worst trial of his country's history and had taken from it only faith in the Union's triumph.

Although some may see Harlan's assertions of faith in this speech as signs of desperation, they are the work of a rhetorical strategist who wanted his main point to be remembered and his speech to end with a bang. The inconsistency that we detect—his support for the war against Philippine independence and his devotion to the idea that God has made of one blood all nations of men—went unobserved by Harlan because his belief in American destiny reconciled the two. We might say that Harlan confused the ideal with the real. The freedom offered in the United States was supposed to take account of man as man, to tolerate no government that did not rest on the consent of the governed, and to recognize the right of all persons within its jurisdiction, of whatever race, to the equal protection of the law in every matter affecting life, liberty, and property. Harlan identified the United States with these standards so strongly that he could not describe reality without reference to them. Only in deciding the Insular Cases was Harlan forced to test what was against what ought to be.

William Jennings Bryan, the standard-bearer of the Democratic Party since his 1896 presidential candidacy, ended up supporting the Treaty of Paris. He was willing to delay a decision on Philippine independence until 1900, when he would make it the "paramount issue of the campaign" for president (although apparently it wasn't).[83] The people could either give their mandate to imperialism by reelecting McKinley or reject the building of a colonial empire by choosing Bryan. The Democratic platform condemned the Philippine-American War.

Many Democrats spoke out in Congress against retaining the islands because that would require extending full rights of citizenship to the inhabitants. Reconstruction had proven that Anglo-Saxon ways of self-government could not be adopted successfully by other races.[84] During the House debates over the proper relationship between the United States and Puerto Rico, a representative from Mississippi was willing to accept the Puerto Ricans as "in the main, of Caucasian blood" but explained that the Filipinos "are of wholly different races of peoples from ours—Asiatics, Malays, negroes and mixed blood. They have nothing in common with us and centuries can not assimilate them."[85] Similarly, the Democratic Party platform defined "desirable territory" as that "which can be erected into States in the Union, and whose people are willing and fit to become American citizens." It concluded that "the Filipinos cannot be citizens without endangering our civilization." Instead of annexation, the Democrats proposed "an immediate declaration of the nation's purpose to give the Filipinos, first, a stable form of government; second, independence, and third, protection from outside interference." The party would repeat the call for independence until 1928.[86]

The Republican Party supported McKinley's extension of American control over the Philippines. Its speakers blamed the Democrats for encouraging the Filipino insurgents. (Southern Democrats especially feared being called unpatriotic.)[87] The Republican platform declared that "wherever sovereign rights were extended it became the high duty of the Government to maintain its authority, to put down armed insurrection, and to confer the blessings of liberty and civilization upon all the rescued peoples." It did not offer citizenship to the Filipinos but only a promise of "the largest measure of self-government consistent with their welfare and our duties."[88] Unlike the Democrats, the McKinley administration always spoke of the island inhabitants' current incapacity for self-rule, "never of inferiority."[89]

Always a party stalwart, Harlan celebrated the Republican victory in 1900, but he had become concerned with the party's position on the insular possessions. During the summer of 1900, Harlan wrote his friend William Howard Taft, who was then in the Philippines as part of the Philippine Commission, that a Democratic triumph would "bring dishonor upon America in its relations with the world."[90] The day before the election, he teased Taft that if Bryan was elected, "look out for bullets that will be directed against you by Aguinaldo, & don't go out doors often." "You can be seen at a good long distance by the allies of Bryan in the Phillipines [sic]," he reminded his oversized friend, "and would make a good mark for a Fillipino [sic], having a modern rifle in his hands, at several hundred yards."[91] Harlan grew serious as he discussed the party's position. He reported to Taft that "many of our Speakers have allowed the party to be put in the position of . . . holding some views about the power of Congress and of the President over our new possessions that may well create (and I think have created) some alarm among the people who do not wish any radical departure from the principles underlying our system of government."[92] For Harlan, the new overseas activities had to follow the historical pattern of republicanism. That was their only justification.

Taft reported from the Philippines that "the result of the election has been wonderfully beneficial in the islands." With no possibility of independence after Bryan's defeat, "the insurrection is rapidly fading out," he wrote Harlan. Taft had never seen the insurgency as anything more than an elevated form of banditry—a "selfish, dishonest system of robbery and murder by the comparatively small element that have insisted on maintaining the revolution." Their "reign of terror" would now come to an end. The real voice of the people, which Taft assumed was friendly toward the United States, would be heard at last: "Now that the people see that they are to be protected they do not hesitate to come out in favor of a civil government under the sovereignty of the United States."[93]

Administering the new territories—which Taft was destined to do—raised serious constitutional questions. Article 4 of the Constitution gives Congress the power "to dispose of and make all needful Rules and Regulations respecting the Territory or other Property belonging to the United States." Two questions arose. First, did other clauses in the Constitution limit that power? Second, did Congress have a constitutional duty to set Puerto Rico and the Philippines on the road to statehood? Prominent legal writers debated the principles and precedents in law reviews and elsewhere. In public discussion, the controversy often boiled down to the question, "Does the Constitution follow the flag?"

The first cases to raise the question of the constitutional status of the island territories revolved around tariff issues. In order to raise revenue to cover administrative costs, Congress proposed to treat Puerto Rico as a foreign country as far as the tariff laws were concerned. But the uniform taxation clause of the Constitution declares that "all Duties, Imposts and Excises shall be uniform throughout the United States." Did this clause apply to the insular territory? Mainland sugar producers and orange growers would have said no, but importers, who had to pay the duty, insisted that it did.

Harlan and former president Benjamin Harrison, who had also supported the war, exchanged troubled letters over the tariff in the spring of 1900. Harlan wrote in March that the tariff "Bill is one of the worst ever conceived by any statesman or politician."[94] Harrison, who refused to campaign for McKinley in the 1900 election, called it a "serious, and it may yet be fatal, blunder." [95] He confided to Harlan that he was receiving a good deal of abuse at the hands of the mainland sugar and tobacco people. But he only spoke out publicly against imperialism after the election of 1900. In a speech published in the *North American Review* in 1901, Harrison explained that "a gentleman connected with the beet-sugar industry, seeing my objections to the constitutionality of the law, and having a friendly purpose to help me over them, wrote to say that the duty [on Puerto Rican sugar] was absolutely needed to protect the [mainland] beet-sugar industry." Harrison responded "that the needs of the beet-sugar industry seemed to me to be irrelevant in a constitutional discussion." [96] Like other opponents of imperialism, Harrison drew a historical analogy to slavery: "It is not a question of kind or unkind treatment, but of human rights; not of the good or bad use of power, but of the power." [97]

In his exchange with Harrison in March 1900, Harlan refused to discuss the constitutional issue. By July, he was aware that the Court "may be called upon to declare the extent of the power of Congress over our new possessions" by ruling on the constitutionality of the tariff law. He wrote Taft that "it is a great question, & worthy of serious, deliberate consideration. I have impressions, but no fixed opinions; for I have not examined the adjudged cases, nor carefully considered the question." [98]

Meanwhile, Taft pressured him to approve the tariff. After hearing a rumor that the justices were leaning toward declaring it unconstitutional, Taft warned Harlan in January 1901 that such a decision "will result in a very narrow colonial policy for the islands and will doubtless require for two or three years that we shall be helped out of the United States Treasury to raise funds enough to carry on the government." [99] Taft wrote again in May to stress the inconvenience of applying the uniform taxation clause to the Philippines and urged Harlan "if there is room for two constructions, to take the one that avoids such a result." [100]

Everyone realized that although the first cases involved tariffs, eventually the Court would have to pass on Congress's power to limit the civil and political rights of the islands' inhabitants. Taft and James Harlan, who was in Puerto Rico, insisted that the island inhabitants were unfit to participate in American political life. Taft wrote Harlan the summer before the election of 1900 that the Filipinos "are in many respects nothing but grown up children." [101] He hoped that the Court would not order Congress to grant them the right to a trial by jury because so few people would be qualified to serve. [102] Although Taft distinguished between behavior and race, he saw little hope of acting on the difference anytime soon. "Three hundred years of Spanish political rule," he wrote Harlan, "has given them to understand that it is the legitimate function of every public official to be bribed, and a proper method for every one having to do with them to bribe them." The Filipinos "need the training of fifty or a hundred years before they shall even realize what Anglo Saxon liberty is."[103] If Harlan replied to these remarks, the letters have not survived. From the bench, he made clear that he believed it was impossible *not* to administer the island territories along constitutional lines.

D. A. DeLima and Company of New York City brought a suit to recover the duties it had been forced to pay on goods imported from Puerto Rico on the grounds that the tariff law violated the uniform taxation clause. The implications of the dispute were tremendous: if this clause did not control Congress when it dealt with the insular possessions, then perhaps neither did the rest of the Constitution.

The Court split embarrassingly over the issue in a set of decisions the whole country was waiting to hear. In late May 1901, it managed to say that Congress both could *and* could not treat Puerto Rico differently from other territories under tariff law. Justice Henry Billings Brown was the swing vote and delivered both majority decisions. In the first decision, *DeLima v. Bidwell*, Harlan was part of the majority.[104] *DeLima* declared that Puerto Rico was not a foreign country under the tariff laws. Brown argued that precedents made clear that after territory came into the possession of the United States it was domestic in nature; logic made it impossible for territory to be both domestic and foreign at the same time.[105] Justice Joseph McKenna dissented, joined by Justices George Shiras Jr. and Edward D. White, and Horace Gray dissented on his own. McKenna wrote that there was a midway status between foreign and domestic territory: territory not yet incorporated into the Union.

In the second decision, *Downes v. Bidwell*, these dissenters formed a majority with Brown. Brown delivered the opinion, then White concurred in the result and Shiras and McKenna joined him. *Downes* approved the Foraker Act, which placed tariffs on Puerto Rican products and organized the island's civil government.[106] It gave Puerto Ricans an elected lower house and an upper house appointed by the U.S. president. This time Brown cited precedents, including *Dred Scott*, to prove that "the Constitution deals with *States*, their people, and their representatives" and that its clauses, including the uniformity clause, only applied to territories when Congress chose to apply them.[107] He admitted that "prohibitions as go to the very root of the power of Congress to act at all" were applicable to these territories, but he refused to declare whether that meant the whole Bill of Rights.[108] White seemed more concerned about rights but was vague: "Even in cases where there is no direct command of the Constitution which applies, there may nevertheless be restrictions of so fundamental a nature that they cannot be transgressed, although not expressed in so many words in the Constitution."[109]

The justices who supported the proimperial interpretation in both decisions voiced a vision of the future at odds with Harlan's. For them, an empire had to be constitutionally possible. White argued in his concurrence to *Downes* that "the consequence [of applying all clauses of the Constitution] would be to entail ruin on the discovered territory and to inflict grave detriment on the United States to arise both from the dislocation of its fiscal system and the immediate bestowal of citizenship on those absolutely unfit to receive it."[110] An interpretation that denied to Congress its full power over the territories, wrote McKenna in his dissent from *DeLima*, "takes this great country out of the world and shuts it up within itself."[111] Linking past to future, Brown warned in *Downes:* "A false step at this time might be fatal to the development of what Chief Justice Marshall called the American Empire."[112] True, Americans had long referred to their country as an empire, but they spoke of an empire of liberty or of reason, of virtue or of love.[113] We might presume that an empire of liberty needed a Bill of Rights.

To calm those who feared that Congress would descend into "centralized despotism" once unleashed from constitutional restraint, Brown offered a further historical argument in *Downes:* "These fears . . . find no justification in the action of Congress in the past century, nor in the conduct of the British Parliament towards its outlying possessions since the American Revolution." He added a racial argument to account for this good behavior: "There are certain principles of natural justice inherent in the Anglo-Saxon character which need no expression in constitutions or statutes to give them effect."[114] This essentialist view of Anglo-Saxonism made the Constitution itself superfluous.

Harlan explained to Taft that "it was not my original purpose to write a dissenting opinion" in *Downes.* He had intended "to stand upon" Chief Justice Melville Fuller's dissent, which Justices David J. Brewer and Rufus W. Peckham also joined.[115] Fuller insisted that the Constitution enumerated the powers it conveyed to the branches of national government and the qualifications of those powers. Precedents made clear that the uniform taxation clause, a qualification on the power of Congress, applied to both states and territories.[116] He condemned the "limbo" in which so-called unincorporated territory would be placed and brushed aside the economic arguments as irrelevant.[117] To argue that new circumstances required a new reading of the Constitution was to fail to appreciate that "the Constitution was framed for ages to come" by the founding fathers.[118] Fuller concluded that "the theory [of unincorporated territory] . . . substitutes for the present system of republican government, a system of domination over distant provinces in the exercise of unrestricted power."[119]

Harlan gave Fuller's dissent his "entire approval."[120] But Harlan told Taft that Brown's and White's opinions had provoked him to write his own dissent: "My friend Brown particularly had said some things which I was unwilling to pass without explicitly referring to them." In order to defend his republican faith, Harlan had to compromise his religious practices: "I am sorry to say, and you will be shocked to learn, that the greater part of my dissent was written on the Sabbath. I stayed away from church to do the work. Horrible! But my ox was in the ditch, & had to be gotten out in some way."[121] A reporter described Harlan's delivery of the dissent: "He threw his words out as if he was shying bricks at an enemy."[122]

White and Brown had voiced ideas about the Constitution's relationship to the people, the American mission, and the nature of Anglo-Saxonism entirely at odds with Harlan's. Brown's contention that the Constitution dealt only with the states defied the tradition of constitutional nationalism dating back to Joseph Story, John Marshall, and James Wilson. Harlan responded that "as this court has often declared, it is a government created by the People of the United States, with enumerated powers, and supreme over States and individuals, with respect to certain objects, throughout the entire territory over which its jurisdiction extends."[123] Harlan found the suggestion that the United States could hold the insular territories under its general powers of sovereignty, as other nations governed their territories, a betrayal of the founders' very purpose in creating a republican government and a betrayal of the people of the United States who had adopted it.

The supremacy of the Constitution was essential to the republican mission, which distinguished the United States from all other countries. White had argued that under the law of nations, the United States might fix the status of any territory as it liked.[124] The exchange that the majority proposed—an empire for the Constitution as it was—did not interest Harlan. "We heard much in argument about the 'expanding future of our country,'" he noted. "It was said that the United States is to become what is called a 'world power'; and that if this Government intends to keep abreast of the times and be equal to the great destiny that awaits the American people, it *must* be allowed to exert all the power that other nations are accustomed to exercise."[125] But the United States was not like other nations: "The idea that the country may acquire territories anywhere upon the earth, by conquest or treaty, and hold them as mere colonies or provinces—the people inhabiting them to enjoy only such rights as Congress chooses to accord to them—is wholly inconsistent with the spirit and genius as well as with the words of the Constitution."[126] The economic necessity of tariffs was irrelevant. "We cannot violate the Constitution," Harlan declared, "in order to serve particular interests in our own or in foreign lands."[127] The political necessity of nonincorporation was also irrelevant. Harlan refused to enter into the debate over the qualification of the insular peoples for citizenship, saying only that such objections should have been thought of when the territory was first acquired. It was too late constitutionally, he implied, to make them now.[128] If the proimperial Court majority triumphed, Harlan feared that "we will . . . pass from the era of constitutional liberty guarded and protected by a written constitution into an era of legislative absolutism."[129] The mission would be abandoned.

The founders had written this Constitution precisely because they had not shared Brown's faith in the genetic fairness of the Anglo-Saxon race. "The wise men who framed the Constitution," Harlan informed the Court, "and the patriotic people who adopted it, were unwilling to depend for their safety upon . . . 'certain principles of natural justice inherent in Anglo-Saxon character.' " "They well remembered," although some of the brethren had apparently forgotten, "that Anglo-Saxons across the ocean had attempted, in defiance of law and justice, to trample upon the rights of Anglo-Saxons on this continent."[130] Behavior, not mere ancestry, determined whether one was living up to one's racial destiny.

If the people now desired to do something that "the fathers never intended," then they had to amend the Constitution.[131] The way in which Harlan told the history of the framing indicated that he did not consider such a solution to the controversy possible. The Constitution linked the republican past with the republican future. The people would never choose a different destiny.

Harlan continued to receive letters like those from Taft about the Philippines. James, then attorney general of Puerto Rico, complained in 1902, "The real problem here is a lack of an educated public conscience"; "when a man commits a crime against the election law, or some other offense of that general public nature, the people that are indignant are those that suffer by it."[132] He argued that "from the practical standpoint, it is for the present impossible in this island to administer the local government along constitutional lines."[133] But such messages had no impact on Harlan's position.

Harlan continued to dissent as the Court expanded on the idea of territorial incorporation. It announced two years later in *Hawaii v. Mankichi* that the Bill of Rights applied only to territory designated by Congress as incorporated into the Union.[134] Again, Fuller dissented and Harlan, Brewer, and Peckham joined him. And again Harlan also dissented on his own because of the "exceptional importance" of the case.[135] He declared himself unable to comprehend what territorial incorporation meant: "It is impossible for me to grasp the thought that that which is admittedly contrary to the supreme law can be sustained as valid."[136] Harlan embraced the popular way of framing the question —whether the Constitution followed the flag. He described the ceremony at

James Shanklin Harlan (1861–1927), the second of Harlan's three sons, practiced law in Chicago. He served as attorney general to Puerto Rico from 1901 to 1903 after the United States gained that territory following the Spanish-American War. His complaint that Puerto Ricans were incapable of serving on juries had no effect on his father's opinion that all of the Bill of Rights applied to the insular possessions. James was a member of the Interstate Commerce Commission from 1906 to 1918. This photograph was taken in 1904. (Photograph by J. C. Strauss; courtesy of the Library of Congress)

the official transfer of the islands to the United States in 1898. At that moment, "when the flag of Hawaii was taken down, by the authority of Hawaii, and in its place was raised that of the United States," every provision of the Constitution went into force. The U.S. minister's words welcoming the Hawaiians as fellow citizens under a common Constitution proved it. The majority's opinion, which gave Congress the power to pick and choose the rights it would extend to the islands' inhabitants, made Congress supreme and the Constitution subordinate to its will. It meant that "under the influence and guidance of commercialism and the supposed necessities of trade, this country had left the old ways of the fathers, as defined by a written Constitution."[137] Harlan then described what the future would hold: "Thus will be engrafted upon our republican institutions, controlled by the supreme law of a written Constitution, a *colonial* system entirely foreign to the genius of our Government and abhorrent to the principles that underlie and pervade the Constitution."[138]

Harlan dissented again in *Dorr v. United States* in 1904 when the Court held that the right to trial by jury was not guaranteed in the Philippines. Justice William R. Day declared that jury trials could not be a constitutional necessity because they would be impossible to administer in a "territory peopled by savages."[139] Peckham wrote a concurrence, which Fuller and Brewer joined, that admitted that *Mankichi* was the controlling authority but opposed it still. Harlan fiercely declared that the implications of the ruling were "utterly revolting to my mind." The majority had interpreted Article 3, Section 2, of the Constitution as though it read: "The trial of all crimes, except in cases of impeachment, *and except where Filipinos are concerned*, shall be by jury." The brethren had clearly forgotten the republican mission. "Such a mode of constitutional interpretation plays havoc with the old-fashioned ideas of the fathers, who took care to say that the Constitution was the supreme law—supreme everywhere, at all times, and over all persons who are subject to the authority of the United States."[140] By 1910, Fuller, Brewer, and Peckham were gone. Their replacements did not share Harlan's fears. When the Court made two proimperial decisions in 1911, Harlan dissented alone.[141] He no longer bothered to explain why.

Faith in an exceptional American destiny shaped Harlan's ideas of the past and the present and ultimately his judicial opinions. In embracing this faith, Harlan shared in an idea common among nineteenth-century Americans. Even historian George Bancroft, who received training from the German historicists themselves, was unable to shake off the idea of a providential destiny for the United States.[142]

The man to whom Harlan had poured out his reading of history, President William McKinley, seems to have reluctantly chosen a course at odds with it. According to McKinley's recollection, when he prayed for guidance about what to do about the Philippine Islands in 1899, he rejected the idea of giving them back to Spain as dishonorable, the idea of giving them to any other European power as commercially unsound, and the idea of giving them up to self-government as unwise. He concluded (still on his knees) that "there was nothing left for us to do but to take them all and to educate the Filipinos, and uplift and Christianize them, and by God's grace do the very best we could by them, as our fellow-men for whom Christ also died."[143] The very best we could do was to provide a set of "inviolable rules" by which the Philippine commissioners were instructed to govern; these included granting the Filipinos the protections found in the first eight amendments to the Constitution, save for the right to a jury trial and the right to bear arms.[144] McKinley believed that he was forwarding the American mission by training the Filipinos for self-government. Taft estimated that they would be ready after no more than three generations. Harlan balked at this delay as a betrayal of the providential trust placed in the United States. Americans may have been better-intentioned imperialists than the Spaniards, but the difference between the United States and other countries was supposed to be one of kind, not degree. One can sense the anomalous position Harlan found his country in from the prayer he offered at the banquet celebrating his twenty-fifth year on the Court in late 1902: "God bless our dear country. God bless every effort to sustain and strengthen it in the hearts of the people of every race subject to its authority or jurisdiction."[145]

Harlan's persistent faith in the American mission may be why he refused to credit the stories of American atrocities in the Philippines. Several courts-martial were held in the spring of 1902, and Senate hearings on the behavior of the American forces ran from January through June of that year.[146] Harlan wrote Senator John C. Spooner in July 1902 that he refused to believe that "the misconduct, if there was misconduct, of a few officers or soldiers" justified any criticism of the army as a whole.[147]

But the Insular Cases troubled him deeply. To explain why the United States had swerved from the path of destiny, Harlan cited two failings that could bring down a Christian or a republic: greed and pride. In his letter to Spooner, Harlan wrote that he had noted "a manifest tendency among the captains of industry, and others of enormous wealth, to make everything subservient to the necessities of *commerce and trade*." "This tendency," he continued, "must be resisted at all hazards, and the nations and peoples of the earth given to understand that America will not under any circumstances, be false to true liberty, as defined and safeguarded by our Constitution."[148] Similarly, during a speech before the Detroit Bar Association in 1908, he warned of the "overweening pride" of those Americans who "delight to talk of being a world power." He urged the listening lawyers instead to "teach the people to stand firmly for those principles which underlie the American system of Constitutional government." [149]

Harlan was not alone in his concern that the taking of colonies was a wrong step. In fact, as time wore on he recognized that he shared ideas with some of the early antiimperialists who had written about atrocities. Moorfield Story, one of the founders of the Anti-Imperialist League, wrote him in 1908, "I have been much delighted and encouraged by your opinions in important cases, of which from time to time I have received copies." [150] Harlan also exchanged copies of his dissenting opinions for copies of the speeches of another opponent of imperialism, Charles Francis Adams Jr. [151]

The difference between Harlan's early criticism of the antiimperialist movement and his later judicial protests against imperialism is striking. Yet both originated from the same source. Like a set of blinders, Harlan's national myth limited his ability to see the present even as it guided him down the righteous path. Harlan could not comprehend the criticisms of the American forces fighting against the Filipinos; nor could he comprehend a constitutional interpretation that allowed Congress to withhold rights from the Filipinos once defeated. The United States could not be wrong in fighting the Filipinos because the United States had a destiny; the Court majority could not be right in refusing them the Bill of Rights for the same reason. Harlan's vision of the American mission determined history, contemporary politics, and constitutional interpretation all at once. He dissented so fiercely in the Insular Cases because he feared the country was selling its birthright for a mess of pottage.

# CHAPTER 6

# This Age of Money Getting

## Constitutional Nationalism and Free Labor

*Justice Harlan of the United States Supreme Court, recently
observed in a promiscuous company that in his opinion half of the
men in Wall Street should be in State's prison. Certain men of
prominence in Wall Street endeavored to get from Judge Harlan
a denial of the remark attributed to him, but he declined to
retract his ugly words.*

—*Illustrated American*, circa 1892

More judicial biographies are started than finished. John M.
Harlan survived at least four unsuccessful attempts before Loren P. Beth
published one in 1992. The sheer number of judicial decisions is part of the
problem. Harlan wrote over 700 opinions for the Court and over 100 dissents
and dissented silently in 100 more cases. He voted in a total of some 14,000
cases.[1] The biographer can choose the controversial or the influential ones,
but it is hard to dismiss many of them as unimportant. Some readers may
think that Beth included the chapter "Other Issues" because scholars hate to
throw away their notes, but many of us would flinch at tossing out the topics of that chapter: the First Amendment, federal criminal prosecutions, the
separation of powers, and personal injury cases. After all, they're all important legal subjects.

Biographers have to impose structure on their subjects' legal careers, and
the well-known or important decisions are natural choices, but one of our
considerations should be what the judges themselves thought. Just as Harlan
recounted a national history in his lectures, so he wrote his own history by
drawing up a list of majority opinions and dissents that he wanted published.
These were the decisions he wanted us to remember. I call them his favorite
decisions, but it might be better to think of them as his legacy. (Those who
like their data raw will find the list in the appendix.)

The list is undated, but Harlan probably wrote it during the summer of
1910. The last decision listed was delivered in the spring of 1910, and Harlan
guessed which volume of the *United States Supreme Court Reports* it would appear in. Growing intimations of mortality may have prompted him to compile

the list. Harlan wrote William Howard Taft in 1892, "My own conclusion, long ago formed, is to stay at my post on the Bench until I die."[2] But by 1906 he confided to Augustus E. Willson that the question of mental competence "is a matter which could not be referred to myself alone" because "an old man will not recognize the fact that he is steadily going down the hill."[3] The deaths of Justice David J. Brewer in March 1910 and Chief Justice Melville Fuller in July 1910 may have prompted Harlan to consider his legacy. Fuller and he had both been born in 1833, and Brewer was born in 1837.

Harlan listed fifty-nine majority opinions and twenty-four dissents. He wrote them down largely in chronological order and gave accurate citations for most. *When* Harlan wrote this list influenced his selection: only eleven decisions predate 1890, whereas thirty were from the 1890s and forty-two were from 1900 to 1910. Although it's true that the Court was getting busier, Harlan probably remembered the more recent cases better. The number of times an issue appears may not indicate its importance; only one income tax decision is listed, but Harlan's letters tell us it meant a lot to him. Some of the decisions are about several issues, so it's hard to know just why Harlan chose them. And, of course, the fact that certain decisions didn't make the list tells us something too (remember *Cumming*'s absence). Despite these limitations, Harlan's list of favorite decisions allows us to understand how he conceived of his work on the Court.

The most striking things about this list are the subjects of the decisions and their relative proportions. The largest group is composed of eighteen decisions (counting opinions for the Court and dissents together) in which Harlan supported the exercise of the state's police power. In thirteen decisions, Harlan attempted to protect interstate commerce from burdens imposed on it by the states. In twelve decisions, he tried to extend protections to criminal defendants, and in three of these cases, he tried to apply the Bill of Rights to the states. The fourth largest group at ten and the one with the largest number of dissents are cases that support civil rights. After that the numbers dwindle: five support nationalism; three each support antitrust legislation, substantive due process, and limits on the rights of fugitives fighting extradition; two oppose forum shopping, that is, working up an excuse for federal jurisdiction in order to escape from the state courts; two announce that the federal judiciary is not bound to follow state judges' interpretations of state law; one supports the federal income tax and another backs liberty of contract. I've lumped the rest under "miscellaneous" because it's not clear which of the issues raised best defines them. One can argue about the relative significance of each decision (does a righteous dissent like *Plessy* count for more than a mild-mannered opinion on railroad-safety regulations?), but the numbers themselves mean something.

Among other things, the numbers tell us that Harlan wanted us to notice his respect for the state's power to protect the health, safety, and morals of its people. One of his police-power favorites compelled an individual to get a smallpox vaccination, and the rest controlled business.[4] In them, Harlan allowed the states to prohibit the sale of liquor, lottery tickets, and margarine (we now know the judge had butter for breakfast).[5] He dismissed complaints from corporations about regulations banning Sunday trains and prohibiting the use of the American flag in advertisements. He upheld laws requiring safety improvements, certain procedures for transferring corporate stock, shorter working days, and the regulation of garbage collection and the shipping of livestock.[6] He told railroad companies that they had to rebuild their bridges and tunnels at their own expense if the common good required changes to the navigable streams they crossed.[7] Harlan spoke for the majority in fifteen out of eighteen of these police-power favorites.

Perhaps Harlan decided to include so many police-power decisions because the Court had received considerable flak by 1910 for striking down such laws. Populists and labor leaders accused it of siding with the plutocrats. By the 1896 presidential election, the Court's record had become a political issue, and Democratic candidate William Jennings Bryan argued that the people needed to have direct control over the judiciary.[8] In the eyes of its critics, the Court protected capitalists by misinterpreting the Constitution.

This period has come to be called the *Lochner* era after *Lochner v. New York*, a 1905 case in which the Court majority struck down a state law that barred bakers from working more than ten hours a day, six days a week. Justice Rufus W. Peckham argued for the majority that the law violated the bakers' Fourteenth Amendment right to liberty of contract. The police power could not justify the law because baking was not a special occupation needing state supervision (like deep-shaft mining), and there was no threat to the public health in the bakers' contracting to work more than ten hours. Peckham concluded that statutes "limiting the hours in which grown and intelligent men may labor to earn their living, are mere meddlesome interferences with the rights of the individual." He meant men literally; women needed protection, but the state did not have the power to act as *pater familias* over male bakers.[9] Harlan dissented from this decision, and two justices joined him in arguing that the evidence on the bad conditions of work and the ill-health and early death of bakers was sufficient to show that the state was rightly exercising its police power. Justice Oliver Wendell Holmes Jr.'s pithier dissent captured people's imaginations, especially when he declared that "the Four-teenth Amendment does not enact Mr. Herbert Spencer's Social Statics." [10] Progressive legal scholars accused the justices of suffering from legal formal-ism, and historians of the New Deal era and later argued that the turn-of-the-century Court was controlled by Social Darwinists unwilling to allow the state to interfere in the unequal battles between the haves and the have-nots. [11] One historian wrote in 1954 that the bench and bar were at the beck and call of an "industrial oligarchy." [12] Harlan was dubbed a paternalist for his trouble in *Lochner*, whereas Holmes, who had made it clear that he did not believe in either economic theory (not believing in things being what he did best), was hailed as a hero by those desiring a more active state. [13]

The trouble with calling Harlan a paternalist and the Court laissez-faire is that neither label sticks very well. The paternalism I have identified in Har-lan in earlier chapters did not apply to white males; it was directed at women as the weaker sex and at blacks as former slaves. Harlan himself rejected the label. In a speech in 1908, he praised Presbyterianism because it encouraged individuality, and he concluded that "it is the strength of individuality that makes men more fitted and determined to oppose the pernicious doctrines of the present day that are called socialism and paternalism." [14]

Similarly, the numbers prove that this wasn't a laissez-faire Court. The ratio of decisions for and against police-power cases found in Harlan's list— fifteen to three—was similar to the record of the Court as a whole. Charles Warren noted in 1913 that the handful of infamous decisions in which the Court struck down police power was vastly outnumbered by decisions in which such laws were upheld. [15] Laissez-faire judges would not have left such a record.

Despite Warren's figures, the power of the paternalist/laissez-faire cate-gories was such that it took some time for scholars to look more closely at the judges and their reasoning. One focus has been Justice Stephen J. Field, who sat on the Court from 1863 until 1897. True, Field was gone by the time of *Lochner*, but his long tenure allowed scholars of the progressive–New Deal tradition to lay part of the blame for *Lochner* at his feet. But Charles W. McCurdy has described Field's background as a Democratic Jacksonian sus-picious of legislation that granted special privileges to any particular class of people (shades of the Bank of the United States!). [16] Field worked out a clear set of rules limiting the power of government to promote or control eco-nomic activity; the public welfare, not the wishes of some interest group, de-termined what the state could do. So it was the much-vilified Field who wrote the decision that saved the lakefront of Chicago from being handed over to a railroad. Field declared that such an alienation of public property was outside the power of the state legislature.[17]

Instead of being either proponents of laissez-faire or proponents of paternalism, the judges in 1905 believed that they could draw a clear line between what was a reasonable exercise of the police power and what was not.[18] In *Lochner*, Peckham with his majority and Harlan with his fellow dissenters were merely disagreeing on where to draw that line. In most other instances, they all agreed. With this insight into nineteenth-century legal thought, the adjective "laissez-faire" may finally have been pried loose from its position in front of the noun "Court."[19]

Harlan, like Field, perceived clear constitutional limits on the state's police power, as we'll see later in this chapter, but there were differences between them. As a Whig turned Republican, Harlan relied ultimately on the providential Constitution and its Fourteenth Amendment, whereas Field, whose political sympathies were Democratic, harkened further back in time to the theory of natural rights. When the Court held in *Geer v. Connecticut* in 1896 that the residents of the state retained common ownership over its wild animals and might ban the killing of game intended for interstate commerce, Field waxed poetic in his dissent over "the trapper on the plains and the hunter in the north" who created property "according to the extent to which [the animals] are subjected by his labor or skill to his use and benefit."[20] Since Connecticut had not been in a state of nature for some time, Field ended by relying squarely on the interstate commerce clause. Harlan wrote only of that clause in his separate dissent. He had little to add to Field's analysis of it. Apparently, he wanted to distance himself from Field's fictional frontiersmen versed in John Locke's labor theory of value. Harlan preferred to rely on the Constitution and would not go beyond that. He didn't have to because he believed that God had had a hand in the Constitution's creation and that the Civil War amendments had constitutionalized the promise of equality found in the Declaration of Independence.

Harlan also differed from Field in his perception that something disturbing was happening to the late-nineteenth-century economy. Field continued to see the market as a place where artisans plied their trades and only government threatened their opportunities by trying to grant privileges to a special few.[21] Field insisted that the state alone could create a monopoly.[22]

Harlan, on the other hand, was convinced that businesspeople were creating monopolies by breaking the laws of free competition and that they threatened the welfare of the Union. He wrote his old friend Augustus Willson in 1905 that "the greatest injury to the integrity of our social organization comes from the enormous power of the corporations." He immediately added, "We must have corporations. We could not get along without them, but we must see they do not corrupt our government and institutions."[23] Bribing legislators for special privileges was a traditional form of corruption, but even more insidious were new business practices, such as the formation of trusts, that denied the average citizen the benefits of free competition.

In Harlan's 1910 list of decisions, we can trace a coherent legal vision. Harlan's constitutionalism drew on both Whig tradition and Republican innovation. The large number of opinions in favor of interstate commerce shows us how the Whig commitment to economic ties among the country's regions was reinvigorated by a new Republican desire to bind the wounded Union together. The interstate commerce clause was part of the original Constitution; the Thirteenth and Fourteenth Amendments were the source of new doctrines that also bound the nation together. The logic that led Harlan to champion civil rights under the amended Constitution guided his decisions on economic issues as well. Doctrines condemned as bald attempts to favor industrial capitalists, such as substantive due process and liberty of contract, represented something else to Harlan: the triumph of the Thirteenth and Fourteenth Amendments and the nationalism they required.

Harlan even expressed his fear of the political power of the new industrial magnates in the antebellum language of free labor ideology. When the Court struck down laws aimed at countering corporate power, Harlan wrote in angry dissents that the country was facing a peril as dangerous as slavery and a judicial error as great as *Dred Scott*. Harlan again used typology to understand a threat to the American mission. Now he seemed genuinely afraid for its success.

The second largest number of decisions on Harlan's list are decisions favoring interstate commerce. The interstate commerce clause was an essential feature of the Constitution designed to stop the states from discriminating against one another's goods as they had under the Articles of Confederation. Harlan had been brought up among Kentucky Whigs who believed that a national market would create general prosperity. They supported Henry Clay's plans for a national bank and internal improvements.[24] Clay's American System would encourage manufacturing by placing a high tariff on imported goods, and the sale of public lands would foster western farming.[25] Domestic manufacturers and farmers would supply each other. Harlan reminded Willson just before the turn of the century, "You know I am a firm believer in the principle of protection and I want such duties imposed as are essential to build up and sustain our industries of every kind and make us wholly independent of the world."[26] Independence from the world economy required that the states turn to one another. Economic nationalism could counter the local feeling that had proven almost fatal in the Civil War.[27] Harlan's favorite decisions on the interstate commerce clause condemned the economic localism that would have undermined this plan.[28]

Because the states might exercise their police powers in ways that had some effect on interstate commerce, the Supreme Court decided early in the nineteenth century that local regulation could affect such commerce as long as it did so indirectly and as long as Congress did not usurp the field with its own regulations.[29] The Court only dealt with the clause five times before 1840, but it became increasingly important as railroads webbed across the country, companies competed across state lines, and the states struck out at each other's corporations and products. The interstate commerce clause had come up a total of 213 times before the Court by 1898, and there were similar increases in other courts.[30]

Harlan's contemporaries noted the importance of the interstate commerce clause in preventing what they called "wars of commercial discrimination among the States."[31] Justice Samuel F. Miller predicted in 1889 that if "that clause were removed tomorrow, this Union would fall to pieces simply by reason of the struggles of each State to make the property owned in other States pay its expenses."[32] An 1898 treatise described the interstate commerce clause as "the peace-maker of the States, . . . perhaps not inaptly compared to the inch of timber which floats the ship, or the half inch of steel that guides the train."[33]

The oldest of Harlan's favorite majority opinions on the clause was *Guy v. Baltimore* in 1879. Here the city of Baltimore argued that a fee on boats carrying out-of-state goods was not an unreasonable charge for use of a wharf constructed at the expense of local taxpayers. Harlan struck it down on the "settled" grounds that "no State can . . . impose . . . more onerous public burdens or taxes" on out-of-state goods "than it imposes upon the like products of its own territory." The Court was not to be fooled by the term "wharfage fee," which was "a mere expedient or device to accomplish, by indirection, what the State could not accomplish by a direct tax, viz., build up its domestic commerce by means of unequal and oppressive burdens upon the industry and business of other States."[34]

In favorite decisions written ten years later, Harlan continued to object to such discrimination, even when the states pleaded that circumstances had changed. In one, the Minnesota legislature tried to pass off as a public health measure an 1889 law that forbade the sale of meat not inspected on the hoof, thus making it practically impossible for anyone to sell meat produced outside the state. Harlan explained to his law class, "The courts were not to be fooled by mere words, and we said in [*Minnesota v. Barber*], as we said in others, that while the state may take care of the public health and public morals and public safety, that may be the form, the mere form of legislative declaration, but the courts would look through the substance of things."[35]

The attorneys for the state had tipped their hand by declaring that "a powerful combine has thrown its gauntlet at the sovereignty of the States and is engaged in a grand duello with both State and nation."[36] This "gigantic moneyed interest" was composed of the Chicago-based meatpackers—Armour, Morris, Swift, and Hammond—who could undersell local packers by using refrigerated cars, economies of scale, and under-the-table railroad rebates.[37] Harlan did not even bother to respond to this complaint, which merely proved that the health benefits the legislature said would follow from the law were a ruse.[38]

Harlan's zeal for commercial nationalism is even more apparent in dissents missing from his list of favorites. When the Court allowed the legislature of North Carolina to put money left over from fees charged for the inspection of commercial fertilizers into the general fund of the state's Department of Agriculture, he dissented.[39] When the Court allowed Texas to bar the entry of livestock from Louisiana after anthrax broke out, he dissented.[40] When the Court allowed Louisiana to prohibit the entrance of boat passengers from quarantined towns in 1902, he joined a dissent.[41]

A majority opinion that did make it onto the list, *Reid v. Colorado* in 1902, indicates that Harlan would have liked owners to have the chance to prove the good health of their livestock. The Colorado law required that animals brought into the state during the sick season be held for ninety days before being sold. Since there was no proof that obeying the regulation entailed "serious embarrassment or unreasonable cost" and since Congress had "left a wide field for the exercise by the States of their power . . . to protect their domestic animals against contagious, infectious and communicable diseases," Harlan found for the state.[42] Perhaps he left the more zealous dissents off the list and included this one as an example of how the police power could be exercised without violating the interstate commerce clause.

Other favorite opinions of Harlan's promoted interstate commerce without invoking the clause. Some involved out-of-state or "foreign" corporations. People with growing businesses wanted to establish a physical presence throughout the Union, sometimes out of practical necessity, as in the case of railroads, and other times in order to compete more successfully against local producers.[43] The legal hurdle was that corporations, as the artificial creations of state charters, entered a state only with its permission. Some legal writers objected to the persistence of this doctrine because all corporations were "formed under similar conditions and complying with substantially similar standards."[44] Harlan seems to have shared this feeling. He acknowledged only grudgingly that foreign corporations entered a state by courtesy.

Harlan tried to make it possible for insurance companies to do business anywhere in the country. Before his arrival, the Court had decided that the sale of insurance policies was not commerce.[45] Cut loose from constitutional restraint, the state legislatures outdid themselves. A professor complained in 1906 of "fifty self-seeking state jurisdictions with conflicting statutes, retaliatory measures, 'hold-up' acts, fake examinations, and unequal if not exorbitant taxation."[46] In *Philadelphia Fire Association v. New York* in 1886, the Court decided that a retaliatory law in New York that taxed a Pennsylvania corporation at the same rate that Pennsylvania taxed New York companies did not violate the equal protection clause of the Fourteenth Amendment.[47] Harlan insisted in dissent that the Constitution required states to at least treat all foreign companies alike. If New York could tax every state's corporations differently, he warned, "such legislation would be a species of commercial warfare by one State against the others."[48]

Even as local officials tried to close their borders to outside competitors, they recognized that foreign companies whose presence was inevitable, such as railroads, telegraph companies, and express shipping companies, might be treated as cash cows.[49] As Harlan told his class in 1898, "one thing is absolutely certain, and that is that there is not a state in this union which would not, if it had the power, support its government from top to bottom by levying tribute or taxes upon the commerce among the states; they have all tried to do it."[50] All states had the power to tax their own corporations, but they wanted to tax foreign corporations working within their borders as well. The problem was how "to avoid the dilemma of goods escaping tax altogether or being subjected to the risk of multiple taxation," as Charles Fairman put it.[51] Property had to have a situs, that is, a single, specific place where it was legally located and taxable.[52] But as economist Edwin R. A. Seligman noted, the "complexities of modern industrial life" were such that "a man may live in one State, may own property in a second, and may carry on business in a third . . . or if he has invested in corporate securities, the corporation may be the creature of another State, and be situated or do business in a third."[53]

The Court did a bad job of sorting it all out. Seligman commented that the Court "has arrived at some very remarkable conclusions," and the writers of one treatise declared that "there is a conflict, both in the decisions and in the grounds upon which they rest."[54] Frederick N. Judson noted in his 1917 treatise that "the difficulty of defining the line where the State and Federal powers meet is illustrated by the frequent dissents in the court and the overruling of decisions by the same judges who pronounced them."[55] One legal scholar concluded in 1919 that the Supreme Court had allowed the "states to impose taxes that from an economic standpoint were levied more or less directly on receipts from interstate commerce" by indulging "in nominalism and conceptualism."[56]

The Court had to struggle with the ingenious taxing schemes of state legislators bent on avoiding constitutional objections. Some states taxed a proportion of real property, such as taxing the railroad cars according to the proportion of a company's track out of all track in the state. Others taxed gross receipts as a proportion of business done in their state. Some taxed companies' capital stock, which was very likely to be located outside their borders. Finally, states tried to tax a franchise to do business, a complete intangible, which they valued in a variety of ways. With rare exceptions, Harlan's position was that anything that came close to double taxation was unconstitutional.[57] He dissented many times when the Court approved state taxation formulas.[58]

Harlan listed two victories in his effort to prevent double taxation. One was *Western Union Telegraph Company v. State of Kansas ex rel. Coleman, Attorney General* in 1910, in which the state had tried to tax the capital stock of a foreign corporation and threatened it with the loss of in-state business if it failed to pay up. Harlan agreed with Western Union that the tax "strikes at the company's entire business wherever conducted and its property wherever located." "If every State should pass a statute similar to that enacted by Kansas," not only would the Court's decisions be nullified, but "the business of the country" would be "thrown into confusion."[59]

This seems to have been the end of unconditional requirements for the entry of foreign corporations. A treatise writer noted that after that time the courts no longer allowed the states to discriminate against foreign corporations.[60] They could now move through the Union under the rules that covered each state's own corporations.

Harlan also encouraged interstate commerce in municipal bond repudiation decisions. True, only one appears on his list of favorites, and such cases did not involve constitutional law, which is the focus of this chapter.[61] Indeed, their absence from the list reflects Harlan's concern for the Constitution. But municipal bond repudiation is worth discussing as an example of how Harlan could encourage trade among the states without invoking the interstate commerce clause itself. It can serve as a warm-up to my treatment of doctrines that appear more frequently on the list whose meaning for understanding Harlan's thought is something other than what is usually assigned.

In municipal bond cases, the townspeople who were trying to repudiate their debt portrayed themselves as the victims of eastern sharpsters, but they're better understood as failed capitalists. They had borrowed money to pay for improvements like railroads or waterworks in order to attract settlers —often small-time land speculators—who might otherwise choose another town.[62] When the economy collapsed, most residents moved out, leaving little to tax and no funds to pay back the money borrowed. Often the town would claim that it had no obligation to pay because the bonds had been issued illegally in the first place.

Harlan and the Court usually sided with the bondholders. Thus supported, the national market in local bonds grew enormously during the nineteenth century.[63] The populists saw these decisions as proof of the brethren's regional prejudice in favor of the East and class prejudice in favor of the wealthy.[64] Justice Miller wrote privately that the municipal bond decisions were "a farce whose result is invariably the same, namely to give more to those who have already, and to take away from those who have little, the little that they have."[65] Harlan was probably moved by his conviction that repudiation undermined commercial nationalism.[66] In a rare decision in which the Court sided with a town, he fretted in dissent that "a declaration by this court that such notes are void . . . will, we fear, produce incalculable mischief" in light of the "enormous" amounts of similar bonds in circulation.[67] A national market for local bonds could exist only if repudiation was controlled.

Harlan helped construct an elaborate set of rules to validate bonds as long as some law authorized their issue.[68] Buyers had to check only whether state constitutions or statutes authorized the issuance of bonds in the first place. These documents were relatively easy to come by, and the result was that buyers who hailed from the eastern part of the country could rely on the Court's upholding the value of bonds issued from the West. If city officials stated on the face of the bonds that all legal requirements for issue had been met (even if they hadn't been met), then the municipality was bound by those statements.[69] Harlan noted in the one municipal bond decision on his list that "these bonds would seem to have been prepared and issued in a manner that concealed their true character, and to mislead investors in that class of securities."[70] Harlan held that the bonds were valid and ordered the locals to pay up.

The victory of bondholders represented the triumph of nationalism over the forces of localism in more than one way. Such decisions represented the triumph of federal over state judges because the Court created its own rules for determining the validity of bonds and rejected the state judiciary's interpretations of state laws.[71]

Harlan listed this municipal bond decision and many other decisions in which he supported commerce among the states because he wanted us to appreciate his nationalism. He also listed several opinions approving the exercise of national power, opinions that otherwise wouldn't attract much attention. Their presence indicates the satisfaction he took in nationalism for its own sake.[72] Harlan wrote Taft in 1893 that "so ardent is our affection for the [local] Government that is closest to us by every day contact, that the National Government, from the time of the adoption of the Constitution, has been compelled to struggle all the time for the right to exercise powers actually granted to it by the Constitution."[73] The Civil War had proven to Harlan that it was the Union, not the states, whose existence was precarious.

The Civil War produced new constitutional language for Harlan to put to the same nationalist use. Earlier chapters have shown how Harlan interpreted the Fourteenth Amendment's effect on black rights. The amendment also affected economic issues, and there were connections between the two kinds of cases in Harlan's mind.

Harlan supported what came to be called substantive due process, one of the most condemned doctrines of the late nineteenth century. The guarantee of due process of law found in the Fifth Amendment required at the very least that all persons in the same situation be accorded the same procedural protections (one accused robber of post offices was supposed to be tried and sentenced in the same way as another). The doctrine of substantive due process under the Fourteenth Amendment required not only that the same procedures be followed by the states but also that the outcome of these procedures—that is, their substance—be fair. This allowed the Court to pass judgment on the rates that the states or their agencies ordered railroads to charge. If rates were set too low, the reasoning went, then the states were simply taking the railroads' property and giving it to their customers. It became the Court's job to make sure that they didn't.

Harlan's contribution to the doctrine's shape was a formula to judge the reasonableness of rates.[74] In *Smyth v. Ames*, an 1898 favorite, Harlan deduced from precedent three principles for judging a state's railroad-rate schedule: railroads were protected under the Fourteenth Amendment's due process and equal protection clauses; state action preventing a railroad from "earning such compensation as under all circumstances is just to it and to the public" violated those clauses; and it was up to the judiciary to decide when violations occurred. He admitted that the question of just compensation "could be more easily determined by a commission composed of persons whose special skill, observation and experience qualifies them to so handle great problems of transportation," but he had confidence in the judiciary's ability to do the job. He added with pride, "This function and duty of the judiciary distinguishes the American system from all other systems of government."[75]

Harlan seemed confident of his ability to dispense economic justice. He wrote that the roads' contention "that a railroad company is entitled to exact such charges for transportation as will enable it, at all times, not only to pay operating expenses, but also to meet the interest regularly accruing upon all its outstanding obligations, and justify a dividend upon all its stock" was a "misconception of the relations between the public and a railroad corporation" because it made "the interests of the corporation . . . the sole test" of the reasonableness of rates. The public's interest had to be considered as well. How were reasonable rates to be arrived at? Although this was "an embarrassing question" in practice, Harlan had some suggestions on how to value fairly the property being used by the public, including "the original cost of construction, the amount expended in permanent improvements, the amount and market value of its bonds and stock, the present as compared with the original cost of construction, the probable earning capacity of the property under particular rates prescribed by statute, and the sum required to meet operating expenses."[76] This list did not exhaust the possibilities.[77]

Scholars working out of the progressive–New Deal tradition have heaped contempt on substantive due process and Harlan's fair-value formula. Charles Fairman argued in 1953 that rate regulation was not a job for the courts because it was too complex and because they had no authority to second-guess the state legislatures on something that was a policy question.[78] Clinton Rossitor in 1971 called the doctrine part of the "Great Train Robbery of American Intellectual History" whereby champions of laissez-faire prevented the states from controlling the roads that monopolized the country's shipping.[79] Carl B. Swisher, Justice Field's early biographer, characterized the doctrine as "another instance where a function of great responsibility was taken out of the hands of the representatives of the people by an irresponsible body, or by a body responsible only to its own interpretation of the law, which is much the same thing."[80] Harlan went along with substantive due process because of his "want of analytical power," according to William Winslow Crosskey.[81] More recently, Harlan's fair-value formula has been criticized as vague or circular on the grounds that a railroad's value is determined by the rates it can charge.[82]

The defense of the doctrine began early on but gained power as the progressive–New Deal critique of the Court proved inadequate. Edwin S. Corwin noted in 1911 that a notion of vested rights—that is, rights that a legislature could not disturb—was voiced well before the Civil War because of "a feeling on the part of judges that to leave the legislature free to pass arbitrary or harsh laws, so long as all the formalities be observed in enforcing such laws, were to yield the substance while contending for the shadow."[83] Other scholars argue that the idea that some rights lay beyond the power of government is reflected in the language of state constitutions echoing the Declaration of Independence and was voiced by abolitionists who relied on natural-rights theory to make their case against slavery.[84] According to a biographer of Chief Justice Morrison R. Waite, who served from 1874 to 1888, "From the very beginning, *all* of the justices regarded due process as furnishing protection against any purely arbitrary actions by government, irrespective of whether the arbitrary act occurred in a trial or in the regulation of property."[85]

As for Harlan's fair-value formula, it wasn't circular, according to Stephen A. Siegel, because everyone involved understood his meaning: "Railroads and utilities were entitled to an equivalent of competitive market returns — morally and politically justified profits — not returns attributable to their monopolistic and legally privileged positions."[86] Harlan's talk of considering the public's and the corporation's interests fit into this general understanding.

As the first part of this chapter made clear, I believe that Harlan's interest in the free flow of commerce among the states prompted many of the choices on his list of favorites. But if we want to understand the particular appeal of a substantive interpretation of the Fourteenth Amendment's due process clause, we need to pay attention to his first encounter with it. This occurred in 1873 when the Court had its first crack at interpreting the Fourteenth Amendment and Harlan was a Kentucky lawyer who had recently been doing some work for the government.

In the *Slaughter-House Cases* in April 1873, the Court considered a Louisiana statute that created a butchering monopoly in the city of New Orleans on the grounds of public health.[87] Former butchers complained that the law abridged their privileges and immunities and deprived them of their liberty and property without due process of law in violation of the Fourteenth Amendment's protections. Writing for the majority, Justice Miller sounded annoyed at the idea that the amendment had any other purpose than the protection of the rights of ex-slaves, and he defined even those rights in the most limited way so as not to "radically [change] the whole theory of the relations of the State and Federal governments to each other and of both these governments to the people."[88] He drew a distinction between state and national citizenship and identified civil rights as primarily a concern of the states rather than the national government. So narrow was Miller's interpretation that one historian accuses him of trying to "repeal" the Fourteenth Amendment "through emasculation."[89]

The dissenting justices responded that the Fourteenth Amendment *had* radically changed the relationship between the states and the national government. Justice Noah H. Swayne saw it as "a new Magna Carta."[90] According to Justice Field, Miller's misinterpretation made the Fourteenth Amendment into "a vain and idle enactment, which accomplished nothing, and most unnecessarily excited Congress and the people on its passage."[91] Granting a monopoly was exactly the kind of abuse of governmental power that Jacksonians had condemned. Denying a butcher his right to labor smacked of the feudalism that the English had finally thrown off and that the American colonists had despised.[92] Field cited Adam Smith (the great eighteenth-century opponent of English mercantilism) in support of his declaration that "the right of free labor" was "one of the most sacred and imprescriptible rights of man."[93] His rhetoric dovetailed with the free labor ideology that had become central to the Republican Party's antislavery effort.[94] Whereas Field relied on the privileges and immunities clause of the Fourteenth Amendment, Justice Joseph P. Bradley emphasized the due process clause. He rejected Miller's citizenship priorities: the adoption of the Fourteenth Amendment *had* made the American "primarily a citizen of the United States, and, secondarily, a citizen of the State where he resides."[95] He defined privileges and immunities as those rights contained in the national Bill of Rights, including the due process clause.[96]

Benjamin H. Bristow wrote Harlan in early May for his reaction. Bristow thought Miller had "frittered away much of [the Fourteenth Amendment's] true value" through his narrow construction. If Miller was right, then "indeed was the late war fought solely for the benefit of Sambo, and all the work of reconstruction has been in his interest." But Reconstruction had a larger purpose in his mind. Bristow was "disposed to deal out favors & benefits, liberally enough to the 'nigger,' but I am not prepared to admit that the white man is not equally entitled to the 'protection of law,' & to the 'privileges & immunities,' secured by the XIV Amendment." Bristow may have been thinking of the white Union men of Kentucky who had been terrorized by ex-Confederates after the war. He may also have been thinking back to the cause they had fought for. To leave civil rights in the hands of the states was to lose the war after the fact. Bristow condemned Miller's version of dual citizenship as "without solid foundation" and "unworthy of Miller's broad & large mind." He ended with the request, "Let me hear what you think of Miller's opinion."[97] But there is no reply among Harlan's papers.

Still, we can guess what he thought. Harlan had fought for the Union and condemned the Ku Klux Klan violence after the war. He may have been as concerned as Bristow over the rights of white men, but consider his situation in April 1873 when the decision was handed down. He had been appointed in

February to help with government prosecutions under the Enforcement Acts of 1870 and 1871.[98] In February and March, he was busy prosecuting white men from Lexington for denying black men the right to vote.[99] He and Bristow discussed the difficulty of getting the circuit judge to take on "men occupying the so-called high social positions that these Lexington Rebels do." [100] Bristow counseled Harlan to wait until Swayne came out to ride circuit. So, at the very time that the Court handed down *Slaughter-House*, Harlan was trying to enforce a law that defined citizenship as primarily national and was waiting for a judge who was willing to help him do it. He wouldn't have approved of a decision that rendered national citizenship virtually meaningless, even if it was white butchers who brought up the question.

When a majority of the Court decided in 1890 that the due process clause of the Fourteenth Amendment guaranteed substantive rights against state action, Harlan was there to witness it.[101] *Chicago, Milwaukee, and St. Paul Railway Company v. Minnesota* turned on neither black civil rights nor white men's right to labor. Instead, the question was whether the state had the power to endow its railroad commission with final say over the rates a road could charge. Justice Samuel Blatchford wrote for the Court that the law was unconstitutional because "it deprives the [railroad] company of its right to a judicial investigation, by due process of law, under the forms and with the machinery provided by the wisdom of successive ages for the investigation judicially of the truth of a matter in controversy." Justice Bradley, who had urged the substantive reading of due process in *Slaughter-House*, thought the Court was wrong to apply it here. He dissented, accompanied by several others, on the grounds that determining the reasonableness of rates was "a legislative question" not open to judicial review.[102]

Harlan was part of the majority in *Chicago, Milwaukee, and St. Paul* and went on to deliver *Smyth v. Ames* and its fair-value formula eight years later and then to place it on his list of favorites in 1910 to indicate his satisfaction with the doctrine. He listed two other decisions supporting substantive due process as well. Because it was a long time from *Slaughter-House* in 1873 to *Smyth* in 1898 and a long way from prosecuting ex-Rebels to working out a formula for reasonable railroad rates, I want to turn to a related doctrine to strengthen my explanation for Harlan's support of substantive due process: nationalization of the Bill of Rights. For Harlan, both doctrines were the logical consequence of the constitutional rebirth of the Union signaled by the Fourteenth Amendment. Harlan listed three decisions supporting each of these doctrines, and the conceptual connections between them should become plain.

Originally, the Bill of Rights applied only to the national government. When the Fourteenth Amendment was passed, there was some talk that its due process clause might apply the Bill of Rights to the states, but eighteenth-century rules of constitutional draftsmanship worked against this. The Fifth Amendment has its own due process clause, which implies that the protections listed in the other original amendments making up the Bill of Rights—such as a grand jury indictment for capital crimes and freedom of the press—are not covered by the phrase "due process of law."[103]

On the other hand, nineteenth-century oratorical style allowed repetition for emphasis, and the congressional Republicans who wrote the amendment might have seen a need to repeat themselves. They thought that they had endowed blacks with civil rights when they emancipated them with the Thirteenth Amendment. But then southern white men passed the black codes. So Congress passed the Civil Rights Act of 1866 and then wrote the Fourteenth Amendment to make sure that the act was constitutional. The whole first section of the amendment reads as variations on a theme repeated in the face of creative opposition.

Whether or not Harlan read the intentions of the drafters of the amendment correctly (and there is a debate on that), he argued that the Fourteenth Amendment renewed the vision of the founding fathers by creating a national standard of rights. Due process became the key to this renewal. Harlan told his law class in 1898 that due process "is not any process that the state chooses to call due process of law because that would make the will of the state final and conclusive." It was up to judges to decide, and they were to look to "what was due process of law at the time when the Constitution was adopted."[104] Harlan explained that "there are some things that we know are not due process of law. There are some things that we know are due process of law, but there is a middle ground between these two, and you are not able to decide." He warned his students that they would "never hear the last of that phrase as long as this is a free country because there are varying circumstances arising and the judges are put to their wits' ends to know whether this, that or the other act transcends the provision of the constitution."[105] The open-endedness of this remark belies Harlan's own practice. When pushed to *his* wits' end, Harlan drew from the Bill of Rights. Every example of due process he offered to his students is found there.[106]

Harlan first voiced the idea of applying the Bill of Rights to the states in his dissent from *Hurtado v. People of California* in 1884, a favorite. Here the Court allowed California to eliminate an indictment by grand jury for capital crimes, a protection found in the Fifth Amendment. Even Justice Stanley Matthews, who spoke for the Court, preferred not to simply invoke the rules of constitutional draftsmanship because that would mean that *no* specific protection in the Bill of Rights was required by due process. Matthews argued instead that due process signified certain fundamental rights that might be protected by "any legal proceeding enforced by public authority, whether sanctioned by age and custom, or newly devised in the discretion of legislative power," as long as it was not partial or arbitrary.[107] Hurtado's prosecution on information filed by the district attorney satisfied due process. That grand jury indictment for capital offenses was a traditional Anglo-American procedure held little weight. Matthews argued, "It is more consonant to the true philosophy of our historical legal institutions to say that the spirit of personal liberty and individual right, which they embodied, was preserved and developed by a progressive growth and wise adaptation to new circumstances and situations of the forms and processes found fit to give, from time to time, new expression and greater effect to modern ideas of self-government."[108] The past could not dictate which liberties were essential in an evolving society.

For Harlan, change occurred in republican history only as a fulfillment of the fathers' plan. If one followed the reasoning of the Court, theoretically none of the specific guarantees of the Bill of Rights were required for due process. Nothing might stop a state from "dispensing with petit juries in criminal cases, and permitting a person charged with a crime involving life to be tried before a single judge, or even a justice of the peace, upon a rule to show cause why he should not be hanged."[109] To Harlan, such alterations of the founders' blueprint were a gross error. It was not merely Hurtado's rights that were at stake but the jury system itself. Harlan feared for the people's traditional role in the administration of justice.

Harlan objected to prosecution on information because it ended popular participation. As Harlan explained to his students, the grand jury "is a given number of men selected by ballot or some impartial mode who come from the whole county, different parts of the county, generally men of the first standing in their neighborhood." These men "come together to inquire whether any crime has been committed in that county since the last term of the court."[110] These citizens have no special legal training. The grand jury is an exercise in republican government; the grand jurors are of the people, and they are the best the people have to offer.

Harlan described prosecution by information. "An information filed by the District Attorney is this," he explained. "He steps into the court and he files the information charging John Jones with the crime of murder. He does that on his own responsibility."[111] So the district attorney did not have to consult with the people before beginning a prosecution on information. In California, criminal prosecutions had been placed in the hands of an expert qualified for the position by legal training, which was exactly why some lawyers liked it.

A significant portion of the bar wanted to do away with the jury system during Harlan's time on the bench. Open any law review from the 1880s onward and you are likely to find an article arguing that the average male citizen was too stupid or too distracted or too prejudiced to do justice. "Book men and learned professors" thought "that a petit jury is a nuisance," Harlan told his class sarcastically.[112] A less-educated group of critics, "men who never read the constitution and never read anything else much," according to Harlan, complained that "there are too many delays in the administration of the criminal laws, and the courts often reverse judgments in criminal cases." He parodied their idea of criminal due process: "End the matter; put this fellow out of the way; if he wasn't guilty he would not be charged; must not have these delays; let some one man decide and end it; if he has to be hung, let him be hung and get it over quick." Such "is the feeling of some," Harlan told his students, but "that is not the idea of the constitution."[113]

Such critics failed to appreciate the essence of republican government enshrined in the Bill of Rights' jury guarantees. "Nothing is more sublime," Harlan once told a reporter, than a jury trial.[114] He invited his law students to "go out into the country among the plain people, walk into a country court-house while the court is being held." This is what they would find: "It is not a rich country. There are no rich people about there. They are all plain people of moderate means, but it is court time and you walk into that court-house and see one man sitting on a bench, the court-house crowded, probably some great case being argued, some great lawyer about to make a speech, a case interesting the public, and the court-house is packed." For Harlan, a jury trial was both a glorious ritual and a concrete expression of republicanism. He tried to convey its significance to his students: "The word of that one man brings that crowd to silence. . . . That one man opens his mouth to talk to that jury, to instruct them as to the case, and that crowd of several hundred people are sitting as quietly as if they were in church, listening to what is being said. It is the majesty of the law." Who were the members of the jury? "Most of them are men of ordinary means and ordinary station." Their very plainness recommended them. The people listening in the courtroom were satisfied with their verdict, and most important, so were the twelve: "The community accepts it, but what do those twelve men feel? Why they go back to their farms in the country with a recognition of the fact that they are part and parcel of the Government under which they live."[115] Harlan repeatedly described juries as making the people part and parcel of the government under which they lived. By placing the jury system in the Bill of Rights, the founders had elevated the plain people to a position of power.

Fulfillment of the founders' plan was the only direction change might take, according to Harlan. The Fourteenth Amendment's due process clause fulfilled their plan by applying the Bill of Rights to the states. It made a more perfect union by nationalizing the Constitution's standard of rights. When the Court reaffirmed its *Hurtado* decision in *Maxwell v. Dow* in 1900 by allowing a jury of eight instead of a jury of twelve for a capital crime, Harlan dissented. He listed *Maxwell* as a favorite dissent and did the same with *Twining v. New Jersey*, in which the Court refused to apply the Fifth Amendment's protection from self-incrimination to the states in 1908.[116]

Like nationalization of the Bill of Rights, the doctrine of substantive due process fits into Harlan's understanding of the Fourteenth Amendment's transformative power. Although Howard Jay Graham has argued that "substantivized due process is essentially constitutionalized natural law," we don't have to reach that far back in theory to explain Harlan's support for it.[117] As I noted earlier, Harlan used only examples from the Bill of Rights in describing due process to his students. Substantive due process was a way of making the states abide by the Fifth Amendment's guarantee that no private property can be taken for public use without just compensation.[118] The three decisions on substantive due process that Harlan listed as favorites acknowledged this. All were opinions for the Court.

In *Covington and Lexington Turnpike Road Company v. Sandford* in 1896, Harlan announced that allowing turnpike rates to be set so low that the company was working for free would be like allowing the state to take property for public use without requiring it to pay for it.[119] Similarly, in *Smyth v. Ames* in 1898, Harlan held that the question of whether railroad rates "are so unreasonably low as to deprive the carrier of its property without such compensation as the Constitution secures, and therefore without due process of law," was a judicial one.[120] But it was in another favorite, *Chicago, Burlington, and Quincy Railroad Company v. Chicago* in 1897, that Harlan was most explicit. He questioned "whether the due process of law enjoined by the Fourteenth Amendment required compensation to be made or adequately secured to the owner of private property taken for public use under the authority of a State." Here were all of the elements of the Fifth Amendment's eminent domain clause. After considering precedent and constitutional law treatises (including Joseph Story's), Harlan concluded that the Fourteenth Amendment did stipulate compensation. "The mere form of the proceeding against the owner . . . cannot convert the process used into due process of law, if the necessary result be to deprive him of his property without compensation." [121]

The Court's rulings on substantive due process amounted to the nationalization of one particular clause found in the Bill of Rights, but Harlan's favorites on other clauses were dissents. He noted the discrepancy between his success in *Chicago, Burlington, and Quincy* and his failure in *Maxwell v.*

*Dow.* He scolded his colleagues: "It would seem that the protection of private property is of more consequence than the protection of the life and liberty of the citizen."[122] Harlan's constitutional nationalism valued both protections because the Bill of Rights did. The Fourteenth Amendment was supposed to fulfill the plan left by the founders.

Harlan's support for liberty of contract can be explained in the same way. It was a doctrine much vilified at the turn of the century and by historians of the progressive–New Deal tradition, but it has been more recently defended by revisionists who have identified its origins in antebellum beliefs. It is also a doctrine that would have particular appeal to Harlan, and it shows up in a variety of decisions on his list of favorites—some dealing with economic questions and some with civil rights. In fact, it is the overlap of issues that deserves our attention.

*Lochner v. New York* is the most infamous of the liberty of contract decisions. As I explained earlier, Harlan dissented from it. He was convinced of the appropriateness of state legislation by descriptions of the poor working conditions of bakers. The state could exercise its police power in this instance without violating the Fourteenth Amendment. Harlan put *Lochner* on his list.

Harlan also listed his majority opinion in *Adair v. United States* in 1908, in which the Court struck down a federal law as a violation of the liberty of contract protected by the due process clause of the Fifth Amendment. The law was part of the Erdman Act, passed in reaction to the Pullman strike of 1894, which had paralyzed the country's railroad system. The idea was to lessen the possibility of strikes by prohibiting the railroads from firing workers on interstate lines for joining unions. Here Harlan acknowledged that the justices had disagreed in *Lochner*, but "there was no disagreement as to the general proposition that there is a liberty of contract which cannot be unreasonably interfered with by legislation." Congress had passed the Erdman Act under its power to regulate interstate commerce, but "what possible legal or logical connection is there between an employee's membership in a labor organization and the carrying on of interstate commerce?"[123] The dissenters answered his question. Employers who fired workers for joining a union might provoke a strike so widespread that interstate commerce would come to a stop. Justice Joseph McKenna stressed that the act provided for arbitration between unions and employers in order to prevent such shutdowns. Justice Holmes argued that unions were at least as important to interstate commerce as safety couplings on railroad cars, which Congress had required and the Court allowed. For Harlan, though, the links were too vague whereas the right of liberty of contract was compelling.

The next year, Roscoe Pound, a professor of law at the University of Chicago who was destined to become the dean of the Law School at Harvard University, published a famous article entitled "Liberty of Contract." Pound tried to explain why judges persisted in voicing the fallacy that—here he quoted Harlan in *Adair*—"the right of the employee to quit the service of the employer, for whatever reason, is the same as the right of the employer, for whatever reason, to dispense with the services of such employee. . . . In all such particulars the employer and the employee have equality of right." [124] Pound listed the reasons why such an idea had survived despite the fact that large corporations now dictated the terms of employment. He blamed "an individualist conception of justice" that preferred a laissez-faire policy and "a mechanical jurisprudence" or formalism "in which conceptions are developed logically at the expense of practical results." [125] These judges stuck to an eighteenth-century antifeudal, antimercantilist philosophy designed to free people to compete in the marketplace. The natural-rights origins of the Bill of Rights encouraged this way of thinking. Pound's critique led the way for the progressive–New Deal school's view of the Court. Harlan was being artificial, academic, impractical, and mechanistic in his reasoning. Or was he?

Harlan *was* a legal formalist who believed that there were set rules for interpretation of the laws and that the Constitution enshrined certain individual rights that no government might violate. But Pound missed the mark by a century in trying to identify the specific impulse for including liberty of contract among those sacred rights. Slavery appeared in Pound's article only as a theoretical issue, but to Harlan it was a practical matter.[126] The Thirteenth and Fourteenth Amendments granted black men the right to liberty of contract. The free labor ideology that Harlan adopted after the Civil War infused his understanding of contract. When Harlan wrote in *Adair* that "it is not within the functions of government—at least in the absence of contract between the parties—to compel any person in the course of his business and against his will to accept or retain the personal services of another, or to compel any person, against his will, to perform personal service for another," he was repeating a lesson he had learned over the course of his political career.[127] The Civil War amendments meant that no one could be forced to labor; instead, all men were now free to contract to labor.[128]

In other decisions found on Harlan's list, the free labor origins of the doctrine of liberty of contract become even clearer. In 1906, Harlan dissented from *Hodges v. United States*, in which the Court decided that a group of whites who had forced black men from their jobs (thus forcing them to break their contracts) could not be prosecuted for violating the Thirteenth Amendment. (In keeping with the state-action doctrine, the Court had found the

Fourteenth Amendment's protections inapplicable.) The wrong done these men, according to the Court, did not amount to slavery, so the federal courts had no jurisdiction. To Harlan, the liberty to make a contract was essential to the positive state of freedom, and he cited as precedent, of all things, the *Civil Rights Cases.* In that decision, Justice Bradley, who was taking pains to show that segregated public accommodations were not a badge or incident of slavery, listed some things that were, including the "disability . . . *to make contracts.*" [129] Since not being able to contract was part of slavery, being able to contract was part of freedom. Forcing a man to break his labor contract was like binding him in peonage, wrote Harlan in his *Hodges* dissent, because "in each case his will is enslaved, because illegally subjected, by a combination that he cannot resist, to the will of others in respect of matters which a freeman is entitled to control in such way as to him seems best." [130] Similarly, when Harlan argued in *Berea College v. Commonwealth of Kentucky* that the Court should strike down a law barring the teaching of black and white students in the same classroom, he cited *Adair* in defense of the freedom to teach.

The most dramatic example on Harlan's list of free labor ideas at work is his dissent from *Robertson v. Baldwin* in 1897. Robertson was a sailor who jumped ship, and Baldwin was the U.S. marshal who delivered him back to his captain. Robertson complained that the federal law authorizing his arrest violated the Thirteenth Amendment's prohibition on slavery and involuntary servitude. His case was weak because traditionally sailors had been forced by law to perform their labor contracts instead of simply being made liable for monetary damages for nonperformance as other contractors were. This made captains' lives easier and sailors' lives harder. Harlan threw aside the Court's citations to several thousand years of maritime law on the grounds that the "enactments of ancient times [including the mutilation and starvation of runaways], enforced by or under governments possessing arbitrary power," could not determine the law of "this free land." These sailors had been "seized, somewhat as runaway slaves were in the days of slavery, and committed to jail without bail." [131] The situation reminded him of those "former days" when "overseers could stand with whip in hand over slaves, and force them to perform personal service for their masters." Thanks to the Court's opinion, "we may now look for advertisements, not for runaway servants as in the days of slavery, but for runaway seamen." [132] According to Harlan, the Civil War amendments signaled a break with this past. Free labor was the rule for adult men.

Harlan's warning in *Robertson* that "a similar rule may be prescribed as to employees upon railroads and steamboats engaged in commerce among the States" was not that far-fetched. [133] An earlier decision, *Arthur v. Oakes,* that isn't on Harlan's list because he decided it while sitting circuit shows the practical application of free labor ideology in industrial settings. During the Pullman strike, one of Harlan's circuit judges held that it was illegal for a union to organize a strike.[134] In a decision that attracted national attention, Harlan pointed out that the Thirteenth Amendment bars a court from ordering one person to perform personal service for another.[135] Free labor ideology, born of the antebellum fight over slavery, survived Reconstruction and lived into the turn of the century as liberty of contract. Industrialization changed its surroundings but not its relevance.[136]

In fact, free labor ideas came into play unnervingly in the late nineteenth and early twentieth centuries in decisions found on Harlan's list. I say unnervingly because a key component of the antislavery thought of the early Republican Party was that slaveholders had organized a slave power conspiracy in order to thwart the founders' wish for eventual emancipation.[137] Just as Harlan had adopted the story of the founders as would-be abolitionists, so he had come to believe in a conspiracy against liberty by slaveholders. As the country industrialized at an unprecedented rate and corporations and financiers gained enormous political and economic power, Harlan saw them as posing a similar threat. He also feared that the Court was playing the same sorry role it had played when it decided *Dred Scott* and capitulated to the slave power.

Slaveholders were villains in part because they refused to labor themselves. Just who made up the virtuous laboring classes of the antebellum North depended on who was talking. The male mechanics and artisans of New York City, for example, believed that only men like themselves qualified. But their masters, middle-class merchants, and professionals also called themselves laboring men. This allowed them not only to rank themselves among the deserving but also to defuse hostility between the classes.[138] Henry Clay's American System was based on the belief that there was a "harmony of interests" among the classes.[139] The protective tariff that helped American manufacturers, for example, would prevent American wages from sinking to the low levels of European wages.[140] In the late nineteenth century, members of all classes continued to claim that they were workers.[141] Even the Knights of Labor welcomed middle-class professionals, although they made a point of excluding lawyers.[142]

*Pollock v. Farmers' Loan and Trust Company (II)* of 1895, a dissent found on Harlan's list of favorites, can serve as a starting point for explaining how he altered free labor ideology to include his own often-maligned profession, applied it to the industrialized age, and identified a new threat to the Union.

The income tax was part of a revenue bill that aimed at redistributing the burden of federal taxation. Up until then, it had fallen most heavily on consumption.[143] Then the Panic of 1893 provoked an economic depression that lasted for four years and prompted congressmen to do something to provide relief and to save themselves and the system from more radical change.[144] Publicity about inequities in wealth paved the bill's way.[145] The bill laid a 2 percent tax on incomes of over $4,000 and exempted charitable, religious, and educational corporations, mutual insurance companies, and mutual banks. After a bitter congressional debate, the Democrats of the agrarian South and West supported the bill, whereas Republicans representing the industrial Northeast opposed it.[146] Once passed, it attracted a firestorm of criticism from the conservative press. The law came before the Supreme Court in *Pollock v. Farmers' Loan and Trust Company*, which was heard twice by the Court in 1895. Both times Harlan dissented.[147]

Several conservative newspapers accused Harlan of acting like a Populist politician when he delivered his dissent in Court.[148] One commented that his sarcasm threw his listeners "into a state of very undignified hilarity."[149] A friendly witness noted his emotion. After a quiet and restrained beginning, "the florid face, hitherto pale, assuming its natural color, reddened even to the high crown of the big bald head; pent up indignation burst its bounds and dominated the man; the judge seemed lost in the statesman and patriot, and thenceforth to the end the tone and manner and gesture even were those of indignant advocacy and fervent protest."[150] Harlan admitted in private the depth of his feeling but denied that he had acted out of turn. He confided to Augustus Willson, "I feel more strongly about this recent decision than any which ever emanated from this court."[151] He insisted that he had not shaken his finger in the face of the chief justice or glared at anyone on the bench, as some reporters had written. He admitted only to turning to confront Justice Field, who was making rude remarks under his breath. Harlan was sure that it was not his tone but his message that "cut to the quick some that held contrary views." The newspaper criticisms were "not because of any harshness of words used by me, but because of the exposure of the dangers that would follow the decision of the court."[152]

The decision turned on whether a tax on the income from personal property and real estate was a direct tax. If it was, it had to be apportioned among the states according to their populations, according to the Constitution. Justice Fuller held for the majority that it was a direct tax, although he admitted that this decision would have a weird effect. Either a rich taxpayer in a wealthy state would pay less than a rich taxpayer in a relatively poor state (there being fewer rich taxpayers to share the burden), or the state would tax the whole population for its portion instead of taxing the wealthy few. Neither option was what Congress had had in mind, and scholars have criticized the decision.[153]

Justices Edward D. White and Harlan pointed out in their dissent that an income tax was not a direct tax according to precedent.[154] Harlan was particularly disturbed by Fuller's dismissal of the federal income tax passed during the Civil War as an emergency measure and his implication that it was unconstitutional.[155] "The supremacy of the nation was reestablished against armed rebellion seeking to destroy its life," Harlan wrote, "but, it seems, that the consummation, so devoutly wished, and to effect which so many valuable lives were sacrificed, was attended with a disregard of the Constitution by which the Union was ordained." [156] Harlan turned Fuller's logic on its head: the founders gave the national government broad taxing powers because they knew wars were inevitable. In his letter to Willson, Harlan wrote that in wartime "all imports would cease," and the federal government would have to turn to an income tax.[157]

The Civil War served as a type for the present controversy in Harlan's eyes, but the main roles were taken by different actors. Harlan refused to acknowledge the sectional appeal and effect of the tax. The battle was not between the different sections but between the plain people and the wealthy.[158] If the income tax had to be apportioned, a state could choose to tax all of its people to pay for levies for which only the wealthy few should be liable. Those who worked for a living would be paying for those who lived off of their investments.

Harlan's description of the inhabitants of "the large cities or financial centres" in terms of taxable classifications was a variation on what Daniel T. Rodgers calls one of industrial America's most vital legends—"the fable of the drones who slipped into the busy, contented hive and found a way to live off the fruits of someone else's labor." [159] Free labor ideology had identified the slaveholders as drones; now Harlan had found others. These ideas were broadly shared. Slavery was the "master metaphor for inequality" for nineteenth-century Americans.[160] Henry Demarest Lloyd voiced his criticisms of big business by echoing Abraham Lincoln: "As true as that a house divided against itself cannot stand, and that a nation half slave and half free cannot permanently endure, is it true that a people who are slaves to market-tyrants will surely come to be their slaves in all else." [161] Labor leader Eugene Debs used the same metaphor.[162] The populists of the West saw themselves "as the new abolitionists." [163] Woman's rights advocates likened married women's inferior legal status to slavery.[164]

Harlan laid out his version of the fable of the drones in his dissent. "In the large cities or financial centres of the country there are persons deriving enormous incomes from the renting of houses that have been erected, not to be occupied by the owner, but for the sole purpose of being rented." This class was joined by the forces of industrial capitalism: "other persons, trusts, combinations, and corporations, possessing vast quantities of personal property, including bonds and stocks of railroad, telegraph, mining, telephone, banking, coal, oil, gas, and sugar-refining corporations, from which millions upon millions of income are regularly derived."[165] All of these industries were monopolized.

Harlan wrote of his loathing for this class in private letters. Railroad tycoon C. P. Huntington was "one of the monster swindlers of this age of money getting," he told his sons. He damned Russell Sage, an associate of financier Jay Gould, as an "unmitigated scamp who loves money more than he does all else on earth." Sage "cannot appreciate or will not appreciate that anything is entitled to consideration in our government except what the opinion of the court calls invested personal property."[166] The wealthy had long been civilly irresponsible. "The fact is the wealth of the country has for years evaded the payment of its fair share of taxes," he confided to Willson. "It is a curious fact in my experience that I never knew a *very* rich man who was not astute in attempting to evade the payment of his proper share of taxes. Those whose *business* in life is to clip coupons from bonds as a general rule are indignant at the thought of their being required to pay taxes."[167]

The tax burden had fallen on other people for too long, according to Harlan's dissent. These were people who owned "neither real estate, nor invested personal property, nor bonds, nor stocks of any kind, and whose entire income arises from the skill and industry displayed by them in particular callings, trades, or professions, or from the labor of their hands, or the use of their brains." These were apparently the plain people. The majority opinion meant the tax burden would fall on "the merchant, the artisan, the workman, the artist, the author, the lawyer, the physician, even the minister of the Gospel, no one of whom happens to own real estate, invested personal property, stocks or bonds."[168] In Harlan's view, the working class, the middle class, and professionals shared a common interest.

In listing the lawyer alongside the artisan and the workman, Harlan ignored the immense differences in income between them. At this point, he was making $10,000 a year as an associate justice, and it was well known that some successful lawyers turned down judgeships because they would mean a substantial drop in their income. Meanwhile, in the early 1890s, laborers averaged $1.39 a day, and factory workers $1.53 a day when they could get work.[169] By grouping lawyers with workmen, Harlan also defied an antilawyer strain in popular American thought dating back to colonial times.[170] Lawyers were viewed during the Gilded Age as tools of the financial and industrial tycoons who amassed absurd amounts of wealth while many people suffered in poverty.[171]

In the eyes of their toughest critics, they were parasites growing fat off of the body politic.[172] Lawyers do feed off of trouble in an adversarial system. Harlan's older brother James welcomed the prospect of his Oklahoma homesteading clients coming into "constant collision" with cattlemen.[173] Was it any wonder that lawyers were accused of making trouble?

In private writings and public speeches, Harlan defended lawyers as workingmen, in fact, as men whose work was essential to the administration of justice. "Every man, no matter how bad he is, or what he may have done," Harlan wrote his son John Maynard in 1894, urging him to take labor leader Eugene Debs on as a client, "is entitled to a lawyer, when he is called into a court." Harlan summed up: "The function of a lawyer is to assist the court." This was how justice was served. "The harder lawyers fight for their clients, keeping within the bounds of decency & integrity, the more certain it is that the court will understand the case & reach correct conclusions."[174] Many elite New York City lawyers, some of them implicated in the worst Gilded Age scandals, went a step further. They worked for legal reform in order to ensure that they would indeed serve the courts. They reasoned that "if legal rights could be made *certain* and procedurally *effective*, the advantages accruing from illegitimate tactics would simply disappear, and lawyers could keep their clients within the law."[175] Harlan's account relied on simple virtue.

Lawyers worked not so much for money as for the glory of serving the Republic. Harlan joined in the general condemnation of inherited wealth and applied it specifically to lawyers. He explained to a group of law students that boys born to riches sank into lethargy. Such young men "manage in some way, 'by hook or crook,' to obtain a license to practice law, and then open up an office. But that is the beginning and the end of their professional career." They were mere idlers. "Their ambition seems to be satisfied," Harlan continued, "if only they can become a member of some lazy club, lead a 'German' [cotillion], own a Tally-Ho Coach, frequent fashionable watering places, and imitate the pronunciation and manners of the people of some other country."[176] From the way Harlan described it, he believed that even *making* money as a lawyer was a sign of moral failing. "There are very few lawyers who have the gift of money-making," Harlan counseled his students. "There are very few lawyers that lay up large estates, and when you find the lawyer who loves money better than he does the practice of his profession it is absolutely certain that he never makes a great lawyer or a good lawyer."[177] Financial success was at odds with civic duty, *the* virtue of his profession.

Lawyers worked for the Republic directly. In a speech before the New York State Bar in 1890, Harlan said, "Upon the integrity, learning and courage of the Bar largely depends the welfare of the country of which they are citizens;

for, of all members of society, the lawyers are best qualified by education and training to devise the methods necessary to protect the rights of the people against the aggressions of power." [178] Indeed, many of the founding fathers had identified themselves as members of the bar.[179] Harlan counted the number of lawyers among past U.S. presidents and cabinet members in a speech before the National Bar Association. "These facts speak volumes in condemnation of the senseless clamor in some quarters against a profession which, at every crisis in the Anglo-American struggle for liberty regulated by law, has furnished defenders of the rights of the people when assailed by arbitrary power." [180] Because the process of self-government was ongoing, lawyers were just as necessary to the Republic as the founders had been. "Let me impress upon you," he told a group of law students, "that you owe it to your high and honorable profession, and to the public that you should not be idlers, but, in the truest sense, *working* men." [181] Civic work gave lawyers a place in free labor ideology.

When Harlan placed lawyers among those whose entire incomes depend on their skill and industry, he contrasted them with people whose investment incomes were targeted by the new tax. Whereas lawyers and judges served the Republic, the leaders of industrial capitalism threatened it. Like many Americans at the turn of the century, Harlan was convinced that the concentrations of wealth produced by unprecedented industrial growth were the result of corruption and dishonesty. This idea grew partly out of free labor ideology's proposition that all hardworking men might eventually improve their situations. "Our paupers today, thanks to free labor, are our yeomen and merchants of tomorrow," the *New York Times* wrote in 1857.[182] But gargantuan corporations betrayed this promise by their very existence. When one company employed thousands, there was little chance that each worker could become an independent entrepreneur. Something had gone wrong. Instead of concluding that free labor thought no longer explained the workings of the economy, Harlan decided that the corporate tycoons were to blame.

He had good reason to think so. Writers exposed corporate misdeeds with alarming frequency during the late nineteenth century. Charles Francis Adams Jr. described the machinations of railroad tycoons in the late 1860s and concluded that "no portion of our system was left untested, and no portion showed itself to be sound." The stock exchange was manipulated, judges and legislators bribed, "and laws, made to order, were bought and sold." [183] Henry Demarest Lloyd's writings on Standard Oil (an article in 1881 and a book in 1894) became the model for a generation of muckrakers.[184] Lloyd observed that John D. Rockefeller had done everything to the Pennsylvania legislature except refine it.[185]

According to popular ideas about the marketplace, the monopolies that resulted broke the normal laws of supply and demand. Harlan joined one of Justice Bradley's concurrences in 1884 that complained, "Monopolies are the bane of our body politic at the present day. In the eager pursuit of gain they are sought in every direction. They exhibit themselves in corners in the stock market and produce market, and in many other ways." [186] In one of his antitrust majority opinions, Harlan himself wrote that "if such combination be not destroyed, all the advantages that would naturally come to the public under the operation of the general laws of competition . . . will be lost." [187]

Economic historians argue today, as economists did at the time, that monopolies are inevitable in certain industries and usually so efficient that they lower prices.[188] One writes that "the causes of oligopoly lay much more in prosaic interrelated forces of technology and markets" than in the evil intentions of corporate leaders.[189] And some in Congress acknowledged at the time that it was possible for an honest businessperson to become a monopolist.[190] But there seemed plenty of evidence, even in the courts, that corporate leaders were bent on cheating the public.

For example, *Addyston Pipe and Steel Company v. United States* in 1899 was a spectacular case in which an employee turned over to the government damning evidence of a price-fixing combination in the pipe industry that had divided up the country into private markets.[191] Each participant was given control over its market, while the rest agreed to offer higher bids only in order to create the semblance of true competition. The 1905 decision in *Swift and Company v. United States* confirmed the existence of collusion in the meatpacking industry as well.[192] These cases exposed business practices that many feared had become commonplace. Harlan wrote in response to a demand for proof of a conspiracy in an 1895 decision: "Men who form and control these combinations are too cautious and wary to make such admissions orally or in writing." [193] Whether through bribery or collusion, the business tycoons of the Gilded Age stood convicted in Harlan's eyes. These were the drones who had cheated the free labor system.

Some cheated, but the system was still sound, according to Harlan's income tax case dissent. Although some Americans turned to socialism as a solution, Harlan remained committed to a capitalist system in which monopolists were prevented from lording it over the plain people. Neither political radicalism nor upper-class reactionism made any sense in a system based on a harmony of interests. He wrote Willson at the time that "the fury of socialism is equalled by the fury with which *mere* millionaires, taking them as a class, and corporations, resent any attempt to make them pay their share of taxes." [194] Harlan explained in his dissent that propertyholders would be best served by diffusing the impulse toward radicalism. "The real friends of property," he wrote, "are not those who would exempt the wealth of the country from bearing its fair share of the burdens of taxation." Harlan defended the law's exemptions for incomes under $4,000: they "do not indicate sympathy on the part of the legislative branch of government with the pernicious theories of socialism, nor show that Congress had any purpose to despoil the rich." Harlan concluded his dissent by charging the Court with favoring the rich at the expense of everyone else, "who ought not to be subjected to the dominion of aggregated wealth any more than the property of the country should be at the mercy of the lawless."[195] The Court had failed to protect the people.

Harlan condemned the income tax decision in his dissent as among the worst the Court had ever delivered. It would "be regarded as a judicial revolution, that may sow the seeds of hate and mistrust among the people of different sections of our common country" because it ignored clear precedent. The Court had disgraced itself in the eyes of the populace, and evil was sure to follow. "I have a deep, abiding conviction, which my sense of duty compels me to express," he wrote, "that it is not possible for this court to have rendered any judgment more to be regretted than the one just rendered." He called for a constitutional amendment in somber language: "If this new departure from the safe way marked out by the fathers and so long followed by this court, is justified by the fundamental law, the American people cannot too soon amend their Constitution."[196] The Sixteenth Amendment placed the country back on the safe way in 1913, two years after Harlan's death.

The public reaction to the income tax decision was strong and mostly hostile.[197] William Jennings Bryan launched an attack on the Court, and the Democratic Party platform of 1896 specifically criticized the decision. Legal progressives and moderates joined in.[198] The *Harvard Law Review* and the *American Law Review* came out against the decision.[199] Rumors of Harlan's political ambitions flew, but he never spoke publicly on the topic and treated it only briefly in his law lectures of 1897–98.[200]

Harlan's private correspondence shows how much the Civil War had shaped his understanding of what had happened in the *Income Tax Case*. Harlan repeatedly compared the decision to *Dred Scott*.[201] Once again the Court had tarnished its public reputation by siding with the forces of tyranny. He feared for the country's safety and for the undoing of the work of emancipation. Harlan told his sons that the decision would "make the freemen of America the slaves of accumulated wealth."[202] He wrote Willson that "my earnestness in this matter was quite as sharp as when the flag was fired upon at Sumter."[203] The historical analogy was common. One of Harlan's former law students wrote him that "before the war, the main business of the Supreme

Standard Oil was one of many large companies criticized at the turn of the century for its monopoly power and its corruption of the political system. This cartoon by Emil Keppler in the 7 September 1898 issue of *Puck* is entitled "Next!" The company is an octopus whose arms have encircled the State House, the Capitol, and the copper and steel industry and whose eyes are on the White House. The U.S. government's prosecution of Standard Oil for violating the Sherman Anti-Trust Act came before the Supreme Court in the Great Trust Cases of 1911. (Courtesy of the Library of Congress)

Court was to uphold slavery; in recent years its main business seems to be to favor aggregated capital and corporate wealth."[204] Just as Harlan had taught his students of the threat to all liberty posed by slaveholders, now he warned the nation of the menace of irresponsible capital.

There are two decisions not on Harlan's list whose absence makes me think that he drew it up in 1910 and never revised it during the year that followed. I cannot imagine that he would have left the Great Trust Cases of 1911 out of an accounting of his legacy to the nation. Other antitrust decisions are on the list, but Harlan's concurrences in the Great Trust Cases were his final declaration of free labor ideology. In these concurrences, Harlan spoke frankly of the Court's evil intentions in promoting a new kind of slavery and of his fears for the American mission.

These decisions turned on the Sherman Anti-Trust Act of 1890, which prohibited "every contract, combination in the form of trust or otherwise, or conspiracy, in restraint of trade or commerce among the several States, or with foreign nations." The law was a reaction to the ineffectiveness of state antitrust statutes after New Jersey changed its incorporation law and offered the trusts a haven in 1889.[205] It was a national solution to a national problem.

One such trust was the American Sugar Refining Company, which tried to bring its share of the national sugar market to 98 percent by buying four refineries. The federal government brought suit to prevent the purchase, but Chief Justice Fuller held in *United States v. E. C. Knight Company* in 1895 that American Sugar had a monopoly in the *manufacture* of refined sugar, not in its *commerce*, and although "commerce succeeds to manufacture," it "is not a part of it." He suggested that the people look to their respective states for protection. Harlan expressed astonishment at the nicety of Fuller's distinction. Since the company bought and sold sugar nationally, it conducted interstate commerce. Purchasers of sugar were faced "with the threat—for it is nothing more nor less than a threat—that they *shall not* purchase what they desire to purchase, *except at the prices fixed by such combinations.*"[206] The operators of the sugar trust would be "satisfied with nothing less than to have the whole population of America pay tribute to them." Countering the massive threat of such monopolies was necessarily and constitutionally a national job. "Suppose another *combination*, organized for private gain and to control prices, should obtain possession of all the large flour mills in the United States," Harlan suggested; "another, of all the salt-producing regions; another, of all the cotton mills; and another, of all the great establishments for slaughtering animals, and the preparation of meats." Then "what power is competent to protect the people of the United States against such dangers except a national power?"[207] By refusing to allow the federal government to prosecute American Sugar, the Court had left the people at the company's mercy.[208]

Harlan's concerns may have been quieted by several later decisions indicating a broader definition of commerce.[209] Then, in his next favorite antitrust decision, *Northern Securities Company v. United States* in 1904, he succeeded in defining an exchange of stocks as a commercial transaction that could be regulated by Congress. The U.S. attorney general had brought suit to prevent two great tycoons—James J. Hill and J. P. Morgan—from combining their competing railroads.[210] The choice of a New Jersey stockholding company to accomplish the merger was an attempt to circumvent the Sherman Act, according to Harlan, but "no device in evasion of its provisions, however skillfully such device may have been contrived, and no combination, by whomsoever formed, is beyond the reach of the supreme law of the land."[211] One newspaper description of Harlan's oral delivery noted that "he placed the emphasis and earnestness upon sentences which characterized in no gentle terms the scheme of the merger."[212] *Northern Securities* caught the popular attention as no other antitrust decision had.[213] Harlan received letters of thanks that were gathered into a family scrapbook.[214] He achieved a victory in another favorite opinion in which he refused to allow a trust to sue one of its contractors by invoking the common law rule that courts will not help those engaged in illegal acts.[215] But these victories were overshadowed by his defeat in the Great Trust Cases.

The central dispute in these cases was the so-called rule of reason. Harlan had acknowledged in *Northern Securities* the importance of deciding whether the Sherman Act forbade every combination in restraint of trade or only those that were unreasonable. He found the choice simple. Either a judge followed the clear meaning of the act and found a combination that had a direct effect on interstate commerce to be unlawful, or the judge indulged in a personal belief that "the general business interests and prosperity of the country will be best promoted if the rule of competition is not applied" and declared that such a combination was not unreasonable.[216] Harlan's remarks must have been directed at Justice Brewer, who warned in his concurrence to *Northern Securities* that he did not believe that the Sherman Act forbade reasonable restraints of trade. The rule of reason had been raised even earlier, but the importance of the issue had not been recognized.[217]

The Great Trust Cases involved two of the largest companies created during the late nineteenth century: Standard Oil and American Tobacco. Standard Oil of Ohio controlled 90 percent of the oil business by 1882. In 1906, the federal government charged it and the thirty-three other companies that had formed Standard Oil of New Jersey with restraining trade, obtaining discriminatory railroad rates, monopolizing oil pipelines, engaging in industrial spying, operating front companies, and making a ridiculous amount of money. American Tobacco of New Jersey eventually swallowed up 250 companies, although only 65 were prosecuted by the federal government for violating the Sherman Act. Chief Justice White, writing for the majority, found these companies' tremendous size suspect. Standard Oil's size "gives rise . . . to the *prima facie* presumption of intent and purpose to maintain the dominancy over the oil industry, not as a result of normal methods of industrial development."[218] He noted the sinister character of the business practices of American Tobacco, especially "the remarkable fact [of] . . . the disbursement of enormous amounts of money to acquire plants, which on being purchased were not utilized but were immediately closed."[219] Clearly, the majority of the Court believed that something other than the law of supply and demand was at work. White declared that both companies had unreasonably restrained interstate trade: Standard Oil was to be dissolved, and American Tobacco dismantled.

Harlan concurred in part to both decisions and dissented because he objected to the Court's interpretation of the term "restraint of trade." This dispute might seem like an argument over mere vocabulary. Here, Harlan identified a *restraint* of trade, whereas the Court found an *unreasonable restraint* of trade, and they agreed that the two trusts must be dismantled. Perhaps in the future when Harlan would find *no restraint* of trade, the Court would find a *reasonable restraint* of trade, and both would agree that the defendant should be let off. But more was at stake than the meaning of the phrase.

The dispute was partly historical. The word "monopoly" had two original meanings: the cornering of a market and a governmental grant of control over a certain trade. The latter definition fell into disuse by the nineteenth century. The phrase "restraint of trade" also dated to early common law. It meant a promise by one economic actor not to compete with another, usually because of the sale of a business and its goodwill, and it was frowned on because the seller might become a public ward.[220] By the seventeenth century, a restraint of trade was legal only if it was part of such a transaction, partial, and reasonable.[221] The common law of the various American states tended to hold "arrangements involving restraints on business competition" illegal.[222] But the term was often shaken loose from its historical moorings by those who objected to antitrust prosecutions. For example, the *New York Times* insisted in 1904 that "copyrights and patents restrain trade, trade is restrained by the attempt of the manufacturer to get for his product more than it has cost him. All these things are lawful."[223]

White announced the rule of reason in *Standard Oil Company of New Jersey et al. v. United States*. Since the Sherman Act did not define monopoly or restraint of trade, "it follows that it was intended that the standard of reason which had been applied at the common law and in this country in dealing with subjects of the character embraced by the statute, was intended to be the measure used."[224] In *United States v. American Tobacco Company*, he explained further. The Sherman Act made illegal "acts or contracts or agreements or combinations which operated to the prejudice of the public interest by *unduly* restricting competition or *unduly* obstructing the due course of trade" (emphasis added). Only this interpretation could give the term "restraint of trade" "a meaning which would not destroy the individual right to contract and render difficult if not impossible any movement of trade in the channels of interstate commerce."[225] If almost every contract was a restraint of trade (and Congress clearly was not bent on destroying the right to contract), then only *unreasonable* restraints of trade could have been targeted.

White circumvented contrary precedents by a verbal sleight of hand.[226] He invoked the word "reason" in its broadest sense: the use of one's rational powers. Whenever the judges had tried alleged violations of the Sherman

Act, "reason was the guide by which the provisions of the act were in every case interpreted." [227] White's pun laid him wide open.

For Harlan, the use of one's reason inevitably led to the conclusion that there was no such thing as a reasonable restraint of trade. He stuck by the idea he had set forth in *Northern Securities* that any judge who labeled a restraint of trade in interstate commerce reasonable was moved by a personal indifference to the dangers of monopolies at odds with the legislative will expressed in the Sherman Act. In his *Standard Oil* concurrence, Harlan underlined that the Sherman Act prohibited "*every* restraint of trade." In his concurrence in *American Tobacco*, he declared that the idea that these decisions followed precedent surprised him "quite as much as would a statement that black was white or white was black." White's pun was insulting. "It is obvious," Harlan wrote in *American Tobacco*, "from the opinions in the former cases, that the majority did not grope about in darkness, but in discharging the solemn duty put on them they stood in the full glare of the 'light of reason.' " [228] Congress had set up a simple rule, he explained in *Standard Oil*, and now the Court was turning it into an infinitely complicated one that "will throw the business of the country into confusion and invite widely-extended and harassing litigation, the injurious effects of which will be felt for many years to come." [229]

These decisions left the country unable to defend itself properly against a threat like that which had caused the Civil War. Harlan noted that the Sherman Act was passed because of the "universal" conviction that although "the Nation had been rid of human slavery . . . the country was in real danger from another kind of slavery sought to be fastened on the American people." This was "the slavery that would result from aggregations of capital in the hands of a few individuals and corporations controlling, for their own profit and advantage exclusively, the entire business of the country, including the production and sale of the necessaries of life." [230] These were the powers Harlan accused of being satisfied with nothing less than tribute from the whole country in *E. C. Knight*.

Why had the Court done this? "Why was it necessary to make an elaborate argument," Harlan asked, "to show that according to the 'rule of reason' the act . . . should be interpreted as if it contained the word 'unreasonable' or the word 'undue'?" Such a serious misreading could only be purposeful. The other justices did not like what Congress had done in the Sherman Act, so they decided to practice "judicial legislation, by inserting in the act the word 'unreasonable.' " [231] Although typology had long explained the progressive course of American history for Harlan, it seemed to have finally failed him. He was now unsure that victory would follow the battle against tyranny. The federal judiciary no longer knew its place within the constitutional system. He wrote in *Standard Oil* that "after many years of public service at the National Capital, . . . I am impelled to say that there is abroad, in our land, a most harmful tendency to bring about the amending of constitutions and legislative enactments by means alone of judicial construction." Harlan's faith in the happy end of the mission was shaken. He warned that "to overreach the action of Congress merely by judicial construction, that is, by indirection, is a blow at the integrity of our governmental system and in the end will be proven most dangerous to all." [232]

When Harlan delivered his concurrences from the bench, Justice Charles Evans Hughes noted that "he went far beyond his written opinion, launching out into a bitter invective, which I thought most unseemly." President Taft, Harlan's friend, wrote his daughter that Harlan's concurrence was "a nasty, carping and demagogic opinion, directed at the Chief Justice and intended to furnish [Progressive Robert] La Follette and his crowd as much pabulum as possible." [233] Indeed, his concurrences made him a hero of political progressives. The publisher of a Colorado newspaper and a former student confided to him that "whenever we handle this trust question your name brings thunders of applause." [234] Another former law student working for the Progressive ticket in California wrote, "Your praises are proclaimed on the streets and abroad in the land." [235] One scholar writes that "few decisions . . . helped to crystallize criticism of the Court more than" the Great Trust Cases. [236] Family scrapbooks hold letters from plain people who thanked Harlan, including one who was waiting for the day when "men, women and children take their guns and bulldogs to defend their own, and replace law-abiding people in the saddle." [237] These concurrences and the public acclaim that followed prompted journalists to call Harlan the people's judge in his obituaries several months later. [238]

In their efforts to explain Harlan, scholars labeled him. He was a paternalist for dissenting in *Lochner.* He was an advocate of laissez-faire in *Adair.* He was so dim that he supported substantive due process despite his better intentions. Alan F. Westin calls him "a premature New Dealer" for his antitrust decisions — this of a man who remarked in reference to William Jennings Bryan's plan for national insurance on bank deposits, "Could any thing be more dangerous or stupid than that?" [239] Loren Beth came closer to the truth in calling Harlan "the last Whig justice." In Harlan's list of favorites, we can see the Whig-Republican synthesis. Before the war, the Whig commitment to prosperity justified governmental intervention to promote economic change and control its course. After the war, the national character of this intervention was a constitutional imperative. The Thirteenth and Fourteenth

Amendments supported the doctrines of substantive due process and liberty of contract. Even Harlan's criticism of corporate power was couched in free labor ideology. The Whig turned Republican had learned his lessons well.

Although Harlan recognized that corporate scale and power had increased, he did not abandon free labor thought. Other jurists and legal scholars were setting forth a new vision of the economy and society.[240] The rise of the social sciences in the United States and the acceptance of the German historical school of economics led these people to question the basic premises of the American legal system.[241] Roscoe Pound argued in 1909 in his "Liberty of Contract" article for the need to reject an "individualist conception of justice."[242] Felix Frankfurter declared in 1916 that now "the emphasis is shifted to community interests . . . not merely society conceived of as independent individuals dealing at arm's length with one another."[243]

Harlan remained on the other side of the conceptual divide. His support for federal regulation of corporations was based on an old faith in the virtues of free competition rather than a new one in the need for economic cooperation under governmental control. In a letter to Theodore Roosevelt in 1908, Harlan condemned "the political monstrosities (as applied to our National Government) of National Ownership of railroads."[244] Harlan saw the answer to monopoly in the prosecution of those who broke the laws of free competition. Like many Americans of his generation, Harlan retained a simplified view of economic class even as others were complicating their views.[245] There were people who worked and people who lived off of their investments (which they were likely to have acquired in some underhanded way).

By writing his list of favorite decisions, Harlan was drawing attention to the work he had done. The next chapter will look at another legacy he left to the Republic: his sons. It will also lead us back to the household where this book began.

# You May Rightfully Aspire

## Manhood and Success in the Republic

*If my countrymen think that the duties of the great office so long
held by me have been discharged with conscientious regard for the
law, or for what I deemed to be the law, and with an eye single to
the ends of justice and right and truth, my descendants will have
in this estimate of my judicial life a legacy more precious than
any that I could possibly leave them.*

—John Marshall Harlan at a banquet for his

twenty-fifth year on the Supreme Court, 1902

John Marshall Harlan's great grandchildren tell a story about
the second Justice John Marshall Harlan, who sat on the Supreme Court from
1955 to 1971. Harlan the younger was at a Washington, D.C., function when
conversation with a member of a foreign delegation turned to the Court. On
learning of Harlan the elder's tenure there, the foreigner remarked, "Oh, I
had no idea that these positions were hereditary."

High status and public office were not supposed to be hereditary in the
United States.[1] When writers like Thomas Paine sneered at the pretensions
of the British nobility, they dealt a blow to political hierarchy that reverber-
ated within the family. The colonial rebels wanted to wrench the status of
sons apart from that of their fathers and set them on a level footing with
each other.[2]

The revolutionary generation rejected one system of masculine status in
order to create another. Public accomplishment replaced claims to noble
birth. The founding fathers created a new standard for their literal and spiritual sons to aim for, and some men felt the mark was almost impossibly high.[3]
But Harlan was comfortable with it. Consider how the entrance hall of his
Washington, D.C., home was decorated. Portraits of John Marshall, Thomas
Jefferson, John Jay, Alexander Hamilton, and others lined the walls. At the
foot of the stairs, unflustered among such venerable company, was a bust of
Harlan himself. Just as the founders became the model for his countrymen,
so Harlan became a model within his family.

But ideals of manhood changed by the mid-nineteenth century. Historians describe two ideal types, both of which put individual interests first. The masculine achiever was aggressive, independent, and competitive when it came to sex and money-making. The Christian gentleman turned inward toward family and religious life. The first sought world mastery, and the second desired self-mastery.[4]

The Harlans integrated a part of each ideal into their pursuit of government office. Harlan taught his sons that duty to the Republic was their personal obligation. Examples were still plentiful in the late nineteenth century. When Harlan compiled a list of forty-six "great men whom I have seen," it was filled with military men from the Civil War like Ulysses S. Grant, Philip H. Sheridan, George B. McClellan, and John A. Logan (and two Confederates); judges such as Stephen J. Field, Samuel F. Miller, and Joseph P. Bradley; and congressmen, senators, and presidents, including Grover Cleveland, Rutherford B. Hayes, James G. Blaine, and Stephen A. Douglas.[5] His ideal might be called the republican achiever or the republican gentleman. The Harlan men pursued civic distinction aggressively. The self-mastery expressed by a man's piety and morality prepared him to participate in the Republic's project of self-government. A moral man could embark on a legal career, earn public distinction, and end up as a sort of world master by serving the people. In setting out this ideal, Harlan altered his era's belief that men should be financially successful. He explained his own indebtedness not as failure but as the price paid for his efforts to serve his country.

The Harlans' commitment to public service was apparently atypical in the late nineteenth century.[6] But their attempts to integrate the interests of a man's self, his family, and his community demonstrate the robustness of the tradition of public service. The same pattern appeared in the family of John and Abigail Adams and suggests commonalities among families that have made an impact on American history. One thinks of Kentucky's Breckinridges in the nineteenth century, of the Tafts of Ohio, and of the Roosevelts and the Kennedys. Such families hoped to create a natural aristocracy in which the titles were those of public office and one of the main routes to them was through the law.

John and Malvina Harlan had three sons. Richard and James were born before the war, and John Maynard was born in 1864. When Harlan scolded one of them for acting "like the great mass of those who attend colleges" by not putting forth his best effort, he added that "I have fancied that my boys . . . had greater natural gifts than most young men of your age."[7] Harlan demanded an extra measure of achievement. Good citizenship was only a start.

Another story must have circulated for a time in the Harlan family. John's son James wrote a relative in 1879 that he had been "cured" of any notion of inherited importance when he tried to impress a black federal clerk in Washington, D.C., by telling him "what I wanted and *who* I was." The clerk answered, "You would stand a better chance if you were a boot-black."[8] In a land that had banished inherited titles, it wasn't supposed to matter who your father was.

Of course, it still did. Harlan's three sons were acutely aware of the benefits he provided them. The story of the Harlan men displays the tension between opportunity and birth, between social duty and private satisfaction, between professional ambition and personal ethics. The Harlan boys learned at home that their public lives should consist of certain masculine pursuits. The gap between the household and the world was small.[9]

One assumption behind Harlan's ideal of public service was the exclusion of women. The revolutionary era's challenge to hierarchy altered women's status only by valuing them as republican mothers raising citizen sons.[10] When Harlan spoke of the people in their mythic sense or the importance of participation in self-government, he was referring to men. When women fought for access to legal education or to the bar, they received no help from Harlan.[11]

Although the ideal of the nineteenth-century middle class gave a man the role of economic provider for his wife and children, reality was less tidy. Harlan expressed dismay that the death of his father-in-law had not brought him any money.[12] Similarly, when his wife's brother, George W. Shanklin, imagined "the angel I must have for a wife," she was accompanied by a fortune.[13] Wifely angels blessed their husbands with more than love.

Before his appointment to the Supreme Court in 1877, Harlan hustled like any other nineteenth-century city lawyer. He and Benjamin H. Bristow made a play for the local business of railroad entrepreneur Tom Scott in the early 1870s, but mostly they worked on probate and property and an occasional criminal trial.[14] Much of Harlan's legal business was debt collection, but the risks of the market made an impression on him only when it destroyed his own fortune. The failure of banker Jay Cooke triggered the Panic of 1873. "The depreciation of real estate," as Harlan later described it, meant that the land he had bought with thousands of borrowed dollars was now worth little.[15] He would never pay back his creditors.

Harlan had actually gotten into debt earlier, although the depression greatly worsened his situation.[16] During the war, Harlan had asked his commanding officer for permission to take a leave of absence by explaining that "I have *bank* obligations of a (*to me*) large amount, hanging over my head and involving others, which my honor compels me to arrange."[17] When Harlan left Kentucky in 1877 to accept his nomination to the Supreme Court, he owed local banks some $30,000, and well into the 1890s, he continued to negotiate partial repayment through his friend Augustus E. Willson and Shanklin.[18] "One who is broke is broke," Willson counseled in 1880, "and will save further pain and falls to reach ground at once."[19] Harlan requested that all judgments against him be taken in Louisville so that people in Washington, D.C., would be unlikely to hear about them. "The whole situation is so deadly mortifying to me," he wrote in 1880; "I am sometimes surprised that I have been able to stand up at all."[20]

Harlan's early financial problems were compounded by living beyond his means during his years on the bench. He borrowed $750 from his son John Maynard in 1910, explaining, "I am sorely in need of some money which will not surprise you when you think of the increased cost of living."[21] His manner of living was more the problem. His salary was $10,000 when he started as an associate justice, climbed to $12,500 in 1903, and reached $14,500 by the year of his death in 1911.[22] But such a salary did not cover the costs of his life-style. Owning a house that "takes in nearly a whole block" with "a large reception hall" manned by a black butler, bringing his daughters out in Washington, D.C., society, educating his sons first at Princeton University and then in Berlin, and taking his family away each summer to Canada cost more than his salary could bear.[23] He resigned himself to the discrepancy between his income and his style of living. He wrote to Shanklin in 1894, "I wish I had the money to pay off the old debts. But I have not and never expect to have."[24]

Debt made Harlan think of himself as impoverished. He was poor in comparison with his hopes as a young attorney. Harlan continued to purchase real estate on credit. His entire financial life seems to have been premised on his vain hope that no matter how bad things were, "some plan might be devised for my relief."[25] When he died leaving a widow and two unmarried daughters an estate worth only $13,000, the Washington, D.C., community of lawyers discussed what they might do in light of "the unfortunate financial condition in which Mr. Justice Harlan left his family."[26]

Faced with his debt, Harlan redefined the relation between financial success and masculine ethics to his own advantage. The Harlan family tradition of politicking and civic service made this easy to do. To Harlan's mind, his family and his country benefited from his poverty.

The common vision of success, as voiced by Henry Clay, was that of the "enterprising self-made men, who have whatever wealth they possess by patient and diligent labor."[27] Those without fortunes had failed to practice this work ethic. Poverty sprang from vice, although exceptions were made for the victims of calamities: widows, orphans, and accident victims.[28] Harlan added victims of economic calamities to the list, and by doing this, he removed prosperity from the common definition of masculine virtue.

Harlan was one of many to do so during the late nineteenth century, although questioning the relation between wealth and virtue went far back.[29] The middle-class ideal of the Christian gentleman rejected the equation outright. Gilded Age labor radicals and rural populists criticized the economic system as an inequitable distributor of wealth. Harlan, as we've seen, suspected successful businesspeople of corruption and collusion.

Harlan could not erase the stigma of economic failure, but he pleaded that such difficulties be understood with compassion. During one of his constitutional law lectures, Harlan praised the federal bankruptcy laws as regulations that "have their foundation in humanity and in the best welfare of the state." He explained to his students that Congress generally passed them "after the country has passed through a season of distress and financial embarrassment" that produced a set of "men overwhelmed with debt, way beyond their expectations, and way beyond every possibility of [their] ever being worth, if they live to be much older than men live."[30] Indeed, the first bankruptcy law of 1800, repealed in 1803, was a public admission that the economy was unstable.[31] Clay said in 1824 that economic distress was "like the atmosphere which surrounds us—all must inhale it and none can escape it."[32] Notice that Harlan himself used the word "season" in describing an economic depression as though it were akin to a particularly severe winter. In such a situation, "what interest has the state or the public in keeping a man's nose to the grindstone all the while?," he asked.[33]

Although I may be making too much of rhetoric, it seems telling that Harlan imagined himself as the debtor and asked, "If I have run aground and cannot do any more than I have done, why may I not be discharged and made free to start my career in life again?"[34] Perhaps he wanted to suggest to his students that even an upright man might find himself in a state of financial embarrassment. Harlan had once written Shanklin, "If I could call back 10 years I would do so."[35]

The Harlan boys were aware of their father's difficulties. While he was studying at Princeton in 1882, James complained to his father that he was "annoyed for the want of money." His father replied, "That cannot be helped, and what cannot be helped must be borne." Harlan reassured him that "it will not be necessary for you to abandon college because of my poverty for let what may come, I shall take you and John through college."[36]

In a country where money was the usual yardstick of masculine success, a father's financial failure could poison his relationship with his son. Harlan prevented this by defining inherited wealth as an evil, as did many of his contemporaries.[37] He explained in one of his instructive letters that it was unlikely that a "young man who starts upon life with the certainty of a good estate & without the necessity of labor" would become "distinguished or useful." "The men who control the world, & who leave their mark upon the generation in which they live are those who make their own fortunes, and do not depend upon wealth acquired by their parents," he counseled his son James. Unhappy as he was in debt, the judge felt no self-reproach for its effect on his sons. "After all," he concluded, "I think it well for my boys that they will be compelled to make their own living."[38] Similarly, Malvina wrote John Maynard from Warm Sulphur Springs in 1889 about "two or three young married men here this summer, all fine looking fellows—but with nothing to do but drive after pleasure." "It is a pitiful sight to me," she lamented, "to see strong men tired & worn out from doing *nothing*. . . . It makes me fairly ill!" Like her husband, she congratulated herself on her poverty: "I am glad to have had no fortune to give you, only the fortune of a good name & honest blood."[39]

Virtuous poverty was made out to be the result of Harlan's selfless career rather than an accident of his personal circumstances. When Harlan admitted to his brother-in-law in 1894 that he could never pay off his debts, he concluded that there was "nothing to do but 'jog along' in life, working hard, living economically, dying poor."[40] Service to the Republic was at odds with money-making. One day in class, Harlan told his students that congressmen could barely survive on their salaries. Why, then, did they remain in public life? Harlan answered, "I cannot tell, except from the feeling of the ambition that is planted in the breast of every man to live after he is dead and gone in the memory of his fellow citizens." He continued, "I can understand why a man may be willing to give his whole life, and lead a life of poverty and self-denial if by so doing he can make a great name in his country."[41] By serving the Union, a man could achieve civic immortality.

Political theory and family tradition combined to produce Harlan's high estimate of public service and the sacrifices it entailed. A republic relied on the virtues of its male citizens. The highest expression of this involvement was the public service of officeholding. Such service was part of "an internal stream of identity flowing from one generation to the next" that constituted the Harlan "family myth," to borrow David F. Musto's term.[42] The very first American Harlan, John Marshall Harlan's grandfather James, was remembered by his family for rendering the most elemental of public services by helping to found the commonwealth of Kentucky. His son, a congressman and state administrator, kept the idea alive and passed it on. By bestowing the name John Marshall on his son, the second James indicated that he expected his boy to serve his country. Long before his financial troubles, John Harlan had held public office. Service was a family tradition, not an excuse for economic failure. Although the family myth lessened the pressure to gain wealth, it increased the pressure to attain public office.

Harlan's explanation for his financial problems contrasts with his criticism of his older brother for his decline into alcoholism and drug addiction. A man who brought financial *and* public disgrace upon himself and his family was unsuited for any role in a republic. To lack personal virtue was to lack civic virtue, as the early temperance reformers made clear when they modeled themselves on the founding fathers by declaring their independence from drink.[43]

James Harlan's drinking began early. By the time John was leading a regiment in the Civil War, James could not be trusted to handle the business of the family law office. When their father died in early 1863, John resigned his commission in order to keep the office going.[44] When John was appointed to the bench in 1877, he left behind Augustus Willson, whom he had brought into the practice as a young man. Willson decided to join in a partnership with James despite John's doubts.[45] Within a year, Willson was writing worried letters stating that he feared James's "very bad condition" would mean the "destruction of business and all prospects."[46] James's repeated vows to quit drinking followed by his disappearances on "sprees" with his pockets full of important papers reduced Willson to despair. He finally wrote John in 1880, "I would welcome even his death if it would be respectable."[47] But James lived until 1897, perpetually getting on and falling off the wagon.

James's drinking was called many things in family letters: a mania, a weakness, a misfortune, a habit, and a disease. Each term carried a different implication of James's responsibility for drinking, but in the end, family members blamed him for it.[48] James himself confessed that "much" of his trouble "is the result of my own weakness, and I have no claims for excuses and make none."[49]

Unless James stopped drinking, the Harlans reasoned, nothing they did to help him really mattered. Malvina wrote James in 1891 that she "wish[ed] you could realize how hopeless the talk of helping you seems unless you can change your whole course of life."[50] John responded less kindly to a request for a patronage job from James's son Henry, who was also an alcoholic. He was "unwilling to lose any time in helping any one who has deliberately or recklessly set out upon a road that he knows leads to ruin."[51] Henry had deliberately followed in his father's footsteps.

Although James blamed himself, he also believed that being a Harlan made it harder for him. When he lamented his life as "a hard and fruitless one," he particularly mourned the fact that he would probably die "without having done anything worthy of note." [52] What was known of him in Louisville was scandalous. James had destroyed his partnership with Willson and shown up drunk when assigned a temporary judgeship in the local courthouse in 1880.[53] James wrote his brother in 1885 that he was "brought to that point now where I am not ashamed of any kind of labor, so it is honest." [54] But finding a job in Kentucky was impossible, he concluded, because any work other than the law "would attract an attention which would be disagreeable to my family." [55] It was hard for a Harlan to be an inconspicuous failure in Kentucky.

So James left Louisville. He traveled to Kansas City, Missouri, only to learn that his family still hampered him. He had no money to put into a partnership, but he could not work as a salaried law clerk either. He wrote his brother, "I find that I am well known as your brother here as in many places nearer home, and this would make [clerking] disagreeable to you & other members of the family." His way would be easier, he reasoned, "if I were the only one of the name or family." [56] James may have been making excuses, but it must have been hard for the failed older brother of a Supreme Court justice to find a suitable position.

James began drinking again in Kansas City, recovered, and traveled with high hopes to the territory that would become Oklahoma. From there, he begged his brother for money for treatments for what by then had become the double addiction of alcohol and opium.[57] He tried several cures at sanatoriums in 1884 and 1885. He returned to Louisville in the early 1890s, and Willson took responsibility for looking after him. James ended his days in a residence hotel paid for by John.[58]

One wonders about the effect on James of John's success, first as a politician and then as a judge on the country's highest court. James was the one usually known as "Judge Harlan" in Louisville (his brother was dubbed "General" because of his military service). Being the other, lesser Judge Harlan must have galled the older brother who bore *the* name of the family—James was not only their father's name but also that of the first American Harlan. James often boasted of some little success to his brother. "I have made quite a reputation recently by my jury speeches," he wrote in 1882.[59] From Kansas City in 1887, James claimed that even as a clerk, "I could force my way to the front in a short time." [60] In 1888, he wrote that he was headed to Oklahoma "with a confidence I never had before." [61] Such talk was a way of reassuring his brother and himself that he was indeed worthy of the family name.

But James was effectively banished from his brother's presence. After a long correspondence with Willson in 1892, John decided that he would not fund a visit by James because it would be "embarrassing . . . to me here & to my family, if he should get off the track while here." [62] James had not seen his brother in over a decade by the 1890s. In 1894, in a letter discussing Willson's plan to commit James to a hospital, John again refused to have James visit because of his "duties to my children, who are in society, which cannot be ignored." His daughter Ruth was to have a reception that very week in honor of her coming out in society. Harlan wrote Willson that his brother "knows well that there has never been a moment when I was not willing to share all I had with him, & to have him with me, all his & my days, if his life had been such as to have admitted of his being invited here." [63] When James's condition was at its worst in Oklahoma, he stopped addressing his letters to his brother to "Dear John" and used "Dear General" instead. Although dependent on his family until he died, James had ceased to feel that he was one of them.

This painful experience—John once called his brother's condition "the one and only cloud upon my life"—did not stop the justice from drinking or from sending Kentucky bourbon to his friends on the Court. He even joked about the "delightful sensations" his gifts produced.[64] But James's alcoholism did affect John's relationship with his sons.

While visiting John Maynard in Chicago in 1894, Harlan noticed that his son "could take whiskey for a cold without the slightest appreciation that there was any danger in [his] doing so." He reminded his son of "the fact that there are, on both sides of your house, some melancholy instances of ruin coming from the use of stimulants." Drunkenness had ruined many a public career. His uncle James was a case in point, and John also pointed to Kentuckian John Griffen Carlisle, then secretary of the Treasury. Carlisle's chances at the chief justiceship and the presidency had been ruined because of his drinking. John Maynard had a "great career" at stake, his father warned. If he indulged in drink, he would "not achieve all that [he was] capable of doing." [65]

At the time of this letter, John Maynard was some thirty years old, but his father still felt that his advice was in order. Middle-class fathers tried to balance their control against their sons' independence.[66] Instead of ordering his sons to blindly obey his dictates, Harlan insisted that they "cultivate the habit of *reasoning* about everything, that is—to think about every question presented to your mind—look at all sides, and *deliberate* before you reach a conclusion." [67] At the same time, Harlan wanted his sons to obey a set of rules that he intended to enforce. Unbeknownst to John Maynard, his father had written several years earlier to his nephew Henry that "I have made up my mind that if one of my sons ever contracts the habit of drinking, to break off all connection with or responsibility for him, and never allow him to come into my presence." [68] Harlan seems not to have written such a warning to his own sons. Whether the Harlan boys were lucky or vigilant, the family papers reveal no serious problem with alcohol.

When Harlan wrote his sons while they were in college about the benefits they would gain from their lack of ready cash, he also imparted to them an unrelenting work ethic. In long, detailed letters, he told them how and what to study. This pressure to succeed seems to have helped push them through their studies and into professional careers, but it also exacted a toll.

Fatherly control and filial independence played off each other when it came to the boys' choosing a profession. It was a choice of utmost importance to a family in which the men were supposed to gain public office. Unlike his father, who decided his son's profession at birth, John Harlan once allowed that his son James might be a journalist, doctor, or "Railroad King." [69] In truth, he thought all of his boys especially suited to the law. Two of them agreed, but the eldest, Richard, held out despite subtle paternal pressure. When Harlan quizzed Richard in 1870 as to his personal "tastes and inclinations" regarding his career, he emphasized that "I do not mean that you shall write me the notions of any other person, but your own just as they strike your mind." [70] Harlan declared to his son James a decade later that if Richard settled on the ministry, "I shall be satisfied." However, even while acknowledging that Richard "will know best," he repeated to James that "my own judgment is that Richard's field of usefulness lies in the direction of the legal profession, & ultimately of public life." [71] Richard resisted and finally joined the Presbyterian ministry.

Harlan's letters to his sons demanded work, public service, and republican glory. "There is no place in the active stirring civilization of this time, for a drone or a mere pretender," he wrote James in 1880. "Labor, unremitting labor, study, serious constant study, is essential to great success." [72] Two years later, Harlan lamented the time that he had wasted at college and urged that "a young man at your age, should strip himself, so to speak, of every tendency to misuse time, and labor unceasingly for the development of the mind." [73] He recommended Reverend John Todd's *Student's Manual*, which drove home the importance of industry, habit, piety, and politeness with contemporary and historical anecdotes. Various fields of study were recommended as preparation for public life. Harlan urged James to study mathematics because its lessons in cause and effect cultivated one's ability to "explain and discriminate and the man who can do this will make an effective public speaker." [74]

The threat of criticism overshadowed Harlan's clumsy attempts at encouragement. In 1882, he wrote James of his regret "that one of the results of your Christmas vacation, was the belief, upon your part, that you did not enjoy my full confidence." Harlan assured his middle son that "I think your judgment generally is quite valuable, and I have never doubted your success in life." But even this letter contained a note of disappointment doubtless akin to whatever careless word Harlan dropped at Christmas. "I confess," Harlan wrote, "that I have not thought that either you or John [Maynard] are putting forth your best efforts. While you stand well, you should hold a higher rank in your class."[75] James must have thought of the unspoken comparison to his older brother Richard, who had been valedictorian.

Harlan's insensitivity to the strain his message placed on his boys may be seen in his reply to a request from James for "a remedy for the *blues*." His advice? "It will go far towards warding them off to grit your teeth, and determine that you will not have them."[76]

When Harlan admitted the difficulty of the task he had set before his sons, he always pointed out that they had had advantages. It was true, he wrote James, that "the young men of this country . . . have, in some respects, more obstacles to contend with than the young men of fifty years ago had. It requires more education, study, & training to lead now than it did fifty years ago."[77] At the same time, the Harlan boys could overcome those problems at their father's literal expense. "Men have become distinguished without acquiring a classical education, and going through the training had at college," the judge noted, "but they would have become more distinguished had their early life been blessed with such training as you can have at Princeton."[78] Harlan counseled James to read the biographies of statesmen in order to appreciate "the difficulties overcome by great men in reaching eminence."[79] Whatever difficulties Harlan's sons faced, they were offered "every possible inducement to win such positions as will enable them to live after they are dead, in the memories of the people everywhere."[80]

Harlan could conjure up an awesome vision of the opportunities open to men in a republic. On James's twenty-first birthday, Harlan shared some of his musings. "It has always been a subject of pleasant thought with me that the privileges which the young men of this day enjoy in our country are immeasurably greater than belong to young men of other countries." Unlike nations in which status was assigned at birth, the United States allowed all men to contend for its most prestigious positions. "Just to think," he wrote, "you may rightfully aspire to the Presidency, to the Chief Justiceship of the U.S., and to a seat in [the] U.S. Senate. Indeed, it is possible, under the Constitution, that you may, in the course of your life, occupy all three positions."[81] The idea that any American boy could grow up to be president held a particularly pointed message for those whose fathers held high office. That sort of expectation turned out to be more than they could handle.

John Maynard, the youngest son, was the most troubled by his father's demands. He was dismissed from Princeton for the second time in 1881 for hazing—a spontaneous attack on a freshman for violating the social conventions of the upperclassmen. John Maynard could not have acted in any way more calculated to enrage his father. In the first place, the two had previously discussed hazing. Harlan wrote James after the incident that John Maynard "knew my abhorrence of Hazing, & heard me say that I could not excuse such conduct." In the second place, hazing was the kind of brutality antithetical to the family myth of paternalism. To refrain from the abuse of power was part of his family identity. So Harlan bemoaned the state of his son's "sense of right and justice and his manliness" with a special pang. It was bad enough that young John had directly disobeyed his father and the rules of the college, but Harlan "was still more horrified that his own sense of propriety would not restrain him." [82] Harlan found it impossible to accept that his youngest son was a bully. He preferred to believe that "John has been led into this thoughtlessly, by others & that he was dragged along as it were without the nerve to put his foot down & say he would not join in." The idea that John Maynard "organized these raids, or that he was the controlling spirit or brain" would have made his father "despair of his being useful to himself, to his family or to his country." [83]

John Maynard backed down. Unlike his uncle James, he did not fall into self-destructive habits or wish that he was without a family name. Two years after his second expulsion, he was back at Princeton, again receiving his father's lengthy instructions in the mail. Harlan advised him that "the first step towards improvement in any one is to recognize the errors, if any, which may have been committed, in the past." He tried to bolster his son's confidence: "That you have made mistakes, or failed to improve opportunities is of course to be regretted. But, at your age, what has been lost may be regained." [84] John Maynard graduated and followed his father into the law. His father, in fact, became the ideal of manhood to which he compared himself.

Because of Harlan's national prominence, the Harlan boys were repeatedly reminded of what they ought to achieve. Malvina filled scrapbooks with clippings about Harlan's decisions and public appearances. Lavish messages arrived like one from the dean of Central Law School in Kentucky declaring that "we rank you with Lincoln, Sumner, Phillips, Beecher, and Garrison" and one from a Mississippi judge who regarded "Mr. Justice Harlan as one of the greatest judges who ever sat on any bench—the equal of Mansfield, Marshall or Field." [85] As the boys reached adulthood, praise of their father became a kind of family currency exchanged in all directions.

When Harlan concurred in the Great Trust Cases in 1911, the press and public lauded him as the only justice with the courage to defend the people. John Maynard wrote his father, "I wish I could see you and tell you face to face what pride I have taken in your dissenting opinion in the Standard Oil case." As the judge's son, he gathered the world's praise: "Many people from all walks of life have spoken to me about it, uniformly in praise of your position. . . . Many of those who have spoken to me have been lawyers, some of whom I haven't passed a word with in years, but they have spoken to me when they would have liked to speak to you yourself."[86] The sons were reminded continually that their father had achieved what the family set down as most admirable. Harlan's judicial legacy was a personal and public one.

Comparisons were drawn especially between John Maynard and his father. Harlan signed himself "John M. Harlan," a practice praised as an expression of his unassuming character by journalists who mistook him for a descendant of Justice John Marshall and a practice that made the comparison with the younger John M. Harlan that much easier. A newspaper in 1892 ran a story entitled "Two Harlans," with a sketch of the justice above one of John Maynard. The first was described as "distinguished," the second as "most promising"; both were lawyers and part-time law instructors.[87] The comparison was unavoidable for all concerned. These pressures took a toll on Justice Harlan's youngest son, just as they had on his brother, as demonstrated by an encounter that occurred after the justice's death.

While riding on a train one day in 1915, John Maynard introduced himself to a stranger who remarked on the Harlan name and praised the judge. Instead of acknowledging his connection, John Maynard savored the praise quietly and then passed it on to his mother in a letter. But the praise left a bittersweet taste in his own mouth because he could not help thinking that he had failed to live up to his father's example. John Maynard wrote his mother, "I have had a lot of people tell me I looked like father, but up to date no one has told me that I was like him, and I am waiting, hoping that someone may feel like saying that to me." He continued, "I am afraid though, that never will or can be said, for a stranger would not have any opinion on the subject and anyone who knew father and knows me could not say it." Unwilling to end his letter so sadly, John Maynard tried to joke his way out of the dilemma by saying, "However, I must try to fool someone into thinking so!"[88] By 1915, it was too late for John Maynard to prove to his father that he was up to the standards of their clan. Several times he had come tantalizingly close.

American Railway Union leader Eugene Debs had come to John Maynard seeking legal counsel following his arrest for violating a federal injunction during the Pullman strike of 1894. Afraid of being tarred with the brush of radicalism and unwilling to lower his fees, John Maynard declined. His father

John Maynard Harlan (1864–1934), the youngest of Harlan's three sons, practiced law in Chicago and New York. He ran unsuccessfully for mayor of Chicago in 1897 and 1905 and for governor of Illinois in 1920. He wrote in 1915, a year before this photograph was taken, "I have had a lot of people tell me I looked like father, but up to date no one has told me that I was like him, and I am waiting, hoping that someone may feel like saying that to me." (Photograph by Moffett; courtesy of the Library of Congress)

fired off two letters detailing why "I think you made a mistake in not accepting Debs' employment." Regardless of his personal opinion of the strike, he should have taken the case since "what you need now is to become *known*. A well-prepared argument in such a cause would do you good."[89] Young John hurried word back to Debs that he had reconsidered, but it was too late. The case went to Clarence Darrow, and the rest, as they say, is history.[90]

In his political campaigns, John Maynard raised hopes in his father that he did not satisfy. Harlan wrote a letter to his granddaughter during John Maynard's fight for the Chicago mayoralty that in one breath described how Abraham Lincoln became president despite his humble origins and in the next reminded her that "next Wednesday [your] Papa, will, it seems, be nominated for Mayor & then will commence a campaign that will attract the attention of the whole country."[91] The judge's aspirations were plain, but his son lost the election. John Maynard was also nominated by his party in 1920 for the Illinois governorship but lost. He would never attain the national prominence that both he and his father craved for him.

Unlike John Maynard, who had shied away from but then allowed himself to be led by his father's example, Richard was seemingly uninjured by paternal pressure during his youth. By becoming valedictorian of his class at Princeton and then going on to prepare for the ministry, he resisted his father in the least rebellious of ways. His valedictory prompted Noah Swayne to write his father: "*Such things cannot be measured by any pecuniary standard. They are above and beyond it!*"[92] Despite his hope that Richard would go on from this triumph to a brilliant career in the law and public life, Harlan consented to his son's choice and financed his graduate education. He considered the clergy's spiritual leadership of the people as important to civic virtue as the work of liberty-loving lawyers.

In his choice of occupation, Richard partook most of the Christian gentleman ideal, which rejected material ambition and turned inward toward spiritual life. Richard served as a minister in several churches and as president of Lake Forest College in Illinois from 1901 to 1906 and then did administrative work at George Washington University. But that work was apparently not enough. The lures of Mammon remained attractive. By 1909, Richard lost almost all of his wife Margaret's trust (worth some $110,000) through bad bets on the stock market. He turned to his brothers for help.

Richard confided the trouble to them in James's office in the Interstate Commerce Commission building. According to John Maynard's deposition given for a resulting lawsuit and written in the third person, "Both James and John were very much shocked by this disclosure, so much so that they both actually wept." The brothers immediately offered whatever funds they had to

Richard Davenport Harlan (1859–1931) was Harlan's eldest son. He was valedictorian of the class of 1881 at Princeton University and graduated from Princeton Theological Seminary in 1885. After serving as pastor at two New York churches, he was president of Lake Forest College in Illinois from 1901 to 1905 and then worked at George Washington University from 1907 to 1910. When he lost almost all of his wife's trust fund through bad bets on the stock market, his brothers offered to help, but arguments over the ownership of bonds devoted to replacing the funds provoked the brothers to sue one another. (Courtesy of Archives, Lake Forest College)

try to cover the losses. The question of Richard's possible criminal liability was never mentioned, John Maynard testified. Above all, "the fear of public scandal was predominant."[93] They must have been horrified at the idea that *this* might be their generation's contribution to the public reputation of the Harlan tribe.

The sons managed to keep the losses from becoming public knowledge for years, but the scandal burst into the open in the 1920s. The Harlan sons fell out over an agreement concerning certain bonds whose interest was set aside to replenish the trust. The question was whether the bonds themselves had changed hands. James proceeded to sue John Maynard in the Illinois courts, and John Maynard responded with a countersuit against James and Richard in the courts of the District of Columbia. Because of the immediate appellate power of the U.S. Supreme Court over the courts of the nation's capital, the Harlan scandal found its way before the bench on which their father had sat.[94]

It is unclear just how much Harlan knew about the financial troubles into which his sons had fallen. He held an extremely low opinion of speculation by the early twentieth century. They could have guessed his displeasure at the situation in light of his adage, "Preserve a good name. You will see in the end that it is a far better asset than a bank account."[95] His concern had some lingering effect. John Maynard thanked Margaret in 1921 for what he called "the one happy aspect of the whole calamity": "the fact that the public disclosure of Richard's error has been postponed until after father and mother had died."[96] The trust scandal inflicted a family wound that took a generation to heal.

There is evidence elsewhere of "a dramatic shift of masculine ideals in nineteenth-century America—the shift from a standard of manhood rooted in the life of the community and the qualities of a man's soul to a standard of manhood based on individual achievement and the male body"—but the Harlan men blended the two impulses.[97] Harlan told a fellow judge that their fate was to "live well, work hard & die poor. Yet I am happy and contented in my lot."[98]

What went unacknowledged was the part luck had played in Harlan's gaining the post with which he made his public reputation. From the early 1870s onward, Harlan and Bristow had been discussing his chances of gaining a spot on the bench. They were not particularly good. Bristow once said, "There are so many *eminent* lawyers who are willing to be immolated on the alter, that the chances of any one man are hardly worth reckoning."[99] If he had never found his way into federal office, Harlan might have languished in Kentucky for years as a perennial Republican candidate. So valued was the appointment that Harlan's friendship with Bristow broke under its weight. Bristow accused

Harlan of taking a prize that was rightfully his.[100] Of course, shrewd political maneuvering was no more a part of Harlan's official formula for success than luck.[101]

Although the Harlan sons felt the strain of their tribe's demands, it would be wrong to depict them as crushed. Even in the letters from their college years, there is evidence of a serious give-and-take between the sons and their father as to "the best mode" of study.[102] Harlan counseled them that it was important to rest and to play, a little anyway, even as he urged them to hit the books. As adults, they corresponded seriously. When John Maynard heard from his mother in 1910 that George Washington University was trying to struggle out of financial chaos by cutting the salaries of its law professors, he wrote his father a letter of advice quite as formidable as anything his father had ever written him.[103] Neither his father's personal success nor his expectations had reduced John Maynard to a nonentity.

Harlan was renowned for his amiable nature, but John Maynard was remembered by his daughter as "an irascible tyrant" and by his grandson Roger Derby as having had an "extraordinarily stormy temperament." [104] It is hard to say whether his bad temper was what prevented him from attaining high office or whether the failure to win high office produced a bad temper. The pressure John Maynard endured, his personal disappointments, and the financial scandal may have taken a toll on him. But as Roger Derby rightly pointed out, his failings are only part of the picture. Better to heed the biography of John Maynard written by his son, Justice John Marshall Harlan the younger, and recognize the public achievements of a man with a substantial legal career and lifelong local political influence. His disappointments, to risk a pun, were relative.

# Conclusion

*The veneration he had for the high place to which he had been called, filled him more and more with an intense ambition to be worthy of it; and while he never reached his own ideal for that position, yet his opinions, even in the earliest years of his services on the bench, won for him, in the judgment of the legal profession, a high place among the great men.*

—Malvina Shanklin Harlan, 1915

Almost everyone knows what it's like to come up with a clever response several hours after an argument. I felt that way after a conference marking the 100th anniversary of Harlan's dissent in *Plessy v. Ferguson* in April 1996 held at Harlan's alma mater, Centre College in Kentucky. A member of the audience asked the panel of scholars what we thought Harlan would do today. In the back of many people's minds was *Hopwood v. State of Texas*, the decision made the month before by the Court of Appeals for the Fifth Circuit that the University of Texas School of Law had violated the Fourteenth Amendment by "giving substantial racial preferences in its admissions program" through affirmative action. Some uneasiness marked the discussion that followed, probably because opponents of affirmative action had been arguing in the press that a color-blind Constitution must bar it and advocates of affirmative action were unhappy that Harlan's words were being invoked by the other side.[1] My worry was that we did history itself a disservice by asking such a question.

I thought it was a silly question because of the reasons we ask it. I think we ask what Harlan would do today, or Thomas Jefferson or Frederick Douglass or anyone else, because we want them to tell us what to do. But they can't because we are on our own and need to take responsibility for our own moral choices. They can't because we are unable to really know what they would do. I told the man in the audience that we can only understand and explain Harlan through the historical circumstances in which he lived. It's impossible to rip him out of those circumstances, stick him in ours, and watch him go.

I had guessed that the man in the audience was a lawyer from the way he had asked the question and from his persistence. I saw him later and we continued to argue in a friendly fashion. He said that the answer to his question was obvious. Many of Harlan's words, he insisted, could be taken directly out of *Plessy* and used today. It was only later that I thought of how I should have responded to that: so great is the chasm between Harlan and us that some of his words in *Plessy* seem to make no sense at all.

Harlan began his dissent by reciting the particulars of the Louisiana statute that prohibited a person of one race from entering a train compartment designated for the use of the other race. He then pointed out that although the law exempted nurses caring for children of a different race, "no exception is made for colored attendants travelling with adults." As a result, "a white man is not permitted to have his colored servant with him in the same coach, even if his condition of health requires" constant attention. Nor was a white woman allowed the services of her black maid.

To us, this seems a strange opening for a judge about to let loose on the injustice and stupidity of racial segregation in public transportation. Was the inability of well-off whites to travel with their black servants really the first and most important objection Harlan could make to racial segregation in public accommodations? Charles Lofgren, in his book about the origins of the *Plessy* case, criticizes Harlan for beginning his dissent in "an unfortunately weak fashion."[2]

But Harlan must have planned carefully the opening barrage of his last full-scale assault on segregation in public accommodations. (There would be another such dissent in 1900 and one in 1910, but both were silent.) He didn't mean it to be weak. It only seems weak now because of the distance between us. Harlan aimed his opening at a subject of particular significance for the brethren of the late-nineteenth-century Supreme Court. As Malvina Harlan explains in her memoirs, "It has always been the custom for the Government to furnish a messenger or personal attendant for each Justice of the Supreme Court. These messengers are always coloured men."[3] Thus, all of the judges had "colored servants" with whom they would not be allowed to travel under Louisiana law, just like the fictional white man on the train. Harlan designed his opening in *Plessy* to appeal specifically to his brethren, to their common sense and personal feeling. He was trying to make them admit what they knew: that it was absurd to force the separation of traveling blacks and whites when they worked with each other every day. Harlan's "court messenger" James Jackson traveled north from Washington, D.C., to Murray Bay in Quebec to spend the summer working for the Harlan family, so it is possible that Harlan had shared a train ride with him. Only by recognizing the circumstances in which Harlan wrote his decisions can we understand what he was doing.

The legal realists are known for their insight into the worldly origins of the law, but the only novelty of their insight lay in their rejection of any transcendent ideal for judges to aim at. Harlan once told his class about the role the Supreme Court justices had played in the disputed presidential election of 1876. A special election commission composed of congressmen and justices was supposed to decide whether Republican Rutherford B. Hayes or Democrat Samuel J. Tilden had won the majority of electoral votes. Harlan described Justice Nathan Clifford, who served on the commission, as "a man who had strong political convictions, but he never meddled in politics, and he did not know what politics he had when he got on the bench." But one day "he met one of his brethren who was not on the commission, and Brother Clifford, with perfect simplicity, said to that brother judge, that he was sick at heart. Why what was the matter. 'Why, up to this time every question that had been considered here, the commission is divided on the line of politics.'" And the fellow judge, who was a Republican himself, agreed, "I observe 'Cliffy' that all of you Democrats vote together every time a vote is cast"—a truth that shocked Justice Clifford. The Court was "supposed to be above party."[4]

Harlan thought that one could act above party. A newspaperman once asked him if it was true, as people said, that he saw no middle ground between right and wrong. Harlan replied with a certain impatience: "I cannot understand why this should be said of me, nor do I know precisely what is meant by the question." He went on to explain that "there are some things so eternally wrong that duty to conscience compels one to condemn them, and not to tolerate half-measures. Such wrongs ought to be avenged or suppressed and be destroyed utterly, and ought never to be condoned." Other times, one could not act so surely and swiftly "although it may be fairly said that there is right on one side and a wrong on the other side." "We must be guided somewhat by the gravity of the matter to be dealt with," he added, "and the presence or absence of any special duty on our part in reference to such matters."[5] Harlan was explaining the relationship between eternal ideals and human circumstances. The fact that circumstances varied did not affect the truth of ideals.

One of my favorite quotations is from the Massachusetts Declaration of Rights. Its Article 29 declares that "it is the right of every citizen to be tried by judges as free, impartial, and independent as the lot of humanity will admit."[6] There's a strain of Christianity in that last phrase. Such a faith allowed people to recognize that their fallen status made it impossible for them to reach the ideal they might set for themselves. Yet that same faith prevented such failure from undermining the strength of those ideals.

When one of the district judges on Harlan's circuit retired, Harlan wrote him a letter voicing his ideal of judgeship. We don't have that letter, but we do have the reply. Judge Romanzo Bunn wrote Harlan, "I do not know as I could say all that you quote from Samuel, though I think I could. At any rate, I can say, as you could say of yourself, that I have never made an unconscientious ruling."[7] The passage that Harlan must have quoted to him from the Old Testament is this:

> And Samuel said unto all Israel . . .
>
> Behold here I am: witness against me before the Lord and before his anointed: whose ox have I taken? or whose ass have I taken? or whom have I defrauded? Whom have I oppressed? or of whose hand have I received any bribe to blind my eyes therewith? and I will restore it to you.
>
> And they said, Thou has not defrauded us, nor oppressed us, neither has thou taken aught of any man's hand.[8]

Judge Bunn may have been unwilling to go metaphorically before Israel as the righteous judge in a fallen world, but he believed that he and Harlan had ruled honestly. Samuel was asking about the easy cases of integrity. He had taken no bribe, confiscated no goods for himself.

This book has been about the hard cases of integrity. Instead of trying to identify Harlan as a man who transcended history and was later vindicated by it, it has tried to show that he was a man with a history. It has searched for the ideals and goals that lie behind the law that the judge pronounced that he had found. Harlan drew on the traditions in which he was raised, struggled through his own experiences, and came to an explanation of what had happened and what would happen to himself and his country. Tradition and circumstance offered him a range of moral choices. The realist remark that the law was what the judge had for breakfast underestimates the effort and creativity of Harlan's work on the republican project.

Judicial biographers' desire to prove that they were writing about great judges was inspired in part by the oldest justification for biography: the attempt to supply models of civic behavior. Harlan recommended that his sons read biographies of "great men."[9] All but one were American statesmen. John P. Kennedy's *Memoirs of the Life of William Wirt* was dedicated "to the young men of the United States, who seek guidance to an honourable fame."[10] M. L. Weems wrote a little poem for the title page of his volume on George Washington: "A Life how useful to his country led! / How loved! while living!—how revered! now dead! / Lisp! lisp! his name, ye children yet unborn! / And with like deeds your own great names adorn."[11] I offer Harlan's history less as a model and more as evidence of the importance of the individual choices made by those participating in the republican project. If it is we who draw on tradition, create standards, and choose goals instead of simply receiving some eternal natural law, then Harlan's history offers the most essential republican message. As he would put it, we are part and parcel of the government under which we live.

# Harlan's List of Opinions for Publication

Harlan listed the following opinions, probably in 1910, with the note, "In book containing my opinions & dissenting opinions publish the following." The list can be found among his papers at the University of Louisville Law School. I have corrected citations when necessary.

## MAJORITY OPINIONS

*Guy v. Baltimore*, 100 U.S. 434 (1879)
*Hopt v. People of the Territory of Utah*, 110 U.S. 574 (1884)
*New Orleans Gas Company v. Louisiana Light Company*, 115 U.S. 650 (1885)
*Mugler v. Kansas*, 123 U.S. 623 (1887)
*Callan v. Wilson*, 127 U.S. 540 (1888)
*Clough v. Curtis, Burkhart v. Reed*, 134 U.S. 361 (1890)
*Cherokee Nation v. Southern Kansas Railway Company*, 135 U.S. 641 (1890)
*Minnesota v. Barber*, 136 U.S. 313 (1890)
*Holden v. Minnesota*, 137 U.S. 483 (1890)
*Brimmer v. Rebman*, 138 U.S. 78 (1891)
*United States v. Texas*, 143 U.S. 621 (1891)
*Field v. Clark*, 143 U.S. 649 (1892)
*Plumley v. Massachusetts*, 155 U.S. 461 (1894)
*Sparf and Hansen v. United States*, 156 U.S. 51 (1895)
*Sweet v. Rechel*, 159 U.S. 380 (1895)
*Rosen v. United States*, 161 U.S. 29 (1896)
*United States v. Texas*, 162 U.S. 1 (1896)
*Gibson v. Mississippi*, 162 U.S. 565 (1896)
*Hennington v. Georgia*, 163 U.S. 299 (1896)
*Covington and Lexington Turnpike Road Company v. Sandford*, 164 U.S. 578 (1896)
*New York, New Haven, and Hartford Railroad Company v. New York*, 165 U.S. 628
    (1897)
*Chicago, Burlington, and Quincy Railroad Company v. Chicago*, 166 U.S. 226 (1897)
*Tindal v. Wesley*, 167 U.S. 204 (1897)
*Douglas v. Kentucky*, 168 U.S. 488 (1897)
*Smyth v. Ames*, 169 U.S. 466 (1898)
*Thompson v. Utah*, 170 U.S. 343 (1898)
*Blake v. McClung*, 172 U.S. 239 (1898)
*Lake Shore and Michigan Southern Railway Company v. Ohio*, 173 U.S. 285 (1899)
*Smith v. Reeves*, 178 U.S. 436 (1900)
*Motes v. United States*, 178 U.S. 458 (1900)
*Scranton v. Wheeler*, 179 U.S. 141 (1900)
*Reid v. Colorado*, 187 U.S. 137 (1902)

*Lottery Case (Champion v. Ames)*, 188 U.S. 321 (1903)

*Louisville and Jeffersonville Ferry Company v. Kentucky*, 188 U.S. 385 (1903)

*Atkin v. Kansas*, 191 U.S. 207 (1903)

*Northern Securities Company v. United States*, 193 U.S. 197 (1904)

*Great Southern Fire Proof Hotel Company v. Jones*, 193 U.S. 532 (1904)

*Jacobson v. Massachusetts*, 197 U.S. 11 (1905)

*California Reduction Company v. Sanitary Reduction Works*, 199 U.S. 306 (1905)

*Chicago, Burlington, and Quincy Railway Company v. People of the State of Illinois ex rel. Drainage Commissioners*, 200 U.S. 561 (1906)

*West Chicago Street Railroad Company v. People of the State of Illinois ex rel. City of Chicago*, 201 U.S. 506 (1906)

*Pettibone v. Nichols*, 203 U.S. 192 (1906)

*Appleyard v. Massachusetts*, 203 U.S. 222 (1906)

*Union Bridge Company v. United States*, 204 U.S. 364 (1907)

*Halter v. Nebraska*, 205 U.S. 34 (1907)

*Homer E. Grafton, Plaintiff in Error, v. United States*, 206 U.S. 333 (1907)

*Adair v. United States*, 208 U.S. 161 (1908)

*Miller and Lux, Incorporated, v. East Side Canal and Irrigation Company*, 211 U.S. 293 (1908)

*Southern Realty Investment Company v. Walker*, 211 U.S. 603 (1909)

*Presidio County, Texas, v. Noel-Young Bond and Stock Company*, 212 U.S. 58 (1909)

*Continental Wall Paper Company v. Louis Voight and Sons Company*, 212 U.S. 227 (1909)

*Hepner v. United States*, 213 U.S. 103 (1909)

*Compton v. State of Alabama*, 214 U.S. 1 (1909)

*Kuhn v. Fairmont Coal Company*, 215 U.S. 349 (1910)

*Henley v. Myers, Receiver of Consolidated Barbed Wire Company*, 215 U.S. 373 (1910)

*Western Union Telegraph Company v. State of Kansas ex rel. Coleman, Attorney General*, 216 U.S. 1 (1910)

*Pullman Company v. State of Kansas ex rel. Coleman, Attorney General*, 216 U.S. 56 (1910)

*International Textbook Company v. Pigg*, 217 U.S. 91 (1910)

*Southwestern Oil Company v. Texas*, 217 U.S. 114 (1910)


DISSENTING OPINIONS

*Civil Rights Cases*, 109 U.S. 3 (1883)

*Cunningham v. Macon and Brunswick Railroad Company et al.*, 109 U.S. 446 (1883)

*Hurtado v. People of California*, 110 U.S. 516 (1884)

*Philadelphia Fire Association v. New York*, 119 U.S. 110 (1886)

*Baldwin v. Franks*, 120 U.S. 678 (1887)

*Bowman v. Chicago and Northwestern Railway Company*, 125 U.S. 465 (1888)

*Louisville, New Orleans, and Texas Railway Company v. Mississippi*, 133 U.S. 587 (1890)

*Ficklen v. Shelby County Taxing District*, 145 U.S. 1 (1892)

*United States v. E. C. Knight Company*, 156 U.S. 1 (1895)

*Pollock v. Farmers' Loan and Trust Company (II)*, 158 U.S. 601 (1895)

*Plessy v. Ferguson*, 163 U.S. 537 (1896)

*Robertson v. Baldwin*, 165 U.S. 275 (1897)

*Hawker v. New York*, 170 U.S. 189 (1898)

*Maxwell v. Dow*, 176 U.S. 581 (1900)

*Hawaii v. Mankichi*, 190 U.S. 197 (1903)

*Dorr v. United States*, 195 U.S. 138 (1904)

*Lochner v. New York*, 198 U.S. 45 (1905)

*Trono v. United States*, 199 U.S. 521 (1905)

*Cox v. Texas*, 202 U.S. 446 (1906)

*Hodges v. United States*, 203 U.S. 1 (1906)

*Berea College v. Commonwealth of Kentucky*, 211 U.S. 45 (1908)

*Twining v. New Jersey*, 211 U.S. 78 (1908)

*Bailey v. State of Alabama (I)*, 211 U.S. 452 (1908)

*Macon Grocery Company v. Atlantic Coast Line Railroad Company*, 215 U.S. 501 (1910)

# NOTES

ABBREVIATIONS

The following abbreviations are used in the notes.

| | |
|---|---|
| AEW | Augustus E. Willson |
| BH | Benjamin Harrison |
| BHB | Benjamin H. Bristow |
| FD | Frederick Douglass |
| GWS | George W. Shanklin |
| HHL | Horace H. Lurton |
| JH | James Harlan (John Marshall Harlan's brother) |
| JMayH | John Maynard Harlan |
| JMH | John Marshall Harlan |
| JMH Lectures | John Marshall Harlan, Constitutional Law Lectures, 1897–98, John Marshall Harlan Papers, Library of Congress, Manuscript Division, Washington, D.C. |
| JoH | Joseph Holt |
| JSH | James Shanklin Harlan |
| LC | Library of Congress, Manuscript Division, Washington, D.C. |
| MRW | Morrison R. Waite |
| MSH | Malvina Shanklin Harlan |
| MSH, "Memories" | Malvina Shanklin Harlan, "Some Memories of a Long Life, 1854–1911," 1915, microfilm, John Marshall Harlan Papers, Library of Congress, Manuscript Division, Washington, D.C. |
| MWF | Melville Weston Fuller |
| RDH | Richard Davenport Harlan |
| UofL | University of Louisville School of Law, Law Library, Louisville, Kentucky |
| WHT | William Howard Taft |
| WM | William McKinley |
| WQG | Walter Q. Gresham |

## INTRODUCTION

1. *Plessy v. Ferguson*, 163 U.S. 537, 559, 562, 560 (1896).

2. *Louisville, New Orleans, and Texas Railway Company v. Mississippi*, 133 U.S. 587 (1890); *Chiles v. Chesapeake and Ohio Railway Company*, 218 U.S. 71 (1910).

3. *Berea College v. Commonwealth of Kentucky*, 211 U.S. 45 (1908).

4. Harlan dissented from *Clyatt v. United States*, 197 U.S. 207 (1905), and *Bailey v. State of Alabama (I)*, 211 U.S. 452 (1908), then was part of the majority in *Bailey v. State of Alabama (II)*, 219 U.S. 219 (1911).

5. *United States v. Harris*, 106 U.S. 629 (1883); *James v. Bowman*, 190 U.S. 127 (1903); *Hodges v. United States*, 203 U.S. 1 (1906).

6. *Pace v. Alabama*, 106 U.S. 583 (1882).

7. *Cumming v. Richmond County Board of Education*, 175 U.S. 528 (1899).

8. "Writing of Judicial Biography," 368.

9. JMH to HHL, 3 July 1910, HHL Papers, LC. Unless otherwise noted, italics in quotations throughout are reproduced from the original source.

10. Horwitz, "Conservative Tradition," 281.

11. Swisher, *Stephen J. Field*, 165. See also ibid., 239.

12. Kens, *Justice Stephen Field*, 10.

13. Hurst, "Who Is the 'Great' Appellate Judge?," 398–400.

14. Fairman, *Mr. Justice Miller*, 197. Fairman lists craftsmanship in "What Makes a Great Justice?," 86.

15. Horwitz, "Conservative Tradition," 277.

16. Knight, "Dissenting Opinions," 484.

17. Westin, "John Marshall Harlan," 705.

18. See Reid, *Chief Justice*, 281.

19. Swisher, *Stephen J. Field*, 433, 431.

20. Swisher, *Roger B. Taney*, 584. For Swisher's New Deal loyalties, see "Judge in Historical Perspective," 385–86. For other examples, see Hurst, *Growth of American Law*, 18, and Levy, *Law of the Commonwealth*, 126.

21. Kens, *Justice Stephen Field*, 269.

22. Levy, *Law of the Commonwealth*, 302.

23. Reid, *Chief Justice*, 100.

24. Fairman, "What Makes a Great Justice?," 70.

25. Beth, "Justice Harlan," 1086.

26. Fairman, *Mr. Justice Miller*, 138. See also ibid., 207–8.

27. McCurdy, "Stephen J. Field," 6–7, and "Justice Field." See Levy, *Law of the Commonwealth*, 67, on Shaw dealing with the Fugitive Slave Law.

28. Levy, *Law of the Commonwealth*, 145, 164, n. 87.

29. Ibid., 164.

30. G. Edward White, *Justice Oliver Wendell Holmes*, 180–81.

31. Newmyer, *Supreme Court Justice Joseph Story*, 119. See also ibid., 383, and Magrath, *Morrison R. Waite*, 203.

32. King, *Melville Weston Fuller*, 129.

33. Yarbrough, *Judicial Enigma*, 179.

34. Beth, *John Marshall Harlan*, 269–71.

35. Holmes has not been the only judge to experience such a reconstruction. See Spillenger, "Reading the Judicial Canon," on Brandeis, and Finkelman, " 'Hooted down the Page of History,' " on Taney.

36. G. Edward White, *Justice Oliver Wendell Holmes*, 355.

37. Waite, "How 'Eccentric' Was Mr. Justice Harlan?"

38. "John Marshall Harlan (1833–1911)," special issue of *Kentucky Law Journal* 46 (Spring 1958).

39. Richard B. Morris, *Encyclopedia of American History*, 671; Bradley, "Who Are the Great Justices?," 24–28; Blaustein and Mersky, *First One Hundred Justices*, 37, 42.

40. On religious faith, compare Brodhead's treatment in *David J. Brewer* to the

essays in "Symposium: Religion and the Judicial Process," especially J. Gordon Hylton's. On literary interests, see King, *Melville Weston Fuller,* 87–93, and Ely, *Chief Justiceship of Melville W. Fuller,* 14–15.

41. Biographies of women, such as Laura Thatcher Ulrich's *Midwife's Tale* on Martha Ballard and Edith B. Gelles's *Portia* on Abigail Adams, have used more uncommon approaches.

42. J. Woodford Howard Jr., "Commentary," 543. See also *New York University Law Review* 70 (June 1995): 556, 560, 730–31.

43. McCurdy, "Justice Field"; Benedict, "Laissez-Faire and Liberty"; Alan Jones, "Thomas M. Cooley and the Interstate Commerce Commission" and "Thomas M. Cooley and 'Laissez-Faire Constitutionalism.'"

44. *Spring Valley Water Works v. Schottler and Others, Supervisors,* 110 U.S. 347, 374 (1884).

45. Paludan, *Covenant with Death*; Schieber, "Federalism and Legal Process"; Benedict, "Preserving Federalism"; Magrath, *Morrison R. Waite,* 153–54.

46. Morton White, *Social Thought in America.*

47. Fredrickson, *Inner Civil War.*

48. G. Edward White, *Justice Oliver Wendell Holmes,* 80–82.

49. Kaczorowski, *Politics of Judicial Interpretation.* See also Gold, *Shaping of Nineteenth-Century Law,* 97–119.

50. Przybyszewski, "Judge Lorenzo Sawyer," 31.

51. Kousser, "Before *Plessy.*"

CHAPTER ONE

1. *Plessy v. Ferguson,* 163 U.S. 537, 559 (1896).

2. Landynski, "John Marshall Harlan," 899.

3. Beth, *John Marshall Harlan,* 231.

4. See McCurry, "Two Faces of Republicanism."

5. Thelan, "Memory and American History," 1120–21.

6. MSH, "Memories," frame 150.

7. Beth, *John Marshall Harlan,* 51; Yarbrough, *Judicial Enigma,* 46–47.

8. Faust, "Altars of Sacrifice."

9. Kerber, "Separate Spheres," 39.

10. MSH, "Memories," frame 106.

11. MSH to JMH, August 1877, JMH Papers, LC.

12. MSH to her children, [27 October] 1911, JMH Papers, LC.

13. Westin, "John Marshall Harlan," 642, 652; Beth, *John Marshall Harlan,* 27; Yarbrough, *Judicial Enigma,* 9; Farrelly, "Harlan's Formative Period," 368.

14. Baradaglio, *Reconstructing the Household,* xi.

15. MSH, "Memories," frames 111–12. Malvina's father, John Shanklin, was well enough disposed to African Americans in Evansville to sell them property for a church for a nominal sum (Bigham, *We Ask Only a Fair Trial,* 10).

16. MSH, "Memories," frame 112.

17. Ibid., frame 115.

18. Ibid., frame 112.

19. Coulter, *Civil War*, 7–8.

20. D. Howard Smith to James Harlan, 4 August 1851, JMH Papers, LC.

21. James Harlan to D. Howard Smith, 5 August 1851, JMH Papers, LC.

22. Rose, "Domestication of Domestic Slavery."

23. MSH, "Memories," frames 114–15.

24. Scott, "Women's Perspective," 175.

25. Rose, "Domestication of Domestic Slavery," 23.

26. Thomas D. Morris, *Southern Slavery*, 182–208.

27. MSH, "Memories," frame 119.

28. Ibid., frames 117, 124.

29. Ibid., frame 124.

30. Ibid., frame 116.

31. Ibid., frame 159.

32. Ibid., frame 115.

33. MSH to JMH, May 1867, JMH Papers, LC.

34. MSH, "Memories," frame 118.

35. Ibid., frame 159.

36. Ibid., frame 157.

37. Ibid., frame 114.

38. Ibid., frame 120.

39. Simmons, *Men of Mark*, 613.

40. Scott, "Women's Perspective," 180.

41. See *Cincinnati Daily Gazette*, 15 October 1881, 4. I thank Professor J. Morgan Kousser for this citation. On this question, see James W. Gordon, "Did the First Justice Harlan Have a Black Brother?"

42. Robert interceded on behalf of a Harlan who had assaulted a black civil servant on 5 November 1871 and discussed Rutherford B. Hayes's disappointing race policy with John on 1 June 1877, JMH Papers, LC.

43. Morrow paraphrased a shortened version of the story in "Talks with Notable Men," which differs in minor details.

44. MSH, "Memories," frame 119.

45. Ibid., frame 155.

46. Ibid., frame 119.

47. Ibid., frames 119, 120.

48. JMH Lectures, 7 May 1898.

49. MSH, "Memories," frame 119. Malvina uses the term "slave-driver," but since slave drivers were generally black, she must have meant a slave trader, both of whom "ranked . . . as the fiends of the regime," according to Genovese, *Roll, Jordan, Roll*, 372.

50. Howe, *Political Culture of the American Whigs*, 133–35.

51. Collins and Collins, *Collins' Historical Sketches*, 1:62. See also Degler, *Other South*, 55–60.

52. T. D. Clark, "Slave Trade," 335.

53. Bancroft, *Slave-Trading*, 128, 376.

54. James W. Gordon, "Did the First Justice Harlan Have a Black Brother?," 160.

55. Henry Harlan to Benjamin Harlan, 25 January 1845, JMH Papers, LC.

56. MSH, "Memories," frame 120.

57. Not all Harlans did. In 1909, John and others wrote President William Howard Taft asking him to pardon W. S. Harlan of Lockhart, Alabama, after his conviction on charges of peonage (series 5, case file 1275, reel 336, WHT Papers, LC). See Daniel, *Shadow of Slavery*, 88–94.

58. MSH, "Memories," frame 120.

59. Ibid., frame 114.

60. Ibid., frames 157–58.

61. Ibid., frame 155.

62. Estate of James Harlan, [1863], JMH Papers, LC.

63. Genovese, " 'Our Family, White and Black,' " 87.

64. MSH, "Memories," frames 108–9.

65. Malvina attended the Glendale Female Seminary outside Cincinnati in 1855 and the Presbyterian Misses Gill's School in Philadelphia in 1853.

66. MSH, "Memories," frames 160–61.

67. See Welter, "Cult of True Womanhood," 151.

68. Matthews, *Just a Housewife*, 34.

69. MSH, "Memories," frame 248.

70. See Degler, *At Odds*, 8–9, and Lebsock, *Free Women of Petersburg*, 28–32.

71. MSH, "Memories," frame 112. Malvina acquiesced to their later move to Louisville despite her desire to return to Evansville (MSH to JMH, 26 May 1867, JMH Papers, LC).

72. Scott, "Women, Religion, and Social Change," 191.

73. Lebsock, *Free Women of Petersburg*, 32. See also Bynum, *Unruly Women*, 71–77, 82–85.

74. Basch, " 'Invisible Women,' " 348; Grossberg, *Governing the Hearth*, 27. See also Censer, " 'Smiling through Her Tears.' "

75. Harlan and Butler, "Treatise on the Law of Marriage."

76. Basch, *In the Eyes of the Law*.

77. See Baym, *Woman's Fiction*, and Hartog, "Mrs. Packard."

78. MSH, "Memories," frame 249.

79. Ibid., frame 204.

80. Ibid., frame 130.

81. Duffield, *Washington in the 90's*, 61; Slayden, *Washington Wife*, 65.

82. MSH, "Memories," frame 235.

83. Ibid., frame 181. John Harlan explained that Lockwood should have known that the federal government doesn't have an answer for every complaint (JMH Lectures, 12 March 1898).

84. MSH, "Memories," frame 250; *First International Congress in America for the Welfare of the Child*.

85. *Bradwell v. the State*, 83 U.S. 130, 141 (1872). Harlan was part of a unanimous majority in *In re Lockwood*, 154 U.S. 116 (1893), which allowed the state courts to decide whether "person" equals "man" in their statutes, so the states could refuse to allow women to join the state bar.

86. *Thompson v. Thompson*, 218 U.S. 611, 620 (1910).

87. JMH to John Harland, 27 February 1911, JMH Papers, LC.

88. Laura served as a social secretary to several presidents' wives. See Yarbrough, *Judicial Enigma*, 226.

89. Quoted in Hartz, "John M. Harlan," 18.

90. This chapter's chronology relies on Coulter, *Civil War*.

91. U.S. Bureau of the Census, *Population of the United States in 1860, Eighth Census*, 179, 184.

92. JMH to JoH, 11 March 1861, JoH Papers, LC.

93. McPherson, *Abraham Lincoln*, 31.

94. Quoted in Collins and Collins, *Collins' Historical Sketches*, 1:87.

95. Stevenson, "General Nelson," 118.

96. JMH, "Civil War of 1861: The Union Cause in Kentucky . . . ," n.d., autobiographical essay, JMH Papers, LC.

97. Coulter, *Civil War*, 100.

98. JMH, "Civil War of 1861: The Union Cause in Kentucky . . . ," n.d., autobiographical essay, JMH Papers, LC.

99. *War of the Rebellion*, 3d ser., 1:801.

100. Ibid., 1st ser., 20:134–41.

101. Coulter, *Civil War*, 145–69; Collins and Collins, *Collins' Historical Sketches*, 1:109.

102. Randall, *Constitutional Problems*, 193–94.

103. Collins and Collins, *Collins' Historical Sketches*, 1:111.

104. Coulter, *Civil War*, 158–59.

105. Ibid., 161.

106. Quoted in Speed, Kelly, and Pirtle, *Union Regiments*, 371.

107. JMH to RDH, 4 July 1911, autobiographical letter, JMH Papers, LC.

108. Collins and Collins, *Collins' Historical Sketches*, 1:146.

109. Quoted in Westin, "John Marshall Harlan," 651.

110. Quoted in Hartz, "John M. Harlan," 29–30.

111. Quoted in Coulter, *Civil War*, 279–80.

112. Hartz, "John M. Harlan," 29.

113. Quoted in ibid., 31.

114. Victor B. Howard, *Black Liberation*, 72–90.

115. Collins and Collins, *Collins' Historical Sketches*, 1:163; *Commonwealth v. John M. Palmer*, 65 Ky. (2 Bush) 570 (1866).

116. *Bowlin v. Commonwealth*, 15 Ky. (2 Bush) 5 (1867); Victor B. Howard, "Black Testimony Controversy."

117. Morrow, "Talks with Notable Men," 6. See also JMH to RDH, 4 July 1911, autobiographical letter, JMH Papers, LC.

118. Malvina wrote to her son James: "I hate to think of decent people belonging to" the Democratic Party (MSH to JSH, 14 November 1880, JMH Papers, LC).

119. J. S. Sinclair to JMH, 30 November 1869, JMH Papers, LC.

120. Wellington Harlan to JMH, 21 January 1868, JMH Papers, LC.

121. Kaczorowski, *Politics of Judicial Interpretation*, 52.

122. JMH, "The Know-Nothing Organization . . . ," n.d., autobiographical essay, JMH Papers, LC.

123. Westin contends similarly that "perhaps more than anything else" Democratic violence swayed Harlan's decisions ("John Marshall Harlan," 659).

124. Coulter, *Civil War*, 359.

125. Low, "Freedmen's Bureau," 254–55, 256.

126. JMH to JSH, 8 October 1881, JMH Papers, LC.

127. MSH, "Memories," frame 101.

128. Quoted in editorial, "General Harlan's Republicanism," *Louisville Daily Commercial*, 1 November 1877, typed copy, JMH Papers, LC.

129. JMH to BHB, 16 September 1871, BHB Papers, LC.

130. BHB to JMH, 22 December 1870, JMH Papers, LC.

131. JMH to BHB, 28 August 1874, BHB Papers, LC. See also ibid., 25 August 1874.

132. JMH to BHB, 10 August 1874, BHB Papers, LC.

133. James D. Hardin to JMH, 16 February 1870, JMH Papers, LC.

134. O. S. Poston to JMH, 12 December 1876, JMH Papers, LC.

135. JMH to BHB, 15 May 1875, BHB Papers, LC.

136. *New York Times*, 31 October 1877, 1, and 28 November 1877, 1.

137. Lewis, "Document," 60–68.

138. Ibid., 70.

139. Quoted in editorial, "General Harlan's Republicanism," *Louisville Daily Commercial*, 1 November 1877, typed copy, JMH Papers, LC.

140. Aunt Charloott to JMH, 5 November 1877, JMH Papers, LC.

141. MSH, "Memories," frames 228–29.

142. Ibid., frame 115.

143. Ibid., frame 228.

144. Ibid., frame 230.

145. Ibid., frames 229–30.


CHAPTER TWO

1. George Johannes to John Marshall Harlan (grandson of JMH), 21 October 1955, JMH Papers, LC.

2. Almon C. Kellog to RDH, 27 May 1930, JMH Papers, UofL.

3. Clipping, *Little Rock Saturday Bee*, 16 April 1895, Family Scrapbook (*Income Tax Case*), JMH Papers, UofL.

4. See, for example, "Justice Harlan's Dissenting Opinion," *New York Times*, 17 May 1911, 6.

5. Clipping, "The Real Justice John M. Harlan on and off the Supreme Bench," *New York World*, 28 May 1911, Family Scrapbook, 1876–1911, JMH Papers, UofL.

6. See Yarbrough, *Judicial Enigma*, 266, n. 43.

7. JMH to Walter C. Clephane, 4 August 1910, JMH Papers, UofL.

8. JMH Lectures, 2 April 1898.

9. Clipping, Clinton W. Gilbert, "Mr. Justice Harlan, the 'Liberal Construc-

tionist,'" [29 or 20?] August 1925, *Washington Daily Mirror*, "John Harlan Derby from His Grandmother Elizabeth Harlan, Christmas 1934" Scrapbook, in the possession of Eve Dillingham.

10. By 1907, Harlan was using Emlin McClain's *Selection of Cases on Constitutional Law* and Thomas M. Cooley's *General Principles of Constitutional Law in the United States of America*, according to the 1907 *George Washington University Bulletin*. He was working on his own book of "select cases on constitutional law" in 1910 (JMH to Walter C. Clephane, 4 August 1910, JMH Papers, UofL).

11. Grey, "Langdell's Orthodoxy," 34.

12. Auerbach, *Unequal Justice*, 96–100, 109–29.

13. Schlegal, "Between the Harvard Founders and the American Legal Realists."

14. Stevens, *Law School*, 40, n. 49.

15. Noll, "Image of the United States," 43.

16. MSH, "Memories," frame 134.

17. Edgington, *History of the New York Avenue Presbyterian Church*, 147.

18. MSH, "Memories," frame 134.

19. Robert Penn Warren, "Legacy of the Civil War," 289.

20. Aaron, *Unwritten War*; Jimerson, *Private Civil War*, 34–49.

21. Peterson, *Lincoln in American Memory*, 24, 30. But children's schoolbooks depicted Lincoln as the savior of the Union (Elson, *Guardians of Tradition*, 204–6).

22. McConnell, *Glorious Contentment*, 193–97; Meier, "Frederick Douglass' Vision," 132; Blight, "'For Something beyond the Battlefield.'"

23. Faust, *Creation of Confederate Nationalism*, 14; Pressly, *Americans Interpret Their Civil War*, 57; Silber, *Romance of Reunion*, 176–78; Wilson, *Baptized in Blood*, 40, 167.

24. Braden, *Oral Tradition*, 66.

25. Buck, *Road to Reunion*, 220–35; Silber, *Romance of Reunion*, 93–123.

26. McConnell, *Glorious Contentment*, 190; Buck, *Road to Reunion*, 236–62.

27. Foster, *Ghosts of the Confederacy*, 145–59; Buck, *Road to Reunion*, 306; Silber, *Romance of Reunion*, 178–85.

28. JMH to John T. Morgan, 10 August 1893, JMH Papers, UofL.

29. JMH to John W. Frazier, 4 August 1898, JMH Papers, LC.

30. Ferguson, *Law and Letters*, 99–100; Forgie, *Patricide in the House Divided*.

31. JMH Lectures, 14 October 1897.

32. Newmyer, *Supreme Court Justice Joseph Story*, 191.

33. JMH Lectures, 7 May 1898.

34. Ibid., 2 April 1898. On the legal status of West Virginia, see Randall, *Constitutional Problems under Lincoln*, 433–76.

35. MSH, "Memories," frame 195.

36. Morrow, "Talks with Notable Men"; clipping, "Desecration of the Sabbath Greatest Evil in Country," unknown Detroit newspaper, June 1908, Family Scrapbook, 1876–1911, 190, JMH Papers, UofL; JMH Lectures, 21 October 1898.

37. Handy, *Undermined Establishment*, 7–29; *Church of the Holy Trinity v. United States*, 143 U.S. 457, 471 (1892).

38. Quoted in Teaford, "Toward a Christian Nation," 128–29.

39. Morrow, "Talks with Notable Men."

40. *Hennington v. Georgia*, 163 U.S. 299, 304 (1896).

41. Clipping, *Christian Observer*, n.d., JMH Papers, UofL; Morrow, "Talks with Notable Men."

42. JMH, speech at Presbyterian Social Union of Philadelphia banquet in response to the toast "The Courts in the American System of Government," 27 March 1905, JMH Papers, UofL.

43. Clipping, "Says He Will Visit Us Again," *Detroit Free Press*, 6 June 1908, Family Scrapbook, 1876–1911, 192, JMH Papers, UofL.

44. Hays, *Presbyterians*, 117.

45. Goen, *Broken Churches*, 73. See also Snay, *Gospel of Disunion*, 115–26.

46. *The Interior*, 8 June 1905, 724; JMH to [leading Presbyterians], 13 February 1905, JMH Papers, UofL.

47. Justice Brewer speech, in "John Marshall Harlan's Twenty-Fifth Anniversary on the United States Supreme Court Banquet Program," JMH Papers, UofL.

48. "James B. Morrow, 'Talks with Notable Men,' *Washington Post*, Feb. 23, 1906" (interview with JMH), typescript, JMH Papers, LC.

49. Luke 16:26.

50. Quoted in Beth, *John Marshall Harlan*, 149–50.

51. Groves, "Centre College," 312, 313–14.

52. Noll, *Princeton Theology*, 11–48; Holifield, *Gentlemen Theologians*, 111–12, 119.

53. "A Course of Reading Recommended by Professor Scott," 14 December 1849, JMH Papers, LC.

54. Meyer, *Instructed Conscience*, 23–24.

55. JMH to MSH, 5 October 1892, JMH Papers, UofL.

56. Bozeman, *Protestants in an Age of Science*, 111–13.

57. Quoted in Ahlstrom, "Scottish Philosophy," 265.

58. Quoted in Groves, "Centre College," 320.

59. George P. Schmidt, *Old Time College President*, 108–43; Meyer, *Instructed Conscience*, vii.

60. Meyer, *Instructed Conscience*, 27. On links between jurisprudence and moral philosophy, see Mark Warren Bailey, "Moral Philosophy."

61. Turner, *Without God, without Creed*, 144–46.

62. Ibid., 179–84; Carter, *Spiritual Crisis*, 23–39.

63. Meyer, "American Intellectuals," 59.

64. "Remarks of Mr. Justice Harlan at the Unveiling, June 19th, 1891, of Memorial Tablets of John C. Young, Lewis W. Green, William L. Breckinridge, and Ormond Beatley, Formerly Presidents of Centre College, Danville, Kentucky," JMH Papers, LC.

65. Herbst, *German Historical School*, 76–97; Turner, *Without God, without Creed*, 146–50.

66. John Maynard was there in 1885–86, Richard in 1890–91 (Herbst, *German Historical School*, 16).

67. Sandeen, "Princeton Theology," 315.

68. See Massa, *Charles Augustus Briggs*.

69. "Remarks of Mr. Justice Harlan at the Unveiling, June 19th, 1891, of

Memorial Tablets of John C. Young, Lewis W. Green, William L. Breckinridge, and Ormond Beatley, Formerly Presidents of Centre College, Danville, Kentucky," JMH Papers, LC.

70. Marty, *The Irony of It All*, 236.

71. Loetscher, *Broadening Church*, 83–89.

72. Grant Gilmore calls the period from the Civil War to World War I the "Age of Faith" and the subsequent period the "Age of Anxiety" in *The Ages of American Law*.

73. Samuel Freeman Miller, *Lectures on the Constitution*, 502.

74. Robertson, *Outline of the Life of George Robertson*, 168.

75. Quoted in Grey, "Langdell's Orthodoxy," 13.

76. Ibid., 22–23; LaPiana, *Logic and Experience*, 70.

77. Newmyer, *Supreme Court Justice Joseph Story*, 244.

78. Siegel, "Historism in Late Nineteenth-Century Constitutional Thought," 1451.

79. LaPiana, "*Swift v. Tyson*," 773–90.

80. Quoted in Siegel, "Joel Bishop's Orthodoxy," 238.

81. Quoted in LaPiana, "Jurisprudence of History and Truth," 545.

82. Sandeen, "Princeton Theology," 315–19.

83. Constitutional law course exam questions, n.d., JMH Papers, LC.

84. "Questions by Mr. Justice Harlan on Constitutional Law," n.d., JMH Papers, LC.

85. MSH to JMH, 13 June 1894, JMH Papers, LC.

86. JMH Lectures, 14 October 1897.

87. JMH to MWF, 17 August 1896, MWF Papers, LC.

88. Clipping, n.d., Family Scrapbook (*Income Tax Case*), JMH Papers, U of L.

89. Almon C. Kellog to RDH, 27 May 1930, JMH Papers, U of L.

90. JMH Lectures, 5 March 1898.

91. Ibid.

92. Ibid., 14 October 1897.

93. JMH, "James Wilson," 502.

94. See Noble, *Historians against History*, and Somkin, *Unquiet Eagle*, 57–65.

95. Nagel, *One Nation Indivisible*, 147–76; Snay, *Gospel of Disunion*, 186–88. For how it was spread, see Elson, *Guardians of Tradition*, 59–62.

96. Hatch, *Sacred Cause of Liberty*; Abanese, *Sons of the Fathers*.

97. Tuveson, *Redeemer Nation*, 52–90; Maclear, "The Republic and the Millennium."

98. Faust, *Creation of Confederate Nationalism*, 29–33; Wolf, *The Almost Chosen People*, 184–85.

99. Tuveson, *Redeemer Nation*, 187–208; Moorhead, *American Apocalypse*; Strout, *New Heavens*, 158–88.

100. Walters, *Antislavery Appeal*, 139–43.

101. JMH Lectures, 29 January 1898.

102. Ibid., 22 January 1898.

103. Ibid., 26 March 1898. Harlan's explanation reads much like William Freeh-

ling's in "The Founding Fathers and Slavery." See also William Cohen, "Thomas Jefferson."

104. JMH Lectures, 29 January 1898.

105. Ibid., 26 March 1898.

106. Ibid., 29 January 1898.

107. Ibid., 22 January 1898.

108. Ibid., 29 January 1898.

109. Ibid., 26 March 1898.

110. Ibid., 29 January 1898.

111. Ibid., 26 March 1898.

112. Ibid., 22 January 1898.

113. Ibid., 21 October 1898.

114. Harlan praised Mason in "Remarks in Response to the Toast, 'The Judicial Power' at Banquet . . . in Commemoration of the 100th Anniversary of John Marshall's Accession to Chief Justice of the United States Supreme Court . . . ," 4 February 1901, JMH Papers, UofL.

115. The other materials were written by Harlan or were family documents (memo, n.d., JMH Papers, LC).

116. JMH Lectures, 21 October 1898. For the circumstances and text, see Rowland, *Life of George Mason*, 1:244–50, 433–41.

117. Quoted in Newmyer, *Supreme Court Justice Joseph Story*, 188.

118. John D. Wright Jr., *Transylvania*, 140–44.

119. Robertson, *Outline of the Life of George Robertson*, 200.

120. Ibid., 198.

121. JMH Lectures, 23 October 1897.

122. See Nelson, "Impact of the Antislavery Movement."

123. Quoted in Walters, *Antislavery Appeal*, 137; Fredrickson, *Inner Civil War*, 58–59.

124. Douglass, "Constitution of the United States."

125. Current, "Lincoln, the Civil War, and the American Mission"; Paludan, "Hercules Unbound."

126. Foner, *Free Soil, Free Labor, Free Men*, 75–76.

127. Jordan, *White over Black*, 304.

128. Davis, *Problem of Slavery*, 178.

129. Eaton, *Freedom of Thought*, 162–95.

130. JMH Lectures, 26 March 1898.

131. Ibid., 7 May 1898.

132. Ibid., 26 March 1898.

133. Ibid., 7 May 1898.

134. Ibid., 26 March 1898.

135. *Dred Scott v. Sanford*, 19 Howard 393 (1857).

136. JMH Lectures, 23 October 1897.

137. Ibid., 12 March 1898. See also ibid., 5 March 1898.

138. Ibid., 7 May 1898.

139. Ibid., 23 October 1897.

140. Ibid., 26 March 1898.

141. Foner, *Free Soil, Free Labor, Free Men*, 294–300.

142. JMH Lectures, 7 May 1898.

143. Horsman, *Race and Manifest Destiny;* Tuveson, *Redeemer Nation*, 125–33.

144. JMH Lectures, 7 May 1898.

145. The university did not admit blacks until 1957, except for a brief period after the Civil War (Kayser, *Bricks without Straw*, 291–92).

146. Collins and Collins, *Collins' Historical Sketches*, 1:272.

147. JMH to BHB, 2 February 1872, BHB Papers, LC.

148. BHB to JMH, 8 February 1872, JMH Papers, LC.

149. Acts 10:34; 1 Peter 1:17.

150. JMH to MRW, 6 August 1885, MRW Papers, LC.

151. JMH to JSH, 23 November 1880, JMH Papers, LC.

152. JMH, speech before House of Representatives, 4 February 1901, JMH Papers, U of L.

153. JMH to E. Murray, 15 December 1895, JMH Papers, U of L. See also JMH Lectures, 5 March 1898, and clipping, "Mr. Justice Harlan's Lectures," *Chicago Herald*, n.d., Malvina Harlan's Scrapbook, 1892–95, JMH Papers, U of L.

154. JMH, speech at Chicago Union League banquet, 22 February 1888, JMH Papers, U of L.

155. John David Smith, *Old Creed for the New South*, 103–96.

156. Hodes, *White Women, Black Men*, 176.

157. G. Edward White, "John Marshall Harlan I," 5–6.

158. Beth, "Justice Harlan," 1104; Knight, "Dissenting Opinions," 484; Westin, "John Marshall Harlan," 705; Porter, "John Marshall Harlan the Elder," 107.

CHAPTER THREE

1. JMH to BHB, 19 June 1876, BHB Papers, LC. See also Thompson, "Bristow Presidential Boom," 28, n. 110, and Webb, *Benjamin Helm Bristow*, 244–48.

2. See McDaniel, "Francis Tillou Nicholls," and Foner, *Reconstruction*, 575–82.

3. JMH to BHB, 13 April 1877, BHB Papers, LC.

4. Williams, *Hayes*, 67, 78.

5. Rutherford B. Hayes to William Henry Smith, 29 December 1877, in JMayH to JMH, 3 February 1910, in the possession of Eve Dillingham. See also Frank, "Appointment of Supreme Court Justices," 206–10, and Ellwood W. Lewis, "Document."

6. *New York Times*, 31 October 1877, 1, and 28 November 1877, 1.

7. JMH to BHB, 16 November 1870, BHB Papers, LC.

8. JMH Lectures, 12 March 1898.

9. Ibid., 19 March 1898.

10. JMH to MWF, 3 May 1888, MWF Papers, LC.

11. Todd, *Story of Washington*, 239–40.

12. JMH to MWF, 24 August 1896, MWF Papers, LC.

13. Clipping, "The Real Justice John M. Harlan on and off the Supreme

Bench," *New York World*, 28 May 1911, Family Scrapbook, 1876-1911, JMH Papers, UofL.

14. Adams and Adams, *Chapters of Erie*, 137.

CHAPTER FOUR

1. Hyman and Wiecek, *Equal Justice under Law*, 395. See also tenBroek, *Antislavery Origins of the Fourteenth Amendment*; Graham, *Everyman's Constitution*; Corwin, *"Higher Law" Background*; and Kaczorowski, "To Begin the Nation Anew." Others argue that racism and federalism prevented a broad definition of civil rights. See, for example, Fairman, "Does the Fourteenth Amendment Incorporate the Bill of Rights?"; Kelly, "Fourteenth Amendment Reconsidered"; Bickel, "Original Understanding"; Paludan, *Covenant with Death*; Berger, *Government by Judiciary*; Benedict, "Preserving Federalism"; and Belz, *Emancipation and Equal Rights*.

2. See Hyman and Wiecek, *Equal Justice under Law*, 396, 398.

3. McCurdy, "Stephen J. Field," 14.

4. See Weschler, "Toward Neutral Principles."

5. *Roberts v. City of Boston*, 59 Mass. 198 (1849). See also Levy and Phillips, "*Roberts* Case."

6. Baradaglio, *Reconstructing the Household*, 176-78.

7. Marjorie M. Norris, "Early Instance of Nonviolence."

8. Quoted in Hartz, "John M. Harlan," 34-35.

9. Quoted in Webb, "Kentucky," 136, n. 125.

10. BHB to JMH, 10 March 1872, JMH Papers, LC.

11. William C. Goodloe to JMH, 25 August 1874, JMH Papers, LC.

12. JMH to BHB, 28 August 1874, BHB Papers, LC. He did approve of equal facilities (Kousser, "Separate but *Not* Equal," 38).

13. Wyatt-Brown, "Civil Rights Act of 1875"; Foner, *Reconstruction*, 504-5, 532-34. On other attempts, see Kelly, "Congressional Controversy over School Segregation."

14. *Charge to the Grand Jury—Civil Rights Act*, 30 Fed. Case 1005 (1875), case no. 18,260, quoted in editorial, "General Harlan's Republicanism," *Louisville Daily Commercial*, 1 November 1877, typed copy, JMH Papers, LC.

15. *Civil Rights Cases*, 109 U.S. 3, 26 (1883). He did not hear *Hall v. DeCuir*, 95 U.S. 485 (1878).

16. *Plessy v. Ferguson*, 163 U.S. 537, 559 (1896).

17. *Louisville, New Orleans, and Texas Railway Company v. Mississippi*, 133 U.S. 587 (1890); *Chiles v. Chesapeake and Ohio Railway Company*, 218 U.S. 71 (1910).

18. See Hartog, "Constitution of Aspiration."

19. *Cumming v. Richmond County Board of Education*, 175 U.S. 528 (1899).

20. *Gong Lum v. Rice*, 275 U.S. 78 (1927).

21. *Pace v. Alabama*, 106 U.S. 583 (1882).

22. *Plessy v. Ferguson*, 163 U.S. 537, 555 (1896).

23. Beth, *John Marshall Harlan*, 235.

24. Harlan began teaching domestic relations, torts, and commercial law in 1891 (JMH to MWF, 17 August 1891, MWF Papers, LC).

25. Harlan and Butler, "Treatise on the Law of Marriage," 830.

26. *The Interior*, 8 June 1905, quoted in MSH, "Memories," frame 236.

27. Gossett, *Race*, 110–14.

28. Collins, *Fourteenth Amendment and the States*, 79.

29. McPherson, *Abolitionist Legacy*, 201.

30. Quoted in editorial, "General Harlan's Republicanism," *Louisville Daily Commercial*, 1 November 1877, typed copy, JMH Papers, LC.

31. *Plessy v. Ferguson*, 163 U.S. 537, 554 (1896).

32. See Murray, *Presbyterians and the Negro*, 163–64, and Thompkins, "Presbyterian Religious Education."

33. Quoted in Murray, *Presbyterians and the Negro*, 198–99.

34. Wilmore, "Identity and Integration," 111.

35. Quoted in Murray, *Presbyterians and the Negro*, 198–99.

36. Quoted in Ferry, "Francis James Grimké," 60–61.

37. Gatewood, *Aristocrats of Color*, 286–87.

38. Ferry, "Francis James Grimké," 171–76.

39. Archibald H. Grimké, "Presbyterian Fall." See also Ferry, "Racism and Reunion," 82–88.

40. "Report of the Committee of Canvass," 61.

41. Bruce, *Archibald Grimké*, 36.

42. Ferry, "Francis James Grimké," 139.

43. Weeks, "Racism, World War I, and the Christian Life," 60.

44. *Civil Rights Cases*, 109 U.S. 3, 21 (1883).

45. Ibid., 22.

46. Tucker, *Dissertation on Slavery*, 17. I learned of Tucker's work in Rose, "Domestication of Domestic Slavery," 20–21.

47. Quoted in Moses, *Golden Age of Black Nationalism*, 40.

48. *Civil Rights Cases*, 109 U.S. 3, 22 (1883).

49. Ibid.

50. Ibid., 21.

51. Ibid., 22.

52. Litwack, *North of Slavery*, 64–97.

53. Berlin, *Slaves without Masters*, 199–216.

54. *Civil Rights Cases*, 109 U.S. 3, 22 (1883).

55. Quoted in Blight, *Frederick Douglass' Civil War*, 13. See also Nieman, "Language of Liberation."

56. Pease and Pease, *They Who Would Be Free*, 3–4.

57. Quoted in Foner, *Reconstruction*, 150.

58. Thomas D. Morris, *Southern Slavery*, 21.

59. *Civil Rights Cases*, 109 U.S. 3, 24–25 (1883).

60. See Kurland and Casper, "*Civil Rights Cases*."

61. MSH, "Memories," frames 188, 190, 191.

62. *Dred Scott v. Sanford*, 19 Howard 393, 407 (1857), quoted by Harlan in *Civil*

*Rights Cases*, 109 U.S. 3, 31 (1883). I quote Harlan's text and ignore minor differences from Taney's.

63. *Dred Scott v. Sanford*, 19 Howard 393, 405 (1857), quoted in ibid., 32.

64. *Dred Scott v. Sanford*, 19 Howard 393, 407 (1857), quoted in ibid., 31. Taney wrote "beings of an inferior order."

65. Ibid., 33.

66. Ibid., 34.

67. Ibid., 41.

68. Ibid., 54, 56.

69. Ibid., 26.

70. JMH to Rutherford B. Hayes, 30 November 1883, Rutherford B. Hayes Presidential Center, Spiegel Grove, Fremont, Ohio.

71. Noah H. Swayne to JMH, 20 November 1883, and JMH to MSH, [1883], Family Scrapbook—*Civil Rights Cases*—1883, U of L.

72. *Civil Rights Cases*, 109 U.S. 3, 62 (1883).

73. Magrath, *Morrison R. Waite*, 154.

74. Swisher, *Stephen J. Field*, 285–87. Field did not believe that black men were entitled by the Fifteenth Amendment to serve jury duty (*Strauder v. West Virginia*, 100 U.S. 303 [1880]; *Ex Parte Virginia*, 100 U.S. 339 [1880]; *Virginia v. Rives*, 100 U.S. 313 [1880]).

75. JMH, "Civil War—1864 . . . ," n.d., autobiographical essay, JMH Papers, LC.

76. Clipping, "Harlan for President," *Louisville Evening Post*, 16 October 1894, Family Scrapbook (*Income Tax Case*), JMH Papers, U of L.

77. Family Scrapbook—*Civil Rights Cases*—1883, JMH Papers, U of L.

78. FD to JMH, 16 October 1883, Family Scrapbook—*Civil Right Cases*—1883, JMH Papers, U of L. See also Blight, " 'For Something beyond the Battlefield' " and *Frederick Douglass' Civil War*, 219–39.

79. FD to JMH, 26 November 1883, FD Papers, LC.

80. Lofgren, *"Plessy" Case*, 196–97.

81. *Hall v. DeCuir*, 95 U.S. 485 (1878).

82. *Louisville, New Orleans, and Texas Railway Company v. Mississippi*, 133 U.S. 587 (1890).

83. *Plessy v. Ferguson*, 163 U.S. 537, 540 (1896), quoted in Lofgren, *"Plessy" Case*, 28–30.

84. *Plessy v. Ferguson*, 163 U.S. 537, 544 (1896).

85. Ibid., 550.

86. Ibid., 551.

87. Ibid.

88. Ibid., 552.

89. Ibid., 563.

90. Ibid., 559–60.

91. Ibid., 557.

92. Ibid.

93. Ibid., 561.

94. Ibid., 554–55.

95. Ibid., 559. The metaphor of color-blindness was borrowed from Albion W. Tourgee's brief for *Plessy*.

96. Ibid., 560.

97. Ibid., 559. Rodolphe Lucien Desdunes, one of the men who organized to test the Louisiana law (see Lofgren, *"Plessy" Case*, 29), claims that Harlan contributed money to the cause, but in light of his view of judicial ethics, that seems incredible (Desdunes, *Our People and Our History*, 141–42).

98. *Plessy v. Ferguson*, 163 U.S. 537, 560 (1896).

99. Among the segregation cases he heard, Harlan dissented in *Louisville, New Orleans, and Texas Railway Company v. Mississippi*, 133 U.S. 587 (1890); he dissented silently in *Chesapeake and Ohio Railway Company v. Kentucky*, 179 U.S. 388 (1900), and *Chiles v. Chesapeake and Ohio Railway Company*, 218 U.S. 71 (1910).

100. Kousser, "Separate but *Not* Equal," 40–42. Kousser notes that others have argued that Harlan's decision was determined by strict construction, poor pleading by counsel, the availability of private schools, his desire to avoid an outright approval of segregated public schools, and his ignorance of the importance of education.

101. Louis R. Harlan, "Desegregation in New Orleans Public Schools."

102. Coulter, *Civil War*, 403; Kousser, "Making Separate Equal," 400–405. Kentucky followed Rabinowitz's model of postwar institutional change in *Race Relations in the Urban South*.

103. Kelly, "Congressional Controversy over School Segregation," 540. See also Frank and Munroe, "Original Understanding," 467.

104. Litwack, *North of Slavery*, 113–52; Stephenson, *Race Distinctions*, 170–90.

105. *Plessy v. Ferguson*, 163 U.S. 537, 544–45, 551 (1896).

106. *Civil Rights Cases*, 109 U.S. 3, 59–60 (1883); *Plessy v. Ferguson*, 163 U.S. 537, 557–58, 561 (1896).

107. *Cumming v. Richmond County Board of Education*, 175 U.S. 528, 543–44 (1899).

108. *Berea College v. Commonwealth of Kentucky*, 211 U.S. 45, 69 (1908).

109. Louis R. Harlan, "Desegregation in New Orleans Public Schools," 672.

110. My account relies on Kousser, "Separate but *Not* Equal."

111. *Cumming v. Richmond County Board of Education*, 175 U.S. 528, 545 (1899).

112. Kousser criticizes Hobbs's "Negro Education" in "Separate but *Not* Equal," 41. Such a suggestion follows the National Association for the Advancement of Colored People's successful pre-*Brown* campaign for equal if separate schools in higher education.

113. *Cumming v. Richmond County Board of Education*, 175 U.S. 528, 545 (1899).

114. Kousser, "Separate but *Not* Equal," 42.

115. Harlan dissented from *Clyatt v. United States*, 197 U.S. 207 (1905), and *Bailey v. State of Alabama (I)*, 211 U.S. 452 (1908), then was part of the majority in *Bailey v. State of Alabama (II)*, 219 U.S. 219 (1911).

116. Kousser writes that this "was quite typical" ("Separate but *Not* Equal," 20, n. 13).

117. *Cumming v. Richmond County Board of Education*, 175 U.S. 528, 542 (1899).

118. Ibid., 538.

119. Most of the members of the committee seem to have been white. Elite blacks were also keen on uplift. See Gatewood, *Aristocrats of Color,* 50–51, and Gaines, *Uplifting the Race.* But they resented the condescension of the Freedmen's Board. See Murray, *Presbyterians and the Negro,* 194. The question of whether elite blacks would support racial separation is addressed later in this chapter.

120. *The Interior,* 8 June 1905, quoted in MSH, "Memories," frame 236. Harlan spoke at popular meetings on Sabbath observance and at one meeting for laypersons but not at the meeting on the freedmen (*Minutes of the General Assembly,* 53, 78, 158).

121. "Report of the Standing Committee on Freedmen," 63.

122. See Meier, *Negro Thought in America,* 85–118, but see also Louis R. Harlan, *Booker T. Washington,* 128–42.

123. "Report of the Standing Committee on Freedmen," 62.

124. Ibid., 63.

125. Higham, "Ideological Anti-Semitism," 120.

126. Eichorn, *Evangelizing the American Jew;* Sarna, "American Jewish Response."

127. Rosenberg, *From Shylock to Svengali,* 73–115; Prawer, *Israel at Vanity Fair,* 416.

128. Harap, *Image of the Jew in American Literature,* 136–88.

129. See Korn, *American Jewry and the Civil War;* Dinnerstein, *Antisemitism in America,* 3–34; and Sarna, "Anti-Semitism and American History."

130. Naomi W. Cohen, *Jews in Christian America;* Sarna, " 'Mythical Jew' "; Gerber, "Anti-Semitism."

131. JMH Lectures, 19 March 1898; Feldman, *Dreyfus Affair,* 26–41.

132. Higham, "Social Discrimination against Jews"; Dinnerstein, *Antisemitism in America,* 35–57.

133. Higham, "Ideological Anti-Semitism," 130–32.

134. Wilmore, *Black Religion and Black Radicalism,* 37; Levine, *Black Culture and Black Consciousness,* 33, 50–51; Diner, *In the Almost Promised Land,* 20–21; Raboteau, "Exodus," 176–82.

135. Quoted in Raboteau, *Slave Religion,* 311–12.

136. Leviticus 25:8–17.

137. Waldo E. Martin Jr., *Mind of Frederick Douglass,* 123, 201.

138. Louis R. Harlan, *Booker T. Washington,* 284. See also ibid., 260, and Louis R. Harlan, "Booker T. Washington's Discovery of Jews."

139. Shankman, "Friend or Foe?"

140. Diner, *In the Almost Promised Land,* 66.

141. See Naomi W. Cohen, *Jews in Christian America,* 94–98; Singerman, "The Jew as Racial Alien"; and Goldstein, " 'Different Blood Flows in Our Veins.' " Patai and Wing write that Jews "always considered themselves, if not a race, at least a greatly enlarged family" (*Myth of the Jewish Race,* 11).

142. Diner, *In the Almost Promised Land,* 166–72.

143. David Levering Lewis, *W. E. B. Du Bois,* 487–90.

144. Higham, "Ethnic Pluralism in Modern American Thought."

145. Eichorn, *Evangelizing the American Jew*, 156.

146. "Report of the Standing Committee on Freedmen," 65.

147. *Berea College v. Commonwealth of Kentucky*, 211 U.S. 45, 59–60 (1908). See also Peck, *Berea's First 125 Years*, 39.

148. Peck, *Berea's First 125 Years*, 50–52.

149. *Berea College v. Commonwealth of Kentucky*, 211 U.S. 45, 46 (1908).

150. Ibid., 67.

151. Ibid., 51.

152. Ibid., 50.

153. Ibid., 68.

154. Ibid., 67.

155. Ibid., 68.

156. Ibid.

157. Peck, *Berea's First 125 Years*, 44.

158. McPherson, *Abolitionist Legacy*, 179–80; H. Shelton Smith, *In His Image*, 266–71.

159. Quoted in H. Shelton Smith, *In His Image*, 239–40.

160. Peck, *Berea's First 125 Years*, 52.

161. McPherson, *Abolitionist Legacy*, 245.

162. *Pace v. Alabama*, 106 U.S. 583, 585 (1882).

163. Grossberg, *Governing the Hearth*, 18–24.

164. Harlan and Butler, "Treatise on the Law of Marriage," 827.

165. Grossberg, *Governing the Hearth*, 137.

166. Stephenson, *Race Distinctions*, 81; Baradaglio, *Reconstructing the Household*, 180–81.

167. Mencke, *Mulattoes and Race Mixture*, 39.

168. Weeks, "Racism, World War I, and the Christian Life," 69.

169. Francis J. Grimké, "A Resemblance and a Contrast between the American Negro and the Children of Israel . . . ," n.d., in Woodson, *Works*, 1:359.

170. Francis J. Grimké, "Victory for the Allies . . . ," 24 November 1918, in Woodson, *Works*, 1:563.

171. Colossians 3:9–11.

172. Francis J. Grimké, "Evangelism and Institutes on Evangelism," 1916, in Woodson, *Works*, 1:525.

173. Sol. C. Dickey to F. J. Grimké, 7 February 1916, in Woodson, *Works*, 4:148.

174. Francis J. Grimké to Sol. C. Dickey, 11 February 1916, in Woodson, *Works*, 4:148–49.

175. Quarles, *Black Abolitionists*, 38.

176. Quoted in Walters, *Antislavery Appeal*, 73. See Toplin, "Between Black and White."

177. Fowler, "Northern Attitudes towards Interracial Marriage," 147.

178. Ibid., 203–4; Kaplan, "Miscegenation Issue."

179. Avins, "Anti-Miscegenation Laws."

180. Walters, *Antislavery Appeal*, 70–87; Pease and Pease, *They Who Would Be Free*, 38–39.

181. Francis J. Grimké, "God and Prayer as Factors in the Struggle," 11 December [1900], in Woodson, *Works*, 1:283.

182. Quoted in Bruce, *Archibald Grimké*, 114, 115.

183. See Fowler, "Northern Attitudes towards Interracial Marriage," 74–75; Bynum, *Unruly Women*, 36–39, 96–97, 107–8; Hodes, *White Women, Black Men*, 147. Miscegenation was more common than we imagine (Mills, "Miscegenation and the Free Negro").

184. Francis J. Grimké, "Lynching—Its Causes: The Crimes of the Negro," 18 June 1899, and "The Atlanta Riot," 7 October 1906, in Woodson, *Works*, 1:303–16, 406–18. See also Brundage, *Lynching in the New South*, 61–62, 66, and on Wells and others, Hodes, *White Women, Black Men*, 187–97.

185. Jacquelyn Dowd Hall, *Revolt against Chivalry*, 129–57.

186. Berry, "Judging Morality," 854. The Klan did punish white Republican men in such situations (Hodes, "Sexualization of Reconstruction Politics," 70).

187. Moon, *Emerging Thought of W. E. B. Du Bois*, 297.

188. Fowler, "Northern Attitudes towards Interracial Marriage," 258–61.

189. Ferry, "Francis James Grimké," 6–7.

190. Francis J. Grimké to Sol. C. Dickey, 11 February 1916, in Woodson, *Works*, 4:148–50.

191. Kelly Miller, *Race Adjustment*, 109.

192. See Wiener, " 'Black Beast Rapist' "; Glenda Elizabeth Gilmore, *Gender and Jim Crow*; and Kinney, *Amalgamation!*

193. *Dred Scott v. Sanford*, 19 Howard 393, 409 (1856).

194. Ferry, "Francis James Grimké," 147–49.

195. Francis J. Grimké, "God and the Race Problem," 3 May 1903, in Woodson, *Works*, 4:364–78.

196. Francis J. Grimké, "Christianity and Race Prejudice," 29 May 1910, in Woodson, *Works*, 4:444.

197. Waldo E. Martin Jr., *Mind of Frederick Douglass*, 222; Pease and Pease, *They Who Would Be Free*, 104–5.

198. Fowler, "Northern Attitudes towards Interracial Marriage," 244–45.

199. Williamson, *New People*, 116–17.

200. Bruce, *Archibald Grimké*, 37–39.

201. Francis J. Grimké, "Second Marriage of Frederick Douglass," 325.

202. Du Bois, "Conservation of Races," 38.

203. Ibid., 43.

204. Meier, *Negro Thought in America*, 190–206. Similarly, see Francis J. Grimké on Josiah Strong in "Fifty Years of Freedom," in Woodson, *Works*, 4:515.

205. Fowler, "Northern Attitudes towards Interracial Marriage," 322, n. 1.

206. JMH to JSH, 23 November 1880, JMH Papers, LC.

207. *Plessy v. Ferguson*, 163 U.S. 537, 563–64 (1896).

208. Ibid., 562.

209. For example, see Lofgren, *"Plessy" Case*, 191–95; Kull, *Color-Blind Constitution*, 121; Beth, *John Marshall Harlan*, 232–34; Yarbrough, *Judicial Enigma*, 160. Some have stressed Harlan's comments about Anglo-Saxonism. See, for example, Maltz, "Only Partially Color-Blind," and Gaines, *Uplifting the Race*, xiii.

210. Gossett, *Race*, 286.

211. See Shelby J. Davidson to JSH, 2 December 1911, JMH Papers, U of L. The program is in the same collection.

212. The list is in JMH Papers, U of L.

213. The other is *Louisville, New Orleans, and Texas Railway Company v. Mississippi*, 133 U.S. 587 (1890).

214. *Motes v. United States*, 178 U.S. 458 (1900), is a majority opinion; the dissents listed are *Baldwin v. Franks*, 120 U.S. 678 (1887), and *Hodges v. United States*, 203 U.S. 1 (1906).

215. *Gibson v. Mississippi*, 162 U.S. 565 (1896). Harlan delivered jury discrimination decisions in *Neal v. Delaware*, 103 U.S. 370 (1880); *Bush v. Kentucky*, 107 U.S. 110 (1882); and *In re Wood*, 140 U.S. 278 (1891). But such decisions mostly drove the practice underground (Rabinowitz, *Race Relations in the Urban South*, 38–41; Ayers, *Vengeance and Justice*, 175–76). Black criminal defendants offering no proof beyond a bare assertion of a statistical skew did not win. See Harlan's decisions in *Charley Smith v. Mississippi*, 162 U.S. 592 (1896), and *Martin v. Texas*, 200 U.S. 316 (1906). Harlan and the Court rejected the idea of a racially prorated jury (*Thomas v. Texas*, 212 U.S. 278, 283 [1909]; JMH to C. P. Barrett, 24 August 1896, copy enclosed in JMH to MWF, 24 August 1896, MWF Papers, LC). See generally Benno C. Schmidt Jr., "Juries, Jurisdiction, and Race Discrimination."

CHAPTER FIVE

1. *Lone Wolf v. Hitchcock*, 155 U.S. 565 (1903). Harlan concurred in the result.

2. JMH Lectures, 19 March 1898.

3. *Elk v. Wilkins*, 112 U.S. 94, 121 (1884).

4. Ibid., 122.

5. Tuveson, *Redeemer Nation*, 136–75; Weinberg, *Manifest Destiny*, 73–77; Horsman, *Race and Manifest Destiny*.

6. William Prescott's *History of the Conquest of Peru* and *History of the Conquest of Mexico* are on a list entitled "Books Read by John Marshall Harlan, Feb. 15th, 1849," JMH Papers, LC. Harlan cites George Bancroft and John Bach McMaster in a speech on James Wilson.

7. Levin, *History as Romantic Art*, 74. See also Goldman, *John Bach McMaster*, 143.

8. Quoted in Fredrickson, *Black Image in the White Mind*, 106.

9. Levin, *History as Romantic Art*, 127–41.

10. Harlan heard of the abuse of Native Americans from his brother-in-law (J. G. Hatchitt to JMH, 28 April, 2 July 1892, JMH Papers, U of L). On the idea of the doomed and noble Native American, see Berkhofer, *White Man's Indian*, 88–92.

11. JMH Lectures, 9 January 1898.

12. Fredrickson, *Black Image in the White Mind*, 245–47.

13. Gossett, *Race*, 205.

14. JMH to JSH, 9 February 1882, JMH Papers, LC.

15. John P. Kennedy, *Memoirs of the Life of William Wirt*, 2:251–55, 294.

16. Stuart Creighton Miller, *Unwelcome Immigrant*, 159–60.

17. See Salyer, *Laws Harsh as Tigers*, 1–32. On Harlan's rulings on these acts, see McClain, *In Search of Equality*, 165–66, 171, 218.

18. JMH Lectures, 19 March 1898.

19. Ibid.

20. *United States v. Wong Kim Ark*, 169 U.S. 649 (1898). Justice Samuel Freeman Miller had voiced similar arguments (*Lectures on the Constitution*, 279).

21. JMH Lectures, 7 May 1898.

22. *Plessy v. Ferguson*, 163 U.S. 537, 561 (1896).

23. See, for example, Maltz, "Only Partially Color-Blind," and Chin, "*Plessy* Myth," esp. 166, n. 102.

24. Harlan mixed racial and cultural arguments in advising his son on a college debate (JMH to JSH, 21 January 1883, JMH Papers, LC). In a silly letter in French, Harlan teased Justice Brewer that "the newspapers say you are once again before the public—this time for defending the fundamental rights of the Chinese to crowd together like ants across our country as they like" (JMH to David J. Brewer, 30 March 1893, Brewer Family Papers, Manuscripts and Archives, Yale University Library, New Haven, Conn.).

25. JMH Lectures, 29 January 1898.

26. Ibid., 30 October 1897.

27. Ibid., 6 November 1897.

28. He then criticized immigrants sprung from foreign penitentiaries who never learned this ("Remarks of Mr. Justice Harlan at the Centennial Banquet, Given at Chicago . . . ," [1889], Malvina Harlan's Scrapbook, 1892–95, JMH Papers, UofL).

29. Quoted in Page Smith, *James Wilson*, 327.

30. The speech is not mentioned in Beth, *John Marshall Harlan*, 249–56, or Yarbrough, *Judicial Enigma*, 190–200.

31. Dorothy Ross, "Historical Consciousness," 924–25.

32. Loewen, *Lies My Teacher Told Me*.

33. See *Hawaii v. Mankichi*, 190 U.S. 197, 240, 243 (1903).

34. JMH Lectures, 14 October 1897.

35. Moorhead, "American Israel."

36. Quoted in Wilkerson, *Public Opinion and the Spanish-American War*, 41.

37. JMH Lectures, 15 January 1898.

38. *New York Herald*, 16 February 1895.

39. JMH Lectures, 19 February 1898.

40. Ibid., 2 April 1898. Harlan then entertained the possibility of taking Canada.

41. He would later reject this idea (clipping, "Justice Harlan's Lectures," *New Haven Daily Register*, 27 May 1899, JMH Papers, LC).

42. Dorothy Ross contrasts Macaulay's historicism with George Bancroft's metahistory in "Historical Consciousness," 918–19.

43. JMH Lectures, 7 May 1898.

44. There were so many recruits among the students that the university rescheduled the exams (Kayser, *Bricks without Straw*, 179–80).

45. See De Santis, "Imperialist Impulse," 66–67, 70–72. Among the most notable authors are William Appleman Williams and Walter LaFeber.

46. JMayH to JMH, 19 April 1898, JMH Papers, U of L.

47. De Santis, "Imperialist Impulse," 67–68. For example, see Nagel, *This Sacred Trust*, 251–59, 298–310, and Merk, *Manifest Destiny*.

48. Field, "American Imperialism," 668.

49. Clipping, "Justice Harlan Here," *Montreal Daily News*, 28 June 1898, Family Scrapbook (*Income Tax Case*), JMH Papers, U of L.

50. JMH to WM, 5 July 1898, WM Papers, LC.

51. Craven, *Legend of the Founding Fathers*, 61.

52. JMH to RDH, 4 July 1911, JMH Papers, LC.

53. JMH to WM, 5 July 1898, WM Papers, LC.

54. McConnell, *Glorious Contentment*, 233.

55. Quoted in Forbes, *Philippine Islands*, 1:123.

56. Weinberg, *Manifest Destiny*, 283–318. My account relies on Pratt, *America's Colonial Experiment*.

57. JMH to WM, 6 February 1899, WM Papers, LC.

58. JMH Lectures, 19 February 1898.

59. JMH to John W. Frazier, 4 August 1898, JMH Papers, LC.

60. Weinberg, *Manifest Destiny*, 310.

61. Lasch, "Anti-Imperialists," 319.

62. Quoted in Tompkins, *Anti-Imperialism*, 125.

63. Welch, *Response to Imperialism*, 56.

64. Twain, "To the Person Sitting in Darkness," 176.

65. Curti, *Roots of American Loyalty*, 140.

66. JMH, "James Wilson," 481.

67. Ibid., 483. For Wilson's position on slavery and equality, see Page Smith, *James Wilson*, 274, 334.

68. Quoted in JMH, "James Wilson," 491.

69. Ibid., 499–500.

70. Ibid., 502.

71. Ibid., 502–3.

72. Welch, *Response to Imperialism*, 49–51.

73. Stuart Creighton Miller, *"Benevolent Assimilation,"* 108.

74. JMH, "James Wilson," 503.

75. Ibid. Quotations are from Acts 10:34, 17:24.

76. JMH, "James Wilson," 503.

77. Ibid., 503–4.

78. Welch, *Response to Imperialism*, 59.

79. Ibid., 89.

80. JMH, "James Wilson," 500, 502.

81. Ibid., 504.

82. Ibid., 503.

83. See Bailey, "Was the Presidential Election of 1900 a Mandate on Imperialism?"

84. Lasch, "Anti-Imperialists," 324.

85. Quoted in Torruella, *Supreme Court and Puerto Rico*, 35.

86. Forbes, *Philippine Islands*, 2:567, 566.

87. Welch, *Response to Imperialism*, 61.

88. Forbes, *Philippine Islands*, 2:570.

89. Welch, *Response to Imperialism*, 103.

90. JMH to WHT, 6 August 1900, WHT Papers, LC.

91. JMH to WHT, 5 November 1900, WHT Papers, LC. Harlan invariably spelled "Philippines" and "Filipino" incorrectly. The Treaty of Paris made the misspelling "Porto Rico" official until 1932 (Cabranes, *Citizenship and the American Empire*, 1, n. 1).

92. JMH to WHT, 5 November 1900, WHT Papers, LC.

93. WHT to JMH, 7 January 1901, WHT Papers, LC.

94. JMH to BH, 3 March 1900, BH Papers, LC.

95. BH to JMH, 12 March 1900, BH Papers, LC. See also Beisner, *Twelve against Empire*, 189–92.

96. Harrison, "Status of Annexed Territory," 17.

97. Ibid., 8.

98. JMH to WHT, 16 July 1900, WHT Papers, LC.

99. WHT to JMH, 7 January 1901, WHT Papers, LC.

100. WHT to JMH, 19 May 1901, WHT Papers, LC.

101. WHT to JMH, 30 June 1900, WHT Papers, LC.

102. WHT to JMH, 7 January 1901, WHT Papers, LC.

103. WHT to JMH, 30 June 1900, WHT Papers, LC.

104. *DeLima v. Bidwell*, 182 U.S. 1 (1901).

105. Ibid., 192.

106. *Downes v. Bidwell*, 182 U.S. 244 (1901). Senator Joseph B. Foraker declared that the act had nothing to do with citizenship (Cabranes, *Citizenship and the American Empire*, 36–37).

107. *Downes v. Bidwell*, 182 U.S. 244, 251 (1901).

108. Ibid., 277.

109. Ibid., 291.

110. Ibid., 306.

111. *DeLima v. Bidwell*, 182 U.S. 1, 218 (1901).

112. *Downes v. Bidwell*, 182 U.S. 244, 286 (1901).

113. Bercovitch, *American Jeremiad*, 113–14.

114. *Downes v. Bidwell*, 182 U.S. 244, 280 (1901).

115. JMH to WHT, 22 July 1901, WHT Papers, LC.

116. *Downes v. Bidwell*, 182 U.S. 244, 358–59 (1901).

117. Ibid., 372.

118. Ibid., 374.

119. Ibid., 373.

120. Ibid., 375.

121. JMH to WHT, 22 July 1901, WHT Papers, LC.

122. Clipping, *Chicago Record Herald*, 15 March 1904, *Northern Securities* Scrapbook, JMH Papers, U of L.

123. *Downes v. Bidwell*, 182 U.S. 244, 378 (1901).

124. Ibid., 311–12.

125. Ibid., 386.

126. Ibid., 380.

127. Ibid., 385.

128. Ibid., 384.

129. Ibid., 379.

130. Ibid., 381.

131. Ibid., 386.

132. JSH to JMH, 22 November 1902, JMH Papers, U of L.

133. JSH to JMH, 3 June 1902, JMH Papers, U of L.

134. Congress never used the term "incorporation" according to Pratt, *America's Colonial Experiment*, 162–63. See also *Rasmussen v. United States*, 197 U.S. 516 (1905), in which the Court held that Alaska was incorporated and Harlan concurred.

135. *Hawaii v. Mankichi*, 190 U.S. 197, 226 (1903).

136. Ibid., 241.

137. Ibid., 239–40.

138. Ibid., 240.

139. *Dorr v. United States*, 195 U.S. 138, 148 (1904).

140. Ibid., 156.

141. *Gavieres v. United States*, 220 U.S. 338 (1911); *Dowdell v. United States*, 221 U.S. 325 (1911).

142. Herbst, *German Historical School*, 99–103; Dorothy Ross, "Historical Consciousness."

143. Quoted in Merk, *Manifest Destiny*, 253. On historians' views of this account, see Ephraim K. Smith, "William McKinley's Enduring Legacy," 232–34.

144. Forbes, *Philippine Islands*, 2:439–45.

145. JMH, speech at banquet for his twenty-fifth year on the Court, [1902], JMH Papers, U of L.

146. Welch, *Response to Imperialism*, 135–47. Racism was a source of some of the abuse (ibid., 101–5; Stuart Creighton Miller, *"Benevolent Assimilation,"* 176–79, 188–89).

147. JMH to John C. Spooner, 14 July 1902, JMH Papers, U of L.

148. Ibid. See also JMH to MWF, 8 July 1901, quoted in King, *Melville Weston Fuller*, 270.

149. Clipping, "Public Honesty the Rule, Says Judge Harlan," June 1908, JMH Papers, U of L.

150. Moorfield Story to JMH, 13 January 1908, JMH Papers, U of L.

151. JMH to Charles Francis Adams, 15, 20 November 1908, 1 March 1910, Charles Francis Adams Papers, Massachusetts Historical Society, Boston, Mass.

CHAPTER SIX

1. Westin, "Mr. Justice Harlan," 117.

2. JMH to WHT, 13 November 1892, WHT Papers, LC.

3. JMH to AEW, 25 September 1906, JMH Papers, LC.

4. *Jacobson v. Massachusetts*, 197 U.S. 11 (1905).

5. Favorite majority opinion on prohibition: *Mugler v. Kansas*, 123 U.S. 623 (1887); dissents on liquor: *Bowman v. Chicago and Northwestern Railway Company*, 125 U.S. 465 (1888), and *Cox v. Texas*, 202 U.S. 446 (1906); majority opinion on lotteries: *Douglas v. Kentucky*, 168 U.S. 488 (1897); majority opinion on federal power against lotteries: *Lottery Case* (*Champion v. Ames*), 188 U.S. 321 (1903); majority opinion on margarine: *Plumley v. Massachusetts*, 155 U.S. 461 (1894).

6. Majority opinions on Sunday trains: *Hennington v. Georgia*, 163 U.S. 299 (1896); on the flag in advertisements: *Halter v. Nebraska*, 205 U.S. 34 (1907); on train-safety regulations: *New York, New Haven, and Hartford Railroad Company v. New York*, 165 U.S. 628 (1897); on garbage-collection contracting: *California Reduction Company v. Sanitary Reduction Works*, 199 U.S. 306 (1905); on the shipping of livestock: *Reid v. Colorado*, 187 U.S. 137 (1902); on stock transfers: *Henley v. Myers, Receiver of Consolidated Barbed Wire Company*, 215 U.S. 373 (1910); on the working day: *Atkin v. Kansas*, 191 U.S. 207 (1903); dissent on the working day: *Lochner v. New York*, 198 U.S. 45 (1905). *Lake Shore and Michigan Southern Railway Company v. Ohio*, 173 U.S. 285 (1899), was a majority opinion regulating train stops.

7. *Chicago, Burlington, and Quincy Railway Company v. People of the State of Illinois ex rel. Drainage Commissioners*, 200 U.S. 561 (1906); *West Chicago Street Railway Company v. People of the State of Illinois ex rel. City of Chicago*, 201 U.S. 506 (1906).

8. Westin, "Supreme Court"; William G. Ross, *Muted Fury*, 29, 34–35.

9. *Lochner v. New York*, 198 U.S. 45, 61, 62 (1905). On the gendered nature of these rights, see Amy Dru Stanley, "Conjugal Bonds and Wage Labor."

10. *Lochner v. New York*, 198 U.S. 45, 75 (1905).

11. See Wall, "*Lochner v. New York*," and Gillman, *Constitution Besieged*, 3–10.

12. Jacobs, *Law Writers and the Courts*, 167. See also Twiss, *Lawyers and the Constitution*, and Goetsch, "Future of Legal Formalism."

13. On Harlan as a paternalist, see G. Edward White, "John Marshall Harlan I," 13.

14. Clipping, *Detroit Free Press*, 6 June 1908, Family Scrapbook, 1876–1911, 192, JMH Papers, U of L.

15. Charles Warren, "Progressiveness of the United States Supreme Court" and "Bulwark to the State Police Power."

16. McCurdy, "Justice Field" and "Stephen J. Field." See also Alan Jones, "Thomas M. Cooley and 'Laissez-Faire Constitutionalism'"; Gold, "Redfield"; Halper, "Christopher G. Tiedeman"; and Fiss, *Troubled Beginnings*, 3–21. Some persist with the old model. See Kens, *Justice Stephen Field*.

17. *Illinois Central Railroad Company v. Illinois*, 146 U.S. 387 (1892).

18. Duncan Kennedy calls this legal classicism in "Toward an Historical Understanding of Legal Consciousness."

19. See Fiss, *Troubled Beginnings*, 155–84.

20. *Geer v. Connecticut*, 161 U.S. 519, 540, 539 (1896).

21. Forbath, "Ambiguities of Free Labor."

22. See Field's dissents in *Munn v. Illinois*, 94 U.S. 113, 148–49 (1877), and in *Spring Valley Water Works v. Schottler and Others, Supervisors*, 110 U.S. 347, 362–63 (1884).

23. JMH to AEW, 1 December 1905, AEW Papers, Filson Club Historical Society, Louisville, Ky.

24. Cole, *Whig Party*, 53; Brown, *Politics and Statesmanship*, 170–87.

25. See Howe, *Political Culture of the American Whigs*, 137–39; Remini, *Henry Clay*, 225–31.

26. JMH to AEW, [May 1895], JMH Papers, U of L. See also JMH to BH, 3 November 1888, BH Papers, LC.

27. This interpretation contrasts with Newmyer's in "Harvard Law School."

28. See Porter, "John Marshall Harlan" and "That Commerce Shall Be Free."

29. *Thompson Willson et al., Plaintiffs in Error, v. Black Bird Creek Marsh Company*, 2 Peters 245 (1829).

30. Prentice and Egan, *Commerce Clause*, 14–15.

31. Ibid., 30.

32. Samuel Freeman Miller, *Lectures on the Constitution*, 81.

33. Prentice and Egan, *Commerce Clause*, 31.

34. *Guy v. Baltimore*, 100 U.S. 434, 439, 443 (1879).

35. JMH Lectures, 8 January 1898.

36. *Minnesota v. Barber*, 136 U.S. 313, 315 (1890).

37. See Yeager, *Competition and Regulation*, 49–110; Porter and Livesay, *Merchants and Manufacturers*, 168–80; Libecap, "Rise of the Chicago Packers," 246–47, 252–54.

38. The other favorite was *Brimmer v. Rebman*, 138 U.S. 78 (1891). Congress reacted by establishing the Federal Meat Inspection Service in 1891 (McCurdy, "American Law," 647–48).

39. *Patapsco Guano Company v. North Carolina Board of Agriculture*, 171 U.S. 345 (1898).

40. *Smith v. St. Louis and Southwestern Railway Company*, 181 U.S. 248 (1901).

41. *Compagnie Française de Navigation à Vapeur v. Louisiana State Board of Health*, 186 U.S. 380 (1902).

42. *Reid v. Colorado*, 187 U.S. 137, 152, 147 (1902).

43. Chandler, *Visible Hand*, 209–39.

44. See Henderson, *Position of Foreign Corporations*, 177.

45. *Paul v. Virginia*, 8 Wall. 168 (1869).

46. Robinson, "Government Regulation of Insurance Companies," 88.

47. Retaliatory laws amounted to a "system national in scope, although state-administered" (Keller, *Life Insurance Enterprise*, 198).

48. *Philadelphia Fire Association v. New York*, 119 U.S. 110, 129 (1886). See dissents by Harlan in *American Smelting and Refining Company v. Colorado ex rel. Lindsley*, 204 U.S. 103 (1907); *New York State v. Roberts*, 171 U.S. 658 (1898); *American Sugar Refining Company v. Louisiana*, 179 U.S. 89 (1900); and *William v. Fears*, 179 U.S. 270 (1900). Harlan tried and failed to invoke liberty of contract in *Hooper v. California*, 155 U.S. 648 (1895). Peckham's definition of liberty in *Allgeyer v. Louisiana*, 165 U.S. 578, 589 (1897), is a paraphrase of *In re Jacobs*, 98 N.Y. 98, 106, which Harlan had quoted in his dissent to *Hooper v. California*, 155 U.S. 648, 662–63 (1895). Harlan dissented from *Nutting v. Massachusetts*, 183 U.S. 553 (1902).

49. Keller, *Affairs of State*, 326–27.

50. JMH Lectures, 8 January 1898.

51. Fairman, *Reconstruction and Reunion, 1864–1888, Part II*, 663.

52. See Diamond, "Citizenship, Civilization, and Coercion," 138.

53. Quoted in Judson, *Treatise on the Power of Taxation*, 535.

54. Seligman, *Essays in Taxation*, 285; Prentice and Egan, *Commerce Clause*, 202.

55. Judson, *Treatise on the Power of Taxation*, 219.

56. Powell, "Indirect Encroachments [V]," 224. See also Sidney Walter Jones, *Treatise*, 624, and Gray, *Limitations of the Taxing Power*, 418.

57. One exception was *Galveston, Harrisburg, and San Antonio Railway Company v. Texas*, 210 U.S. 217 (1908).

58. Harlan dissented from *Pullman's Palace Car Company v. Pennsylvania*, 141 U.S. 18 (1891); *Pittsburgh, Cincinnati, Chicago, and St. Louis Railway Company v. Backus*, 154 U.S. 421 (1894); *American Refrigerator Transit Company v. Hall*, 174 U.S. 70 (1899); *Adams Express Company v. Ohio State Auditor*, 165 U.S. 194 (1897); and *Kidd v. Alabama*, 188 U.S. 730 (1903). Harlan dissented from decisions allowing taxes to be laid on corporate franchises according to some proportional formula in *Horn Silver Mining Company v. New York State*, 143 U.S. 305 (1892), and *Postal Telegraph-Cable Company v. New Hope*, 192 U.S. 55 (1904). Harlan saw his reasoning adopted in a favorite case, *Louisville and Jeffersonville Ferry Company v. Kentucky*, 188 U.S. 385 (1903).

59. *Western Union Telegraph Company v. State of Kansas ex rel. Coleman, Attorney General*, 216 U.S. 1, 30–31, 37 (1910). See also Henderson, *Position of Foreign Corporations*, 130. Another favorite majority opinion on the taxation of capital stock was *International Textbook Company v. Pigg*, 217 U.S. 91 (1910). Fuller and Joseph McKenna dissented.

60. See Henderson, *Position of Foreign Corporations*, 111. See also a favorite dissent, *Ficklen v. Shelby County Taxing District*, 145 U.S. 1 (1892), and a favorite majority opinion, *Blake v. McClung*, 172 U.S. 239 (1898).

61. *Presidio County, Texas, v. Noel-Young Bond and Stock Company*, 212 U.S. 58 (1909).

62. Monkkonen, "Politics of Municipal Indebtedness," 135.

63. Dillon, *Law of Municipal Bonds*, 7. Two favorite dissents concerned state bonds: *Tindal v. Wesley*, 167 U.S. 204 (1897), and *Cunningham v. Macon and Brunswick Railroad Company et al.*, 109 U.S. 446 (1883). Harlan refused to allow state officials to claim sovereign immunity from suits by individuals despite the Eleventh Amendment. See *Louisiana v. Jumel*, 107 U.S. 711 (1882); *New Hampshire v. Louisiana et al.*, 108 U.S. 76 (1882); *Antoni v. Greenhow*, 107 U.S. 769 (1883); and *In re Ayers*, 123 U.S. 443 (1887). Harlan did an embarrassed about-face when the railroads used his logic to win injunctions against state officials trying to enforce rate schedules. See *Ex parte Young*, 209 U.S. 123 (1908).

64. Westin, "Supreme Court," 5–9.

65. Quoted in Fairman, *Reconstruction and Reunion, 1864–1888, Part I*, 923; Fairman, *Mr. Justice Miller*, 207–36.

66. He did mock bondholders' complaints (JMH to WHT, 13 November 1892, WHT Papers, LC).

67. *Brenham v. German American Bank*, 144 U.S. 173, 197 (1892).

68. Municipal and state bonds were commercial paper under the law merchant, which meant that buyers had certain responsibilities if they expected protection from the courts. See Harlan in *Wilkes County v. Coler,* 190 U.S. 107 (1903). The Court allowed curative legislation. See two decisions by Harlan: *Thompson v. Perrine,* 103 U.S. 806 (1880), and *Grenada County Supervisors et al. v. Brogden et al.,* 112 U.S. 261 (1884).

69. See Harlan's decisions in *Evansville v. Dennett,* 161 U.S. 434 (1896), and *Waite v. Santa Cruz,* 184 U.S. 302 (1902). However, see the importance of "clear and unambiguous" statements or recitals as they were called in *[Independent] School District v. Stone,* 106 U.S. 183, 187 (1882), in which the bondholder was left without remedy by Harlan speaking for the Court. False recitals could not create power. See Harlan for the majority in *Northern Bank of Toledo v. Porter Township Trustees,* 110 U.S. 608 (1884). However, he objected to the slighting of exact form with his silent dissent from *Supervisors of Calhoun County v. Galbraith,* 99 U.S. 214 (1878). See also *County of Schuyler v. Thomas,* 99 U.S. 169 (1878).

70. *Presidio County, Texas, v. Noel-Young Bond and Stock Company,* 212 U.S. 58, 72 (1909).

71. Harlan announced for the Court that the federal courts did not have to follow state rules in two other favorites: *Great Southern Fire Proof Hotel Company v. Jones,* 193 U.S. 532 (1904), and *Kuhn v. Fairmont Coal Company,* 215 U.S. 349 (1910).

72. *Cherokee Nation v. Southern Kansas Railway Company,* 135 U.S. 641 (1890); *United States v. Texas,* 143 U.S. 621 (1891); *United States v. Texas,* 162 U.S. 1 (1896); *Scranton v. Wheeler,* 179 U.S. 141 (1900); *Union Bridge Company v. United States,* 204 U.S. 364 (1907).

73. JMH to WHT, 24 April 1893, JMH Papers, Uof L.

74. He first voiced his idea in his dissent to *Railroad Commission Cases* or *Stone et al. v. Farmers' Loan and Trust Company,* 116 U.S. 307, 337 (1886). See his majority opinion in *Covington and Lexington Turnpike Road Company v. Sandford,* 164 U.S. 578, 597 (1896).

75. *Smyth v. Ames,* 169 U.S. 466, 526, 527, 528 (1898). Fuller and McKenna took no part. Harlan may have made his peace with the Court's gutting of the powers of the Interstate Commerce Commission (ICC). His last ICC dissent was *Interstate Commerce Commission v. Alabama Midland Railway Company,* 168 U.S. 144 (1897). Then *Smyth v. Ames* came in 1898 and solved the problem: rates would be regulated, but by the Court instead of the commission. Harlan put one ICC dissent on his list: *Macon Grocery Company v. Atlantic Coast Line Railroad Company,* 215 U.S. 501 (1910).

76. *Smyth v. Ames,* 169 U.S. 466, 543, 544, 546–47 (1898).

77. See also Harlan's opinion in *San Diego Land and Town Company v. National City,* 174 U.S. 739, 754–56 (1899).

78. Fairman, "So-called Granger Cases," 670.

79. Rossitor, *Conservatism in America,* 128.

80. Swisher, *Stephen J. Field,* 395.

81. Crosskey, *Politics and the Constitution,* 1147.

82. Cook, "History of Rate-Determination," 302; Hale, " 'Fair-Value' Merry-

Go-Round;" Horwitz, *Transformation of American Law, 1870–1960*, 162; Fiss, *Troubled Beginnings*, 207–10.

83. Corwin, "Doctrine of Due Process of Law," 374.

84. See Graham, *Everyman's Constitution*, 242–65, and tenBroek, *Antislavery Origins of the Fourteenth Amendment*, for this last point.

85. Magrath, *Morrison R. Waite*, 196.

86. Siegel, "Understanding the *Lochner* Era," 231.

87. *Slaughter-House Cases*, 16 Wall. 36 (1873). See also Hyman and Wiecek, *Equal Justice under Law*, 475–82.

88. *Slaughter-House Cases*, 16 Wall. 36, 78 (1873).

89. Beth, "*Slaughter-House Cases*," 504.

90. *Slaughter-House Cases*, 16 Wall. 36, 125 (1873).

91. Ibid., 96.

92. Ibid., 101–5.

93. Ibid., 110.

94. Forbath, "Ambiguities of Free Labor."

95. *Slaughter-House Cases*, 16 Wall. 36, 113 (1873).

96. Ibid., 118. Chief Justice Samuel Chase also dissented.

97. BHB to JMH, 4 May 1873, JMH Papers, LC.

98. Westin, "John Marshall Harlan," 664.

99. David R. Smith to JMH, 11 February 1873, JMH Papers, LC; H. H. Adams to BHB, 21 March 1873, BHB Papers, LC.

100. BHB to JMH, 2 March 1873, JMH Papers, LC.

101. The Court resisted substantive due process in *Munn v. Illinois* or the *Granger Cases*, 94 U.S. 113 (1877). For other decisions, see Fiss, *Troubled Beginnings*, 185–204. On the normality of rate regulation, see George H. Miller, *Railroads and the Granger Laws*, 31, and Goodrich, *Government Promotion of American Canals and Railroads*.

102. *Chicago, Milwaukee, and St. Paul Railway Company v. Minnesota*, 134 U.S. 418, 457, 463 (1890). When a new Louisiana constitution outlawed the butchering monopoly and the Court upheld it, Harlan joined Bradley's concurrence, which emphasized the Fourteenth Amendment, rather than Field's, which stressed natural rights: *Butchers' Union Slaughter-House and Live-Stock Landing Company v. Crescent City Live-Stock Landing and Slaughter-House Company*, 111 U.S. 746 (1884).

103. These are the rules of identity (i.e., a term used in one place means the same thing when used again) and of nonsuperfluousness (i.e., nothing is repeated). See Fairman, "Does the Fourteenth Amendment Incorporate the Bill of Rights?," and Frank and Munroe, "Original Understanding," and Kaczorowski, "Searching for the Intent of the Framers." Corwin held that the Fourteenth Amendment was supposed to incorporate the Bill of Rights ("Supreme Court and the Fourteenth Amendment").

104. JMH Lectures, 7 May 1898.

105. Ibid., 23 April 1898.

106. See ibid., 7 May, 23 April 1898.

107. *Hurtado v. People of California*, 110 U.S. 516, 537 (1884).

108. Ibid., 530.

109. Ibid., 548.

110. JMH Lectures, 12 March 1898.

111. Ibid.

112. Ibid.

113. Ibid., 15 January 1898.

114. Clipping, "Our Law Supreme," *Chicago Inter-Ocean*, n.d., Malvina Harlan's Scrapbook, 1892–95, JMH Papers, U of L.

115. JMH Lectures, 30 April 1898.

116. *Maxwell v. Dow*, 176 U.S. 581 (1900); *Twining v. New Jersey*, 211 U.S. 78 (1908). Harlan listed seven cases not involving the Fourteenth Amendment in which he supported due process in criminal cases.

117. Graham, *Everyman's Constitution*, 249.

118. Others have noted this. See Horwitz, *Transformation of American Law, 1870–1960*, 158, and Hovenkamp, *Enterprise and American Law*, 94.

119. *Covington and Lexington Turnpike Road Company v. Sandford*, 164 U.S. 578, 598 (1896).

120. *Smyth v. Ames*, 169 U.S. 466, 526 (1898).

121. *Chicago, Burlington, and Quincy Railroad Company v. Chicago*, 166 U.S. 226, 235, 236–37 (1897).

122. *Maxwell v. Dow*, 176 U.S. 581, 614 (1900).

123. *Adair v. United States*, 208 U.S. 161, 174, 178 (1908).

124. Pound, "Liberty of Contract," 454, quoting Harlan in *Adair v. United States*, 208 U.S. 161, 174–75 (1908).

125. Pound, "Liberty of Contract," 457.

126. Ibid., 484.

127. *Adair v. United States*, 208 U.S. 161, 174 (1908).

128. See McCurdy, "Roots of 'Liberty of Contract' Reconsidered"; Mensch, "History of Mainstream Legal Thought"; and Amy Dru Stanley, "Conjugal Bonds and Wage Labor."

129. Quoted in *Hodges v. United States*, 203 U.S. 1, 31 (1906).

130. Ibid., 34.

131. *Robertson v. Baldwin*, 165 U.S. 275, 294, 296, 288 (1897).

132. Ibid., 303.

133. Ibid., 302.

134. *Farmers' Loan and Trust Company v. Northern Pac. R. Company et al.*, 60 Fed. 803 (1894) (C.C.E.D.Wi.).

135. *Arthur et al. v. Oakes et al.*, 63 Fed. 310 (1894) (7th Cir.).

136. *Arthur et al. v. Oakes et al.* controlled what had become the abuse of the injunction power during strikes (Paul, *Conservative Crisis*, 122).

137. Foner, *Free Soil, Free Labor, Free Men*, 87–102.

138. Wilentz, *Chants Democratic*, 157–58, 274. See also Foner, *Free Soil, Free Labor, Free Men*, 15.

139. Howe, *Political Culture of the American Whigs*, 138–39; Burke, *Conundrum of Class*, 54.

140. Foner, *Free Soil, Free Labor, Free Men*, 18–20.

141. Rodgers, *Work Ethic in Industrial America*, 228–30.

142. Laurie, *Artisans into Workers*, 149.

143. The income tax was part of the Wilson-Gorman Tariff Act of 1894; the tax on higher incomes would replace revenues lost through a lowering of the tariff (Keller, *Affairs of State*, 307–8).

144. Robert Stanley, *Dimensions of Law*, 111–19.

145. Buenker, *Income Tax*, 28–29.

146. Ratner, *American Taxation*, 172–81. On popular support, see Robert Stanley, *Dimensions of Law*, 123–24.

147. The first time, some of the income tax clauses were declared unconstitutional, the Court was split four to four on the rest, and only Harlan and Justice Edward D. White dissented (*Pollock v. Farmers' Loan and Trust Company [I]*, 157 U.S. 429 [1895]). The second time around, Justices Henry Billings Brown and Howell Edmunds Jackson dissented, as did White and Harlan again (*Pollock v. Farmers' Loan and Trust Company [II]*, 158 U.S. 601 [1895]).

148. See clippings, *Boston Daily Globe*, 20 March 1895, and *New York Sun*, 22 March 1895, Family Scrapbook (*Income Tax Case*), JMH Papers, Uof L.

149. Clipping, *Evening Star*, 20 May 1895, Family Scrapbook (*Income Tax Case*), JMH Papers, Uof L.

150. Henry H. Ingersoll, "The Revolution of 20th May 1895," paper presented to the Tennessee Bar Association, 19 July 1895, JMH Papers, Uof L.

151. JMH to AEW, [May 1895], JMH Papers, Uof L.

152. JMH to JSH and JMayH, 24 May 1895, JMH Papers, Uof L.

153. Buenker, *Income Tax*, 19; Kelly, Harbison, and Belz, *American Constitution*, 413–14; Ratner, *American Taxation*, 201; Beth, *Development of the American Constitution*, 157; Fiss, *Troubled Beginnings*, 95–98.

154. See *Hylton, Plaintiff in Error, v. United States*, 3 Dallas 171 (1796), and *Scholey v. Rew*, 23 Wall. 331 (1874).

155. *Springer v. United States*, 102 U.S. 586 (1880). See also WHT to JMH, 27 May 1895, JMH Papers, Uof L.

156. *Pollock v. Farmers' Loan and Trust Company (II)*, 158 U.S. 601, 663 (1895).

157. JMH to AEW, [May 1895], JMH Papers, Uof L.

158. *Pollock v. Farmers' Loan and Trust Company (II)*, 158 U.S. 601, 676–77 (1895).

159. Rodgers, *Work Ethic*, 211.

160. Foner, "Meaning of Freedom in the Age of Emancipation," 438.

161. Lloyd, *Wealth against Commonwealth*, 521.

162. See Lloyd, "Speech at the Reception to Eugene Debs"; Debs, "Liberty"; and Bewig, "*Lochner v. the Journeymen Bakers of New York*," 433–34.

163. Pollack, *Just Polity*, 63.

164. Elizabeth B. Clark, "Matrimonial Bonds," 30–34.

165. *Pollock v. Farmers' Loan and Trust Company (II)*, 158 U.S. 601, 672–73 (1895).

166. JMH to JSH and JMayH, 24 May 1895, JMH Papers, Uof L.

167. JMH to AEW, [May 1895], JMH Papers, Uof L.

168. *Pollock v. Farmers' Loan and Trust Company (II)*, 158 U.S. 601, 673 (1895).

169. Montgomery, *Fall of the House of Labor,* 69.

170. Charles Warren, *History of the American Bar,* 211–24; Chroust, *Rise of the Legal Profession,* 2:15–30.

171. See Auerbach, *Unequal Justice,* 31–35.

172. See Hurst, *Growth of American Law,* 249–52; Bloomfield, "Lawyers and Public Criticism."

173. JH to JMH, 19 June 1888, JMH Papers, U of L.

174. JMH to JMayH, 16 July 1894, JMH Papers, LC. For the actual roles lawyers played, see Hurst, *Growth of American Law,* 333–75.

175. Robert W. Gordon, " 'The Ideal and the Actual in the Law,' " 57.

176. JMH, speech to law students, n.d., JMH Papers, U of L.

177. JMH Lectures, 20 November 1897. This is much like Robertson, *Outline of the Life of George Robertson,* 209.

178. JMH, "Remarks of Mr. Justice Harlan at the Centennial Judiciary Banquet in New York, Given by the Bar Association of That State, on the 4th of February, 1890," JMH Papers, LC. See also "Remarks of Mr. Justice Harlan at the Banquet Given by Members of the Bar in Honor of Mr. Justice Brown," 31 May 1906, JMH Papers, U of L, and clipping, "Public Honesty the Rule, Says Judge Harlan," June 1908, JMH Papers, U of L.

179. Friedman, *History of American Law,* 88.

180. JMH, National Bar Association speech, n.d., JMH Papers, LC.

181. JMH, speech to law students, n.d., JMH Papers, U of L.

182. Quoted in Foner, *Free Soil, Free Labor, Free Men,* 16.

183. Adams and Adams, *Chapters of Erie,* 95.

184. Destler, *American Radicalism,* 136–59.

185. Quoted in Mason, *Brandeis and the Modern State,* 113.

186. *Butchers' Union Slaughter-House v. Crescent City Slaughterhouse,* 111 U.S. 746, 766 (1884). Harlan also defined an exclusive city grant to a gas-lighting company as a legitimate contract but not an exercise of the police power. See *New Orleans Gas Company v. Louisiana Light Company,* 115 U.S. 650 (1885), a favorite case. See also Dudden, "Men against Monopoly," 587.

187. *Northern Securities v. United States,* 193 U.S. 197, 327 (1904). See also *United States v. E. C. Knight Company,* 156 U.S. 1, 25 (1895). See Peritz, *Competition Policy in America,* 9–58.

188. Letwin, *Law and Economic Policy in America,* 71–77.

189. Yeager, *Competition and Regulation,* 241. See also Chandler, *Scale and Scope,* 25–26; McGraw, "Rethinking the Trust Question," 19–24; Tennant, *American Cigarette Industry,* 49.

190. Peritz, *Competition Policy in America,* 22–23.

191. *Addyston Pipe and Steel Company v. United States,* 175 U.S. 211 (1899). Harlan heard this case in May 1897 while sitting for a week with Judges William Howard Taft and Horace H. Lurton in Nashville. See Phillips, "Tennessee and the U.S. Court of Appeals," and *United States v. Addyston Pipe and Steel Company et al.,* 85 Fed. 271 (1898). See also Harlan's opinion in *Connolly v. Union Sewer Pipe Company,* 184 U.S. 540 (1902), and one of his favorites, *Continental Wall Paper Company v. Louis Voight and Sons Company,* 212 U.S. 227 (1909).

192. *Swift and Company v. United States*, 196 U.S. 375 (1905).

193. *United States v. E. C. Knight Company*, 156 U.S. 1, 43 (1895).

194. JMH to AEW, [May 1895], JMH Papers, UofL.

195. *Pollock v. Farmers' Loan and Trust Company (II)*, 158 U.S. 601, 676, 675, 685 (1895).

196. Ibid., 664–65, 671–72.

197. Ratner, *American Taxation*, 212–14; Westin, "Supreme Court," 22–24.

198. Paul, *Conservative Crisis*, 221.

199. Ratner, *American Taxation*, 214.

200. Clipping, *Washington Post*, 27 May 1895, Family Scrapbook (*Income Tax Case*), JMH Papers, UofL; JMH Lectures, 5 February 1898.

201. See JMH to William A. Woods, 28 May 1895, and JMH to JSH and JMayH, 24 May 1895, JMH Papers, UofL.

202. JMH to JSH and JMayH, 24 May 1895, JMH Papers, UofL.

203. Quoted in Westin, "Mr. Justice Harlan," 121. Westin cites JMH to AEW, 1 June 1895, AEW Papers, Filson Club Historical Society, Louisville, Ky., but that is incorrect. It may be the missing first page of a letter at JMH Papers, UofL, that I have tentatively dated May 1895.

204. H. C. Evans to JMH, 27 May 1895, JMH Papers, UofL. See also Henry H. Ingersoll, "The Revolution of 20th May 1895," paper presented to the Tennessee Bar Association, 19 July 1895, JMH Papers, UofL.

205. McCurdy, "*Knight* Sugar Decision," 322–23; Urofsky, "Proposed Federal Incorporation," 163–64.

206. *United States v. E. C. Knight Company*, 156 U.S. 1, 12, 36–37 (1895). The general source is Eichner, *Emergence of Oligopoly*, 185–86, who approves of Harlan's dissent.

207. *United States v. E. C. Knight Company*, 156 U.S. 1, 43, 45 (1895).

208. On Attorney General Richard Olney's role, see Fisher, "*Knight* Case Revisited," 371, versus McCurdy, "*Knight* Sugar Decision," 329–30, n. 94.

209. See *Swift and Company v. United States*, 196 U.S. 375 (1905), and David Gordon, "*Swift and Co. v. United States*." In the meantime, Harlan dissented from *Hopkins v. United States*, 171 U.S. 578 (1898), a suit brought against members of the Kansas City Live Stock Exchange. On the outcome, see Fisher, "*Knight* Case Revisited," 381–83, versus Yeager, *Competition and Regulation*, 184.

210. The stock swap was designed to protect both companies from a raid (Letwin, *Law and Economic Policy in America*, 195, 210–11). Harlan threw out the state suit against consolidation in *Minnesota v. Northern Securities Company*, 194 U.S. 48 (1904).

211. *Northern Securities Company v. United States*, 193 U.S. 197, 347 (1904).

212. Clipping, *Chicago Record Herald*, 15 March 1904, *Northern Securities* Scrapbook, JMH Papers, UofL.

213. Thorelli, *Federal Antitrust Policy*, 563.

214. *Northern Securities* Scrapbook, JMH Papers, UofL.

215. *Continental Wall Paper Company v. Louis Voight and Sons Company*, 212 U.S. 227 (1909). See, similarly, *Connolly v. Union Sewer Pipe Company*, 184 U.S. 540 (1902).

216. *Northern Securities Company v. United States*, 193 U.S. 197, 337 (1904); Peritz, " 'Rule of Reason' in Anti-Trust Law."

217. See White's dissent in *United States v. Trans-Missouri Freight Association*, 166 U.S. 290, 346–47 (1897). See also *United States v. Joint Traffic Association*, 171 U.S. 505 (1898), in which Horace Gray, George Shiras, and White dissented silently.

218. *Standard Oil Company of New Jersey et al. v. United States*, 221 U.S. 1, 75 (1911).

219. *United States v. American Tobacco Company*, 221 U.S. 106, 165–66 (1911).

220. Thorelli, *Federal Antitrust Policy*, 14, 18–19.

221. Bringhurst, *Antitrust and the Oil Monopoly*, 158.

222. Thorelli, *Federal Antitrust Policy*, 40.

223. Reprinted in clipping, *Washington Evening Star*, 15 March 1904, *Northern Securities* Scrapbook, JMH Papers, U of L.

224. *Standard Oil v. United States*, 221 U.S. 1, 60 (1911).

225. *United States v. American Tobacco Company*, 221 U.S. 106, 179, 180 (1911).

226. *United States v. Trans-Missouri Freight Association*, 166 U.S. 290 (1897); *United States v. Joint Traffic Association*, 171 U.S. 505 (1898).

227. *Standard Oil v. United States*, 221 U.S. 1, 65 (1911).

228. *United States v. American Tobacco Company*, 221 U.S. 106, 191, 192 (1911).

229. *Standard Oil v. United States*, 221 U.S. 1, 102 (1911).

230. Ibid., 83.

231. Ibid., 90. Bringhurst agrees with Harlan in *Antitrust and the Oil Monopoly*, 158, whereas William Howard Taft held that the Court was right in *Anti-Trust Act*, 89–90.

232. *Standard Oil v. United States*, 221 U.S. 1, 105 (1911).

233. Quoted in Fiss, *Troubled Beginnings*, 31, n. 39.

234. William Glasman to JMH, 8 October 1911, JMH Papers, U of L.

235. Rolfe L. Thompson to JMH, 31 May 1911, JMH Papers, U of L.

236. William G. Ross, *Muted Fury*, 44.

237. John W. Gaines to JMH, 10 August 1911, JMH Papers, U of L.

238. See, for example, clippings, James W. Davis, "A Friend of the Court," *American Magazine*, [1911], and *Washington Times*, 14 October 1911, Supreme Court Scrapbook 10, Records of the Supreme Court of the United States, Record Group 267, National Archives, Washington, D.C.

239. Westin, "Mr. Justice Harlan," 118; JMH to AEW, 17 July 1908, AEW Papers, Filson Club Historical Society, Louisville, Ky.

240. See Morton White, *Social Thought in America*, 59–75; Jones, "Law and Economics v. a Democratic Society"; Ernst, "Free Labor."

241. See Fine, *Laissez-Faire and the General Welfare State*, and Dorothy Ross, *Origins of American Social Science*.

242. Pound, "Liberty of Contract," 457.

243. Frankfurter, "Hours of Labor," 367.

244. JMH to Theodore Roosevelt, 25 June 1908, JMH Papers, U of L.

245. Blumin, *Emergence of the Middle Class*, 285–90.

1. Byars, "Making of the Self-Made Man," 52.

2. See Jordan, "Familial Politics," and Burrows and Wallace, "American Revolution," 213.

3. Forgie, *Patricide in the House Divided;* Breitenbach, "Sons of the Fathers."

4. Rosenberg, "Sexuality, Class, and Role in Nineteenth Century America"; Rotundo, "Learning about Manhood" and *American Manhood.* Rotundo also includes the late-nineteenth-century masculine primitive. This literature studies middle-class northerners but seems more applicable than the work on white southerners focusing on the planter elite.

5. JMH, "Great Men Whom I Have Seen," n.d., JMH Papers, UofL.

6. Greene, *America's Heroes,* table 1, 52, table 8, 153.

7. JMH to JSH, 26 January 1882, JMH Papers, LC.

8. JSH to GWS, 30 March 1879, JMH Papers, UofL.

9. Kerber, "Separate Spheres," 39.

10. Norton, *Liberty's Daughters;* Kerber, *Women of the Republic.*

11. See *In re Lockwood,* 154 U.S. 116 (1893); Weisberg, " 'Barred from the Bar' "; and Grossberg, "Institutionalizing Masculinity."

12. JMH to Colonel Thomas Bullitt, 17 October 1880, Letter Press Book, 1878–81, JMH Papers, UofL.

13. GWS to JMH, 16 December 1880, JMH Papers, UofL.

14. See BHB to JMH, 10, 12 March 1872, and other letters of that year, JMH Papers, LC.

15. See JMH to Colonel Thomas Bullitt, 17 October 1880, Letter Press Book, 1878-81, JMH Papers, UofL.

16. Malvina noted in her memoirs that her bridegroom had to borrow $500 "for the expenses of our wedding and for our start in life" (MSH, "Memories," frame 109).

17. JMH to Major General Calvin Goddard, 21 January 1863, Combined Military Service Record, U.S. Army Archives, National Archives, Washington, D.C.

18. Harlan's wife's father canceled a $10,000 note of John's in his will (John Shanklin's will, 16 October 1875, JMH Papers, LC).

19. AEW to JMH, 30 June 1880, JMH Papers, LC. See also AEW to JMH, 3 August 1895, JMH Papers, LC.

20. JMH to Colonel Thomas Bullitt, 17 October 1880, Letter Press Book, 1878-81, JMH Papers, UofL.

21. JMH to JMayH, 20 May 1910, in the possession of Lauren Derby.

22. Epstein, Segal, Spaeth, and Walker, *Supreme Court Compendium,* 42, table 1-9.

23. Clippings, "Our Modern Daniels," *Washington Post,* 6 May 1895, Supreme Court Scrapbook 4, and "The Real Justice John M. Harlan on and off the Supreme Bench," *New York Herald,* 28 May 1911, Supreme Court Scrapbook 10, Records of the Supreme Court of the United States, Record Group 267, National Archives, Washington, D.C.

24. JMH to GWS, 19 November 1894, JMH Papers, LC.

25. JMH to Colonel Thomas Bullitt, 17 October 1880, Letter Press Book, 1878–81, JMH Papers, UofL.

26. Clipping, *New York Age*, 6 January 1912, JMH Papers, UofL; John B. Larner to WHT, 2 December 1911, WHT Papers, LC.

27. Quoted in Wyllie, *Self-Made Man in America*, 10.

28. Rodgers, *Work Ethic*, 222–28.

29. Weiss, *American Myth of Success*, 6.

30. JMH Lectures, 15 January 1898.

31. Harlan missed the fact that federal bankruptcy law was supposed to hold the states in line (Coleman, *Debtors and Creditors in America*, 274).

32. Quoted in Warren, *Bankruptcy in United States History*, 38.

33. JMH Lectures, 15 January 1898.

34. Ibid.

35. JMH to GWS, 19 November 1894, JMH Papers, LC.

36. JMH to JSH, 11 January 1881 [1882?], JMH Papers, LC.

37. Dubbert, *Man's Place*, 142.

38. JMH to JSH, 13 July 1882, JMH Papers, LC.

39. MSH to JMayH, 13 September 1889, in the possession of Lauren Derby.

40. JMH to GWS, 19 November 1894, JMH Papers, LC.

41. JMH Lectures, 20 November 1897.

42. Musto, "Continuity across Generations," 124.

43. Rorabaugh, *Alcoholic Republic*, 194–95, 200–201.

44. JMH to RDH, autobiographical letter, 4 July 1911, JMH Papers, LC.

45. AEW to RDH, 11 April [1930], JMH Papers, LC.

46. AEW to JMH, 24 March 1879, JMH Papers, UofL.

47. AEW to JMH, 17 April 1880, JMH Papers, LC.

48. See AEW to JMH, 24 March 1879; JH to JMH, 29 June 1880, 25 February 1882; and AEW to JMH, 12 September 1880, JMH Papers, UofL. See also Levine, "Discovery of Addiction," and Mendelson and Mello, *Alcohol Use and Abuse*, 229–49.

49. JH to JMH, 29 June 1880, JMH Papers, UofL.

50. Malvina's words were copied into a letter sent to her by James on 22 March 1891, JMH Papers, LC.

51. JMH to Henry Harlan, 10 July 1889, JMH Papers, UofL.

52. JH to JMH, 29 June 1880, JMH Papers, UofL.

53. AEW to JMH, 19 May 1880, JMH Papers, UofL.

54. JH to JMH, 21 October 1885, JMH Papers, UofL.

55. JH to JMH, 16 May 1887, JMH Papers, UofL. See also ibid., 15 July 1887.

56. JH to JMH, 26 August 1887, JMH Papers, UofL.

57. W. H. Acers to JMH, 25 March 1891, JMH Papers, LC. Acers wrote other letters that year. On opium addiction, see Musto, *American Disease*, 1–6. James may have taken opium for a cure (Mendelson and Mello, *Alcohol Use and Abuse*, 47, n. 25).

58. JMH to AEW, 14 December 1892, JMH Papers, UofL; AEW to RDH, 11 April [1930], JMH Papers, LC.

59. JH to JMH, 4 February 1882, JMH Papers, UofL.

60. Ibid., 26 August 1887.

61. Ibid., 19 June 1888.

62. JMH to AEW, 27 April 1892, JMH Papers, UofL.

63. Ibid., 11 December 1894.

64. Ibid., 23 July 1892; JMH to Joseph P. Bradley, 23 February 1889, JMH Papers, UofL.

65. JMH to JMayH, 7 February 1894, JMH Papers, LC.

66. Mintz, *Prison of Expectations*, 38.

67. JMH to [RDH], 12 July 1870, JMH Papers, LC.

68. JMH to Henry Harlan, 10 July 1889, JMH Papers, UofL.

69. JMH to RDH, 29 October 1882, JMH Papers, LC.

70. JMH to [RDH], 12 July 1870, JMH Papers, LC.

71. JMH to JSH, 11 January 1881 [1882?], JMH Papers, LC.

72. Ibid., 11 September 1880. See also JMH to JMayH, 2 October 1887, in the possession of Lauren Derby.

73. JMH to [JSH], 26 January 1882, JMH Papers, LC.

74. JMH to JSH, 11 September 1880, JMH Papers, LC.

75. Ibid., 9 February 1882.

76. Ibid. Harlan partakes much here of the stern Victorian father. See Dubbert, *Man's Place*, 141.

77. JMH to JSH, 23 November 1880, JMH Papers, LC.

78. Ibid., 11 September 1880.

79. Ibid., 9 February 1882.

80. Ibid., 23 November 1880.

81. Ibid., 25 November 1882.

82. Ibid., 8 October 1881. Victorian parents emphasized "internal as opposed to external enforcement of values" (Mintz, *Prison of Expectations*, 38).

83. JMH to JSH, 8 October 1881, JMH Papers, LC.

84. JMH to JMayH, 2 October 1883, in the possession of Lauren Derby.

85. Albert S. White to JMH, 3 December 1907, JMH Papers, UofL; Edgar A. Bancroft to JMH, 17 December 1910, JMH Papers, LC.

86. JMayH to JMH, 19 May 1911, JMH Papers, UofL.

87. Clipping, *Louisville Post*, 11 August 1892, Family Scrapbook (*Income Tax Case*), JMH Papers, UofL.

88. JMayH to MSH, 4 December 1915, "John Harlan Derby . . ." Scrapbook, in the possession of Lauren Derby.

89. JMH to JMayH, 16 July 1894, JMH Papers, LC. See also Tussey, *Eugene Debs Speaks*, 48.

90. John Maynard was apparently in on the case at the local level (JSH to JMH, 30 July 1894, JMH Papers, LC).

91. JMH to Elizabeth Harlan, 12 February 1905, in the possession of Lauren Derby.

92. Noah Swayne to JMH, 5 July 1880, JMH Papers, UofL.

93. "Memorandum of Conference with Defendant John Indicating What His Testimony Will Be," n.d., in the possession of Lauren Derby.

94. *Harlan v. Harlan*, 281 Fed. 602 (Court of Appeals of the District of Columbia) (1922); *John Maynard Harlan v. James Harlan*, 263 U.S. 681 (1923). This latter decision merely declared the case moot because the sons had come to an agreement.

95. Quoted in clipping, J. J. Dickinson, "Justice Harlan's Death Premonition," *Los Angeles Examiner*, 20 October 1911, JMH Papers, U of L.

96. JMayH to Margaret Harlan, 9 July 1921, in the possession of Eve Dillingham.

97. Rotundo, "Body and Soul," 23.

98. JMH to WQG, 11 June 1885, WQG Papers, LC.

99. BHB to JMH, 26 November 1872, JMH Papers, LC.

100. See AEW to RDH, 11 April [1930], JMH Papers, LC, and Webb, *Benjamin Helm Bristow*, 244–72.

101. But it was the usual way one got judgeships. See Botein, " 'What We Shall Meet Afterwards in Heaven.' "

102. JMH to [JSH], 26 January 1882, JMH Papers, LC.

103. JMayH to JMH, 19 July 1910, JMH Papers, LC.

104. Roger Derby to author, 30 January 1989; Roger Derby, sketch of Roger Alden Derby, 1 July 1988.


CONCLUSION

1. See, for example, "Harlan Had It Right," *Forbes*, 3 June 1996, 24; "Assembly Resolution Denounced as Fascist," *San Francisco Chronicle*, 24 May 1996, A19; "Discrimination Liberals," *New York Times*, 6 May 1996, A15; letters to the editor, *New York Times*, 8 May 1996, A22; and *Chronicle of Higher Education*, 29 March 1996, B2–3.

2. Lofgren, *"Plessy" Case*, 191.

3. MSH, "Memories," frame 229. See also Duffield, *Washington in the 90's*, 110–11.

4. JMH Lectures, 19 February 1898.

5. "James B. Morrow, 'Talks with Notable Men,' *Washington Post*, Feb. 28, 1906" (interview with JMH), typescript, JMH Papers, LC.

6. See Levy, *Law of the Commonwealth*, 282.

7. Romanzo Bunn to JMH, 18 January 1905, JMH Papers, U of L.

8. 1 Samuel 12:1–4.

9. JMH to JSH, 9 February 1882, JMH Papers, LC.

10. John P. Kennedy, *Memoirs of the Life of William Wirt*, 1:v.

11. Weems, *Life of George Washington*. The other books were on Walter Scott, John Adams, Henry Clay, and Sargent S. Prentiss, and another was on Washington.

# BIBLIOGRAPHY

PRIMARY SOURCES

*Manuscript Sources*

Boston, Massachusetts
  Massachusetts Historical Society
    Charles Francis Adams Papers
Fremont, Ohio
  Rutherford B. Hayes Presidential Center, Spiegel Grove
Louisville, Kentucky
  Filson Club Historical Society
    Augustus E. Willson Papers
  University of Louisville School of Law, Law Library
    John Marshall Harlan Papers
New Haven, Connecticut
  Yale University Library, Manuscripts and Archives
    Brewer Family Papers
Washington, D.C.
  Library of Congress, Manuscript Division
    Benjamin H. Bristow Papers
    Frederick Douglass Papers
    Melville Weston Fuller Papers
    Walter Q. Gresham Papers
    John Marshall Harlan Papers
    Benjamin Harrison Papers
    Joseph Holt Papers
    Horace H. Lurton Papers
    William McKinley Papers
    William Howard Taft Papers
    Morrison R. Waite Papers
  National Archives
    Records of the Supreme Court of the United States
    U.S. Army Archives

*Published Works*

Adams, Charles Francis, Jr., and Henry Adams. *Chapters of Erie.* 1886. Reprint, Ithaca: Cornell University Press, 1956.
Bryce, James. *The American Commonwealth.* 2 vols. New York: Macmillan, 1919.
Coudert, Frederic R. "Judicial Constitutional Amendment as Illustrated by the Devolution of the Institution of the Jury from a Fundamental Right to a Mere Method of Procedure." *Yale Law Journal* 13 (1904): 331–65.
Debs, Eugene. "Liberty." In *Writings and Speeches of Eugene V. Debs,* edited by Arthur M. Schlesinger Jr., 6–20. New York: Hermitage Press, 1948.

Desdunes, Rodolphe Lucien. *Our People and Our History.* Trans. Sister Dorothea Olga McCantes. Baton Rouge: Louisiana State University Press, 1973. Originally published as *Nos hommes et notre histoire* (1911).

Douglass, Frederick. "The Constitution of the United States: Is It Pro-Slavery or Anti-Slavery?" (1860). In *Life and Writings of Frederick Douglass,* 5 vols., edited by Philip S. Foner, 2:467–80. New York: International Publishers, 1950.

Du Bois, W. E. B. "The Conservation of Races." In *The Oxford W. E. B. Du Bois Reader,* edited by Eric J. Sundquist, 37–47. New York: Oxford University Press, 1996.

Duffield, Isabel McKenna. *Washington in the 90's.* San Francisco: Press of the Overland Monthly, 1929.

*The First International Congress in America for the Welfare of the Child, Held under the Auspices of the National Congress of Mothers at Washington D.C., March 10th to 17th, 1908.* Washington, D.C.: National Congress of Parents and Teachers, 1908.

Frankfurter, Felix. "Hours of Labor and Realism in Constitutional Law." *Harvard Law Review* 29 (1916): 353–73.

Grimké, Archibald H. "The Presbyterian Fall." *New York Age* 20 (April 1905): 1.

Grimké, Francis J. "The Second Marriage of Frederick Douglass." *Journal of Negro History* 19 (July 1934): 324–29.

Harlan, John Marshall. "James Wilson and the Formation of the Constitution." *American Law Review* 34 (July–August 1900): 481–504.

Harlan, John Marshall, and Charles Henry Butler. "Treatise on the Law of Marriage." In *Cyclopedia of Law and Procedure,* 40 vols., edited by William Mack, 26:821–926. New York: American Law Book Company, 1907.

Harrison, Benjamin. "The Status of Annexed Territory and Its Free Civilized Inhabitants." *North American Review* 172 (1901): 1–22.

Hays, Reverend George P. *Presbyterians: A Popular Narrative of Their Origins, Progress, Doctrines, and Achievements.* New York: J. A. Hill, 1892.

Kennedy, John P. *Memoirs of the Life of William Wirt, Attorney-General of the United States.* 2 vols. Philadelphia: Lew and Blanchard, 1850.

Kurland, Philip B., and Gerhard Casper. "*Civil Rights Cases,* 109 U.S. 3." In *Landmark Briefs and Arguments of the Supreme Court of the United States: Constitutional Law,* 8:305–94. Arlington, Va.: University Publications of America, 1975.

Lloyd, Henry Demarest. "Speech at the Reception to Eugene Debs" (1895). In *Men: The Workers,* 179–93. New York: Doubleday, Page, 1909.

———. *Wealth against Commonwealth.* New York: Harper & Brothers, 1894.

Miller, Kelly. *Race Adjustment: Essays on the Negro in America.* New York: Neale, 1908.

Miller, Samuel Freeman. *Lectures on the Constitution of the United States.* 1893. Reprint, Littleton, Colo.: Fred B. Rothman, 1980.

*Minutes of the General Assembly of the Presbyterian Church in the United States of America,* n.s., vol. 5, no. 2. Philadelphia: Office of the General Assembly, 1905.

Moon, Henry Lee, ed. *The Emerging Thought of W. E. B. Du Bois: Essays and Editorials from "The Crisis."* New York: Simon and Schuster, 1972.

Morrow, James. "Talks with Notable Men." *Washington Post*, 25 February 1906, 6.

Pound, Roscoe. "Liberty of Contract." *Yale Law Journal* 18 (1909): 454–87.

"Report of the Committee of Canvass" (22 May 1905). In *Minutes of the General Assembly of the Presbyterian Church in the United States of America*, n.s., 5, no. 2:60–61. Philadelphia: Office of the General Assembly, 1905.

*The Report of the Philippine Commission (Schurman)* (31 January 1900). 4 vols. Washington, D.C.: Government Printing Office, 1900.

"Report of the Standing Committee on Freedmen" (22 May 1905). In *Minutes of the General Assembly of the Presbyterian Church in the United States of America*, n.s., 5, no. 2:61–66. Philadelphia: Office of the General Assembly, 1905.

Robertson, George. *An Outline of the Life of George Robertson.* Lexington, Ky.: Transylvania, 1876.

Robinson, Maurice H. "Government Regulation of Insurance Companies." In *Proceedings of the American Political Science Association, 1906*, 3:80–195. Lancaster, Pa.: Wickersham Press, 1907.

Slayden, Ellen Maury. *Washington Wife: Journal of Ellen Maury Slayden from 1897–1919.* New York: Harper & Row, 1962.

Taft, William Howard. *The Anti-Trust Act and the Supreme Court.* New York: Harper & Row, 1914.

Todd, Charles Burr. *The Story of Washington: The National Capital.* New York: G. P. Putnam's Sons, 1889.

Tucker, St. George. *A Dissertation on Slavery, with Proposal for the Gradual Abolition of It, in the State of Virginia.* 1796. Reprint, Westport, Conn.: Negro University Press, 1970.

Tussey, Jean Y., ed. *Eugene Debs Speaks.* New York: Pathfinder Press, 1972.

Twain, Mark. "To the Person Sitting in Darkness." *North American Review* 172 (February 1901): 161–76.

U.S. Bureau of the Census. *Population of the United States in 1860, Eighth Census.* Washington, D.C.: Government Printing Office, 1864.

*War of the Rebellion: A Compilation of the Official Records of the Union and Confederate Armies.* Washington, D.C.: Government Printing Office, 1880–1907.

Warren, Charles. "A Bulwark to the State Police Power: The United States Supreme Court." *Columbia Law Review* 13 (1913): 667–95.

———. "The Progressiveness of the United States Supreme Court." *Columbia Law Review* 13 (1913): 294–313.

Weems, M. L. *The Life of George Washington, with Curious Anecdotes Equally Honourable to Himself, and Exemplary to His Young Countrymen.* Philadelphia: Joseph Allen, 1847.

Williams, T. Harry, ed. *Hayes: The Diary of a President, 1875–1881.* New York: David McKay, 1964.

Woodson, Carter G., ed. *The Works of Francis J. Grimké.* 4 vols. Washington, D.C.: Associated Publishers, 1942.

SECONDARY SOURCES

*Books*

Aaron, Daniel. *The Unwritten War: American Writers and the Civil War.* New York: Knopf, 1973.

Abanese, Catherine L. *Sons of the Fathers: The Civil Religion of the American Revolution.* Philadelphia: Temple University Press, 1976.

Auerbach, Jerold. *Unequal Justice: Lawyers and Social Change in Modern America.* New York: Oxford University Press, 1976.

Ayers, Edward L. *Vengeance and Justice: Crime and Punishment in the Nineteenth Century South.* New York: Oxford University Press, 1984.

Bancroft, Frederic. *Slave-Trading in the Old South.* Baltimore: J. H. Furst, 1931.

Baradaglio, Peter W. *Reconstructing the Household: Families, Sex, and the Law in the Nineteenth-Century South.* Chapel Hill: University of North Carolina Press, 1995.

Basch, Norma. *In the Eyes of the Law: Women, Marriage, and Property in Nineteenth-Century New York.* Ithaca: Cornell University Press, 1982.

Baym, Nina. *Woman's Fiction: A Guide to Novels by and about Women in America, 1820–1870.* Ithaca: Cornell University Press, 1978.

Beisner, Robert L. *Twelve against Empire: The Anti-Imperialists, 1898–1900.* New York: McGraw-Hill, 1968.

Belz, Herman. *Emancipation and Equal Rights: Politics and Constitutionalism in the Civil War Era.* New York: Norton, 1978.

———. *Reconstructing the Union: Theory and Policy during the Civil War.* Ithaca: Cornell University Press, 1969.

Bercovitch, Sacvan. *The American Jeremiad.* Madison: University of Wisconsin Press, 1978.

Berger, Raoul. *Government by Judiciary: The Transformation of the Fourteenth Amendment.* Cambridge: Harvard University Press, 1977.

Berkhofer, Robert F., Jr. *The White Man's Indian: Images of the American Indian from Columbus to the Present.* New York: Knopf, 1978.

Berlin, Ira. *Slaves without Masters: The Free Negro in the Antebellum South.* New York: Random House, 1974.

Beth, Loren P. *The Development of the American Constitution, 1877–1917.* New York: Harper & Row, 1971.

———. *John Marshall Harlan: The Last Whig Justice.* Lexington: University Press of Kentucky, 1992.

Bigham, Darrel E. *We Ask Only a Fair Trial: A History of the Black Community in Evansville, Indiana.* Bloomington: Indiana University Press, 1987.

Blaustein, Albert P., and Roy M. Mersky. *The First One Hundred Justices: Statistical Studies on the Supreme Court of the United States.* Hamden, Conn.: Archon, 1978.

Blight, David W. *Frederick Douglass' Civil War: Keeping Faith in Jubilee.* Baton Rouge: Louisiana State University Press, 1989.

Blumin, Stuart M. *The Emergence of the Middle Class: Social Experience in the American City, 1760–1900.* Cambridge: Cambridge University Press, 1989.

Bozeman, Theodore Dwight. *Protestants in an Age of Science: The Baconian Ideal and Ante-bellum American Religious Thought.* Chapel Hill: University of North Carolina Press, 1977.

Braden, Waldo W. *The Oral Tradition in the South.* Baton Rouge: Louisiana State University Press, 1979.

Bringhurst, Bruce. *Antitrust and the Oil Monopoly: The "Standard Oil" Cases, 1890–1911.* Westport, Conn.: Greenwood Press, 1979.

Brodhead, Michael J. *David J. Brewer: The Life of a Supreme Court Justice, 1837–1910.* Carbondale: Southern Illinois University Press, 1994.

Brown, Thomas. *Politics and Statesmanship: Essays on the American Whig Party.* New York: Columbia University Press, 1985.

Bruce, Dickson D., Jr. *Archibald Grimké: Portrait of a Black Independent.* Baton Rouge: Louisiana State University Press, 1993.

Brundage, W. Fitzhugh. *Lynching in the New South: Georgia and Virginia, 1880–1930.* Urbana: University of Illinois Press, 1993.

Buck, Paul. *The Road to Reunion, 1865–1900.* Boston: Little, Brown, 1937.

Buenker, John D. *The Income Tax and the Progressive Era.* New York: Garland, 1985.

Bullock, Henry Allen. *A History of Negro Education in the South: From 1619 to the Present.* Cambridge: Harvard University Press, 1967.

Burke, Martin J. *The Conundrum of Class: Public Discourse on the Social Order in America.* Chicago: University of Chicago Press, 1995.

Bynum, Victoria E. *Unruly Women: The Politics of Social and Sexual Control in the Old South.* Chapel Hill: University of North Carolina Press, 1992.

Cabranes, José A. *Citizenship and the American Empire: Notes on the Legislative History of the United States Citizenship of Puerto Ricans.* New Haven, Conn.: Yale University Press, 1979.

Carter, Paul A. *The Spiritual Crisis of the Gilded Age.* De Kalb: Northern Illinois University Press, 1971.

Chandler, Alfred D., Jr. *Scale and Scope: The Dynamics of Industrial Capitalism.* Cambridge: Belknap Press of Harvard University Press, 1990.

———. *The Visible Hand: The Managerial Revolution in American Business.* Cambridge: Belknap Press of Harvard University Press, 1977.

Chroust, Anton-Hermann. *The Rise of the Legal Profession in America.* 2 vols. Norman: University of Oklahoma Press, 1965.

Cohen, Naomi W. *Jews in Christian America: The Pursuit of Religious Equality.* New York: Oxford University Press, 1992.

Cole, Arthur C. *The Whig Party in the South.* Washington, D.C.: American Historical Association, 1913.

Coleman, Peter J. *Debtors and Creditors in America: Insolvency, Imprisonment for Debt, and Bankruptcy, 1607–1900.* Madison: State Historical Society of Wisconsin, 1974.

Collins, Charles Wallace. *The Fourteenth Amendment and the States: A Study of the Operation of the Restraint Clauses of Section One of the Fourteenth Amendment to the Constitution of the United States.* 1912. Reprint, New York: DaCapo Press, 1974.

Collins, Lewis, and Richard H. Collins. *Collins' Historical Sketches of Kentucky.* 2 vols. Covington, Ky.: Collins, 1882.

Corwin, Edward S. *The "Higher Law" Background of American Constitutional Law.* 1928. Reprint, Ithaca: Cornell University Press, 1965.

Cott, Nancy. *The Bonds of Womanhood: "Woman's Sphere" in New England, 1780–1835.* New Haven, Conn.: Yale University Press, 1977.

Coulter, E. Merton. *The Civil War and Readjustment in Kentucky.* 1926. Reprint, Gloucester, Mass.: Peter Smith, 1966.

Craven, Wesley Frank. *The Legend of the Founding Fathers.* New York: New York University Press, 1956.

Crosskey, William Winslow. *Politics and the Constitution in the History of the United States.* 2 vols. Chicago: University of Chicago Press, 1953.

Curti, Merle. *The Roots of American Loyalty.* New York: Columbia University Press, 1946.

Daniel, Pete. *The Shadow of Slavery: Peonage in the South, 1901–1969.* Urbana: University of Illinois Press, 1972.

Davis, David Brion. *The Problem of Slavery in the Age of Revolution, 1770–1823.* Ithaca: Cornell University Press, 1975.

Degler, Carl N. *At Odds: Woman and the Family in America from the Revolution to the Present.* New York: Oxford University Press, 1980.

————. *The Other South: Southern Dissenters in the Nineteenth Century.* 1974. Reprint, Boston: Northeastern University Press, 1982.

Destler, Chester McArthur. *American Radicalism, 1865–1901.* 1946. Reprint, Chicago: Quadrangle Books, 1966.

Dillon, John F. *The Law of Municipal Bonds.* St. Louis: G. I. Jones, 1876.

Diner, Hasia R. *In the Almost Promised Land: American Jews and Blacks, 1915–1935.* Westport, Conn.: Greenwood Press, 1977.

Dinnerstein, Leonard. *Antisemitism in America.* New York: Oxford University Press, 1994.

Dubbert, Joe L. *A Man's Place: Masculinity in Transition.* Englewood Cliffs, N.J.: Prentice Hall, 1979.

Eaton, Clement. *Freedom of Thought in the Old South.* Durham, N.C.: Duke University Press, 1940.

Edgington, Frank E. *A History of the New York Avenue Presbyterian Church.* Washington D.C.: New York Avenue Presbyterian Church, 1961.

Eichner, Alfred S. *The Emergence of Oligopoly: Sugar Refining as a Case Study.* Baltimore: Johns Hopkins University Press, 1969.

Eichorn, David Max. *Evangelizing the American Jew.* Middle Village, N.Y.: Jonathan David, 1978.

Elson, Ruth Miller. *Guardians of Tradition: American Schoolbooks of the Nineteenth Century.* Lincoln: University of Nebraska Press, 1964.

Ely, James W. *The Chief Justiceship of Melville W. Fuller, 1888–1910.* Columbia: University of South Carolina Press, 1995.

Epstein, Lee, Jeffrey A. Segal, Harold J. Spaeth, and Thomas G. Walker, eds. *The Supreme Court Compendium: Data, Decisions, and Developments.* 2d ed. Washington, D.C.: Congressional Quarterly, 1996.

Fairman, Charles. *Mr. Justice Miller and the Supreme Court, 1862–1890.* Cambridge: Harvard University Press, 1939.

——. *Reconstruction and Reunion, 1864–1888, Part I.* Vol. 6 of *History of the Supreme Court of the United States.* New York: Macmillan, 1971.

——. *Reconstruction and Reunion, 1864–1888, Part II.* Vol. 7 of *History of the Supreme Court of the United States.* New York: Macmillan, 1987.

Faust, Drew Gilpin. *The Creation of Confederate Nationalism: Ideology and Identity in the Civil War South.* Baton Rouge: Louisiana State University Press, 1988.

Fehrenbacher, Don E. *The "Dred Scott" Case: Its Significance in American Law and Politics.* New York: Oxford University Press, 1978.

Feldman, Egal. *The Dreyfus Affair and the American Conscience, 1895–1906.* Detroit: Wayne State University Press, 1981.

Ferguson, Robert A. *Law and Letters in American Culture.* Cambridge: Harvard University Press, 1984.

Fine, Sidney. *Laissez-Faire and the General Welfare State: A Study of Conflict in American Thought, 1865–1901.* 1956. Reprint, Ann Arbor: University of Michigan Press, 1976.

Fiss, Owen M. *Troubled Beginnings of the Modern State, 1888–1910.* Vol. 8 of *History of the Supreme Court of the United States.* New York: Macmillan, 1993.

Foner, Eric. *Free Soil, Free Labor, Free Men: The Ideology of the Republican Party before the Civil War.* New York: Oxford University Press, 1970.

——. *Reconstruction: America's Unfinished Revolution, 1863–1877.* New York: Harper & Row, 1988.

Forbes, W. Cameron. *The Philippine Islands.* 2 vols. Boston: Houghton Mifflin, 1928.

Forgie, George B. *Patricide in the House Divided: A Psychological Interpretation of Lincoln and His Age.* New York: Norton, 1979.

Foster, Gaines M. *The Ghosts of the Confederacy: Defeat, the Lost Cause, and the Emergence of the New South, 1865–1913.* New York: Oxford University Press, 1987.

Fredrickson, George M. *The Black Image in the White Mind: The Debate on Afro-American Character and Destiny.* 1971. Reprint, Middletown, Conn.: Wesleyan University Press, 1987.

——. *The Inner Civil War: Northern Intellectuals and the Crisis of Union.* New York: Harper & Row, 1965.

Freehling, Alison G. *Drift toward Dissolution: The Virginia Slavery Debate of 1831–1832.* Baton Rouge: Louisiana State University Press, 1982.

Freyer, Tony Allan. *Forums of Order: The Federal Courts and Business in American History.* Greenwich, Conn.: JAI Press, 1979.

Friedman, Lawrence M. *A History of American Law.* New York: Simon and Schuster, 1973.

Friedman, Lawrence M., and Robert V. Percival. *The Roots of Justice: Crime and Punishment in Alameda County, California, 1870–1910.* Chapel Hill: University of North Carolina Press, 1981.

Gaines, Kevin K. *Uplifting the Race: Black Leadership, Politics, and Culture in the Twentieth Century.* Chapel Hill: University of North Carolina Press, 1996.

Gaston, Paul M. *The New South Creed: A Study in Southern Mythmaking.* New York: Knopf, 1970.

Gatewood, Willard B. *Aristocrats of Color: The Black Elite, 1880 to 1920.* Bloomington: Indiana University Press, 1990.

Genovese, Eugene D. *Roll, Jordan, Roll: The World the Slaves Made.* New York: Random House, 1976.

Gillman, Howard. *The Constitution Besieged: The Rise and Demise of Lochner Era Police Powers Jurisprudence.* Durham, N.C.: Duke University Press, 1993.

Gilmore, Glenda Elizabeth. *Gender and Jim Crow: Women and the Politics of White Supremacy in North Carolina, 1896–1920.* Chapel Hill: University of North Carolina Press, 1996.

Gilmore, Grant. *The Ages of American Law.* New Haven, Conn.: Yale University Press, 1977.

Goen, C. C. *Broken Churches, Broken Nation: Denominational Schisms and the Coming of the Civil War.* Macon, Ga.: Mercer University Press, 1985.

Gold, David M. *The Shaping of Nineteenth-Century Law: John Appleton and Responsible Individualism.* New York: Greenwood Press, 1990.

Goldman, Eric F. *John Bach McMaster, American Historian.* Philadelphia: University of Pennsylvania Press, 1943.

Goodrich, Carter. *Government Promotion of American Canals and Railroads, 1800–1890.* New York: Columbia University Press, 1960.

Gossett, Thomas F. *Race: The History of an Idea in America.* New York: Schocken Books, 1965.

Graham, Howard Jay. *Everyman's Constitution: Historical Essays on the Fourteenth Amendment, the "Conspiracy Theory," and American Constitutionalism.* Ithaca: Cornell University Press, 1977.

Gray, James M. *Limitations of the Taxing Power.* San Francisco: Bancroft-Whitney, 1906.

Green, Constance. *The Secret City: A History of Race Relations in the Nation's Capital.* Princeton, N.J.: Princeton University Press, 1967.

Greene, Theodore P. *America's Heroes: The Changing Models of Success in American Magazines.* New York: Oxford University Press, 1970.

Grossberg, Michael. *Governing the Hearth: Law and the Family in Nineteenth-Century America.* Chapel Hill: University of North Carolina Press, 1985.

Hall, Jacquelyn Dowd. *Revolt against Chivalry: Jessie Daniel Ames and the Women's Campaign against Lynching.* New York: Columbia University Press, 1979.

Handy, Robert T. *Undermined Establishment: Church-State Relations in America, 1880–1920.* Princeton, N.J.: Princeton University Press, 1991.

Harap, Louis. *The Image of the Jew in American Literature: From Early Republic to Mass Immigration.* Philadelphia: Jewish Publication Society of America, 1974.

Harlan, Louis R. *Booker T. Washington: The Wizard of Tuskegee, 1901–1915.* New York: Oxford University Press, 1983.

Harris, Robert J. *The Quest for Equality: The Constitution, Congress, and the Supreme Court.* Baton Rouge: Louisiana State University Press, 1960.

Hatch, Nathan. *The Sacred Cause of Liberty: Republican Thought and the Millennium in Revolutionary New England.* New Haven, Conn.: Yale University Press, 1977.

Henderson, Gerard Carl. *The Position of Foreign Corporations in American Constitutional Law: A Contribution to the History and Theory of Juristic Persons in Anglo-American Law.* Cambridge: Harvard University Press, 1918.

Herbst, Jurgen. *The German Historical School in American Scholarship: A Study in the Transfer of Culture.* Ithaca: Cornell University Press, 1965.

Higham, John. *Strangers in the Land: Patterns of American Nativism, 1865–1925.* 1955. Reprint, New York: Atheneum, 1972.

Hodes, Martha. *White Women, Black Men: Illicit Sex in the Nineteenth-Century South.* New Haven, Conn.: Yale University Press, 1997.

Holifield, E. Brooks. *The Gentlemen Theologians: American Theology in Southern Culture, 1795–1860.* Durham, N.C.: Duke University Press, 1978.

Horsman, Reginald. *Race and Manifest Destiny: The Origins of American Racial Anglo-Saxonism.* Cambridge: Harvard University Press, 1981.

Horwitz, Morton J. *The Transformation of American Law, 1780–1860.* Cambridge: Harvard University Press, 1977.

———. *The Transformation of American Law, 1870–1960: The Crisis of Legal Orthodoxy.* New York: Oxford University Press, 1992.

Hovenkamp, Herbert. *Enterprise and American Law, 1836–1937.* Cambridge: Harvard University Press, 1991.

Howard, Victor B. *Black Liberation in Kentucky: Emancipation and Freedom, 1862–1884.* Lexington: University Press of Kentucky, 1983.

Howe, Daniel Walker. *The Political Culture of the American Whigs.* Chicago: University of Chicago Press, 1979.

Hoxie, Frederick E. *A Final Promise: The Campaign to Assimilate the Indians, 1880–1920.* Cambridge: Harvard University Press, 1967.

Hurst, James Willard. *The Growth of American Law: The Law Makers.* Boston: Little, Brown, 1950.

———. *Law and the Conditions of Freedom in the Nineteenth Century United States.* Madison: University of Wisconsin Press, 1956.

Hyman, Harold M., and William M. Wiecek. *Equal Justice under Law: Constitutional Development, 1835–1875.* New York: Harper & Row, 1982.

Ireland, Robert M. *The County Courts in Antebellum Kentucky.* Lexington: University Press of Kentucky, 1972.

Jacobs, Clyde E. *Law Writers and the Courts: The Influence of Thomas M. Cooley, Christopher G. Tiedeman, and John F. Dillon upon American Constitutional Law.* Berkeley: University of California Press, 1954.

Jenkins, William S. *Pro-Slavery Thought in the Old South.* Chapel Hill: University of North Carolina Press, 1935.

Jimerson, Randall C. *The Private Civil War: Popular Thought during the Sectional Conflict.* Baton Rouge: Louisiana State University Press, 1988.

Jones, Sidney Walter. *A Treatise on the Law of Telegraph and Telephone Companies.* Kansas City, Mo.: Vernon Law Book Company, 1906.

Jordan, Winthrop D. *White over Black: American Attitudes toward the Negro, 1550–1812*. Chapel Hill: University of North Carolina Press, 1968.

Judson, Frederick N. *A Treatise on the Power of Taxation State and Federal in the United States*. St. Louis: F. H. Thomas Law Book Company, 1917.

Kaczorowski, Robert J. *The Politics of Judicial Interpretation: The Federal Courts, Department of Justice, and Civil Rights, 1866–1876*. Dobbs Ferry, N.Y.: Oceana Publications, 1985.

Kayser, Elmer Louis. *Bricks without Straw: The Evolution of George Washington University*. New York: Appleton-Century-Crofts, 1970.

Keller, Morton. *Affairs of State: Public Life in Nineteenth Century America*. Cambridge: Belknap Press of Harvard University Press, 1977.

———. *The Life Insurance Enterprise, 1885–1910: A Study in the Limits of Corporate Power*. Cambridge: Belknap Press of Harvard University Press, 1963.

Kelly, Alfred H., Winfred A. Harbison, and Herman Belz. *The American Constitution: Its Origins and Development*. 6th ed. New York: Norton, 1983.

Kens, Paul. *Justice Stephen Field: Shaping Liberty from the Gold Rush to the Gilded Age*. Lawrence: University Press of Kansas, 1997.

Kerber, Linda. *Women of the Republic: Intellect and Ideology in Revolutionary America*. Chapel Hill: University of North Carolina Press, 1980.

Kerr, James Edward. *The Insular Cases: The Role of the Judiciary in American Expansionism*. Port Washington, N.Y.: Kennikat Press, 1982.

King, Willard L. *Melville Weston Fuller: Chief Justice of the United States, 1888–1910*. New York: Macmillan, 1950.

Kinney, James. *Amalgamation!: Race, Sex, and Rhetoric in the Nineteenth-Century American Novel*. Westport, Conn.: Greenwood Press, 1985.

Korn, Bertram Wallace. *American Jewry and the Civil War*. Philadelphia: Jewish Publication Society of America, 1951.

Kousser, J. Morgan. *Dead End: The Development of Nineteenth-Century Litigation on Racial Discrimination in the Schools*. Oxford: Clarendon Press, 1986.

Kull, Andrew. *The Color-Blind Constitution*. Cambridge: Harvard University Press, 1992.

LaPiana, William P. *Logic and Experience: The Origins of Modern American Legal Education*. New York: Oxford University Press, 1994.

Laurie, Bruce. *Artisans into Workers: Labor in Nineteenth-Century America*. New York: Hill & Wang, 1989.

Lebsock, Suzanne. *The Free Women of Petersburg: Status and Culture in a Southern Town, 1784–1860*. New York: Norton, 1984.

Letwin, William. *Law and Economic Policy in America: The Evolution of the Sherman Anti-Trust Act*. 1954. Reprint, New York: Random House, 1965.

Levin, David. *History as Romantic Art: Bancroft, Prescott, Motley, and Parkman*. Stanford: Stanford University Press, 1959.

Levine, Lawrence W. *Black Culture and Black Consciousness: Afro-American Folk Thought from Slavery to Freedom*. New York: Oxford University Press, 1977.

Levy, Leonard. *The Law of the Commonwealth and Chief Justice Shaw*. New York: Oxford University Press, 1957.

Lewis, David Levering. *W. E. B. Du Bois: Biography of a Race, 1868–1919.* New York: Henry Holt, 1993.

Linderman, Gerald F. *The Mirror of War: American Society and the Spanish-American War.* Ann Arbor: University of Michigan Press, 1974.

Litwack, Leon F. *Been in the Storm So Long: The Aftermath of Slavery.* New York: Knopf, 1980.

———. *North of Slavery: The Negro in the Free States, 1790–1860.* Chicago: University of Chicago Press, 1961.

Loetscher, Lefferts A. *The Broadening Church: A Study of Theological Issues in the Presbyterian Church since 1869.* Philadelphia: University of Pennsylvania Press, 1954.

Loewen, James W. *Lies My Teacher Told Me: Everything Your American History Textbook Got Wrong.* New York: New Press, 1995.

Lofgren, Charles A. *The "Plessy" Case: A Legal-Historical Perspective.* New York: Oxford University Press, 1987.

Logan, Rayford B. *The Betrayal of the Negro: From Rutherford B. Hayes to Woodrow Wilson.* 1954. Reprint, New York: Collier Books, 1956.

McClain, Charles J. *In Search of Equality: The Chinese Struggle against Discrimination in Nineteenth-Century America.* Berkeley: University of California Press, 1994.

McConnell, Stuart. *Glorious Contentment: The Grand Army of the Republic, 1865–1900.* Chapel Hill: University of North Carolina Press, 1992.

McPherson, James M. *The Abolitionist Legacy: From Reconstruction to the NAACP.* Princeton, N.J.: Princeton University Press, 1975.

———. *Abraham Lincoln and the Second American Revolution.* New York: Oxford University Press, 1990.

Magrath, C. Peter. *Morrison R. Waite: The Triumph of Character.* New York: Macmillan, 1963.

Marsden, George M. *The Soul of the American University: From Protestant Establishment to Established Nonbelief.* New York: Oxford University Press, 1994.

Martin, Waldo E., Jr. *The Mind of Frederick Douglass.* Chapel Hill: University of North Carolina Press, 1978.

Marty, Martin E. *The Irony of It All, 1893–1919.* Vol. 1 of *Modern American Religion.* Chicago: University of Chicago Press, 1986.

Mason, Alpheus Thomas. *Brandeis and the Modern State.* Princeton, N.J.: Princeton University Press, 1933.

Massa, Mark Stephen. *Charles Augustus Briggs and the Crisis of Historical Criticism.* Minneapolis: Fortress Press, 1990.

Matthews, Glenna. *"Just a Housewife": The Rise and Fall of Domesticity in America.* New York: Oxford University Press, 1987.

May, Glenn Anthony. *Social Engineering in the Philippines: The Aims, Execution, and Impact of American Colonial Policy, 1900–1913.* Westport, Conn.: Greenwood Press, 1980.

Meier, August. *Negro Thought in America, 1880–1915: Racial Ideologies in the Age of Booker T. Washington.* Ann Arbor: University of Michigan Press, 1963.

Mencke, John G. *Mulattoes and Race Mixture: American Attitudes and Images, 1865–1918.* Ann Arbor: UMI Research Press, 1979.

Mendelson, Jack H., and Nancy K. Mello. *Alcohol Use and Abuse in America.* Boston: Little, Brown, 1985.

Merk, Frederick. *Manifest Destiny and Mission in American History: A Reinterpretation.* 1963. Reprint, New York: Vintage Books, 1966.

Meyer, D. H. *The Instructed Conscience: The Shaping of the American National Ethic.* Philadelphia: University of Pennsylvania Press, 1972.

Miller, George H. *Railroads and the Granger Laws.* Madison: University of Wisconsin Press, 1971.

Miller, Stuart Creighton. *"Benevolent Assimilation": The American Conquest of the Philippines, 1899–1903.* New Haven, Conn.: Yale University Press, 1982.

———. *The Unwelcome Immigrant: The American Image of the Chinese, 1785–1882.* Berkeley: University of California Press, 1969.

Minger, Ralph Eldin. *William Howard Taft and United States Foreign Policy: The Apprenticeship Years, 1900–1908.* Urbana: University of Illinois Press, 1975.

Mintz, Steven. *A Prison of Expectations: The Family in Victorian Culture.* New York: New York University Press, 1983.

Montgomery, David. *The Fall of the House of Labor: The Workplace, the State, and American Labor Activism, 1865–1925.* Cambridge: Cambridge University Press, 1987.

Moorhead, James H. *American Apocalypse: Yankee Protestants and the Civil War, 1860–1869.* New Haven, Conn.: Yale University Press, 1978.

Morgan, Philip D. *Slave Counterpoint: Black Culture in the Eighteenth-Century Chesapeake and Lowcountry.* Chapel Hill: University of North Carolina Press, 1998.

Morris, Richard B., ed. *Encyclopedia of American History.* New York: Harper & Brothers, 1953.

Morris, Thomas D. *Southern Slavery and the Law, 1619–1860.* Chapel Hill: University of North Carolina Press, 1996.

Moses, Wilson Jeremiah. *The Golden Age of Black Nationalism, 1850–1925.* Camden, Conn.: Archon Books, 1978.

Murray, Andrew E. *Presbyterians and the Negro: A History.* Philadelphia: Presbyterian Historical Society, 1966.

Musto, David F. *The American Disease: Origins of Narcotic Control.* New Haven, Conn.: Yale University Press, 1973.

Nagel, Paul C. *One Nation Indivisible: The Union in American Thought, 1776–1861.* New York: Oxford University Press, 1964.

———. *This Sacred Trust: American Nationality, 1798–1898.* New York: Oxford University Press, 1971.

Newmyer, R. Kent. *Supreme Court Justice Joseph Story: Statesman of the Old Republic.* Chapel Hill: University of North Carolina Press, 1985.

Nieman, Donald G. *To Set the Law in Motion: The Freedmen's Bureau and the Legal Rights of Blacks, 1865–1868.* Millwood, N.Y.: KTO Press, 1979.

Noble, David W. *Historians against History: The Frontier Thesis and the National*

*Covenant in American Historical Writing since 1830.* Minneapolis: University of Minnesota Press, 1965.

Noll, Mark A., ed. *The Princeton Theology, 1812–1921: Scripture, Science, and Theological Method from Archibald Alexander to Benjamin Breckinridge Warfield.* Grand Rapids, Mich.: Baker Book House, 1983.

Norton, Mary Beth. *Liberty's Daughters: The Revolutionary Experience of American Women, 1750–1800.* Boston: Little, Brown, 1980.

Paludan, Phillip S. *A Covenant with Death: The Constitution, Law, and Equality in the Civil War Era.* Urbana: University of Illinois Press, 1975.

Patai, Raphael, and Jennifer Patai Wing. *The Myth of the Jewish Race.* New York: Scribner, 1975.

Paul, Arnold. *Conservative Crisis and the Rule of Law: Attitudes of Bench and Bar, 1887–1895.* Ithaca: Cornell University Press, 1960.

Pease, Jane H., and William H. Pease. *They Who Would Be Free: Blacks' Search for Freedom, 1830–1861.* New York: Atheneum, 1974.

Peck, Elisabeth S. *Berea's First 125 Years, 1855–1980.* Lexington: University Press of Kentucky, 1982.

Peritz, Rudolph J. R. *Competition Policy in America, 1888–1992.* New York: Oxford University Press, 1996.

Peterson, Merrill D. *The Jefferson Image in the American Mind.* New York: Oxford University Press, 1960.

———. *Lincoln in American Memory.* New York: Oxford University Press, 1993.

Pole, J. R. *The Pursuit of Equality in American History.* Berkeley: University of California Press, 1978.

Pollack, Norman. *The Just Polity: Populism, Law, and Human Welfare.* Urbana: University of Illinois Press, 1987.

Porter, Glenn, and Harold C. Livesay. *Merchants and Manufacturers: Studies in the Changing Structure of Nineteenth-Century Marketing.* Baltimore: Johns Hopkins University Press, 1971.

Pratt, Julius W. *America's Colonial Experiment: How the United States Gained, Governed, and in Part Gave Away a Colonial Empire.* New York: Prentice-Hall, 1950.

Prawer, S. S. *Israel at Vanity Fair: Jews and Judaism in the Writings of W. M. Thackeray.* Leiden: E. J. Brill, 1992.

Prentice, E. Parmalee, and John G. Egan. *The Commerce Clause of the Federal Constitution.* Chicago: Callaghan, 1898.

Pressly, Thomas J. *Americans Interpret Their Civil War.* Princeton, N.J.: Princeton University Press, 1954.

Quarles, Benjamin. *Black Abolitionists.* New York: Oxford University Press, 1969.

Rabinowitz, Howard N. *Race Relations in the Urban South, 1865–1890.* New York: Oxford University Press, 1978.

Raboteau, Albert J. *Slave Religion: The "Invisible Institution" in the Antebellum South.* New York: Oxford University Press, 1978.

Randall, J. G. *Constitutional Problems under Lincoln.* Rev. ed. Gloucester, Mass.: Peter Smith, 1963.

Ratner, Sidney. *American Taxation: Its History as a Social Force in Democracy.* New York: Norton, 1942.

Reid, John Phillip. *Chief Justice: The Judicial World of Charles Doe.* Cambridge: Harvard University Press, 1967.

Remini, Robert V. *Henry Clay: Statesman for the Union.* New York: Norton, 1991.

Rodgers, Daniel T. *Work Ethic in Industrial America, 1850–1920.* Chicago: University of Chicago Press, 1978.

Rorabaugh, W. J. *The Alcoholic Republic: An American Tradition.* New York: Oxford University Press, 1979.

Rosenberg, Edgar. *From Shylock to Svengali: Jewish Stereotypes in English Fiction.* Stanford: Stanford University Press, 1960.

Ross, Dorothy. *The Origins of American Social Science.* Cambridge: Cambridge University Press, 1991.

Ross, William G. *A Muted Fury: Populists, Progressives, and Labor Unions Confront the Courts, 1890–1937.* Princeton, N.J.: Princeton University Press, 1994.

Rossitor, Clinton. *Conservatism in America: The Thankless Persuasion.* New York: Knopf, 1971.

Rotundo, E. Anthony. *American Manhood: Transformations in Masculinity from the Revolution to the Modern Era.* New York: Basic Books, 1993.

Rowland, Kate Mason. *The Life of George Mason, 1725–1792.* 2 vols. New York: G. P. Putnam's Sons, 1892.

Rudwick, Elliot M. *W. E. B. Du Bois: Propagandist of the Negro Protest.* New York: Atheneum, 1968.

Ryan, Mary. *Cradle of the Middle Class: The Family in Oneida County, New York, 1790–1865.* Cambridge: Cambridge University Press, 1981.

Salyer, Lucy E. *Laws Harsh as Tigers: Chinese Immigrants and the Shaping of Modern Immigration Laws.* Chapel Hill: University of North Carolina Press, 1995.

Schmidt, George P. *The Old Time College President.* New York: Columbia University Press, 1930.

Seligman, Edwin R. A. *Essays in Taxation.* 10th ed. New York: Macmillan, 1928.

Silber, Nina. *The Romance of Reunion: Northerners and the South, 1865–1900.* Chapel Hill: University of North Carolina Press, 1993.

Simmons, William J. *Men of Mark, Eminent, Progressive, and Rising.* 1887. Reprint, New York: Arno Press and the New York Times, 1968.

Smiley, David L. *Lion of White Hall: The Life of Cassius M. Clay.* Madison: University of Wisconsin Press, 1962.

Smith, H. Shelton. *In His Image, but . . . : Racism in Southern Religion, 1780–1910.* Durham, N.C.: Duke University Press, 1972.

Smith, John David. *An Old Creed for the New South: Pro-Slavery Ideology and Historiography, 1865–1918.* Westport, Conn.: Greenwood Press, 1985.

Smith, Page. *James Wilson, Founding Father, 1742–1798.* Chapel Hill: University of North Carolina Press, 1956.

Snay, Mitchell. *Gospel of Disunion: Religion and Separatism in the Antebellum South.* Chapel Hill: University of North Carolina Press, 1997.

Somkin, Fred. *Unquiet Eagle: Memory and Desire in the Idea of American Freedom, 1815–1860*. Ithaca: Cornell University Press, 1967.

Speed, Thomas, R. M. Kelly, and Alfred Pirtle. *The Union Regiments of Kentucky*. Louisville, Ky.: Courier-Journal Job Printing Company, 1897.

Stanley, Robert. *Dimensions of Law in the Service of Order: Origins of the Federal Income Tax, 1861–1913*. New York: Oxford University Press, 1993.

Stephenson, Gilbert Thomas. *Race Distinctions in American Law*. New York: D. Appleton, 1910.

Stevens, Robert. *Law School: Legal Education in America from the 1850s to the 1980s*. Chapel Hill: University of North Carolina Press, 1983.

Strout, Cushing. *The New Heavens and New Earth: Political Religion in America*. New York: Harper & Row, 1974.

Swisher, Carl B. *Roger B. Taney*. 1935. Reprint, Hamden, Conn.: Archon Books, 1961.

———. *Stephen J. Field: Craftsman of the Law*. 1930. Reprint, Hamden, Conn.: Archon Books, 1963.

tenBroek, Jacobus. *The Antislavery Origins of the Fourteenth Amendment*. Berkeley: University of California Press, 1951.

Tennant, Richard B. *The American Cigarette Industry: A Study in Economic Analysis and Public Policy*. New Haven, Conn.: Yale University Press, 1950.

Thorelli, Hans B. *The Federal Antitrust Policy: Origination of an American Tradition*. Stockholm: Boktryckeriet P. A. Norstedt & Söner, 1955.

Tompkins, E. Berkeley. *Anti-Imperialism in the United States: The Great Debate, 1890–1920*. Philadelphia: University of Pennsylvania Press, 1970.

Torruella, Juan R. *The Supreme Court and Puerto Rico: The Doctrine of Separate and Unequal*. Rio Piedras: Editorial de la Universidad de Puerto Rico, 1985.

Trelease, Allen W. *White Terror: The Ku Klux Klan Conspiracy and Southern Reconstruction*. New York: Harper & Row, 1971.

Turner, James. *Without God, without Creed: The Origins of Unbelief in America*. Baltimore: Johns Hopkins University Press, 1985.

Tuveson, Ernst. *Redeemer Nation: The Idea of America's Millennial Role*. Chicago: University of Chicago Press, 1968.

Twiss, Benjamin R. *Lawyers and the Constitution: How Laissez-Faire Came to the Supreme Court*. 1942. Reprint, Princeton, N.J.: Princeton University Press, 1962.

Vaughn, William Preston. *Schools for All: Blacks and Public Education in the South, 1865–1877*. Lexington: University Press of Kentucky, 1974.

Walters, Ronald G. *The Antislavery Appeal: American Abolitionism after 1830*. Baltimore: Johns Hopkins University Press, 1976.

Warren, Charles. *Bankruptcy in United States History*. Cambridge: Harvard University Press, 1935.

———. *A History of the American Bar*. Boston: Little, Brown, 1911.

Webb, Ross A. *Benjamin Helm Bristow: Border State Politician*. Lexington: University Press of Kentucky, 1969.

Weinberg, Albert K. *Manifest Destiny: A Study of Nationalist Expansionism in American History*. 1935. Reprint, Gloucester, Mass.: Peter Smith, 1958.

Weiss, Richard. *The American Myth of Success: From Horatio Alger to Norman Vincent Peale.* New York: Basic Books, 1969.

Welch, Richard E., Jr. *Response to Imperialism: The United States and the Philippine-American War, 1899–1902.* Chapel Hill: University of North Carolina Press, 1979.

White, G. Edward. *Justice Oliver Wendell Holmes: Law and the Inner Self.* New York: Oxford University Press, 1993.

White, Morton. *Social Thought in America: The Revolt against Formalism.* New York: Viking, 1949.

Wilentz, Sean. *Chants Democratic: New York City and the Rise of the American Working Class, 1788–1850.* New York: Oxford University Press, 1984.

Wilkerson, Marcus M. *Public Opinion and the Spanish-American War: A Study in War Propaganda.* 1932. Reprint, New York: Russell & Russell, 1967.

Williamson, Joel. *New People: Miscegenation and Mulattoes in the United States.* New York: Free Press, 1980.

Wilmore, Gayraud. *Black Religion and Black Radicalism: An Interpretation of the Religious History of the Afro-American People.* 2d ed. Maryknoll, N.Y.: Orbis Books, 1983.

Wilson, Charles Reagan. *Baptized in Blood: The Religion of the Lost Cause, 1865–1920.* Athens: University of Georgia Press, 1980.

Wolf, William J. *The Almost Chosen People: A Study of the Religion of Abraham Lincoln.* Garden City, N.Y.: Doubleday, 1959.

Wood, Forrest G. *The Arrogance of Faith: Christianity and Race in America from the Colonial Era to the Twentieth Century.* New York: Knopf, 1990.

Woodward, C. Vann. *The Strange Career of Jim Crow.* 1955. Reprint, New York: Oxford University Press, 1975.

Wright, George C. *Life behind a Veil: Blacks in Louisville, Kentucky, 1865–1930.* Baton Rouge: Louisiana State University Press, 1985.

Wright, John D., Jr. *Transylvania: Tutor to the West.* Lexington: University Press of Kentucky, 1975.

Wyllie, Irvin. *The Self-Made Man in America: The Myth of Rags to Riches.* New York: Free Press, 1954.

Yarbrough, Tinsley E. *Judicial Enigma: The First Justice Harlan.* New York: Oxford University Press, 1994.

Yeager, Mary. *Competition and Regulation: The Development of Oligopoly in the Meat Packing Industry.* Greenwich, Conn.: JAI Press, 1981.

Younger, Richard D. *The People's Panel: The Grand Jury in the United States, 1863–1941.* Providence, R.I.: American History Research Center, Brown University Press, 1963.

*Articles*

Abraham, Henry J. "John Marshall Harlan: A Justice Neglected." *Virginia Law Review* 41 (November 1955): 871–91.

Ahlstrom, Sydney E. "The Scottish Philosophy and American Theology." *Church History* 24 (1955): 257–72.

Avins, Alfred. "Anti-Miscegenation Laws and the Fourteenth Amendment: The Original Intent." *Virginia Law Review* 52 (1966): 1224–55.

Bailey, Thomas A. "Was the Presidential Election of 1900 a Mandate on Imperialism?" *Mississippi Valley Historical Review* 24 (1937): 43–52.

Basch, Norma. " 'Invisible Women': The Legal Fiction of Marital Unity in Nineteenth-Century America." *Feminist Studies* 5 (Summer 1979): 346–66.

Benedict, Michael Les. "Laissez-Faire and Liberty: The Re-Evaluation of the Meaning and Origins of Laissez-Faire Constitutionalism." *Law and History Review* 3 (Fall 1985): 293–331.

———. "Preserving Federalism: Reconstruction and the Waite Court." *Supreme Court Review* (1978): 39–79.

Berry, Mary Francis. "Judging Morality: Sexual Behavior and Legal Consequences in the Late Nineteenth-Century South." *Journal of American History* 78 (December 1991): 835–56.

Beth, Loren P. "Justice Harlan and the Uses of Dissent." *American Political Science Review* 49 (December 1955): 1085–1104.

———. "The *Slaughter-House Cases*—Revisited." *Louisiana Law Review* 23 (1963): 487–505.

Bewig, Matthew S. "*Lochner v. the Journeymen Bakers of New York*—The Journeymen Bakers, Their Hours of Labor, and the Constitution: A Case Study in the Social History of Legal Thought." *American Journal of Legal History* 38 (October 1994): 413–41.

Bickel, Alexander. "The Original Understanding and the Segregation Decision." *Harvard Law Review* 69 (1955): 1–65.

Blight, David W. " 'For Something beyond the Battlefield': Frederick Douglass and the Struggle for the Memory of the Civil War." *Journal of American History* 75 (March 1989): 1156–78.

Bloomfield, Maxwell. "Lawyers and Public Criticism: Challenge and Response in Nineteenth-Century America." *American Journal of Legal History* 15 (October 1971): 269–87.

Botein, Stephen. " 'What We Shall Meet Afterwards in Heaven': Judgeship as a Symbol for Modern American Lawyers." In *Professions and Professional Ideologies in America*, edited by Gerald L. Geison, 49–69. Chapel Hill: University of North Carolina Press, 1983.

Bradley, Robert C. "Who Are the Great Justices and What Criteria Did They Meet?" In *Great Justices of the United States Supreme Court: Ratings and Case Studies*, edited by William D. Pederson and Norman W. Provizer, 1–31. New York: Peter Lang, 1993.

Breitenbach, William. "Sons of the Fathers: Temperance Reformers and the Legacy of the American Revolution." *Journal of the Early Republic* 3 (Spring 1983): 69–82.

Burrows, Edwin G., and Michael Wallace. "The American Revolution: The Ideology and Psychology of National Liberation." *Perspectives in American History* 6 (1972): 167–306.

Canfield, Monte, Jr. " 'Our Constitution Is Color-Blind': Mr. Justice Harlan and Modern Problems of Civil Rights." *University of Missouri at Kansas City Law Review* 32 (Summer 1964): 292–321.

Censer, Jane Turner. "'Smiling through Her Tears': Ante-Bellum Southern Women and Divorce." *American Journal of Legal History* 25 (January 1981): 24–47.

Chin, Gabriel J. "The *Plessy* Myth: Justice Harlan on the Chinese Cases." *Iowa Law Review* 82 (October 1996): 151–82.

Clark, Elizabeth B. "Matrimonial Bonds: Slavery and Divorce in Nineteenth-Century America." *Law and History Review* 8 (Spring 1990): 25–54.

Clark, T. D. "The Slave Trade between Kentucky and the Cotton Kingdom." *Mississippi Valley Historical Review* 21 (1934): 331–42.

Cohen, William. "Thomas Jefferson and the Problem of Slavery." *Journal of American History* 56 (1969): 503–26.

Cook, Franklin H. "History of Rate-Determination under Due Process Clause." *University of Chicago Law Review* 11 (1944): 297–337.

Corwin, Edward S. "The Doctrine of Due Process of Law before the Civil War." *Harvard Law Review* 24 (1911): 366–460.

———. "The Supreme Court and the Fourteenth Amendment." *Michigan Law Review* 7 (1909): 643–72.

Current, Richard N. "Lincoln, the Civil War, and the American Mission." In *The Public and the Private Lincoln: Contemporary Perspectives*, edited by Cullom Davis, Charles B. Strozier, Rebecca Monroe Veach, and Geoffrey C. Ward, 137–46. Carbondale: Southern Illinois University Press, 1979.

De Santis, Hugh. "The Imperialist Impulse and American Innocence, 1865–1900." In *American Foreign Relations: A Historiographical Review*, edited by Gerald K. Haines and J. Samuel Walker, 65–90. Westport, Conn.: Greenwood Press, 1981.

Diamond, Stephen. "Citizenship, Civilization, and Coercion: Justice Holmes on the Tax Power." In *The Legacy of Oliver Wendell Homes, Jr.*, edited by Robert W. Gordon, 115–54. Stanford: Stanford University Press, 1992.

Dudden, Arthur P. "Men against Monopoly: The Prelude to Trust-Busting." *Journal of the History of Ideas* 18 (1957): 587–93.

Ellis, Elmer. "Public Opinion and the Income Tax, 1860–1900." *Mississippi Valley Historical Review* 27 (1940): 227–35.

Ernst, Daniel. "Free Labor, the Consumer Interest, and the Law of Industrial Disputes, 1885–1900." *American Journal of Legal History* 36 (January 1992): 19–37.

Fairman, Charles. "Does the Fourteenth Amendment Incorporate the Bill of Rights?: The Original Understanding." *Stanford Law Review* 2 (1949): 5–173.

———. "The So-Called Granger Cases, Lord Hale, and Justice Bradley." *Stanford Law Review* 5 (1953): 587–679.

———. "What Makes a Great Justice?: Mr. Justice Bradley and the Supreme Court, 1870–1892." *Boston University Law Review* 30 (1950): 49–102.

Farrelly, David G. "Harlan's Formative Period: The Years before the War." *Kentucky Law Journal* 46 (Spring 1958): 367–406.

Faust, Drew Gilpin. "Altars of Sacrifice: Confederate Women and the Narratives of War." *Journal of American History* 76 (1990): 1200–1228.

Fehrenbacher, Don E. "Only His Stepchildren." In *Lincoln in Text and Context: Collected Essays*, 95–112. Stanford: Stanford University Press, 1987.

Ferry, Henry Justin. "Racism and Reunion: A Black Protest by Francis James Grimké." *Journal of Presbyterian History* 50 (Summer 1972): 77–88.

Field, James A., Jr. "American Imperialism: The Worst Chapter in Almost Any Book." *American Historical Review* 83 (1978): 644–68.

Finkelman, Paul. " 'Hooted down the Page of History': Reconsidering the Greatness of Chief Justice Taney." *Journal of Supreme Court History* (1994): 83–102.

Fisher, Joe A. "The *Knight* Case Revisited." *Historian* 35 (1973): 365–83.

Foner, Eric. "The Meaning of Freedom in the Age of Emancipation." *Journal of American History* 81 (September 1994): 435–60.

Forbath, William E. "The Ambiguities of Free Labor: Labor and Law in the Gilded Age." *Wisconsin Law Review* (1985): 773–94.

Frank, John P. "The Appointment of Supreme Court Justices: Prestige, Principles, and Politics." *Wisconsin Law Review* (1941): 172–210.

Frank, John P., and Robert F. Munroe. "The Original Understanding of 'Equal Protection of the Laws.' " *Washington University Law Quarterly* (Summer 1972): 421–78.

Frantz, Laurent B. "Congressional Power to Enforce the 14th Amendment against Private Acts." *Yale Law Journal* 72 (July 1964): 1353–84.

Fredrickson, George M. "A Man but Not a Brother: Abraham Lincoln and Racial Equality." *Journal of Southern History* 41 (February 1975): 38–58.

Freehling, William. "The Founding Fathers and Slavery." *American Historical Review* 77 (1972): 81–93.

Genovese, Eugene. " 'Our Family, White and Black': Family and Household in the Southern Slaveholders' World View." In *In Joy and in Sorrow: Women, Family, and Marriage in the Victorian South, 1830–1900*, edited by Carol Bleser, 69–87. New York: Oxford University Press, 1991.

Gerber, David A. "Anti-Semitism and Jewish-Gentile Relations in American Historiography and the American Past." In *Anti-Semitism in American History*, edited by David A. Gerber, 3–54. Urbana: University of Illinois Press, 1986.

Goetsch, Charles C. "The Future of Legal Formalism." *American Journal of Legal History* 24 (1980): 221–56.

Gold, David M. "Redfield, Railroads, and the Roots of 'Laissez-Faire Constitutionalism.' " *American Journal of Legal History* 27 (1983): 254–68.

Goldstein, Eric L. " 'Different Blood Flows in Our Veins': Race and Jewish Self-Definition in Late Nineteenth Century America." *American Jewish History* 85 (March 1997): 29–55.

Gordon, David. "*Swift and Co. v. United States:* The Beef Trust and the Stream of Commerce Doctrine." *American Journal of Legal History* 28 (1984): 244–79.

Gordon, James W. "Did the First Justice Harlan Have a Black Brother?" *Western New England Law Review* 15 (1993): 159–238.

Gordon, Robert W. " 'The Ideal and the Actual in the Law': Fantasies and Practices of New York City Lawyers, 1870–1910." In *The New High Priests: Lawyers in Post–Civil War America*, edited by Gerard W. Gawalt, 51–74. Westport, Conn.: Greenwood Press, 1984.

Gordon, Sanford. "Attitudes towards Trusts prior to the Sherman Act." *Southern Economic History* 30 (1963): 156–67.

Grey, Thomas C. "Langdell's Orthodoxy." *University of Pittsburgh Law Review* 45 (Fall 1983): 1–53.

Grossberg, Michael. "Institutionalizing Masculinity: The Law as a Masculine Profession." In *Meanings for Manhood: Masculinity in Victorian America*, edited by Mark Carnes and Clyde Griffin, 133–51. Chicago: University of Chicago Press, 1990.

Groves, Walter A. "Centre College: The Second Phase, 1830–1857." *Filson Club History Quarterly* 24 (October 1950): 311–34.

Hale, Robert L. "The 'Fair-Value' Merry-Go-Round, 1898–1938: A Forty-Year Journey from Rates-Based-on-Value to Value-Based-on-Rates." *Illinois Law Review* 33 (1939): 517–31.

Hall, Kermit L. "The 'Route to Hell' Retraced: The Impact of Popular Election on the Southern Appellate Judiciary, 1832–1920." In *Ambivalent Legacy: A Legal History of the South*, edited by D. J. Bodenhamer and J. W. Ely, 229–55. Jackson: University Press of Mississippi, 1984.

Halper, Louise A. "Christopher G. Tiedeman, 'Laissez-Faire Constitutionalism,' and the Dilemmas of Small-Scale Property in the Gilded Age." *Ohio State Law Journal* 51 (1990): 1349–84.

Harlan, Louis R. "Booker T. Washington's Discovery of the Jews." In *Region, Race, and Reconstruction*, edited by J. Morgan Kousser and James M. McPherson, 267–79. New York: Oxford University Press, 1982.

———. "Desegregation in New Orleans Public Schools during Reconstruction." *American Historical Review* 67 (April 1962): 663–75.

Hartog, Hendrik. "The Constitution of Aspiration and 'The Rights That Belong to Us All.' " *Journal of American History* 74 (December 1987): 1013–34.

———. "Mrs. Packard on Dependency." *Yale Journal of Law and the Humanities* 1 (December 1988): 79–103.

Hartz, Louis. "John M. Harlan in Kentucky, 1855–1877: The Story of His Pre-Court Political Career." *Filson Club Historical Quarterly* 14 (January 1940): 17–40.

Higham, John. "Ethnic Pluralism in Modern American Thought." In *Send These to Me: Jews and Other Immigrants in Urban America*, 196–320. New York: Atheneum, 1975.

———. "Ideological Anti-Semitism in the Gilded Age." In *Send These to Me: Jews and Other Immigrants in Urban America*, 116–37. New York: Atheneum, 1975.

———. "Social Discrimination against Jews, 1830–1930." In *Send These to Me:*

*Jews and Other Immigrants in Urban America*, 138–73. New York: Atheneum, 1975.

Hobbs, Edward H. "Negro Education and the Equal Protection of the Laws." *Journal of Politics* 14 (August 1952): 488–511.

Hodes, Martha. "The Sexualization of Reconstruction Politics: White Women and Black Men in the South after the Civil War." In *American Sexual Politics: Sex, Gender, and Race since the Civil War*, edited by John C. Fout and Maura Shaw Tantillo, 59–74. Chicago: University of Chicago Press, 1993.

Horwitz, Morton J. "The Conservative Tradition in the Writing of American Legal History." *American Journal of Legal History* 17 (1973): 275–94.

Howard, J. Woodford, Jr. "Commentary on Richard A. Posner's 'Judicial Biography.'" In "Judicial Biography Symposium," special issue of *New York University Law Review* 70 (June 1995): 533–48.

Howard, Victor B. "The Black Testimony Controversy in Kentucky, 1866–1972." *Journal of Negro History* 58 (April 1973): 140–65.

Hurst, Willard. "Who Is the 'Great' Appellate Judge?" In "The Writing of Judicial Biography: A Symposium," special issue of *Indiana Law Journal* 24 (1948): 394–400.

Hylton, J. Gordon. "David Josiah Brewer and the Christian Constitution." In "Symposium: Religion and the Judicial Process," special issue of *Marquette Law Review* 81 (1998): 417–25.

Innes, Reginald H. "Relation of Insurance to the Commerce Clause in the Federal Constitution." *American Law Register* 48 (1900): 717–33.

Jones, Alan R. "Law and Economics v. a Democratic Society: The Case of Thomas M. Cooley, Charles H. Cooley, and Henry C. Adams." *American Journal of Legal History* 36 (April 1992): 119–38.

———. "Thomas M. Cooley and 'Laissez-Faire Constitutionalism': A Reconsideration." *Journal of American History* 53 (1967): 751–71.

———. "Thomas M. Cooley and the Interstate Commerce Commission: Continuity and Change in the Doctrine of Equal Rights." *Political Science Quarterly* 81 (1966): 602–27.

Jordan, Winthrop. "Familial Politics: Thomas Paine and the Killing of the King, 1776." *Journal of American History* 60 (September 1973): 294–308.

Kaczorowski, Robert J. "Searching for the Intent of the Framers of the Fourteenth Amendment." *Connecticut Law Review* 5 (Winter 1972–73): 368–98.

———. "To Begin the Nation Anew: Congress, Citizenship, and Civil Rights after the Civil War." *American Historical Review* 92 (February 1987): 45–68.

Kaplan, Sidney. "The Miscegenation Issue in the Election of 1864." *Journal of Negro History* 34 (July 1949): 274–343.

Kelly, Alfred H. "Clio and the Court: An Illicit Love Affair." *Supreme Court Review* (1965): 119–58.

———. "The Congressional Controversy over School Segregation, 1867–1875." *Journal of American History* 64 (April 1959): 537–63.

———. "The Fourteenth Amendment Reconsidered: The Segregation Question." *Michigan Law Review* 54 (June 1956): 1049–86.

Kennedy, Duncan. "Toward an Historical Understanding of Legal Consciousness: The Case of Classical Legal Thought in America, 1850–1940." *Research in Law and Sociology* 3 (1980): 3–24.

Kerber, Linda. "Separate Spheres, Female Worlds, Woman's Place: The Rhetoric of Women's History." *Journal of American History* 75 (June 1988): 9–39.

Knight, Thomas Jefferson. "Dissenting Opinions of John Marshall Harlan." *American Law Review* 51 (July–August 1917): 481–506.

Kousser, J. Morgan. "Before *Plessy*, before *Brown:* The Development of the Law of Racial Integration in Louisiana and Kansas." In *Toward a Usable Past: Liberty under State Constitutions*, edited by Paul Finkelman and Steve E. Gottlieb, 213–70. Athens: University of Georgia Press, 1991.

———. "Making Separate Equal: Integration of Black and White Schools Funds in Kentucky." *Journal of Interdisciplinary History* 10 (1980): 399–428.

———. "Separate but *Not* Equal: The Supreme Court's First Decision on Racial Discrimination in Schools." *Journal of Southern History* 46 (1980): 17–44.

Kutler, Stanley. "Raoul Berger's Fourteenth Amendment: A History or Ahistorical?" *Hastings Constitutional Law Quarterly* 6 (1979): 511–26.

Landynski, Jacob W. "John Marshall Harlan and the Bill of Rights: A Centennial View." *Social Research* 49 (Winter 1982): 899–962.

LaPiana, William P. "The Jurisprudence of History and Truth: Conservative Legal Thought in the Gilded Age." *Rutgers-Camden Law Journal* 23 (1992): 519–59.

———. "*Swift v. Tyson* and the Brooding Omnipresence in the Sky: An Investigation of the Idea of Law in Antebellum America." *Suffolk University Law Review* 20 (Winter 1986): 771–832.

Lasch, Christopher. "The Anti-Imperialists, the Philippines, and the Inequality of Man." *Journal of Southern History* 24 (August 1958): 319–31.

Levine, Harry Gene. "The Discovery of Addiction: Changing Conceptions of Habitual Drunkenness in America." *Journal of Studies on Alcohol* 39 (1978): 143–74.

Levy, Leonard, and Harlan B. Phillips. "The *Roberts* Case: Source of the 'Separate but Equal' Doctrine." *American Historical Review* 56 (1951): 510–18.

Lewis, Ellwood W. "Document: The Appointment of Mr. Justice Harlan." *Indiana Law Review* 29 (Fall 1953): 46–74.

Libecap, Gary D. "The Rise of the Chicago Packers and the Origins of Meat Inspection and Antitrust." *Economic Inquiry* 30 (1992): 242–62.

Lively, Robert A. "The American System." *Business History Review* 29 (March 1955): 81–96.

Low, W. A. "The Freedmen's Bureau in the Border States." In *Radicalism, Racism, and Party Realignment: The Border States during Reconstruction*, edited by Richard O. Curry, 245–64. Baltimore: Johns Hopkins University Press, 1969.

McCurdy, Charles W. "American Law and the Marketing Structure of the

Large Corporation, 1875–1890." *Journal of Economic History* 38 (September 1978): 639–49.

———. "Justice Field and the Jurisprudence of Government-Business Relations: Some Parameters of Laissez Faire Constitutionalism, 1863–1897." *Journal of American History* 61 (1975): 970–1005.

———. "The *Knight* Sugar Decision of 1895 and the Modernization of American Corporation Law, 1869–1903." *Business History Review* 53 (1979): 304–42.

———. "The Roots of 'Liberty of Contract' Reconsidered: Major Premises in the Law of Employment, 1867–1937." *Supreme Court Historical Society Yearbook* (1984): 20–33.

———. "Stephen J. Field and the American Judicial Tradition." In *The Fields and the Law*, 5–19. San Francisco: U.S. District Court for the Northern District of California Historical Society/Federal Bar Council, 1986.

McCurry, Stephanie. "The Two Faces of Republicanism: Gender and Pro-Slavery Politics in Antebellum South Carolina." *Journal of American History* 78 (March 1992): 1245–64.

McDaniel, Hilda Mulvey. "Francis Tillou Nicholls and the End of Reconstruction." *Louisiana Historical Quarterly* 32 (April 1949): 357–513.

McGraw, Thomas K. "Rethinking the Trust Question." In *Regulation in Perspective: Historical Essays*, edited by Thomas K. McGraw, 1–44. Cambridge: Harvard University Press, 1981.

Maclear, J. F. "The Republic and the Millennium." In *The Religion of the Republic*, edited by Elyn A. Smith, 183–216. Philadelphia: Fortress Press, 1971.

Maltz, Eric. "Only Partially Color-Blind: John Marshall Harlan's View of Race and the Constitution." *Georgia State Law Review* 12 (1996): 973–1016.

Meier, August. "Frederick Douglass' Vision of America: A Case Study in Nineteenth-Century Negro Protest." In *Freedom and Reform*, edited by Harold Hyman and Leonard Levy, 127–48. New York: Harper & Row, 1967.

Mensch, Elizabeth. "The History of Mainstream Legal Thought." In *The Politics of Law: A Progressive Critique*, edited by David Kairys, 18–39. New York: Pantheon, 1982.

Meyer, D. H. "American Intellectuals and the Victorian Crisis of Faith." In *Victorian America*, edited by Daniel Walker Howe, 59–77. Philadelphia: University of Pennsylvania Press, 1976.

Mills, Gary B. "Miscegenation and the Free Negro in Antebellum 'Anglo' Alabama: A Re-Examination of Southern Race Relations." *Journal of American History* 68 (June 1981): 16–34.

Monkkonen, Eric H. "The Politics of Municipal Indebtedness and Default, 1850–1936." In *The Politics of Urban Fiscal Policy*, edited by Terrance J. McDonald and Sally K. Ward, 125–59. Beverly Hills: Sage Publications, 1984.

Moorhead, James H. "The American Israel: Protestant Tribalism and Universal Mission." In *Many Are Chosen: Divine Election and Western Nationalism*, edited by William R. Hutchinson and Hartmut Lehmann, 147–72. Minneapolis: Fortress Press, 1994.

Musto, David F. "Continuity across Generations: The Adams Family Myth." In *New Directions in Psychohistory*, edited by Mel Albin, 117–29. Lexington, Mass.: D. C. Heath, 1980.

Nelson, William E. "The Impact of the Antislavery Movement upon Styles of Judicial Reasoning in Nineteenth Century America." *Harvard Law Review* 87 (January 1974): 513–66.

Newmyer, R. Kent. "Harvard Law School, New England Legal Culture, and the Antebellum Origins of American Jurisprudence." *Journal of American History* 74 (1987): 814–35.

Nieman, Donald G. "The Language of Liberation: African Americans and Equalitarian Constitutionalism, 1830–1850." In *The Constitution, Law, and American Life: Critical Aspects of the Nineteenth Century Experience*, edited by Donald G. Nieman, 59–85. Athens: University of Georgia Press, 1992.

Noll, Mark A. "The Image of the United States as a Biblical Nation, 1776–1865." In *The Bible in America: Essays in Cultural History*, edited by Nathan O. Hatch and Mark A. Noll, 39–58. New York: Oxford University Press, 1982.

Norris, Marjorie M. "An Early Instance of Nonviolence: The Louisville Demonstrations of 1870–1871." *Journal of Southern History* 32 (November 1966): 496–503.

Paludan, Phillip S. "Hercules Unbound: Lincoln, Slavery, and the Intentions of the Framers." In *The Constitution, Law, and American Life: Critical Aspects of the Nineteenth Century Experience*, edited by Donald G. Nieman, 1–22. Athens: University of Georgia Press, 1992.

Peritz, Rudolph J. "The 'Rule of Reason' in Anti-Trust Law: Property Logic in Restraint of Competition." *Hastings Law Journal* 40 (1980): 285–342.

Phillips, Henry. "Tennessee and the U.S. Court of Appeals for the Sixth Circuit." *Tennessee Historical Quarterly* 33 (1974): 22–33.

Porter, Mary Cornelia Aldis. "John Marshall Harlan the Elder and Federal Common Law: A Lesson from History." *Supreme Court Review* (1972): 103–34.

———. "That Commerce Shall Be Free: A New Look at the Old Laissez-Faire Court." *Supreme Court Review* (1977): 135–59.

Powe, L. A., Jr. "Rehearsal for Substantive Due Process: The Municipal Bond Cases." *Texas Law Review* 53 (May 1975): 738–56.

Powell, Thomas Reid. "Indirect Encroachments on Federal Authority by the Taxing Powers of the States [V]." *Harvard Law Review* 32 (1919): 234–65.

Przybyszewski, Linda C. A. "The Dilemma of Judicial Biography or Who Cares Who Is the Great Appellate Judge?: Gerald Gunther on Learned Hand." *Law and Social Inquiry* 12 (Winter 1996): 135–71.

———. "Judge Lorenzo Sawyer and the Chinese: Civil Rights Decisions in the Ninth Circuit." *Western Legal History* 1 (Winter/Spring 1988): 23–56.

———. "Mrs. John Marshall Harlan's Memories: Hierarchies of Gender and Race in the Household and the Polity." *Law and Social Inquiry* 18 (Summer 1993): 453–78.

Raboteau, Albert J. "Exodus, Ethiopia, and Racial Messianism: Texts and Contexts of African American Chosenness." In *Many Are Chosen: Divine*

*Election and Western Nationalism,* edited by William R. Hutchinson and
Hartmut Lehmann, 175–95. Minneapolis: Fortress Press, 1994.

Rose, Willie Lee. "The Domestication of Domestic Slavery." In *Slavery and
Freedom,* edited by William W. Freehling, 18–36. New York: Oxford
University Press, 1982.

Rosenberg, Charles E. "Sexuality, Class, and Role in Nineteenth Century
America." In *The American Man,* edited by Elizabeth H. and Joseph H. Pleck,
219–54. Englewood Cliffs, N.J.: Prentice Hall, 1980.

Ross, Dorothy. "Historical Consciousness in Nineteenth-Century America."
*American Historical Review* 89 (October 1984): 909–28.

Rotundo, E. Anthony. "Body and Soul: Changing Ideals of American
Middle-Class Manhood." *Journal of Social History* 16 (Summer 1983): 23–38.

———. "Learning about Manhood: Gender Ideals and the Middle-Class Family
in Nineteenth-Century America." In *Manliness and Morality: Middle-Class
Masculinity in Britain and America, 1800–1940,* edited by J. A. Mangan and
James Walvin, 35–51. New York: St. Martin's Press, 1987.

Sandeen, Ernest R. "The Princeton Theology: One Source of Biblical
Literalism in American Protestantism." *Church History* 31 (September 1962):
307–21.

Sarna, Jonathan. "The American Jewish Response to Nineteenth-Century
Christian Missions." *Journal of American History* 68 (June 1981): 35–51.

———. "Anti-Semitism and American History." *Commentary* 71 (March 1981):
42–47.

———. "The 'Mythical Jew' and the 'Jew Next Door' in Nineteenth-Century
America." In *Anti-Semitism in American History,* edited by David A. Gerber,
57–78. Urbana: University of Illinois Press, 1986.

Schieber, Harry N. "Federalism and Legal Process: Historical and
Contemporary Analysis of the American System." *Law and Society Review* 14
(1980): 663–722.

Schlegal, John Henry. "Between the Harvard Founders and the American Legal
Realists: The Professionalization of the American Law Professor." *Journal of
Legal Education* 35 (September 1985): 311–25.

Schmidt, Benno C., Jr. "Juries, Jurisdiction, and Race Discrimination: The Lost
Promise of *Strauder v. West Virginia.*" *Texas Law Review* 61 (May 1983):
1401–99.

Scott, Anne Firor. "Women, Religion, and Social Change in the South, 1830–
1930." In *Making the Invisible Woman Visible,* 92–121. Urbana: University of
Illinois Press, 1984.

———. "Women's Perspective on the Patriarchy of the 1850s." In *Making the
Invisible Woman Visible,* 175–89. Urbana: University of Illinois Press, 1984.

Shankman, Arnold. "Friend or Foe?: Southern Blacks View the Jew, 1880–1935."
In *"Turn to the South": Essays on Southern Jewry,* edited by Nathan M.
Kaganoff and Melvin I. Urofsky, 105–23. Charlottesville: University of
Virginia Press, 1979.

Siegel, Stephen A. "Historism in Late Nineteenth-Century Constitutional
Thought." *Wisconsin Law Review* (1990): 1431–1547.

————. "Joel Bishop's Orthodoxy." *Law and History Review* 13 (Fall 1995): 215–59.

————. "Understanding the *Lochner* Era: Lessons from the Controversy over Railroad and Utility Rate Regulation." *Virginia Law Review* 70 (1984): 187–263.

Singerman, Robert. "The Jew as Racial Alien: The Genetic Component of American Anti-Semitism." In *Anti-Semitism in American History*, edited by David A. Gerber, 103–28. Urbana: University of Illinois Press, 1986.

Smith, Ephraim K. "William McKinley's Enduring Legacy: The Historiographical Debate on the Taking of the Philippine Islands." In *The Spanish-American War and Its Aftermath*, edited by James C. Bradford, 205–49. Annapolis: Naval Institute Press, 1993.

Spillenger, Clyde. "Reading the Judicial Canon: Alexander Bickel and the Book of Brandeis." *Journal of American History* 79 (June 1992): 125–51.

Stanley, Amy Dru. "Conjugal Bonds and Wage Labor: Rights of Contract in the Age of Emancipation." *Journal of American History* 75 (September 1988): 471–500.

Stevenson, Daniel. "General Nelson, Kentucky, and Lincoln Guns." *Magazine of American History* 10 (August 1883): 115–39.

Swinney, Everette. "Enforcing the Fifteenth Amendment, 1870–1877." *Journal of Southern History* 27 (1962): 202–18.

Swisher, Carl B. "The Judge in Historical Perspective." In "The Writing of Judicial Biography: A Symposium," special issue of *Indiana Law Journal* 24 (1948): 381–86.

"Symposium: Religion and the Judicial Process—Legal, Ethical, and Empirical Dimensions." Special issue of *Marquette Law Review* 81 (Winter 1998).

Teaford, Jon C. "Toward a Christian Nation: Religion, Law, and Justice Strong." *Journal of Presbyterian History* 54 (Winter 1976): 422–37.

Thelan, David. "Memory and American History." *Journal of American History* 75 (March 1989): 1117–29.

Thompkins, Robert E. "Presbyterian Religious Education among Negroes, 1864–1891." *Journal of the Presbyterian Historical Society* 29 (September 1951): 145–71.

Thompson, E. Bruce. "The Bristow Presidential Boom of 1876." *Mississippi Valley Historical Review* 32 (June 1945): 3–30.

Toplin, Robert. "Between Black and White: Attitudes toward Southern Mulattoes, 1830–1861." *Journal of Southern History* 45 (May 1979): 185–200.

Urofsky, Melvin I. "Proposed Federal Incorporation in the Progressive Era." *American Journal of Legal History* 26 (1982): 160–83.

Waite, Edward F. "How 'Eccentric' Was Mr. Justice Harlan?" *Minnesota Law Review* 37 (February 1953): 173–87.

Wall, Joseph F. "*Lochner v. New York:* A Study in the Modernization of Constitutional Law." In *American Industrialization, Economic Expansion, and the Law*, edited by Joseph R. Frese and Jacob Judd, 113–41. Tarrytown, N.Y.: Sleepy Hollow Press, 1981.

Warren, Robert Penn. "The Legacy of the Civil War: Meditations on the

Centennial" (1961). In *A Robert Penn Warren Reader*, edited by Albert Erskine, 270–310. New York: Vintage Books, 1988.

Watt, Richard F., and Richard M. Orkiloff. "The Coming Vindication of Mr. Justice Harlan." *Illinois Law Review* 44 (1949): 13–40.

Webb, Ross A. "Kentucky: 'Pariah among the Elect.'" In *Radicalism, Racism, and Party Realignment: The Border States during Reconstruction*, edited by Richard O. Curry, 105–45. Baltimore: Johns Hopkins University Press, 1969.

Weeks, Louis B. "Racism, World War I, and the Christian Life: Francis J. Grimké in the Nation's Capital." In *Black Apostles: Afro-American Clergy Confront the Twentieth Century*, edited by Randall K. Burkett and Richard Newman, 59–69. Boston: G. K. Hall, 1978.

Weisberg, D. Kelly. "'Barred from the Bar': Women and Legal Education in the U.S., 1870–1880." *Journal of Legal Education* 28 (1977): 485–507.

Welter, Barbara. "The Cult of True Womanhood, 1820–1860." *American Quarterly* 18 (Summer 1966): 151–74.

Weschler, Herbert. "Toward Neutral Principles of Constitutional Law." *Harvard Law Review* 73 (1959): 10–35.

Westin, Alan F. "The First Justice Harlan: A Self-Portrait from His Private Papers." *Kentucky Law Journal* 46 (Spring 1958): 321–66.

———. "John Marshall Harlan and the Constitutional Rights of Negroes: The Transformation of a Southerner." *Yale Law Journal* 66 (April 1957): 637–710.

———. "Mr. Justice Harlan." In *Mr. Justice*, rev. ed., edited by Allison Dunham and Philip B. Kurland, 93–128. Chicago: University of Chicago Press, 1964.

———. "The Supreme Court, the Populist Moment, and the Campaign of 1896." *Journal of Politics* 15 (1953): 3–41.

White, G. Edward. "The Canonization of Holmes and Brandeis: Epistemology and Judicial Reputations." In "Judicial Biography Symposium," special issue of *New York University Law Review* 70 (June 1995): 576–621.

———. "John Marshall Harlan I: The Precursor." *American Journal of Legal History* 19 (January 1975): 1–21.

Wiener, Jonathan M. "The 'Black Beast Rapist': White Racial Attitudes in the Postwar South." *Reviews in American History* 13 (June 1985): 222–26.

Wilmore, Gayraud. "Identity and Integration: Black Presbyterians and Their Allies in the Twentieth Century." In *The Presbyterian Predicament: Six Perspectives*, edited by Milton J. Coalter, John W. Mulder, and Louis B. Weeks, 109–33. Louisville: Westminster/John Knox Press, 1990.

"The Writing of Judicial Biography: A Symposium." Special issue of *Indiana Law Journal* 24 (1948).

Wyatt-Brown, Bertram. "The Civil Rights Act of 1875." *Western Political Quarterly* 18 (December 1965): 763–75.

*Dissertations and Theses*

Bailey, Mark Warren. "Moral Philosophy and the U.S. Supreme Court, 1860–1910." Ph.D. dissertation, University of Western Ontario, 1996.

Byars, Ronald P. "The Making of the Self-Made Man: The Development of

Masculine Roles and Images in Antebellum America." Ph.D. dissertation, Michigan State University, 1979.

Clark, Floyd Barzilia. "The Constitutional Doctrines of Justice Harlan." Ph.D. dissertation, Johns Hopkins University, 1915.

Ferry, Henry Justin. "Francis James Grimké: Portrait of a Black Puritan." Ph.D. dissertation, Yale University, 1970.

Fowler, David H. "Northern Attitudes towards Interracial Marriage: A Study of Legislation and Public Opinion in the Middle Atlantic States and the States of the Old Northwest." Ph.D. dissertation, Yale University, 1963.

Martin, Asa Earl. "The Anti-Slavery Movement in Kentucky prior to 1850." Ph.D. dissertation, Cornell University, 1917.

Owen, Thomas Lewis. "The Pre-Court Career of John Marshall Harlan." Master's thesis, University of Louisville, 1970.